THE ATTIC ORATORS

FROM

ANTIPHON TO ISAEOS.

THE ATTIC ORATORS

FROM

ANTIPHON TO ISAEOS.

BY

R. C. JEBB, M.A.

FELLOW AND LATE TUTOR OF TRINITY COLLEGE, CAMBRIDGE, AND
PUBLIC ORATOR IN THE UNIVERSITY:
PROFESSOR OF GREEK IN THE UNIVERSITY OF GLASGOW.

*Translator of the Characters of Theophrastus: Author of Commentaries on the Electra
and Ajax of Sophocles, and of Translations into Greek and Latin Verse.*

VOL. I.

NEW YORK
RUSSELL & RUSSELL · INC
1962

L. C. CATALOG CARD NO: 62—8230

ὡς ἀνὴρ ἔκδαμος ὁδοιπορέων αὐγάζεται   στρ.
γλυπτοὺς τεχνιτῶν τῶν πάρος ἔργα κολοσσούς,
ἀσύχοις μορφαῖσι νόον φθιμένων ἐξαγγελλομένους ἔτ' ἐούσιν,
οὐδὲ φρεσὶν δύναταί πω συμμαθεῖν
οἶος ἄρ' ἦν ὁ βίος
ὁπόθεν θ' αἱ φροντίδες
τῶν τάδ' ἐξειργασμένων·

ἀλλὰ λεύσσων θέλγεται ἐς τέλος ἐν θυμῷ λαβὼν   ἀντ.
κάλλος τι πάνταρχον, σκοπέει δὲ πανῆμαρ
τὰν προσώποις φαιδρὸν ἐφεζομέναν τοῖς ἡμιθέοισι γαλάναν
καὶ μελέων ἁβρὸν εὐρύθμων σθένος,
ἐκ δ' ὀλόλυξε χαρείς,
μακρός, ὦ κλεινοί, χρόνος
ὕμμε μὴ κάμνοι σέβων·

ὧδ', ἀείμναστοι στομάτων Διὶ τερπνῶν ῥήσιες,   ἐπ.
ἲς μένει ὑμετέρα, θαῦμ' ἀνδράσιν ἀλλοδαποῖς
οἳ σέλας οὐκ ἴδομεν χρυσανίου
τᾷ πρὶν ἐφ' Ἑλλάδι Φοίβου,
οὐδὲ πάτραν ἀνακαρύξαί κεν ἔχοιμεν Ἀθάνας.
ὕμμι γὰρ ἀέλιον μέν φαμι δεδυγκέναι, οὐδ' ἔμμεν σκότον,
ἀλλὰ λάμπους' ἀθάνατοι χάριτες
λευκὰν πρὸς ἀκτῖν' Ἑσπέρου.

PREFACE.

THE first object of this book is to offer a contribution to a chapter in the history of Greek Literature which has perhaps received less attention than its importance deserves. The oratorical branch of Attic prose has a more direct and more fruitful relation to the general development than modern analogies would suggest. To trace the course of Athenian oratory from its beginnings as an art to the days of its decline is, necessarily, to sketch the history of Greek prose expression in its most widely influential form, and to show how this form was affected by a series of causes, political or social.

The second object of the book is to supply an aid to the particular study of the Attic orators before Demosthenes. The artistic development of Attic oratory is sketched as a whole. But a separate and minute treatment is given only to Antiphon, Andokides, Lysias, Isokrates and Isaeos. The period thus specially determined has more than a correspondence with a practical need: it has an inner unity, resting on grounds which are stated in the Introduction and which are illustrated at each stage of the subsequent inquiry.

As regards the former and larger of these two purposes, the writer may venture to hope that his attempt, however imperfect, will be recognised at least as one for which, in this country, there is room. The History of Greek Literature by Otfried Müller— translated and continued by Donaldson—had been carried only to Isokrates when the author died, at the early age of forty-three, in 1840. Müller's chapters on 'The beginnings of regular Political and Forensic Oratory among the Athenians' (XXXIII), on 'The new cultivation of Oratory by Lysias' (XXXV), and on 'Isokrates' (XXXVI) are, relatively to the plan of his work, very good : that is, they state clearly the chief characteristics of each writer separately. But this very plan precluded a full examination of each writer's works, and even a full discussion of his style. Nor does Müller appear to have regarded Oratory otherwise than as strictly a department, or adequately to have conceived its relation to the universal prose literature. The materials for a more comprehensive estimate had already been brought together in Westermann's *Geschichte der Beredsamkeit,* which carries the chronicle of technical rhetoric and of eloquence to the days of Chrysostom. But this great work is rather a storehouse of references than properly a history ; and, owing to its vast compass and its annalistic method, gives too little space, proportionally, to the best period of Athens. Westermann's thesaurus and Müller's sketch have recently been supplemented by the excellent works of Dr F. Blass: (1) 'Die Attische Beredsamkeit von Gorgias bis zu Lysias,' 1868: (2) 'Isokrates und Isaios', 1874—of which the latter came into my hands only after my own chapters on Isokrates were almost wholly printed. I desire here to record in general terms my obligations to both these works. Particular debts are in every case, so far as I know, acknowledged on the page where they occur.

For the analyses of the orations it seemed best to adopt no uniform scale, but to make them more or less full according to the interest of the subject-matter or the nature of its difficulties. In analysing the works of Isokrates, which abound in matter of literary or historical value, I have endeavoured to give the whole of the contents in a form easy of access, and, at the same time, to preserve the most characteristic features of expression. A careful analysis, whether copious or not, is necessarily to some extent a commentary, since the analyst must exhibit his view of the relation in which each part of the writer's meaning stands to the rest.

In this sense, I hope that the analyses will serve my second and more special purpose—to help students of these five orators who have nothing but a Greek text before them. Critical scholarship in

England has done some of its best work on the orators before Demosthenes. The names of John Taylor, Markland, Robert Tyrwhitt, Dobree, Dobson, Churchill Babington—to mention only a few—are proof enough. But it is long since the orators before Demosthenes have been taken into the ordinary course of reading at our schools and universities. The commentary of Mr Sandys on Isokrates *Ad Demonicum* and *Panegyricus* is (so far as I know) alone in this country. Frohberger's selections from Lysias, Schneider's selections from Isokrates, Rauchenstein's selections from Lysias and from Isokrates, Bremi's selections from Lysias and from Aeschines, are representative of the German feeling that these Greek orators should be read by ordinary students. The principal reason why they have dropped out of school and university favour among ourselves is perhaps not difficult to assign. Demosthenes and (in his measure) Aeschines have a political and historical interest of a kind which every one recognises, and which lends dignity to ancient prose in the eyes of a public that is rather political than philological. Many speeches which Demosthenes did not write have long been studied among us in the belief that they were composed by that statesman; while, on the other hand, comparatively few know, or comprehend, the conjecture of Mr Freeman that every Athenian ekklesiast was equal in political intelligence to an average Member of Parliament. In truth, an oration taken at hazard from Antiphon, Andokides, Lysias, Isokrates or Isaeos, will often be poor food for the mind if it is read alone. What is necessary to make it profitable is some idea of the world in which it was spoken. These orators who were not conspicuous actors in history must be read, not fragmentarily or in the light of notes which confine themselves to explaining what are termed 'allusions,' but more systematically, and with some general comprehension of the author and the age. Brougham, one of the best and most diligent critics of ancient oratory, himself tells us that he could not read Isaeos :—'the total want of interest in the subject, and the minuteness of the topics, has always made a perusal of them so tedious as to prevent us from being duly sensible of the force and keenness with which they are said to abound.' If, however, Brougham had considered Isaeos, not as merely a writer on a series of will-cases, but as the oldest and most vivid witness for the working of inchoate testation in a primitive society, and, on the other hand, as the man who, alone, marks a critical phase in the growth of Attic prose, it is conceivable that Brougham should have thought Isaeos worthy of the most attentive perusal.

The present attempt to aid in giving Attic Oratory its due place in the history of Attic Prose was begun in the summer of 1870, and has since employed all the time that could be spared to it from the severe and almost incessant pressure of other occupations. In addition to the works of Dr Blass, I would name the exhaustive work of Arnold Schäfer, *Demosthenes und seine Zeit*, as one which has been my constant help. M. Perrot's 'L'Éloquence Politique et Judiciaire à Athènes : 1ère Partie, Les Précurseurs de Démosthène,' and Mr Forsyth's *Hortensius*, also claim my gratitude. Among particular aids, I must mention the Essay on Isokrates, by M. Havet, prefixed to M. Cartelier's translation of the περὶ ἀντιδόσεως,—an acknowledgement which is the more due since, by an inadvertence for which I would fain atone, the essay is ascribed at p. 45 of my second volume, not to its true author, but to the scholar whose memory he has so loyally served. The article of Weissenborn on Isaeos in Ersch and Gruber's Encyclopaedia, the editions of Isaeos by Schömann and Scheibe, and the edition of the two Speeches On the Crown by MM. Simcox, must be added to the list. I am glad that my Introduction was not printed too soon to profit by some of Mr Watkiss Lloyd's remarks on Perikles. The authorities, general or particular, not specified above will be found in a list which is subjoined. If an obligation anywhere remains unacknowledged, I would beg my readers to believe that it is by an

oversight which I should rejoice to have the opportunity of repairing.

Last, though not least, I have to thank my
friend Mr Sandys for his help in revising some of
the earlier sheets of the book for the press, as well
as for several valuable suggestions.

It seems probable that the study of antiquity,
especially of the Greek and Latin languages and
literatures, so far from declining, is about to enter
on a larger and a more truly vigorous life than it
has had since the Revival of Letters. That study
has become, in a new and fuller sense, scientific.
The Comparative Method, in its application to
Language, to Literature, to Mythology, to Political
or Constitutional History, has given to the classics
a general interest and importance far greater than
they possessed in the days when the devotion
which they attracted was most exclusive. For the
present, indeed, during a time of transition, the
very breadth of the view thus opened is apt to be
attended by a disadvantage of its own. So long as
the study given to ancient Greece or Rome was
practically confined to the short periods during
which the literature of either was most brilliant,
this study was often narrow, perhaps, but it was
usually searching and sympathetic. The great
masters in each kind were known at close quarters.
Their excellence was not something taken on credit

as giving them their claim to a place in a rapid survey. It was apprehended and felt. Paradoxes as to their relative merits were, therefore, not so easily commended to educated opinion in the name of a revolt from academical prescription. I remember to have seen an ingenious travesty of 'The Last Days of Pompeii,' in which the sorcerer Arbaces had occasion to recite the praises of his countrymen, the Egyptians. 'The Greeks,' Arbaces sang, 'are wonderfully clever; but *we* have invented the Greeks.' Goethe said that Winckelmann had 'found' the antique; but it appears sometimes to be forgotten that this merit is essentially distinct from that intimated by the Egyptian. In the meantime, I am persuaded that anyone will be doing useful work who makes a contribution, however slight, to that close study of the *best* Greek literature which ought ever to be united with attention to the place of Greece in the universal history of the mind. In these things, as in greater still, the words are true, 'Securus iudicat orbis terrarum'.

The University, Glasgow,
November, 1875.

EDITIONS AND AUTHORITIES.

I. CLASSICAL TEXTS.

1. *Greek.*

Oratores Attici.	J. G. Baiter and Hermann Sauppe, 1850. Vol. I.: Antiphon, Andokides, Lysias, Isokrates, Isaeos, Lykurgos, Aeschines, Deinarchos, Demosthenes. Vol. II.: Scholia to Isokrates, Aeschines, Demosthenes, and the Fragments of the Orators, from Gorgias to Demetrios Phalereus, arranged, with comments, by Sauppe. Hypereides, ed. F. Blass, 1869 (Teubner).—For the text, I have consulted also :—1. *Oratores Attici*, ed. Imm. Bekker, 1828.—2. *Oratores Attici*, ed. G. S. Dobson, with notes by H. Stephens, J. J. Scaliger, J. Taylor, J. Markland, J. J. Reiske, A. Auger, &c. 1828.— 3. Antiphon, Andokides, Deinarchos, ed. F. Blass, and Isaeos, ed. C. Scheibe, in Teubner's series.
Aristotle.	Imm. Bekker, edition of the Imperial Academy of Berlin, 1831—1870. The *Rhetoric*, with Commentary, L. Spengel, 1867.
Athenaeos.	J. Schweighauser, 1801—1804.
Comicorum Fragmenta.	F. H. Bothe, 1855 (Didot).
Diodoros.	L. Dindorf and C. Müller (Didot).
Diogenes Laertios.	C. G. Cobet, 1862 (Didot).
Dionysios of Halikarnassos.	J. J. Reiske, 1774. (Also text in the series of C. Tauchnitz, 1829.)
Eunapios.	Βίοι φιλοσόφων καὶ σοφιστῶν. J. F. Boissonade, Amsterdam, 1822.
Harpokration.	W. Dindorf, 1850.
Hesychios.	J. Alberti, 1746.
Lucian.	Imm. Bekker, 1853.
Pausanias.	L. Dindorf (Didot), 1845.
Philostratos.	C. L. Kayser, 1844.
Photios.	Imm. Bekker, 1824.
Plato.	J. G. Baiter, J. C. Orelli, and A. G. Winckelmann, 1842.
Plutarch, *Parallel Lives.*	Imm. Bekker, 1855.
[Plutarch] *Lives of the Ten Orators.*	In Plutarchi *Moralia*, ed. F. Dübner (Didot), 1868.

Pollux.	Imm. Bekker, 1846.
Rhetores Graeci.	(1) For Anaximenes, Aphthonios, Aristeides *Rhetoric*, Demetrios περὶ ἑρμηνείας, Hermogenes, Longinus, Theon, and the writer περὶ ὕψους:—*Rhetores Graeci*, ed. L. Spengel, 3 vols., 1853. (2) For the scholia, and for the lesser writers generally :— *Rhetores Graeci*, ed. C. Walz, 9 vols., 1832.
Sextus Empiricus.	πρὸς τοὺς μαθηματικοὺς ἀντιρρητικοί. J. A. Fabricius, Leipzig, 1718.
Stobaeos.	*Anthology*, 4 vols. ; *Eclogues*, 2 vols., ed. A. Meineke (Teubner), 1860.
Strabo.	C. Müller and F. Dübner (Didot), 1853.
Suidas.	G. Bernhardy, 1853.
Thucydides.	Imm. Bekker, 2nd ed., 1868.
Xenophon.	G. Sauppe, 1865.

2. *Latin.*

Cicero.	*Opera omnia* (with the incerti *Rhet. ad Herennium*) C. F. A. Nobbe, Leipzig, 1869.
„	*Rhetorica* (*De Inventione*, l. II.), with the *Rhet. ad Her.*, F. Lindemann, Leipzig, 1828.
„	*De Oratore*, l. III. C. W. Piderit, Leipzig, 4th ed. 1873.
„	*Brutus de claris oratoribus*, C. W. Piderit, Leipzig, 2nd ed. 1875.
„	*Partitiones Oratoriae*, C. W. Piderit, Leipzig, 1867.
„	*De Optimo Genere Oratorum*, (with *Orator*,) O. Jahn, Berlin, 3rd ed. 1869.
Gellius.	Mart. Hertz (Teubner), 1853.
Lucilius, Fragments of.	In L. Müller's *Saturarum Reliquiae*, 1872.
Quintilian.	E. Bonnell (Teubner), 1868 ; commentary—Spalding, Buttmann, Bonnell, and Zumpt; bks. I—VI. Leipzig, 1798—1834.
Rhetorica ad Herennium.	F. Lindemann (see above), Leipzig, 1828.
De Oratoribus Dialogus.	In Tacitus, ed. J. G. Orelli, 1846.

II. Other Authorities[1].

Belin de Ballu, J. N.	*Histoire Critique de l'Éloquence chez les Grecs.* Paris, 1813.
Barthélemy, J. J.	*Voyage du jeune Anacharsis en Grèce.* Paris, 1788.
Becker, A. G.	*Andokides, übersetzt und erläutert.* 1832.
Beckhaus, H.	*Xenophon der jüngere und Isokrates.* Posen, 1872.
Benseler, G. E.	*De Hiatu in Oratoribus Atticis et Historicis Graecis.* 1841.
Berbig, F.	*Ueber das genus dicendi tenue des Redners Lysias.* Cüstrin, 1871.
	Isokrates Werke, Griechisch und Deutsch. 1854.
Blair, H.	*Lectures on Rhetoric and Belles Lettres.* London, 1783.

[1] The following list does not claim to represent the literature of the subject. My purpose has been to set down every book—whether it has been expressly quoted or not—to which I am conscious of having owed help.

Blass, F.	*Die Attische Beredsamkeit von Gorgias bis zu Lysias.* Leipzig, 1868.
„	*Isokrates und Isaios.* 1874.
„	*Die Griechische Beredsamkeit in dem Zeitraum von Alexander bis auf Augustus.* 1865.
Boeckh, A.	*Die Staatshaushaltung der Athener.* 2nd ed. 1851.
Boehnecke, G.	*Demosthenes, Lykurgos, Hyperides und ihr Zeitalter.* 1864.
Brause, R. T.	*De aliquot locis Isocratis.* Freiburg, 1843.
Bremi, J. H.	*Lysiae et Aeschinis Orationes selectae.* 1826.
Brougham, Lord.	*Rhetorical and Literary Dissertations and Addresses.* 1856.
Campbell, G.	*The Philosophy of Rhetoric.* 7th edit., 1823.
Cartelier, A.	*Le Discours d Isocrate sur lui-même* (with Introduction by E. Havet), 1862.
Clinton, H. Fynes.	*Fasti Hellenici.* 3 vols. 1834—1851.
Cobet, C. G.	*Novae Lectiones.* 1858.—*Variae Lectiones.* 1873.
Cope, E. M.	*The Sophists*, in Journ. of Class. and Sacred Philology, I. 145: *On the Sophistical Rhetoric, ib.* II. 129, III. 253.
„	*Introduction to Aristotle's Rhetoric,* 1867.
„	*Plato's Gorgias, literally translated, with an Introductory Essay.* 1864.
Cowell, Herbert.	*Tagore Law Lectures for* 1870. Calcutta, 1870.
Cox, G. W.	*History of Greece,* Vols. I. and II., 1874.
Curtius, E.	*History of Greece,* translated by A.W.Ward. 5 vols., 1868—1872.
Dobree, P. P.	*Adversaria.* 2 vols., 1831.
Dyer, T. H.	*Ancient Athens.* 1873.
Eckert, H.	*De Epitaphio Lysiae falso tributo.* Berlin. 1865 (?).
Ernesti, J. C. T.	*Lexicon Technologiae Graecorum Rhetoricae.* 1795.
Finlay, G.	*Greece under the Romans,* B.C. 146—A.D. 716. 2nd ed., 1857.
Forsyth, W.	*Hortensius: an Historical Essay on the Office and Duties of an Advocate.* 1874.
Francken, C. M.	*Commentationes Lysiacae.* Utrecht, 1865.
Franz, J.	*Dissertatio de locis quibusdam Lysiae arte critica persanandis.* Munich, 1830.
Freeman, E. A.	*Historical Essays.* Second Series, 1873.
„	*History of Federal Government.* Vol. I., *The Greek Federations,* 1863.
Frohberger, H.	*Lysias ausgewählte Reden.* 1868.
Gladstone, W. H.	*Studies on Homer.* 1858.
Grote, G.	*History of Greece,* ed. 1870.
Hager, Herman.	*Quaestionum Hyperidearum capita duo.* Leipzig, 1870.
„	*De Graecitate Hyperidea.*
Hecker, A.	*De Oratione in Eratosthenem XXXvirum Lysiae falso tributa.* 1847—8.
Henn, P.	*De Isocrate rhetore.* Köln, 1861.
Holmes, A.	*Demosthenes De Corona.* 1871.
Hölscher, L.	*Quaestiunculae Lysiacae.* Herford, 1857.
Hume, D.	*Essay XII., Of Eloquence.*
Jones, Sir W.	*The Speeches of Isæus, with a Prefatory Discourse,* &c. 1779.

Jowett, B. | The Dialogues of Plato, translated into English, with Analyses and Introduction. 1st ed., 1871, and 2nd ed., 1875.
Kirchhoff, A. | Andocidea, in Hermes, I. 1—20.
Kyprianos, A. | Τὰ Ἀπόρρητα τοῦ Ἰσοκράτους. Athens, 1871.
Le Beau, A. | Lysias Epitaphios als echt erwiesen. Stuttgart, 1863.
Leloup, P. J. | Prolegomena in Isocratis Philippicum. 1825.
Liebmann, J. A. | De Isaei Vita et Scriptis. Halle, 1831.
Lightfoot, J. B. | On Hyperides, in Journ. of Class. and Sacred Philology, IV. p. 318, 1859.
Ljungdahl, S. | De transeundi generibus quibus utitur Isocrates commentatio. Upsala, 1871.
Lloyd, W. W. | The Age of Pericles. 1874.
Macaulay, Lord. | On the Athenian Orators (in Miscellaneous Writings, Vol. I.) 1860.
Madvig, J. N. | Adversaria, vol. I.
Maine, H. S. | Ancient Law. 5th ed., 1874.
Meier and Schömann. | Der Attische Process. 1824.
Mitchell, T. | Indices Graecitatis Oratorum Graecorum (after Reiske). 1828.
Müller, K. O. | History of the Literature of Ancient Greece, translated and continued by J. W. Donaldson. 1858.
Mure, W. | A Critical History of the Language and Literature of Ancient Greece. 1857.
Oncken, W. | Isokrates und Athen. Heidelberg, 1862.
Ottsen, P. G. | De rerum inventione ac dispositione quae est in Lysiae atque Antiphontis orationibus. Flensburg, 1847.
Overbeck, J. | Geschichte der Griechischen Plastik. 1869.
„ | Die Antiken Schriftquellen zur Gesch. der Bildenden Künste bei den Griechen. 1868.
Paley, F. A., and J. E. Sandys. | Select Private Orations of Demosthenes. Part I. Cambridge, 1874.
Pater, W. H. | Studies in the History of the Renaissance. 1873.
Perrot, G. | L'Eloquence Politique et Judiciaire à Athènes: Première Partie, Les Précurseurs de Démosthène. 1873.
„ | Démosthène et ses Contemporains (Revue des Deux Mondes, June 15, 1873).
Pfund, J. G. | De Isocratis Vita et Scriptis. Berlin, 1833.
Philippi, A. | Beiträge zu einer Geschichte des Attischen Bürgerrechtes. Berlin, 1870.
Rauchenstein, R. | Ausgewählte Reden des Lysias. 1864.
„ | Isokrates, Panegyricus, Areopagiticus. 1864.
Roelfzema, C. H. | Annotationes in Isocratis Evagoram. Gröningen, 1837.
B. H. |
Ruhnken, D. | Historia Critica Oratorum Graecorum, in his Opuscula.
„ | Disputatio de Antiphonte, ib.
Sandys, J. E. | Isocrates. Ad Demonicum et Panegyricus, 1868.
Sanneg, P. | De Schola Isocratea. Halle, 1867.
Schäfer, A. | Demosthenes und seine Zeit. 1856.
Schirach, G. B. | De vita et genere scribendi Isocratis. 1766.
Schmitz, P. J. A. | Animadversiones in Isocratis Panathenaicum. Marburg, 1835.
Schneider, O. | Isokrates ausgewählte Reden. 1860.

Schömann, G. F.	*Commentarii in Isaeum* (appended to an edit. of the text). Greisswald, 1831.
Schröder, H. P.	*Quaestiones Isocrateae duae.* Utrecht, 1859.
Sidgwick, H.	*The Sophists:* in Journal of Philology, IV. p. 288, 1872.
Simcox, G. A. Simcox, W. H.	{ *The Orations of Demosthenes and Aeschines On the Crown, with Introductory Essays and Notes,* 1872.
Sluiter, J. O.	*Lectiones Andocideae* (with C. Schiller's notes), 1834.
Spengel, L.	Συναγωγὴ Τεχνῶν, *sive Artium Scriptores.* 1828.
Stallbaum, G.	*Lysiaca ad illustrandas Phaedri Platonici origines.* 1851.
Starke, F. A. H.	*De Isocratis Orationibus Forensibus Commentationis Specimen.* 1845.
Strang, J. G.	*Kritische Bemerkungen zu den Reden des Isokrates.* 1831.
Symonds, J. A.	*Studies of the Greek Poets.* 1873.
„	*Renaissance in Italy : Age of the Despots.* 1875.
Taylor, John.	*Lectiones Lysiacae* (in Dobson's *Oratores Attici,* vol. II. pp. 94—158, 1828).
Télfy, J. B.	Συναγωγὴ τῶν 'Αττικῶν νόμων. Pesth, 1868.
Thirlwall, C.	*History of Greece,* ed. of 1855.
Thompson, W. H.	*On the Philosophy of Isocrates, and his Relation to the Socratic Schools.* Appendix II. to edition of Plato's *Phaedrus,* 1868. Also the Introductions to the *Phaedrus* and the *Gorgias* (1871), and the Commentary on both Dialogues.
Volkmann, R.	*Die Rhetorik der Griechen und Römer.* Berlin, 1872.
Wackernagel, W.	*Poetik, Rhetorik und Stilistik.* Halle, 1873.
Weijers, F. V.	*Diatribe in Lysiae Orationem in Nicomachum.* Leyden, 1839.
Weil, H.	*Les Harangues de Démosthène* (with Introd. and Commentary), 1873.
Weissenborn, H.	*Isäus,* in Ersch and Gruber's Encyclopaedia, Section II., Part 38, pp. 286—310.
Westermann, A.	*Geschichte der Griechischen Beredsamkeit.* 1835.
Whately, R.	*Elements of Rhetoric.* 7th ed., 1866.
Wilkins, A. S.	*National Education in Greece.* 1873.

CONTENTS.

CHAPTER I.

ANTIPHON.—LIFE.

CHAPTER II.

ANTIPHON.—STYLE.

CHAPTER III.

ANTIPHON.—WORKS.

CHAPTER IV.

ANDOKIDES.—LIFE.

CHAPTER V.

ANDOKIDES.—STYLE.

CHAPTER VI.

ANDOKIDES.—WORKS.

CHAPTER VII.

LYSIAS.—LIFE.

CHAPTER VIII.

LYSIAS.—STYLE.

CHAPTER IX.

LYSIAS.—WORKS.

THE EXTANT COLLECTION.—EPIDEICTIC AND DELIBERATIVE SPEECHES.

CHAPTER X.

LYSIAS.—WORKS.

FORENSIC SPEECHES IN PUBLIC CAUSES.

CHAPTER XI.

LYSIAS.—WORKS.

FORENSIC SPEECHES IN PRIVATE CAUSES—MISCELLANEOUS WRITINGS.—FRAGMENTS.

CORRIGENDA.

Vol. I. p. 66, in the note, right-hand column, line 8 from bottom, for
'*Cirrh.*' read '*Cir.*'

„   „   92, in l. 3 from bottom, for 'point' read 'part'.

„   „   130, in l. 11 from bottom, for 'in 507' read 'in or about 509.'

„   „   143, in l. 13 from top, for 444 B.C., read 'early in 443 B.C.'

„   „   180, in note 3, for 'Griesch.' read 'Griech.'

„   „   201, in l. 4 from top, 'For Andokides' read 'Against Andokides.'

„   „   226, in note 4 to p. 225, ll. 3 and 2 from end, for *Lysae...Niko-
machum*, read *Lysiae...Nicomachum.*

„   „   246, in l. 1 of *Analysis*, for 'The first' read 'The speaker first'.

„   „   248, in the note, ll. 4 and 8, for στρατικήν, 'Pyrpolinicen', read
στρατιωτικήν, 'Pyrgopolinicen'.

Vol. II. „   9, in l. 16 from top, for ἀλαζόνεια read ἀλαζονεία.

„   „   31, in l. 2 from top, for 345 read 355.

„   „   75, in l. 7 from top, for 'Praxiteles' read 'Polykleitos'.

„   „   82, in l. 4 from top, for 'Against Alkibiades,' read 'For Alkibiades.'

„   „   101, in l. 10 from top, omit '(5)'.

„   „   119, in note, l. 3, for 'Ericthonius' read 'Erichthonios'.

„   „   120, in note, l. 2 from bottom, for παρέκβασεις read παρεκβάσεις.

„   „   156, in note, l. 5, for 423 B.C. read 421 B.C.

„   „   185, in note 3, l. 6, for 'Ochos' read 'Mnemon'.

„   „   193, in l. 14, for 'the speech' read 'this speech'.

„   „   201, in note 3 to p. 200, l. 11, for 464—355 read 464—455.

„   „   217, in l. 3 from top, for 'Kyclades' read 'Kyklades.'

„   „   273, in l. 12 from top, for 'Philistos' read 'Philiskos'.

„   „   351, place the reference to Note 1 at 'civil strife,' in l. 7 from top,
not at 'Olynthians,' in l. 16.

„   „   400, l. 3 from top, for 337 read 336.

„   „   439, l. 14 from bottom, for τρίβη read τριβή.

Vol. I., *p.* 26, *note* 1.—Read the Note thus :—'Thuc. III. 82. Hermogenes
(περὶ ἰδεῶν I. cap. VI.) remarks that σεμνὴ λέξις depends more on ὀνόματα, sub-
stantives and adjectives, than on ῥήματα, verbs. Thus, he says, in this
sentence of Thucydides, the whole effect is wrought by the ὀνόματα. And
so verbal adjectives (ἀπὸ ῥημάτων εἰς ὄνομα πεποιημένα) are preferred to relative
clauses with the verb. (*E.g.* τόλμα ἀλόγιστος is σεμνότερον than ὅστις τολμῶν
οὐ λογίζεται.)'—[This, I now believe with Ernesti *s. v.* ὄνομα, is the ὀνομαστικὴ
σεμνότης—as opposed to ῥηματική—here meant by Hermogenes.]

ANNALS.

Olympiads and Archons.	B.C.		
72. Diognetos	492		Fleet of Mardonios destroyed off Athos.
2. Hybrilides	491		Persian heralds sent by Dareios to demand earth and water from the Greek cities.
3. Phaenippos	490	Pindar Πυθ. 7 and (?) 12. Aeschylos fights at Marathon.	Persians, under Artaphernes and Datis, invade Greece: Hippias lands with them at Marathon. Athenian victory.
4. Aristides	489		Expedition of Miltiades to Paros: his disgrace and death.
73. Anchises	488	Pheidias born?	
2.	487	Simonides of Keos flourishes.	
3.	486	Pindar Πυθ. 3.	Death of Dareios: Xerxes king of Persia.
4. Philokrates	485	Gorgias, Protagoras and Tisias born about this time.	Gelon becomes tyrant of Syracuse.
74. Leostratos	484	Pindar Ολυμπ. 10 and 11. Epicharmos writes Comedy at Syracuse. Aeschylos begins to be eminent in Tragedy. Herodotos born.	
2. Nikodemos	483		Aristeides ostracised.
3.	482		
4. Themistokles	481		
75. Kalliades	480	Antiphon born. Pindar Ισθμ. 7. Euripides born. (Aeschylos was now 45, and Sophokles 15.)	Amnesty at Athens before Salamis i. 125. Second Persian invasion. Xerxes crosses Hellespont. Battles of Thermopylae, Artemision and Salamis.
2. Xanthippos	479		Athenians reject the offers of Mardonios: he occupies Athens. Battles of Plataea and Mykale. Athenian ἀρχή founded. Athens rebuilt and Peiraeus fortified: Walls of Themistokles.

Olympiads and Archons.	B.C.		
3. Timosthenes	478	History of Herodotos ends at siege of Sestos (spring).	Hieron succeeds Gelon as tyrant of Syracuse: Korax flourishes in his reign (cf. 466 B.C.). Pausanias recalled from Byzantium to Sparta.
4. Adeimantos	477		Formation of Delian Confederacy under headship of Athens: tribute assessed on members by Aristeides. Treason and death of Pausanias.—Kleisthenean constitution begins to be developed through the ναυτικὸς ὄχλος: Fourth Class made eligible for archonship: boards for internal administration multiplied (ἀγοράνομοι, ἀστύνομοι, &c.).
76. Phaedon	476	Phrynichos tragicus victor with Φοίνισσαι.	Athenians take Eion, reconquer Lemnos, reduce Skyros and Karystos.
2. Dromokleides	475		
3. Akestorides	474		
4. Menon	473		
77. Chares	472	Pindar Ὀλυμπ. 1 and 12. Death of Pythagoras aet. 99. Aeschylos Πέρσαι.	Thrasydaeos, tyrant of Agrigentum, expelled: Empedokles opposes the restoration of the tyranny, I. cxx.
2. Praxiergos	471	Thucydides born.	Themistokles ostracised.
3. Demotion	470		
4. Apsephion	469		
78. Theagenides	468	Pindar Ὀλυμπ. 6. Sophokles gains his first tragic victory, aet. 28. Sokrates born.	Death of Aristeides.
2. Lysistratos	467		Thrasybulos succeeds Hieron as tyrant of Syracuse.
3. Lysanias	466	Korax begins to teach Rhetoric at Syracuse: I. cxxi.—Pindar Πυθ. 4 and 5. Diagoras of Melos flor.	Thrasybulos expelled from Syracuse: Gelonian dynasty overthrown and a democracy established. Naxos revolts from Athens and is subjugated.
4. Lysitheos	465		Athenian colonists destroyed by Thracians near Ennea Hodoi: II. 189. Thasos revolts from Athens: is reduced 463 B.C. Death of Xerxes: Artaxerxes I. (Μακρόχειρ) king (—425 B.C.).
79. Archidemides	464	Pindar Ὀλυμπ. 7 and 13.	Helots rise against Spartans (—455 B.C.): quarrel between Athens and Sparta: alliance between Athens and Argos.
2. Tlepolemos	463		
3. Konon	462		
4. Evippos	461		Megara joins Athenian alliance: Long Walls of Megara built.

Olympiads and Archons.	B.C.		
80. Phrasiklei-des	460	Parmenides visits Athens. Zenon of Elea ('inventor of Dialectic', Arist.) flor. Hippokrates the physician born. Demokritos born.	Kephalos, father of Lysias, invited to settle at Athens by Perikles? I. 142. Revolt of Egypt from Persia (—455 B.C.).
2. Philokles	459	Lysias born, acc. to [Plut.] and Dionys. (cf. 444 B.C.) I. 143.—Thrasymachos of Chalkedon born?	Reforms of Ephialtes II. 208.
3. Bion	458	Aeschylos Ὀρεστεία.	Kimon ostracised?
4. Mnesithei-des	457		Long Walls of Athens begun. Embitterment of the conservative party: murder of Ephialtes.—Athenians defeated at Tanagra by Lacedaemonians and allies.—Athenians defeat Boeotians at Oenophyta. Athenian empire at its greatest extent
81. Kallias	456	Pindar Ὀλυμπ. 9. Death of Aeschylos aet. 69.	Kimon recalled from exile. Long Walls of Athens completed.
2. Sosistratos	455	First tragedy, Πελιάδες, of Euripides, aet. 36.	Destruction of Athenian armament sent to help Inaros II. 189. Persians reduce all Egypt except the fens held by Amyrtaeos.—Ithome surrenders to Sparta (cf. 464 B.C.): Tolmides, στρατηγός, settles expelled Helots at Naupaktos.—Athens conquers Aegina.
3. Ariston	454		Death of Alexander I. (φιλέλλην) of Macedon (498 B.C.—): accession of Perdikkas.
4. Lysikrates	453		
82. Chaerepha-nes	452	Pindar Ὀλυμπ. 4 and 5.	
2. Antidotos	451	Ion of Chios, tragic poet, begins to exhibit.	
3. Euthyde-mos	450	Krates comicus and Bakchylides lyricus flor. Anaxagoras aet. 50 withdraws from Athens: he had taught Perikles and Euripides.	FiveYears'Truce between Athens and Sparta I. 130. Athens sends 60 ships to help Amyrtaeos in Egypt.
4. Pedieus	449		Siege of Citium in Cyprus by Kimon: cf. II. 189. His death. Athenian victory at the Cyprian Salamis. Alleged treaty ('of Kallias') between Athens and Persia, II. 157 Alkibiades born?
83. Philiskos	448	Kratinos comicus flor.	
2. Timarchi-des	447		Death of Themistokles.—Athenians under Tolmides defeated by Boeotians at Koroneia. Athenians evacuate Boeotia: their ἀρχή begins to break up.

Olympiads and Archons.	B.C.		
3. Kallimachos	446		
4. Lysimachides	445	Iktinos and Kallikrates, architects, flor.	Euboea and Megara revolt from Athens. Lacedaemonians under Pleistoanax invade Attica. Thirty Years' Truce between Athens and Sparta: Andokides, grandfather of the orator, an envoy, I. 132.
84. Praxiteles	444	Date for birth of Lysias placed between this year and 436 by C. F. Hermann and Blass, I. 144 (cf. 459 B.C.). Pheidias aet. 44 has superintendence of the public art-works of Athens.	Foundation of Thurii (I. 143), by Athenian colonists, on the site of Sybaris.
2. Lysanias	443	Death of Pindar aet. 79. Herod. aet. 43 goes to Thurii: Lysias either now or later.	Thucydides, son of Melesias, ostracised: aristocratic party broken up.
3. Diphilos	442	Euripides aet. 49 gains, for the first time, the first prize in tragedy.	
4. Timokles	441		
85. Myrochides	440	Andokides born, I. 71. Decree to put down Comedy (ψήφισμα τοῦ μὴ κωμωδεῖν). Sophokles Ἀντιγόνη (in the year of his στρατηγία).	Revolt of Samos from Athens: Andokides avus and Sophokles command with Perikles against Samos, I. 72. Samos surrenders in 9th month. Appeal of Samians to Lacedaemonians: congress at Sparta: Corinthians insist on the principle of non-interference with an autonomous city.
2. Glaukines	439		
3. Theodoros	438	Parthenon completed and dedicated: Pheidias aet. 50. — Euripides Ἄλκηστις.—Kalamis, sculptor, flor.	
4. Euthymenes	437	Pheidias goes to Elis. Decree against Comedy repealed.	
86. Lysimachos	436	Isokrates born, II. 2. The Zeus at Olympia completed by Pheidias. Propylaea of Athens begun.	The people of Epidamnos apply to their metropolis Corcyra: help is refused, and they apply to Corinth.
2. Antilochides	435	Phrynichos comicus begins to write. Polygnotos, painter, flor.	Corinthian army admitted into Epidamnos: sea-fight between Corinthians and Corcyraeans: Epidamnos capitulates to Corcyraeans.
3. Chares	434		
4. Apseudes	433		Embassies to Athens from Corcyra and from Corinth: Athens makes a defensive alliance with Corcyra: 10

Olympiads and Archons.	B.C.		
			Athenian ships sent to Corcyra under Lakedaemonios son of Kimon.
87. Pythodoros	432	Pheidias and Aspasia prosecuted ἀσεβείας: Pheidias dies in prison— Anaxagoras also persecuted: he withdraws to Lampsakos.	Corcyraeans, supported by Athenians, defeated in a sea-fight by Corinthians (spring).— Athenians blockade Pydna and Potidaea.—Congress at Sparta (autumn): a large majority of the allies vote for war with Athens.
2. Euthydemos	431	Perikles speaks the ἐπιτάφιος of those who had fallen in the first year of the war. Euripides Μήδεια. Xenophon born.	Peloponnesian demands rejected by Athens.—*Beginning of Peloponnesian War.*—Theban attempt on Plataea.—First invasion of Attica under Archidamos.—Brasidas, now first heard of, rescues Methone from Athenians.
3. Apollodoros	430	Polykleitos, sculptor, flor.	*Year 2 of War.*—Second invasion of Attica.—Plague at Athens.—Perikles unpopular: he is fined, but re-elected strategos.
4. Epameinon	429	Damon, musician, flor. II. 145. Plato born (May).—Death of Perikles (autumn). Eupolis writes Comedy.	*Year 3 of War.*—Potidaea surrenders on conditions (cf. 332 B.C.)—Phormion, commanding Athenian fleet, gains two victories in Corinthian gulf.
88. Diotimos	428		*Year 4 of War.*—Lesbos, except Methymna, revolts: Athenians besiege Mytilene. —Third invasion of Attica, led by Kleomenes.
2. Eukleides	427	Gorgias visits Athens as chief envoy of Leontini, I. cxxv. Tisias accompanies him, acc. to Paus. Aristophanes begins to satirize the New Culture in his Δαιταλεῖς—a contrast between the old school and the new.	*Year 5 of War.*—Plataea destroyed by Sparta, II. 176.— Fourth invasion of Attica, led by Kleomenes.—Mytilene taken by Athenians, I. 56: massacre proposed by Kleon and averted by Diodotos.— Strife at Corcyra between oligarchs and demos (summer). Athens sends help to Leontini.
3. Euthynos	426	Aristophanes Βαβυλώνιοι— a plea for the allies against Kleon, &c.	*Year 6 of War.*—Athenians purify Delos and restore the Panionic festival, to be held there every 4 years.
4. Stratokles	425	Aristophanes Ἀχαρνεῖς. Zeuxis, painter, flor.	*Year 7 of War.*—Corcyraean demos, helped by Eurymedon and Athenians, storm Istone: massacre of oligarchs.—Fifth invasion of Attica led by Agis II. — Demosthenes occupies Pylos. Spartan hoplites blockaded in Sphakteria: Kleon

Olympiads and Archons.	B.C.		
			takes the island, and brings Spartan prisoners to Athens. —Death of Artaxerxes I. (465 B.C.—See next year.)
89. Isarchos	424	Aristophanes Ἱππεῖς.	Year 8 of War.—Defeat of Athenians by Thebans at Delium.—Brasidas in Thrace: he gains Akanthos, Amphipolis, Stageiros, Torone.—Congress of Sicilian Greeks at Gela: Hermokrates denounces Athenian aggression. Accession of Dareios II. (Νόθος—405 B.C.) after a contest.
2. Ameinias	423	Thucydides, the historian, is banished, or withdraws from Athens, in consequence of his failure to save Amphipolis (January?). Returns to Athens in 403. Aristophanes Νεφέλαι (1st edit.).	Year 9 of War.—Brasidas in Thrace: Skione and Mende revolt from Athens.—Truce for a year.
3. Alkaeos	422	Aristophanes Σφῆκες.	Year 10 of War.—Torone recovered by Kleon. Battle of Amphipolis: Kleon and Brasidas killed.—Number of Athenian males above the age of 20 was at this time about 20,000: total civic population (excluding μέτοικοι and slaves) about 82,000: average attendance in Ekklesia, about 5000.
4. Aristion	421	Eupolis in his Κόλακες brings in Protagoras as then living at Athens.	Year 11 of War.—Peace 'of Nikias,' for 50 years, nominally valid down to 414, but not accepted by Boeotians, Corinthians or Megarians.
90. Astyphilos	420	Isaeos born II. 262. Plato comicus flor.	Year 12 of War.—Separate treaty of Sparta with (1) Boeotians, (2) Argives.—Alkibiades contrives to alienate the Argives from Sparta: defensive alliance between Athens, Argos, Elis and Mantineia.
2. Archias	419		Year 13 of War.—Alkibiades στρατηγός: he makes a progress through Achaia.—Invasion of Epidauros by Argives.
3. Antiphon	418		Year 14 of War.—Spartans invade Argos. Argives, with Alkibiades, attack Orchomenos: Spartans come to the defence of Tegea. Battle of Mantineia (cf. 362 B.C.): Com-

Olympiads and Archons.	B.C.		
			plete victory of Spartans over Argives and Athenians. Oligarchical conspiracy of the Thousand at Argos.
4. Euphemos	417	Antiphon or. 5 περὶ τοῦ Ἡρώδου φόνου, I. 59	*Year 15 of War.*—Rising of Argive demos against oligarchs. —Athenian expedition to get back Amphipolis: Perdikkas of Macedon breaks faith, and the plan fails.—Ostracism of Hyperbolos, I. 134—the tenth, and last, recorded exercise of ostracism since its institution by Kleisthenes about 509 B.C. (Cf. I. 137.)
91. Arimnestos	416	Agathon tragicus flor.	*Year 16 of War.*—Athenians take Melos, II. 156. Victories of Alkibiades at Olympia? II. 227.—Embassy to Athens from Egesta, asking help against Selinus. Athenian envoys sent to Egesta.
2. Chabrias	415	Andokides banished, under the decree of Isotimides, I. 75. Fictitious date of [Andok.] or. 4 κατὰ Ἀλκιβιάδου, I. 134. Sokrates flor., *aet.* 53: Plato is now 14: Alkibiades circ. 34, Xenophon circ. 16.—Euripides Τρωάδες.	*Year 17 of War.*—Envoys return from Egesta: Sicilian Expedition voted.—Mutilation of the Hermae, just as fleet is going to sail for Sicily (May), I. 73—(Athenian ambitions in 415: II. 188.) — Alkibiades accused of profaning Mysteries.—*Expedition sails for Sicily* under Nikias, Lamachos and Alkibiades.—Excitement caused at Athens by disclosures of Diokleides and Andokides. Alkibiades condemned to death in his absence.—Nikias misses his chance of investing Syracuse.
3. Peisandros	414	Aristophanes Ὄρνιθες.	*Year 18 of War.*—*Second campaign in Sicily.* Lamachos killed. Gylippos enters Syracuse. Nikias writes to Athens for help.
4. Kleokritos	413		*Year 19 of War.*—Dekeleia in Attica fortified by Lacedaemonians, II. 188, who ravage Attica. Formal end to the truce of 421. Beginning of the second chapter of the War, called the Δεκελεικὸς or Ἰώνιος πόλεμος (− 404 B.C.)— *Third campaign in Sicily.* Sea-fight at Syracuse: Athenian fleet destroyed. Death of Nikias and of Demosthenes.

Olympiads and Archons.	B.C.		
			Death of Perdikkas, King of Macedon (454 B.C.—); accession of Archelaos (—399 B.C.).
92. Kallias	412	Antiphon or. 6 περὶ τοῦ χορευτοῦ? I. 63.—Lysias and his brother Polemarchos driven from Thurii, come to Athens.—Euripides 'Ελένη, 'Ανδρομέδα. Kallimachos, sculptor, flor.	Year 20 of War.—Revolt of Lesbos from Athens, I. 58. Revolt of Euboea, II. 263. Revolt of Chios, II. 160. Pedaritos commands there for Sparta, II. 198. Revolt of Miletos. Oropos seized by Boeotians, II. 179. Athenians lose a sea-fight off Knidos, II. 351.—Samian demos, true to Athens, rises against the oligarchs. Athenian fleet musters at Samos: Spartan Astyochos defeats Charmînos. Alkibiades takes refuge from Spartans with Tissaphernos: his overtures to the Athenian leaders.
2. Theopompos	411	First return of Andokides to Athens, I. 79. Antiphon dies, I. 13. Xenophon begins his 'Ελληνικά with the manœuvres at the Hellespont just after the battle of Kynossema: cf. 362 B.C. Aristophanes Λυσιστράτη, Θεσμοφοριάζουσαι.	Year 21 of War.—Government of the Four Hundred, I. 7: (March —June.)—Eratosthenes (Lys. or. 12) active at the Hellespont for the oligarchs: I. 266.—Athenian victory at Kynossema.—Evagoras begins to reign? II. 110.
3. Glaukippos	410	Second return of Andokides to Athens: or. 2. περὶ τῆς ἑαυτοῦ καθόδου, I. 109.—Dramatic date of Plato Φαῖδρος? II. 3.—History of Thucydides breaks off after the battle of Kyzikos.	Year 22 of War.—Thrasyllos commands on coast of Asia Minor, I. 297.—Second form of the Trierarchy brought in — συντριηραρχία: cf. 357, 340 B.C.—Athenians attack and recover Kyzikos: death of Spartan admiral Mindaros. — Kleophon δημαγωγός: Athens rejects Spartan offers of peace.
4. Diokles	409	Sophokles Φιλοκτήτης.	Year 23 of War.—Athenian campaign under Thrasyllos in Lydia. — Messenians in Pylos surrender to Sparta.—Megara recovers Nisaea.
93. Euktemon	408	Euripides 'Ορέστης. Aristophanes Πλοῦτος (1st edit.: cf. 388 B.C.).	Year 24 of War.—Alkibiades recovers Selymbria and Byzantium for Athens.—Troops under Thrasyllos defeated at Ephesos, I. 297.
2. Antigenes	407	Lysias or. 20 ὑπὲρ Πολυστράτου? I. 217.	Year 25 of War.—Alkibiades returns to Athens, is chosen στρατηγός and leads the procession to Eleusis.—Antiochos, the pilot of Alkibiades, defeated by Lysander off

Olympiads and Archons.	B.C.		
			Notion. Alkibiades plunders Kyme. He is deposed from his στρατηγία: ten new Generals are chosen.
3. Kallias	406	Death of Euripides.	*Year 26 of War.*—Dionysios I. becomes tyrant of Syracuse, II. 171.—Kallikratidas (successor of Lysander) storms Methymna and blockades Konon in Mytilene. Complete victory of Athenians at Arginusae: death of Kallikratidas.—Theramenes accuses the Generals: six are put to death, Sokrates protesting.
4. Alexias	405	Death of Sophokles. Aristophanes Βάτραχοι. Dramatic date of Plato Γοργίας.	*Year 27 of War.*—Battle of Aegospotami (late autumn). The Areiopagos takes measures for public safety, II. 212. Konon escapes to Evagoras. Death of Dareios II. (424 B.C.—): Artaxerxes II. (Μνήμων—359 B.C.) succeeds him.
94. Pythodorus	404	Polemarchos, brother of Lysias, put to death by the Thirty (May); Lysias escapes to Megara, I. 148: cf. 265.—Isokrates leaves Athens for Chios, II. 6.	Theramenes brings the terms of peace from Sparta. Agoratos informs, I. 269. Athens surrenders to Lysander. Kritias and Eratosthenes are among the five ἔφοροι, and then among the xxx., I. 266. Tyranny of the Thirty begins (April). Thrasybulos advances from Phyle to Peiraeus. The Thirty deposed in 8th month (Dec.). Theramenes put to death in autumn, II. 6.—Death of Alkibiades aet. circ. 45.
2. *Eukleides*	403	Proposal to give Lysias the citizenship defeated by Archinos, I. 151. Lysias or. 12 κατὰ 'Ερατοσθένους, I. 261.—Lysias or. 34 περὶ τοῦ μὴ καταλῦσαι τὴν πολιτείαν, I. 211. Isokrates returns to Athens, II. 6. Isokrates or. 21 πρὸς Εὐθύνουν, II. 219.	Thrasybulos and the exiles in the Peiraeus are at war with the Ten; but are in possession of Athens before the end of July.—Democracy formally restored in September.—Law of Aristophon, II. 328.— Knights who had served under the Thirty are required to refund their κατάστασις, I. 246.—Expedition from Athens to Eleusis, to dislodge the Thirty, I. 252.
3. Mikon	402	Third and final return of Andokides to Athens. Lysias or. 21 δωροδοκίας ἀπολογία, I. 219. Lysias or. 24 ὑπὲρ τοῦ ἀδυνάτου? I. 255.	

Olympiads and Archons.	B. C.	
4. Xenaenetos	401	Isokrates or. 18 πρὸς Καλλίμαχον, II. 232. Lysias or. 25 δήμου καταλύσεως ἀπολογία, I. 250. Sophokles Οἰδίπους ἐπὶ Κολωνῷ: brought out by Sophokles nepos.	Expedition of Cyrus the younger, II. 161, 173. Battle of Kunaxa and death of Cyrus (autumn).—Retreat of the Greeks: they reach Armenia in the winter.—War between Lacedaemon and Elis.
95. Laches	400	Parrhasios, painter, flor.	Campaign of Thimbron in Asia Minor, II. 161. The Greeks in their retreat reach Kotyora on the Euxine 8 months after battle of Kunaxa.
2. Aristokrates	399	Andokides or. 1 περὶ τῶν μυστηρίων, I. 114.—Death of Sokrates, I. 153.—Lysias or. 30 κατὰ Νικομάχου, I. 224.—[Lys.] or. 6 κατὰ 'Ανδοκίδου, I. 281.—Plato withdraws to Megara.—Lys. or. 13 κατὰ 'Αγοράτου, I. 269.	Proceedings before the Areiopagos against men formerly of the xxx., I 296. Derkyllidas supersedes Thimbron in Asia Minor, II. 161.—Death of Archelaos of Macedon (413 B.C.—); his son Orestes succeeds, but is dispossessed (396 B.C.) by his guardian Aeropos. See 394.
3. Ithykles	398	Ktesias brought his Περσικά to this year.	Second campaign of Derkyllidas in Asia Minor.
4. Suniades	397	Lysias or. 17 περὶ δημοσίων χρημάτων [better περὶ τῶν 'Ερἀτωνος χρημάτων] I. 300 Isokrates or. 17 περὶ τοῦ ξεύγους, II. 228.	Third campaign of Derkyllidas in Asia Minor: he is about to invade Karia when he meets the satraps and makes an armistice with Tissaphernes.
96. Phormion	396		Beginning of ὁ περὶ 'Ρόδον πόλεμος between Persia and Sparta (—394 B.C.), II. 160. First campaign of Agesilaos in Asia Minor, II. 161.
2. Diophantos	395	Lysias or. 18 περὶ δημεύσεως τῶν τοῦ Νικίου ἀδελφοῦ, I. 229. Plato aet. 34 returns to Athens. His Γοργίας written between this year and 389. Lysias or. 7 περὶ τοῦ σηκοῦ? I. 289.	Athenian expedition to relieve Haliartos, I. 247. Alkibiades the younger takes part, I. 257, and Lysander is killed.—Second campaign of Agesilaos.
3. Eubulides	394	[Lysias] or. 9 ὑπὲρ τοῦ στρατιωτοῦ, I. 232. Isokrates or. 20 κατὰ Λοχίτου, II. 215.—(or. 393) or. 19 'Αιγινητικός, II. 217: or. 17 Τραπεξιτικός, II. 222.	Beginning of Corinthian War (—390 B.C.), II. 161. Naval campaigns of Konon (Lys. or. 19), I. 235.—Battle of Corinth. Agesilaos in Boeotia (autumn), I. 247. Battle of Knidos, II. 160. — Dionysios I. hard pressed by Carthaginians, II. 198. — Amyntas II. of Macedon begins to reign, II. 158.

Oiympiads and Archons.	B.C.		
4. Demostratos	393	Lysias or. 3 κατὰ Σίμωνος, I. 277. Polykrates κατηγορία Σωκρατους, II. 94. (—391) Isaeos the pupil of Isokrates, II. 264.	Long Walls of Athens restored by Konon, I. 83. Lechaeum, western port of Corinth, taken by Lacedaemonians, II. 352.
97. Philokles	392	Lysias or. 16 ὑπὲρ Μαντιθέου? I. 245. Isokrates begins to teach. First period of his School, 392—378 B. C. : II. 10.—Aristophanes 'Εκκλησιάζουσαι.	
2. Nikoteles	391	(—390 B. C.) Isokrates or. 11 Βούσιρις, II. 93: or. 13 κατὰ σοφιστῶν, II. 127.	Plenipotentiaries sent by Athens to treat for peace at Sparta, I. 83 (winter 391—390).
3. Demostratos	390	Andokides or. 1 περὶ τῆς πρὸς Λακεδαιμονίους εἰρήνης (spring), I. 128.—Isokrates visits Gorgias in Thessaly, II. 5. Isaeos or. 5 περὶ τοῦ Δικαιογένους κλήρου, II. 348. Skopas, sculptor, and Theopompos, last poet of Old Comedy, flor.	Thrasybulos the Steirian receives Amadokos I. and Seuthes into the alliance of Athens, II. 168 : descends the coast of Asia Minor, II. 346.
4. Antipatros	389	Lysias or. 28 κατὰ 'Εργοκλέους, I. 221. Lysias or. 27 κατὰ 'Επικράτους? I. 222. Lysias or. 29 κατὰ Φιλοκράτους, I. 240. Aeschines born. Plato aet. 40 first visits Sicily. His Πολιτεία was begun before this year.	Death of Thrasybulos the Steirian, I. 246. Athenian expedition to aid Evagoras, I. 236.—Conquests of Dionysios I. in Sicily and Magna Graecia, II. 163 (389—387 B. C.).
98. Pyrrhion	388	Lysias or. 33 'Ολυμπιακός, I. 204. Aristophanes Πλοῦτος—second (the extant) edition, marking the transition to Middle Comedy; cf. 408 B. C. Polykrates eminent as a teacher of Rhetoric, II. 95.	388—387 B. C., Diotimos commands in Hellespont, I. 237. Dionysios I. of Syracuse sends an embassy to Olympia : I. 155.
2. Theodotos	387	Lysias or. 19 περὶ τῶν 'Αριστοφάνους χρημάτων, I. 235.	Eight triremes under Thrasybulos the Kollytean taken by Antalkidas, near Abydos, I. 243.—Peace of Antalkidas, II. 151
3. Mystichides	386	Lysias or. 22 κατὰ τῶν σιτοπωλῶν? I. 227. Plato aet. 43 begins to teach in the Academy?	Plataea rebuilt by Sparta as a stronghold against Thebes, II. 176.
4. Dexitheos	385		Mantineia destroyed by Lacedaemonians, II. 152.—Beginning of war between Evagoras and Artaxerxes II., II. 158.

Olympiads and Archons.	B.C.		
99. Diotrephes	384	(—383 B.C.) Lys. or. 10 κατὰ Θεομνήστου, I. 293. Demosthenes born (Schäfer). Aristotle born: Plato *aet.* 45.	
2. Phanostratos	383		Olynthos besieged by Lacedaemonians, II. 150.—Beginning of Olynthian War (— 379), II. 158. Kotys becomes King of Thracian Odrysae. Iphikrates goes against him with Athenian force: then makes peace with him, II. 337.
3. Evandros	382	Lysias or. 26 κατὰ 'Ευάνδρου, I. 242.	The Kadmeia seized by Lacedaemonians, II. 152.—Philip of Macedon, son of Amyntas II., born : cf. 359 B.C.
4. Demophilos	381	(—380 B.C.) Lysias frag. cxx. f. (Sauppe) ὑπὲρ Φερενίκου, I. 312.	
100. Pytheas	380	Lysias (I. 155).	Phlius besieged by Lacedaemonians, II. 150.
2. Nikon	379	Gorgias and Aristophanes die about this time.	End of Olynthian War, II. 158.
3. Nausinikos	378	(—376 B.C.) Isokrates companion and secretary of Timotheos, II. 10. These orators flourish;— Kallistratos, Leodamas, Thrasybulos and Kephalos of Kollytos, II. 372.	Athens at the head of a new Naval Confederacy, II. 10.— Financial reform: establishment of the 20 συμμορίαι for payment of war-tax, II. 30. Θηβαϊκὸς πόλεμος (II. 331) begins (— 371 B.C.). Invasions of Boeotia by Agesilaos and Kleombrotos, II. 176.
4. Kallias	377	(—371 B.C.) Isaeos or. 10 περὶ τοῦ 'Αριστάρχου κλήρου, II. 333.	Agesilaos invades Boeotia. — Thebes begins to reorganise the Boeotian Confederacy, II. 178.
101. Charisandros	376	—351, Second period of the school of Isokrates, II. 10. Death of Antisthenes, II. 103.	End of war (385—) between Evagoras and Artaxerxes II., II. 158. Kleombrotos invades Boeotia.
2. Hippodamos	375	Isaeos or. 8 περὶ τοῦ Κίρωνος κλήρου? II. 327. Araros (son of Aristophanes) and Eubulos, earliest poets of Middle Comedy.	Timotheos sails round Peloponnesos: Corcyra and other cities of the Ionian Sea join the Athenian League.
3. Sokratides	374	Isokrates or. 2 πρὸς Νικοκλέα, II. 87.	—370 B.C., Jason of Pherae tagos of Thessaly, II. 18. Death of Evagoras king of the Cyprian Salamis, II. 107. Congress at Sparta. Peace between Athens and Sparta, II. 178 : Thebes excluded from it, *ib.* 181.
4. Asteios	373	Isokrates or. 14 Πλαταϊκός, II. 176.	Plataea destroyed. Walls of Thespiae razed by Thebans,

Olympiads and Archons.	B.C.		
			ii. 177—9. At this time Oropos belonged to Athens, *ib.* : cf. 412 B.C.—Timotheos deposed from his στρατηγία and accused by Iphikrates and Kallistratos. — Iphikrates, Chabrias, Kallistratos chosen Generals.
102. Alkisthenes	372	Isokrates or. 1 πρὸς Δημόνικον? ii. 84 : or. 3 Νικοκλῆς ἢ Κύπριοι, ii. 90.	
2. Phrasikleides	371		Battle of Leuktra, July 6, ii. 196. General Peace (excluding the Thebans) concluded at Sparta ('Peace of Kallias'), June 16, ii. 141.—Jason of Pherae enters Greece as mediator.
3. Dysniketos	370	Isokrates or. 10 Ἑλένης ἐγκώμιον, ii. 100.	Jason assassinated, ii. 18. First march of Epameinondas into Peloponnesos : invasion of Laconia : foundation of Megalopolis and of the new Messene, ii. 194.
4. Lysistratos	369	Isaeos or. 9 περὶ τοῦ Ἀστυφίλου κλήρου, ii. 330.	Second march of Epameinondas into Peloponnesos. First expedition sent by Dionysios I. of Syracuse to help the Corinthians and Spartans : Athens also forms friendly relations with him.—Death of Amyntas II. of Macedon : accession of his eldest son Alexander II. (brother of Philip).
103. Nausigenes	368	Isokrates *Epist.* 1 Διονύσῳ, ii. 238.	Second expedition sent by Dionysios I. Pelopidas imprisoned by Alexander of Pherae : released by Epameinondas.—Philip (*aet.* 14) sent by Ptolemaeos as a hostage to Thebes : lives there till 365 B.C. — Alexander II. of Macedon put to death by usurper Ptolemaeos (—365 B.C.).
2. Polyzelos	367	Dionysios I. gains tragic prize with Λύτρα Ἕκτορος. Plato *aet.* 62 visits Sicily for second time. Aristotle *aet.* 17 comes to Athens, where he lives till Plato's death in 347.	Death of Dionysios I. of Syracuse, ii. 19. His son Dionysios II. succeeds him. Third march of Epameinondas into Peloponnesos.—Timotheos again in command of Athenian fleet.
3. Kephisodoros	366	Isokrates or. 6 Ἀρχίδαμος, ii. 193. Demosthenes comes of age : his studies with Isaeos probably begin, ii. 267.	Sparta refuses to recognise Messene. Corinth, Epidauros and Phlius make peace for themselves with Thebes, ii. 193.

Olympiads and Archons.	B.C.		
4. Chion	365	Isokrates or. 9 'Εναγόρας? II. 106.	Oropos revolts from Athens and is occupied by the Thebans. Kallistratos and Chabrias impeached for the Oropos affair by Leodamas, Philostratos Κολωνεύς, and (?) Hegesippos :—acquitted. Timotheos reduces Samos (where κληροῦχοι are established), Sestos and Krithote. —Perdikkas III. (second son of Amyntas II. and brother of Philip) King of Macedon (— 359 B.C.).
104. Timokrates	364	(—363 B.C.) Isaeos or. 6 περὶ τοῦ Φιλοκτήμονος κλήρου, II. 343.	Timotheos succeeds to the command of Iphikrates in Thrace: takes Methone, Pidna, Potidaea, Torone. Expedition of Pelopidas into Thessaly: his death.
2. Charikleides	363	Demosthenes or. 27 κατὰ 'Αφόβου α', or. 28 κατὰ 'Αφόβου β', II. 301.	Campaign of Timotheus against Kotys and Byzantines: his return to Athens.
3. Molon	362	Demosthenes or. 30 πρὸς 'Ονήτορα α', or. 31 πρὸς 'Ονήτορα β', II. 301. Plato's third visit to Sicily. Xenophon closes his 'Ελληνικά (411 B.C.—) at the battle of Mantineia.	Fourth and last march of Epameinondas into Peloponnesos. Battle of Mantineia (July 3) ; death of Epameinondas. General peace, excluding Sparta.—Autokles Athenian commander at the Hellespont.
4. Nikophemos	361	Demosthenes or. 41 πρὸς Σπουδίαν, or. 55 πρὸς Καλλικλέα, II. 301. Deinarchos born.	Archidamos III. succeeds his father Agesilaos as a king of Sparta, II. 19.—Kallistratos flies from Athens to Thasos : Thasians recolonise Datos, II. 185. Aristophon δημαγωγός.
105. Kallimedes	360	(—353 B.C.) Isaeos or. 1 περὶ τοῦ Κλεωνόμου κλήρου, II. 319. Hypereides κατ' Αὐτοκλέους, II. 381. Praxiteles, sculptor, flor.	War between Artaxerxes II. and his satrap Orontes : Athens supports the latter II. 185.
2. Eucharistos	359	Isaeos or. 11 περὶ τοῦ 'Αγνίου κλήρου, II. 354. Demosthenes trierarch. Isokrates Epist. VI τοῖς 'Ιάσονος παισίν, II. 241.	Death of Artaxerxes II. (Μνήμων, 405 B.C.—) Accession of Artaxerxes III. (*Ωχος—337 B.C.).—Perdikkas III. of Macedon killed in battle with Illyrians : contest for throne: accession of Philip (—336 B.C.). —Alexander of Pherae murdered by his wife Thebe's half-brothers, Tisiphonos, Peitholaos and Lykophron, II. 241. Kotys, king of Thracian Odrysae, murdered : his son Ker-

Olympiads and Archons.	B.C.		
			sobleptes prevails, in a contest for the succession, over Berisades and Amadokos II., II. 185.
3. Kephisodotos	358		
4. Agathokles	57		Chios, Kos, Rhodes, Byzantium revolt from Athens. Social War begins (— 355 B.C.), II. 183. Philip takes Amphipolis, II. 185. Treaty between Chares and Kersobleptes: Thracian Chersonese (except Kardia) ceded to Athens, *ib.* Third form of the Trierarchy brought in by the συμμορίαι of Periandros: cf. 410 B.C.
106. Elpines	356	Isaeos frag. XVI (Sauppe) ὑπὲρ Εὐμάθους, II. 367. Demosthenes or. 54 κατὰ Κόνωνος? II. 300. Isokrates *Epist.* IX 'Αρχιδάμῳ, II. 243. Alexis writes Comedy.	Philip victor at Olympia: takes and destroys Potidaea: founds Philippi. Alexander the Great born. Chares defeats a Persian force, II. 206.
2. Kallistratos	355	Isokrates or. 8 περὶ τῆς εἰρήνης (or συμμαχικός): or. 7 'Αρεοπαγιτικός, II. 202. Demosthenes or. 22 κατὰ 'Ανδροτίωνος, II. 301. Aristotle may have taught Rhetoric as early as this year.	Social War ends (midsummer), II. 183.—Phocian (or Sacred) War begins (— 346 B.C.).— Oligarchies set up at Corcyra, Chios, Mytilene, &c., II. 248.
3. Diotimos	354	Death of Xenophon? Isaeos or. 2 περὶ τοῦ Μενεκλέους κλήρου, II. 336. Dem. or. 14 περὶ τῶν συμμοριῶν, II. 301, 373, or. 20 πρὸς Λεπτίνην, II. 301.	Eubulos becomes financial minister of Athens (ταμίας τῆς κοινῆς προσόδου), II. 27: cf. 338 B.C.—Timotheos brought to trial: dies at Chalkis.— Kallistratos returns to Athens (cf. 361 B.C.) :—his death, II. 186.—The Generals Ipikrates, Menestheus and Timotheos arraigned by Aristophon and Chares.
4. Eudemos	353	Isokrates or. 15 περὶ τῆς ἀντιδόσεως, II. 134. Isaeos or. 7 περὶ τοῦ 'Απολλοδώρου κλήρου, II. 324.	Philip marches along the Thracian coasts, and takes Abdera and Maroneia.—Philip takes Methone : is defeated in Thessaly by Onomarchos.
107. Aristodemos	352	Demosthenes or. 16 ὑπὲρ Μεγαπολιτῶν, or. 24 κατὰ Τιμοκράτους, or. 23 κατὰ 'Αριστοκράτους, or. 36 ὑπὲρ Φορμίωνος, II. 300. Theodektes tragicus flor. Theopompos, historian, flor.	Philip re-enters Thessaly: defeats Phocians under Onomarchos (who is killed), and advances to Thermopylae : finds it held by Athenians, and retires. He marches to Heraeon on Propontis: dictates peace to Kersobleptes, makes alliance with Kardia, Perinthos and Byzantium.—

Olympiads and Archons.	B.C.		
			He frees Pherae from the Tyranny, II. 241.
2. Thessalos	351	Demosthenes or. 4 κατὰ Φιλίππου α´, II. 301: or. 15 ὑπὲρ τῆς 'Ροδίων ἐλευθερίας.	Death of Mausolos. Artemisia proposes a contest of oratory: Theopompos the historian gains the prize, II. 11. Idrieus, brother of Mausolos, succeeds Artemisia as dynast of Karia, II. 173.—Philip marches against the Molossian Arybbas.
3. Apollodoros	350	(—338.) Third period of the school of Isokrates, II. 10. Demosthenes or. 39 πρὸς Βοιωτὸν περὶ τοῦ ὀνόματος, II. 300. Isokrates Epist. IX τοῖς Μυτιληναίων ἄρχουσιν, II. 248. Death of Isaeos? II. 269.	Euboeans ally themselves with Athens. Phokion leads Athenians to support Plutarchos of Eretria : battle of Tamynae.—Apollodoros tried and condemned for proposing to apply the θεωρικὸν to the war. —First help sent by Athens to Olynthos.
4. Kallimachos	349	Demosthenes or. 26 κατὰ Μειδίου, or. 1 'Ολυνθιακὸς α´, or. 2 'Ολυνθιακὸς β´.	Philip makes war on Olynthos and the Chalkidic towns. Alliance between Olynthians and Athens.—Second Athenian expedition, under Chares, to help them.
108. Theophilos	348	Demosthenes or. 3 'Ολυνθιακὸς γ´.	Philip besieges Olynthos—third Athenian expedition, under Chares, to help it:—Philip takes Olynthos : destroys it and the 32 Chalkidic towns of its Confederacy.
2. Themistokles	347	[Dem.] or. 40 πρὸς Βοιωτὸν περὶ προικός. Death of Plato aet. 82. Aristotle leaves Athens and goes to Hermeias of Atarneus.	Philip renews war with Kersobleptes (cf. 352)—which he ends in 346 by dictating a peace. Athenian troops under Chares sent to Thrace.— Mytilene returns into alliance with Athens.
3. Archias	346	Isokrates or. 5 Φίλιππος (April), II. 167. Demosthenes or. 5 περὶ εἰρήνης (August).	Envoys (Philokrates, Aeschines, Demosthenes, &c.) sent by Athens to Philip. — Philip goes to Thracian War.—Antipater and Parmenion negociate with Athenian envoys. —Peace 'of Philokrates' ratified on part of Athens and allies (April).—Second Athenian embassy to await Philip at Pella : he returns and takes the envoys to Pherae : ratifies peace there (end of June).—Philip occupies Phocis : end of Phocian War. Philip becomes a member of Amphictyonic Council, and thereby a Greek Power.
4. Eubulos	345	Demosthenes or. 37 πρὸς	Philip marches against Illyrii,

Olympiads and Archons.	B.C.		
		Παντaίνετιν, or. 38 πρὸs Nαυσίμαχον, II. 300. Aeschines or. 1 κατὰ Τιμάρχου. Isokrates *Epist.* VII. Τιμοθέῳ, II. 246. The Δηλιακός of Hypereides (cf. II. 385 *n.*) earlier than 344: Sauppe II. 285 f.	Dardani, Triballi.—Timoleon of Corinth goes againstDionysios II. of Syracuse.
109. Lykiskos	344	Demosthenes or. 6 κατὰ Φιλίππου β'. Aristotle removes from Atarneus to Mytilene. Ephoros, historian, flor.	Timoleon frees Sicily.—Philip begins to meddle in Peloponnesos. Demosthenes goes thither to counteract him. Embassy, in remonstrance, from Philip, Argos and Messene to Athens.
2. Pythodotos	343	Demosthenes or. 19, and Aeschines or. 2, περὶ τῆς παραπρεσβείας. Antiphanes still writing Comedy.	Philokrates is accused by Hypereides: goes into exile.— Aeschines is accused by Demosthenes of malversation in the embassy (346 B.C.), but is acquitted.
3. Sosigenes	342	Hegesippos ([Dem.] or. 7) περὶ ʾΑλοννήσου. Isokrates *Epist.* II. Φιλίππῳ a', II. 250: *Epist.* V. ʾΑλεξάνδρῳ, II. 252. Aristotle begins to teach Alexander. Menander born.	Philip sets up tetrarchies in Thessaly. — His letter to Athens about Halonnesos.— Alliance between Euboean Chalkis and Athens.—Beginning of Philip's Third Thracian War (—339 B.C.): cf. 352, 347 B.C.
4. Nikomachos	341	Demosthenes or. 8 περὶ τῶν ἐν χερσοννήσῳ, or. 9 κατὰ Φιλίππου γ'. Aphareus tragicus flor. down to this time.	Feud between Kardia and Attic kleruchi of Chersonese.— Philip supports Kardia: Diopeithes, Athenian General, ravages Thracian seaboard. Letter of Philip to Athens about the Chersonese.—Philip approaches Perinthos.—Demosthenes envoy to Byzantium: its alliance with Athens.
110. Theophrastos	340	Isokrates *Epist.* IV. ʾΑντιπάτρῳ, II. 253. Anaximenes ʾΡητορικὴ [πρὸs ʾΑλέξανδρον]?	Philip besieges Perinthos and Byzantium:—Athenians under Chares support Byzantines.—Philip's ultimatum: Athens, on proposal of Demosthenes, declares war.— Fourth form of the Trierarchy brought in by law of Demosthenes, equalising the burden on taxable capital: cf. 410, 357 B.C.
2. Lysimachides	339	Isokrates or. 12 Παναθηναϊκός, II. 113. Xenokrates begins to teach in the Academy.	Aeschines and Meidias go as πυλαγόραι to Amphictyonic Council: Amphictyons make war on Lokrians of Amphissa.—Second Athenian force sent to help Byzantium:

Olympiads and Archons.	B.C.		
			Philip raises the siege.—Amphictyons make Philip their General (Oct.). He returns to Greece, defeats mercenaries under Chares and Proxenos, and destroys Amphissa.
3. Chaerondas	338	Isokrates *Epist.* III. Φιλίππῳ β′, II. 235. Death of Isokrates, II. 31. (—326 B.C.) Lykurgos, the orator, is ταμίας τῆς κοινῆς προσόδου, II. 375.	Commissioners (including Demosthenes) appointed to restore fortifications of Athens: Demosthenes administers the θεωρικόν.—Immediately after destroying Amphissa, Philip hands over the Achaean Naupaktos to the Aetolians: then enters Phokis, and occupies Kytinion and Elateia (Feb.?).
4. Phrynichos	337	(Jan.?) At the annual winter Festival of the Dead in the outer Kerameikos, Demosthenes speaks the epitaph of those who fell at Chaeroneia. [Not extant: the Demosthenic or. 60 is spurious.]	Battle of Chaeroneia: μεταγειτνίωνος ἑβδόμῃ (Aug. 2? Curt. v. 436 Eng. tr. *n.*). Peace 'of Demades' between Philip and Athens. End of Athenian Naval Hegemony: Congress of Corinth: Hellenic League under Macedonian Hegemony: Philip Hellenic General against Persia. — Artaxerxes III. (Ὦχος) dies: Arses succeeds him.
111. Pythodemos	336	Ktesiphon proposes (March) that Demosthenes should be crowned at the Great Dionysia. Aeschines gives notice of an action παρανόμων against Ktesiphon. Deinarchos begins his activity as λογογράφος.	Death of Arses: Dareios III. King of Persia (—330 B.C.). Parmenion and Attalos open the Persian War in Asia. Philip assassinated at Aegae (early in August). Alexander the Great becomes king of Macedon.—He enters Greece: Thessaly, Amphictyons, Athens and Congress of Corinth acknowledge his hegemony.
2. Euaenetos	335	The surrender of Demosthenes. Lykurgos, &c. is demanded from Athens by Alexander:—Demades helps to arrange a peace.	Parmenion repulsed in Asia by Memnon, who takes Ephesos. — Thebans rise against Macedon: Alexander takes and destroys Thebes (autumn).
3 Ktesikles	334	Aristotle settles at Athens and teaches in the Lykeion.—His Ῥητορική certainly later than 338 B.C.	Alexander sets out for Persian War, and crosses Hellespont: wins battle of Granikos (May): reduces Aeolis and Ionia: takes Miletos and Halikarnassos: and advances to Gordion in Phrygia.
4. Nikokrates	333		Alexander routs Dareios III. at Issos (Oct.).
112. Niketes	332		Alexander besieges Tyre; takes it (July): takes Gaza: occupies Egypt: founds Alexan-

Olympiads and Archons.	B.C.		
			dria : winters at Memphis.
2. Aristopha-nes	331	Lysippos, sculptor, flor. With his school began a decline of Sculpture, parallel to that of Oratory. Cf. II. 445. Kallisthenes of Stageiros, who went with Alexander to Asia, represents the decay of taste in oratorical prose.	Alexander crosses Euphrates (July) ; routs Dareios at Arbela (Oct.) ; marches to Babylon, Susa and Persepolis.
3. Aristophon	330	(August?) Demosthenes or. 18 περὶ τοῦ στεφάνου, Aeschines or. 3 κατὰ Κτησιφῶντος, II. 398. — Aeschines leaves Athens. Lykurgos κατὰ Λεωκράτους, II. 376. Demades administers the θεωρικόν.—[Dem.] or. 17 περὶ τῶν πρὸς Ἀλέξανδρον συνθηκῶν (by Hegesippos ?). Hypereides ὑπὲρ Εὐξενίππου? II. 387.	Spartans, under Agis III., rise against Macedon : are defeated at Megalopolis by Antipater ; and accept Macedonian hegemony : death of Agis III. —Alexander pursues Dareios, who is murdered by Bessos in Parthia :—enters Hyrcania, Drangiania, and Aracosia : founds Alexandria ad Caucasum (Kandahar?).
4. Kephisophon	329		Alexander enters Baktria and Sogdiana ; takes Marakanda (Samarkand) : crosses the Oxus and advances to Jaxartes : founds Alexandria Eschate (Khojend?).—Returns to winter-quarters in Baktria.
113. Euthykritos	328	Between 330 and 326 B.C. (Schäfer) there was a great dearth at Athens, during which Demosthenes administered the σιτωνία.	Alexander subdues Sogdiana.— Slays Kleitos at Marakanda. —Harpalos sends supplies of corn to Athens, and receives the citizenship.
2. Hegemon	327		Alexander crosses the Indus and enters the Punjaub.
3. Chremes	326	End of financial administration of Lykurgos (338 B.C. —) : Menesaechmos becomes ταμίας. Fictitious date of the speech περὶ τῆς δωδεκαετίας (i.e. 338—326 B.C.): not by Demades, Sauppe II. 312.	Alexander defeats Porus. — Begins his river-voyage southwards through India.
4. Antikles	325		Alexander reaches mouth of Indus about July.—Sets out on march westward in Aug., and reaches capital of Gedrosia in Oct.—Nearchos sails for Persian Gulf in Oct.— Harpalos, the profligate treasurer of Alexander, crosses

Olympiads and Archons.	B.C.		
			from Asia to Attica:—is warned from the Peiraeus, and goes to Taenaron.
114. Hegesias	324	Deinarchos or. 1 κατὰ Δημοσθένους, or. 2 κατὰ ’Αριστογείτονος, or. 3 κατὰ Φιλοκλέους, II. 373. Hypereides κατὰ Δημοσθένους.—Death of Lykurgos (before midsummer).	Alexander celebrates the Dionysia at Susa. — Death of Hephaestion at Ekbatana.—Athens decrees divine honours to Alexander.—Demosthenes ἀρχιθέωρος at Olympia (July). —Areiopagos directs that Demosthenes, Philokles, Demades, &c. be prosecuted for taking bribes from Harpalos. —Demosthenes is fined and imprisoned:—escapes to Aegina.
2. Kephisodoros	323	Epikuros aet. 18 comes to Athens.	Alexander holds court at Babylon and receives the embassies.—His death, June 8. Lamian War, promoted by Hypereides. — Leosthenes of Athens defeats Antipater at Herakleia and besieges him in Lamia.
3. Philokles	322	Hypereides ἐπιτάφιος, II. 389. Death of Hypereides (Oct. 5). Death of Demosthenes (Oct. 12). Aristotle retires to Chalkis, and dies there (Oct. ?). Theophrastos succeeds him in the Lykeion.	Leosthenes killed before Lamia. Antiphilos succeeds to command of the Greeks and defeats Leonnatos. — Decisive victory of Macedonians at Krannon (Aug. 5).—Hellenic League breaks up. Athens submits to Antipater. On proposal of Demades, the Ekklesia pronounces Demosthenes, Hypereides, &c., traitors.
4. Archippos	321	New Comedy beginning.—Menander aet. 21 ’Οργή (his first play).—Philemon, Diphilos comici flor.	Alexander's Empire divided among his Generals. Ptolemy founds a monarchy in Egypt (306) B.C. The descendants of Seleukos found a kingdom in Asia, which afterwards shrinks up into Syria. In Macedonia there is confusion till about 272 B.C.: then the house of Antigonos reigns till 168 B.C., when Rome abolishes the kingdom.
115. Neaechmos	320		
2. Apollodoros	319		Death of Antipater.
3. Archippos	318	Death of Demades.—Demetrios Phalereus flor. Decline of Oratory begins.	

Olympiads.	B.C.		
116. 4.	314	Death of Aeschines.	
120. 1.	300	Kleitarchos of Soli, representative of the florid Asianism.	
			306—285. Ptolemy Soter.
122. 3.	290	Hegesias of Magnesia, the so-called founder of Asianism, flor.	
127. 3.	270	Theokritos, Bion, Moschos flor.	285—247. Ptolemy Philadelphos.
129. 1.	264	Timaeos of Tauromenion (now *aet.* circ. 70, resident at Athens since about 310 B.C.) brought his History down to this year. He represents the epigrammatic Asianism.	280—251. First period of Achaean League. 247—222. Ptolemy Euergetes.
130. 1.	260	Kallimachos, the poet, librarian of Alexandria.	
132. 3. —157. 3.	250 150	A period of almost total darkness in the history of Greek Oratory. When light returns, Asianism is fully dominant, but a reaction to Atticism is just beginning.	205—181. Ptolemy Epiphanes. 197. Battle of Kynoskephalae. The Greek allies of Rome, though nominally free, are henceforth practically dependent.
145. 1.	200	Aristophanes librarian of Alexandria.	
146. 3.	194	Apollonios Rhodios librarian of Alexandria.	
156. 1.	156	Aristarchos librarian of Alexandria.	
158. 3.	146	Polybios brought his History from 264 B.C. (where Timaeos left off) to this year.	Corinth destroyed. The Achaean cities become formally subject to Rome. 145. Polybios legislates for the Achaean cities.
165. 1.	120	Hierokles and Menekles represent the epigrammatic Asianism in its maturity.	
166. 3.	114	Hortensius born.	
167. 3.	110	Approximate date for Hermagoras of Temnos [usually put much too late —by Clinton, about 62 B.C. See Cic. *de Invent.* I. 8, written about 84 B.C., which shows that Hermagoras was then *long* dead: Blass die Griech. Ber. von Alex. bis zu Aug., pp.84 f.] —Hermagoras founds the Scholiastic Rhetoric, and thus prepares the way for Atticism. Apollonios ὁ μαλακός eminent as a teacher of Rhetoric at Rhodes.	

Olympiads.	B.C.		
168. 3.	106	Cicero born.	
170. 1.	100	Established fame of the Rhodian eclectic school of Oratory,—Attic in basis, but with Asian elements. Julius Caesar born. Greek Rhetoric is already thoroughly fashionable at Rome.	
171. 2.	95	Apollonios, surnamed Molon (Cicero's master), eminent at Rhodes.	
172. 1.	92	L. Plotius and others open schools at Rome for the teaching of Rhetoric, no longer in Greek, but in Latin.	
173. 3.	86		Sulla takes Athens.
174. 1.	84	Cicero *De Inventione?*	
3.	82	Caius Licinius Calvus born.	
175. 1.	80	The *Rhetorica ad Herennium* (incerti) not earlier than this year.—Aeschilos of Knidos and Aeschines of Miletos represent the florid Asianism. Cf. 120 B.C.	
175. 2.	79	Cicero, *aet.* 27, at Athens.	
177. 4.	69	Hortensius, the Roman representative of Asianism, is Consul. After this time he comes little forward as a speaker; and leaves the field to Cicero, the representative of the Rhodian eclecticism.	
181. 2.	55	Cicero *De Oratore.* Calvus represents pure Atticism of the Lysian type.	
182. 3.	50	Apollodoros of Pergamos and Theodoros of Gadara are rival masters of Scholastic Rhetoric.	
183. 1.		Death of Calvus.	
2.	46	Cicero *Brutus.* Cicero *Orator.*	
4.	44	Cicero *De Optimo Genere Oratorum.*	Death of Caesar.
184. 1.	43	Death of Cicero.	
187. 3.	30	Didymos of Alexandria, grammarian and critic, flor.	Octavianus (Augustus Caesar) begins to govern the Republic as Emperor.
188. 4.	25	Dionysios of Halikarnassos and Caecilius of Calacte, a Sicilian Greek, flourish at Rome as scholars and critics. Victory of Atti-	

Olympiads.	B.C.		
		cism over Asianism complete and nearly universal.	
189. 4.	21		Athens deprived of its jurisdiction over Eretria and Aegina: Confederacy of the free Laconian cities formed by Augustus.
191. 3.	A.D. 14		Death of Augustus.
192. 3.	18	Strabo (born 66 B.C.) published his γεωγραφικά about this year.	
213. 2.	74	Tacitus *Dialogus De Oratoribus*.	69—79. Vespasian.
214. 4.	80	The βίοι τῶν δέκα ῥητόρων, wrongly ascribed to Plutarch, were perhaps compiled about this time, chiefly from Caecilius.	
217. 2.	90	Plutarch flor. Quintilian flor.	81—96. Domitian. 98—117. Trajan.
230. 3.	143	Herodes Atticus, the master in Greek oratory of Marcus Aurelius and Lucius Verus, is made consul *aet.* 40, by Antoninus Pius. — Favorinus and Fronto flor.	117—138. Hadrian. His visits to Athens, 122—135. 138—161. Antoninus Pius.
234. 4.	160	Lucian, a Syrian of Samosata, writes the best Attic Greek since Hypereides. — Aulus Gellius *Noctes Atticae.*—Pausanias the geographer, Ptolemy the astronomer, Polyaenos (Στρατηγήματα), and Galen flor.	161—180. Marcus Aurelius.
237. 2.	170	Publius Aelius Aristeides, of Mysia, in his Παναθηναικός and ἱεροὶ λόγοι, imitates the Attic models of ἐπίδειξις. Hermogenes makes a complete digest of the Scholastic Rhetoric since Hermagoras of Temnos (110 B.C.). It is contained in his περὶ στάσεων, περὶ ἰδεῶν, περὶ εὑρέσεως, περὶ μεθόδου δεινότητος, προγυμνάσματα (in *Rhetores Graeci*, II. Spengel). Hermog. was the chief authority on his subject till Aphthonios.	
242. 2.	190	Athenaeos Δειπνοσοφισταί. Dio Cassius flor. — The ὀνομαστικόν of Julius Pol-	

Olympiads.	A.D.		
		lux drawn up about this time.	
247. 2.	210	Tertullian flor.	
249. 4.	220	Origen flor.	
251. 1.	225	Sextus Empiricus πρὸς τοὺς μαθηματικοὺς ἀντιρρητικοί: a controversy with the professors of (1) grammar and history, (2) rhetoric, (3) geometry, (4) arithmetic, (5) astrology, (6) music. — Diogenes Laertios φιλόσοφοι βίοι.	
253. 3.	235	Philostratos βίοι σοφιστῶν. Aelian flor.	
264. 4.	280	Timaeos λέξεις Πλατωνικαί.	
259. 4.	260	Longinus (Διονύσιος Κάσσιος Λογγῖνος) flor. His τέχνη ῥητορική is printed in *Rhet. Graec.*, ii. 298 f., ed. Spengel. [The treatise *On the Sublime* (περὶ ὕψους, *ib.* 245 f.) *may* be his, and is at least of about this date. The ground of the doubt is that the oldest MS. has Διονυσίου (certainly not the Halikarnassian) ἤ Λογγίνου: another, ἀνωνύμου.]	284—305. Diocletian.
			306. Flavius Valerius Constantinus (the Great) begins to reign.
273. 3.	315	Aphthonios προγυμνάσματα (in *Rhet. Graec.* ii. Spengel). This book superseded Hermogenes in the schools. At the Revival of Letters it again became a text-book of Rhetoric, saec. xvi. and xvii.	323—337. Constantine makes Christianity the religion* of the Empire, and builds Constantinople as its new capital.
282. 2.	350	Libanios of Antioch ὑποθέσεις εἰς τοὺς Δημοσθένους λόγους, βίος Δημοσθένους: μελέται: προγυμνασμάτων παραδείγματα, &c.—Gregory of Nazianzos: Athanasios flor.	361—363. Julian Emperor. 379—395. Theodosios the Great.
289. 4.	380	Aelius Theon, of Alexandria, προγυμνάσματα (in *Rhet. Graec.* ii. Speng.). [The only clue to his date is that he certainly used both Hermog. and Aphthonios, though he does not name them; and pro-	

Olympiads.	A. D.		
		bably wrote while the popularity of the latter was fresh. Cf. Walz, *Rhet. Graec.* vol. v. pp. 137 f.]	
		Eunapios of Sardis, βίοι φιλοσόφων καὶ σοφιστῶν.	390—420. The Pagan religion prohibited, and (except in the rural districts) extinguished.
293. 2.	394		Olympic Games abolished under Theodosios I.
	395		The Empire divided between the Caesar of the West and the Caesar of the East.
	397	Ioannes, surnamed Χρυσόστομος, archbishop of Constantinople.	
	480	Ioannes Stobaeos, 'Ανθολόγιον 'Εκλογαί.	
	800		Charles, king of the Franks, crowned Emperor of Rome.
	858	Photios raised to the patriarchate, Dec. 25, βιβλιοθήκη, λεξέων συναγωγή.	
	988		Cherson, the last of the Greek Commonwealths, submits to Wladimir of Russia.
	1050	? Byzantine 'Ετυμολογικὸν μέγα.	
	1100	? Suidas λέξεις.	
		Harpokration's Lexicon to the Ten Orators (λέξεις τῶν ι' ῥητόρων) was used both by the compilers of the Etymologicum and by Suidas. Its author has been identified (1) with the Harpokration who taught Lucius Verus, about 150 A.D.: (2) with the poet and teacher praised by Libanios, about 350 A.D.: (3) with the Harpokration of Mendes mentioned by Athenaeos —whom Schweighäuser (*ad* XIV. 648 b) identifies with the friend of Julius Caesar.	

INTRODUCTION.

IN the reign of Augustus, when Rome had become *The Augustan Atticism.* the intellectual no less than the political centre of the earth, a controversy was drawing to a close for which the legionaries cared less than their master, but which for at least fifty years had been of some practical interest for the Forum and the Senate, and which for nearly three centuries had divided the schools of Athens, of Pergamos, of Antioch, of Alexandria, of all places where men spoke and wrote a language which, though changed from the glory of its prime, was still the idiom of philosophy and of art. This controversy involved principles by which every artistic creation must be judged; but, as it then came forward, it referred to the standard of merit in prose literature, and, first of all, in oratory. Are the true models those Attic writers of the fifth and fourth centuries, from Thucydides to Demosthenes, whose most general characteristics are, the subordination of the form to the thought, and the avoidance of such faults as come from a misuse of ornament? Or have these been surpassed in brilliancy, in freshness of fancy, in effective force by those writers, belonging sometimes to the schools or cities of Asia Minor, sometimes to Athens itself or to Sicily, but collectively called 'Asiatics,' who flourished between Demosthenes and Cicero? This was the question of Atticism against Asianism. For a long time Asianism had been predominant. But, in the last century of the Republic, the contest had centred at Rome, at Rome it was fought out, and the voice that decided the strife of the schools was the same that commanded the nations. If the Roman genius for art had little in common with the Greek, if it was ill-fitted to apprehend the Greek subtleties, it had pre-eminently that sound instinct in large art-questions which goes with directness of character, with the faculty of creating and maintaining order and with reverence for the majesty of law. A ruling race may not always produce the greatest artists or the finest critics. But in a broad issue between a pure and a false taste its collective opinion is almost sure to be found on the right side. Rome pronounced for Atticism.

Caecilius and Diony-sios. Among the Greeks then living in the Imperial City were two men, united by friendship, by community of labours and by zeal for the Atticist revival; symbols, by birth-place, of influences which in the past had converged upon the Athens of Perikles from Sicily and the Ionian East,—Caecilius of Calacte and Dionysios of Halikarnassos, now met in that new capital of civilised mankind to which the arts, too, of Athens were passing. Both were scholars of manifold industry, in history, in archæ-ology, in literary criticism, in technical rhetoric, and in a field which the catalogues of the libraries had left almost untouched—discrimination between the genuine and the spurious works of Attic writers. Both wrote upon the Attic orators, but with a difference of plan which is instructive.

The lost work of Caecilius was entitled περὶ χα- ρακτῆρος τῶν δέκα ῥητόρων, *On the Style of the Ten Orators.* These ten were Antiphon, Andokides, Lysias, Isokrates, Isaeos, Lykurgos, Aeschines, Demosthenes, Deinarchos. Now, Caecilius, and his contemporary Didymos, the grammarian and critic of Alexandria, are the earliest writers who know this decade. Dionysios takes no notice whatever of the canon thus adopted by his friend. He seems never to have heard of the number 'ten' in connexion with the Attic orators. But from the first century A.D. onwards the decade is established. It is attested, for instance, by the Lives of the Ten Orators, wrongly ascribed to Plutarch, but probably composed about 80 A.D.; by Quintilian; by the neoplatonist Proklos, about 450 A.D.; and by Suidas, about 1100 A.D.—from whom it appears that, in his time, the grammarians had added a second list of ten to the first. The origin of the canon is unknown. It has been ascribed to Caecilius himself, mainly on the ground that it is not heard of before his time. It has been referred to Aristophanes the Byzantine, librarian at Alexandria about 200 B.C., or to his successor Aristarchos, about 156 B.C.,—by whom a canon of the poets, at least, was certainly framed. Another view is that it arose simply from the general tendency to reduce the number of distinguished names in any field to

Caecilius on the Attic Orators.

The decade.

a definite number,—the tendency that gives the Seven Sages of Greece, the Seven Champions of Christendom, and the like. This last theory may safely be rejected. The decade includes at least three names which this kind of halo can never have surrounded—Andokides, Isaeos and Deinarchos. It excludes other orators who, though inferior as artists, would have had a stronger popular claim, such as Kallistratos of Aphidnae, the chief organiser of the Athenian Confederacy in 378, of whom Demosthenes said, when asked whether he or Kallistratos were the better speaker, 'I, on paper—Kallistratos on the platform',—his opponents, Leodamas of Acharnae, Aristophon of Azenia, Thrasybulos and Kephalos of Kollytos,—or that vigorous member of the anti-Macedonian party, Polyeuktos of Sphettos. Clearly, this canon was framed once for all by a critic or a school from whose decree contemporary opinion allowed no appeal, was adopted by successive generations, and ultimately secured the preservation of the writings which it contained, while others, not so privileged, were neglected, and at last suffered to perish. The decade was probably drawn up by Alexandrian grammarians in the course of the last two centuries before our era: but there is no warrant for connecting it with any particular name[1].

Dionysios on the Attic Orators.

Dionysios, as has been said, altogether ignores the decade. If we supposed that Caecilius was its

[1] On the history of the decade, see Ruhnken, *Historia Critica Oratorum Graecorum*, who brings together the ancient authorities; Meier, *Comment. Andoc.* IV. 140; and the observations in Blass, *Die Griechische Beredsamkeit in dem Zeitraum von Alexander bis auf Augustus* (Berlin, 1865) p. 193.

author, and that, when Dionysios wrote, Caecilius had not yet made his selection, the fact would be explained. But the double supposition involves the strongest improbability. Even if Caecilius had been the framer of the decade, it can hardly be doubted that at least the idea must have been known through him to his intimate friend Dionysios before the latter had completed the series of works which we possess, and that we should find some trace of it in those long lists of orators which Dionysios frequently gives. The truth probably is that Dionysios was perfectly aware of this arbitrary canon, but disregarded it, because it was not a help, but a hindrance, to the purpose with which he studied the Attic orators.

Nothing is more characteristic of Dionysios as a critic than his resolution not to accept tradition as such, but to bring it to the test of reason. This comes out strikingly, for instance, in his distrust of merely prescriptive or titular authenticity when he is going through the list of an ancient writer's works. Now, his object in handling the Attic orators was *His object in handling them.* not to complete a set of biographies or essays, but to establish a standard for Greek prose, applicable alike to oratory and to every other branch of composition. He considers the orators, accordingly, less as individual writers than as representatives of tendencies. He seeks to determine their mutual relations, and, with the aid of the results thus obtained, to trace a historical development. The orators whom he chose as, in this sense, representative were six in number —Lysias, Isokrates, Isaeos, Demosthenes, Hypereides, Aeschines. We have his treatises on Lysias, Isokrates, and Isaeos. We have also the first part of his treatise on Demosthenes—that part in which he discusses expression as managed by Demosthenes; the second part, in which he discussed the Demosthenic handling of subject-matter, has perished with his discourses on Hypereides and Aeschines. The treatise on Deinarchos, it need hardly be said, is bibliographical, and has nothing to do with the other series.

His classification— the εὑρεταί and the τελειωταί.

Dionysios considers his six orators as forming two classes. Between these classes the line is clearly drawn. Lysias, Isokrates, Isaeos are εὑρεταί, inventors,—differing indeed, in degree of originality, but alike in this, that each struck out a new line, each has a distinctive character of which the conception was his own. Demosthenes, Hypereides, Aeschines, are τελειωταί, perfecters,—men who, having regard to the historical growth of Attic prose, cannot be said to have revealed secrets of its capability, but who, using all that their predecessors had provided, wrought up the several elements in a richer synthesis or with a subtler finish[1].

Plan of this book.

The task which I have set before me is to consider the lives, the styles and the writings of Antiphon, Andokides, Lysias, Isokrates and Isaeos, with a view to showing how Greek oratory was developed, and thereby how Greek prose was moulded, from the outset of its existence as an art down to the point at which the organic forces of Attic speech were matured, its leading tendencies determined, and its destinies committed, no longer to discoverers, but to those who should crown its perfection or

[1] Dionys. *De Deinarch.* c. 1; cf. c. 5.

initiate its decay. The men and the writings that mark this progress will need to be studied systematically and closely. It is hoped that much which is of historical, literary or social interest will be found by the way. But the great reward of the labour will be to get, if it may be, a more complete and accurate notion of the way in which Greek prose grew. It will not be enough, then, if we break off when the study of Isaeos has been finished. It will be necessary to look at the general characteristics of the mature political oratory built on those foundations at which Isaeos was the latest worker. It will be necessary to conceive distinctly how Isaeos and those before him were related to Lykurgos, Hypereides, Aeschines, Demosthenes. Nor must we stop here. The tendencies set in movement during the fifth and fourth centuries B. C. were not spent before they had passed into that life of the Empire which sent them on into the modern world. The inquiry which starts from the Athens of Perikles has no proper goal but in the Rome of Augustus.

At the outset, it is well to clear away a verbal hindrance to the comprehension of this subject in its right bearings. The English term 'orator,' when it is not used ironically, is reserved for one who, in relation to speaking, has genius of an order analogous to that which entitles a man to be seriously called a poet. The term 'oratory,' though the exigencies of the language lead to its often being used as a mere synonym for 'set speaking,' is yet always inconveniently coloured with the same suggestion either of

The English word 'orator'

irony or of superlative praise. The Roman term *orator*, 'pleader,' had this advantage over ours, that it related, not to a faculty, but to a professional or official attitude. It could therefore be applied to any one who stood in that attitude, whether effectively or otherwise. Thus the Romans could legitimately say 'mediocris' or 'malus orator,' whereas, in English, the corresponding phrases are either incorrect or sarcastic. Even the Romans, however, seem to have felt that their word was unsatisfactory, and to have confessed this sense by using ' dicere,' 'ars
dicendi,' as much as possible. But the Greeks had a word which presented the man of eloquence, not, like the English word, as a man of genius, nor like the Roman word, as an official person, but simply as a *speaker*, ῥήτωρ. This designation was claimed by those Sicilian masters who taught men how to speak : at Athens it was given especially to the habitual speakers in the public assembly : in later times it was applied to students or theorists of Rhetoric. What, then, is the fact signified by this double phenomenon—that the Greeks had the word *rhetor*,
and that they did not apply it to everybody? It is this : that, in the Greek view, a man who speaks may, without necessarily having first-rate natural gifts for eloquence, or being invested with office, yet deserve to be distinguished from his fellows by the name of a *speaker*. It attests the conception that speaking is potentially an *art*, and that one who speaks may, in speaking, be an *artist*.

This is the fundamental conception on which rests, first, the relation between ancient oratory and ancient prose; secondly, the relation between ancient and modern oratory.

The relation between ancient oratory and ancient prose, philosophical, historical or literary, is necessarily of the closest kind. Here our unfortunate word 'oratory,' with its arbitrary and perplexing associations, is a standing impediment to clearness of view. The proposition will be more evident if it is stated thus:—In Greek and Roman antiquity, that prose which was written with a view to being *spoken* stood in the closest relation with that prose which was written with a view to being *read*. Hence the historical study of ancient oratory has an interest wider and deeper than that which belongs to the study of modern oratory. It is that study by which the practical politics of antiquity are brought into immediate connexion with ancient literature.

Relation between ancient Oratory and ancient Prose.

The affinities between ancient and modern oratory have been more often assumed than examined. To discuss and illustrate them with any approach to completeness would be matter for a separate work. We must try, however, to apprehend the chief points. These shall be stated as concisely as possible, with such illustrations only as are indispensable for clearness.

Relation between Ancient and Modern Oratory.

Ancient oratory is a fine art, an art regarded by its cultivators, and by the public, as analogous to sculpture, to poetry, to painting, to music and to acting. This character is common to Greek and Roman oratory; but it originated with the Greeks, and was only acquired by the Romans. The evidence for this character may be

Ancient Oratory a fine art.

I. *Internal evidence.* considered as internal and external[1]. The internal
1. *Finish of form.* evidence is that which is afforded by the ancient
orations themselves. First, we find in these, con-
sidered universally, a fastidious nicety of diction,
of composition and of arrangement, which shows
that the attention bestowed on their form, as distinguished from their matter, was both disciplined
2. *Repeti- tions.* and minute. Secondly, we find the orator occasionally repeating shorter or longer passages—not always
striking passages—from some other speech of his
own, with or without verbal amendments; or we
find him borrowing such passages from another
orator. Thus Isokrates, in his *Panegyrikos*, borrowed
from the *Olympiakos* of Lysias, and from the so-called
Lysian Epitaphios. Demosthenes, in the speech
against Meidias, borrowed from speeches of Lysias,
of Isaeos and of Lykurgos, in like cases of outrage.
In many places Demosthenes borrowed from himself.
This was done on the principle that τὸ καλῶς εἰπεῖν
ἅπαξ περιγίγνεται, δὶς δὲ οὐκ ἐνδέχεται: *A thing can
be well said once, but cannot be well said twice*[2].
That is, if a thought, however trivial, has once been
perfectly expressed, it has, by that expression, become a morsel of the world's wealth of beauty.
The doctrine might sometimes justify an artist in
repeating *himself*; as an excuse for appropriation, it
omits to distinguish the nature of the individual's
property in a sunset and in a gem; but, among
Greeks, at least, it was probably not so much indolence

---

[1] Some of the chief heads of the evidence are given by Brougham, *Dissertation on the Eloquence of the Ancients.*

[2] Theon (who disputes the maxim) προγυμνάσματα c. 1 (*Rhet. Graec.* II. 62, ed. Spengel).

as solicitude for the highest beauty, even in the least
details, that prompted such occasional plagiarisms.

Thirdly, we find that the orators, in addressing *Speakers criticise each other's style.*
juries or assemblies, criticise each other's style.
Aeschines, in a trial on which all his fortunes depended, quotes certain harsh or unpleasant figures of
speech which, as he alleges, Demosthenes had used.
'How,' he cries to the jurors, 'how, men of iron, can
you have supported them?' And then, turning in
triumph to his rival, 'What are these, knave? ῥήματα
ἢ θαύματα; metaphors or monsters[1]?' When a poet,
a painter or a musician thus scrutinises a brother
artist's work, the modern world is not surprised.
But a modern advocate or statesman would not
expect to make a favourable impression by exposing
in detail the stylistic shortcomings of an opponent.

The external evidence is supplied by what we *II. External evidence.*
know of the orators, of their hearers and of their
critics. Already, before the art of Rhetoric had *1. Training of speakers.*
become an elaborate system, the orators were ac-
customed to prepare themselves for their task by
laborious training, first in composition, then in delivery. They make no secret of this. They are
not ashamed of it. On the contrary, they avow it
and insist upon it. Demosthenes would never
speak extemporarily when he could help it; he was
unwilling to put his faculty at the mercy of fortune[2]. 'Great is the labour of oratory,' says Cicero,

---

[1] Aesch. *In Ctes.* §§ 166 f.

[2] ἐπὶ τύχῃ ποιεῖσθαι τὴν δύναμιν,
Plut. *Demosth.* c. 9: who observes
that this was certainly not from
want of nerve, since, in the opinion

of many contemporaries, Demosthenes showed *more* τόλμα and
θάρσος when he spoke without
premeditation. His habitual re-
luctance to do so is, however, well

2. *Apprecia-
tion shown
by hearers.* 'as is its field, its dignity and its reward.' Nor
were the audiences less exacting than the speakers
were painstaking. The hearers were attentive, not
merely to the general drift or to the total effect, but
to the particular elegance. Isokrates speaks of 'the
antitheses, the symmetrical clauses and other figures
which lend brilliancy to oratorical displays, compel-
ling the listeners to give clamorous applause'[1].
Sentences, not especially striking or important in
relation to the ideas which they convey, are praised
by the ancient critics for their artistic excellence[2].

3. *Pamph-
lets in the
oratorical
form.* Further, when an orator, or a master of oratorical
prose, wished to publish what we should now call a
pamphlet, the form which he chose for it, as most
likely to be effective, was that, not of an essay, but
of a speech purporting to be delivered in certain
circumstances which he imagined. Such are the
Archidamos, the *Areopagitikos* and the *Symmachikos*
of Isokrates in the Deliberative form, and his speech
On the Antidosis in the Forensic. Such again is the

---

attested. See Plut. *l. c. c.* 8, and the
story in [Plut.] *Vitt. X. oratt.,
Dem.* § 69. To the reproach, ὅτι
ἀεὶ σκέπτοιτο, he answered:—αἰσχυ-
νοίμην γὰρ ἂν εἰ τηλικούτῳ δήμῳ
συμβουλεύων αὐτοσχεδιάζοιμι. The
compiler naïvely adds, τοὺς δὲ
πλείστους λόγους εἶπεν αὐτοσχεδιά-
σας, εὖ πρὸς αὐτὸ πεφυκώς,—a
fact perfectly consistent with laborious preparation for all *grave*
occasions.

[1] Isokr. *Panath.* (Or. XII.) § 2.
[2] *E.g.* Cic. *in Verr.* Act. II. Lib.
v. c. xxxiii, *Stetit soleatus praetor
populi Romani cum pallio pur-*

*pureo tunicaque talari, mulier-
cula nixus, in litore:* praised by
Quint. VIII. 3 § 64 for ἐνάργεια,
artistic *vividness:* (not, as Brougham
says in alluding to it, *Dissert. on
the Eloquence of the Ancients,*
p. 42, for 'fine and dignified composition.')—Cic. *Orator,* c. 63 § 214,
speaking of the rhythmical effect
of the dichoreus, $- \smile - \smile$, at the end
of a sentence, quotes from the tri-
bune Carbo, *Patris dictum sa-
piens temeritas filii comprobavit:*
and adds,—'The applause drawn
from the meeting by this dichoreus
was positively astonishing.'

famous Second Philippic of Cicero.　Then we know 4. *Collections of commonplaces.* that orators compiled, for their own use, collections of exordia or of commonplaces, to be used as occasion might serve.　Such was that *volumen prooemiorum* of Cicero's which betrayed him into a mistake which he has chronicled.　He had sent Atticus his treatise 'De Gloria' with the wrong exordium prefixed to it—one, namely, which he had already prefixed to the Third Book of the Academics.　On discovering his mistake, he sends Atticus a new exordium, begging him to 'cut out the other, and substitute this[1].'

Lastly, the ancient critics habitually compare the 5. *Ancient critics compare Oratory with Sculpture or Painting.* pains needful to produce a good speech with the pains needful to produce a good statue or picture. When Plato wishes to describe the finished smoothness of Lysias, he borrows his image from the sculptor, and says ἀποτετόρνευται.　Theon says :—' Even as for him who would be a painter, it is unavailing to observe the works of Apelles and Protogenes and Antiphilos, unless he tries to paint with his own hand, so for him who would become a speaker there is no help in the speeches of the ancients, or in the copiousness of their thoughts, or in the purity of their diction, or in their harmonious composition, no, nor in lectures upon elegance, unless he disciplines himself by *writing* from day to day[2].'　Lucilius, from

---

[1] Cic *ad Att.* XVI. 6 § 4, quoted by Brougham, *Dissert.* p. 36. As to the 'προοίμια of Demosthenes' there noticed, it is now well known that they were not drawn up by Demosthenes. The scholastic compiler, whoever he was, took some of them from Demosthenes, some from other orators, and probably wrote some himself : Schäfer, *Dem. u. seine Zeit*, III. App. p. 129.

[2] Theon, προγυμνάσματα c. 1, (*Rhet. Graec.* I. p. 62 ed. Spengel.)

whom Cicero borrows the simile, compares the phrases,
lexeis, each fitted with nicety to its setting in a
finished sentence, with the pieces, *tesserulae*, laid
in a mosaic [1]. But among the passages, and they
are innumerable, which express this view there is
one in Dionysios that can never be too attentively
Dionysios
περὶ συνθέ-
σεως, c. 25. considered by those who wish to understand the
real nature of ancient, and especially of Attic, oratory.
He is explaining and defending—partly with a
polemical purpose at which we shall have to glance
by and by—that minute and incessant diligence
which Demosthenes devoted to the perfecting of his
orations. It is not strange, says the critic, 'if a
man who has won more glory for eloquence than
any of those that were renowned before him, who
is shaping works for all the future, who is offering
himself to the scrutiny of all-testing Envy and
Time, adopts no thought, no word, at random, but
takes much care of both things, the arrangement
of his ideas and the graciousness of his language :
seeing, too, that the men of that day produced
discourses which resembled no common scribblings,
but rather were like to carved and chiselled forms,—
I mean Isokrates and Plato, the Sophists. For
Isokrates spent on the *Panegyrikos*, to take the
lowest traditional estimate, ten years; and Plato
ceased not to smooth the locks, and adjust the

---

[1] Lucilius *ap.* Cic. *De Oratore*
III. § 171 :

> *Quam lepide lexeis compostae!*
>   *ut tesserulae omnes*
> *arte pavimento atque emble-*
>   *mate vermiculato.*

The satirist was mocking T.

Albucius, who wished himself to
be thought 'plane Graecus' (Cic.
De Fin. I. 1 § 8), and was alluding
especially to the Isokratics. No
one, certainly, could say of Lucilius
what he said of Albucius.

tresses, or vary the braids, of his comely creations,
even till he was eighty years old[1]. All lovers of
literature are familiar, I suppose, with the stories
of Plato's industry, especially the story about the
tablet which, they say, was found after his death,
with the first words of the *Republic*—κατέβην χθὲς
εἰς Πειραιᾶ μετὰ Γλαύκωνος τοῦ Ἀρίστωνος—arranged
in several different orders. What wonder, then,
if Demosthenes also took pains to achieve euphony
and harmony, and to avoid employing a single word,
or a single thought, which he had not weighed? *It
seems to me far more natural that a man engaged in
composing political discourses, imperishable memorials
of his power, should neglect not even the smallest
detail, than that the generation of painters and sculptors, who are darkly showing forth their manual tact
and toil in a corruptible material, should exhaust the
refinements of their art on the veins, on the feathers,
on the down of the lip and the like niceties[2].'* Repeating this passage, slightly altered, in the essay
on Demosthenes, Dionysios adds that we might indeed marvel if, while sculptors and painters are thus
conscientious, 'the artist in civil eloquence (πολιτικὸς
δημιουργός) neglected the smallest aids to speaking
well—*if indeed these be the smallest[3].'*

It has already been observed that this feeling *This con-
about speaking is originally Greek; and it is worth* *ception is
originally
Greek.*

---

[1] The language here—τοὺς ἑαυτοῦ
διαλόγους κτενίζων καὶ βοστρυχίζων
καὶ πάντα τρόπον ἀναπλέκων—is not,
perhaps, mere tautology. κτενίζων
may be the general term; while
βοστρυχίζων refers to the addition,
and ἀναπλέκων to the retrench-
ment, of luxuriance.

[2] Dionys. περὶ συνθέσεως ὀνομάτων, c. 25.

[3] Dionys. *De Demosth.* c. 51.

*Its basis—
the ideali-
sation of
man.* while to consider how it arose.   That artistic sense which distinguished the Greeks above all races that the world has known was concentrated, in the happy pause of development to which we owe their supreme works, on the idealisation of man. Now, λόγος, speech, was recognised by the Greeks as the distinctive attribute of man[1].   It was necessary, therefore, that, at this stage, they should require in speech a clear-cut and typical beauty analogous to that of the idealised human form. This was the central and primary motive, relatively to which all others were subsidiary or accidental.

*Secondary
motives:
(1) the oral
tradition
of poetry:* But, of these secondary motives, two at least demand a passing notice.   First, the oral tradition of poetry and the habit of listening to poetical recitation furnished an analogy which was present to people's minds when they saw a man get up to make a set speech; they expected his words to have something like the coherence, something like the plastic outline, something even like the music of the verses which they were wont to hear flow from the lips of *(2) The
civil im-
portance of
speech.* his counterpart, the rhapsode.   Secondly, in the Greek cities, and especially at Athens, public speaking had, by 450 B. C., become so enormously important, opened so much to ambition, constituted a safeguard so essential for security of property and person, that not only was there the most various

---

[1] Aristotle uses this consideration to enforce the 'defensive' use of Rhetoric:—πρὸς δὲ τούτοις ἄτοπον εἰ τῷ σώματι μὲν αἰσχρὸν μὴ δύνασθαι βοηθεῖν ἑαυτῷ, λόγῳ δ᾽ οὐκ αἰσχρόν· ὃ μᾶλλον ἴδιον ἐστιν ἀνθρώπου τῆς τοῦ σώματος χρείας, *Rhet.* I. 1. On λόγος as the distinction of man, see a splendid passage in Isokrates, *Antid.* (Or. xv.) §§ 252—257.

inducement to cultivate it, but it was positively
dangerous to neglect it. Further, since in a law-court (3) Competition.
it was unavailing for the citizen that he could speak
well unless the judges thought that he spoke better
than his opponent, the art of persuasion was studied
with a competitive zeal which wrought together
with the whole bent of the Greek genius in securing
attention to detail.

It will now be useful to look at some of the broad *Characteristics of Modern Oratory.*
characteristics of modern oratory and of the modern
feeling towards it; but only in so far as these will help
our present purpose—namely, to elucidate the nature of ancient oratory. The first thing that strikes
one is how completely modern life has redressed the
complaint made by the earliest philosophical theorist
of rhetoric. Aristotle opens his treatise with the ob- *Aristotle on the three instruments of Rhetorical Proof:*
servation that, whereas there are three instruments
of rhetorical persuasion—the ethical, the pathetic
and the logical—his predecessors have paid by far the
most attention to the second, and have almost totally
neglected the third, though this third is incompara-
bly the most important,—indeed, the only one of the
three which is truly scientific. The logical proof is
the very body, $\sigma\hat{\omega}\mu\alpha$, of rhetorical persuasion,—everything else, appeal to feeling, attractive portrayal of
character, and so forth, is, from the scientific point of
view, only $\pi\rho\sigma\theta\acute{\eta}\kappa\eta$, appendage. This is essentially *His estimate is that of the Modern World.*
the modern, especially the modern Teutonic, theory
of oratory, and the modern practice is in harmony
with it. The broadest characteristic of modern ora- *Modern Oratory puts the $\lambda o\gamma\iota\kappa\grave{\eta}$ $\pi\acute{\iota}\sigma\tau\iota\varsigma$ first.*
tory, as compared with ancient, is the predominance
of a sustained appeal to the understanding. Hume,

with general truth, declares the attributes of Greek
oratory to be 'rapid harmony, exactly adjusted to
the sense', 'vehement reasoning, without any appearance of art', 'disdain, anger, boldness, freedom,
involved in a continual stream of argument[1]'—a
description, it must be observed, which should at all
events be limited to the deliberative and forensic
orators contemporary with Demosthenes. Brougham,
however, states the case both more accurately and
in terms of wider application, when he observes that
in ancient oratory there are scarcely any long chains
of elaborate reasoning; what was wanted to move, to
rouse, and to please the hearers, was rather a copious
stream of plain, intelligible observations upon their
interests, appeals to their feelings, reminiscences
from the history, especially the recent history, of
their city, expositions of the evils to be apprehended
from inaction or from impolicy, vindications of the
orator's own conduct, demonstrations of the folly
which disobeys, or of the malice which assails him[2].
Aristotle himself, it may be observed, the very champion of the enthymeme, is the strongest witness to the
truth of this. He impresses upon the student of
Rhetoric that a speaker must ever remember that he
is addressing the vulgar ; he must not expect them
to be capable of a far-reaching ratiocination, he must
not string syllogism to syllogism, he must administer
his logic temperately and discreetly[3]. Now, in contrast with this, long and elaborate chains of reasoning,

---

[1] Essay XII., *Of Eloquence.*

[2] *Dissertation On the Eloquence
of the Ancients,* pp. 48, 58.

[3] See (*e.g.*) *Rhet.* I. 2 §§ 12, 13
(ὁ γὰρ κριτὴς ὑπόκειται εἶναι ἁπλοῦς,
κ.τ.λ.) : II. 22 §§ 2 ff., III. 17 § 6, etc.

or expositions of complicated facts, have been the very essence of the great efforts and triumphs of modern oratory; the imagery and the pathos heighten the effect, but would go only a very little way if the understandings of the hearers had not, in the first place, been convinced. We are here again reminded of the basis on which ancient oratory rested. The *The modern speaker has no distinct acceptance as an artist.* modern speaker comes before his audience with no *a priori* claim to be regarded as an artist whose display of his art may be commendable and interesting in itself. Cicero's speech for Archias, which is ex- *The ancients less strict about logical relevance.* quisitely composed, but of which not more than one-sixth is to the purpose, or his speech for Publius Sextus, in which the relevant part bears a yet smaller proportion to the whole, could not have been delivered in a British court of justice [1]. There is usually, however, an important difference, which will be noticed by and by, between the nature of Greek and that of Roman irrelevance. On the other hand, the modern exaction of consecutive and intelligible reasoning becomes, of course, less severe the more nearly the discourse approaches to the nature of a display. Still, this logical vigilance, with a comparative indifference to form, is, on the whole, the first great characteristic of modern oratory, and has, of course, become more pronounced since the system of reporting for the Press has been perfected, as it is *Influence of newspaper reporting.* now, in many cases, far more important for the speaker to convince readers than to fascinate hearers. The characteristic which comes next in degree of significance for our present object is the habitual

[1] Brougham, *l. c.,* p. 46.

Modern feeling that a great speech must be extemporary.

presumption that the speech is extemporary. Even where there has been the most laborious preparation, even where the fact of such preparation is notorious, it is generally felt to be essential to impressiveness that the fact of *verbal* premeditation should be kept out of sight, and on the part of the hearers it is considered more courteous to ignore it. A certain ridicule attaches to a speech which, not having been delivered, is published,—the sense of something ludicrous arising partly from the feeling, ' What an absurd disappointment', but also from the feeling, 'Here are the bursts which would have

Sources of this feeling: 1. *The failures of Premeditation.*

electrified the audience'. One thing which has helped to establish this feeling is the frequent failure of those who have attempted verbal premeditation ; a failure probably due less often to defective memory or nerve than to neglect of a department in which the ancient orators were most diligent, and in which, moreover, they were greatly assisted by the plastic forms among which they lived, by the share of musical training which they ordinarily possessed, and by the draping of the himation or the toga—delivery, in respect both of voice and of action. When a premeditated speech is rendered lifeless or ludicrous by the manner in which it is pronounced, the modern mind at once recurs to its prejudice against Rhetoric—that is, against the Rhetoric of the later schools—and a contempt is generated for those who deign to labour beforehand on words

2. *The Hebraic basis of Christian education.*

that should come straight from the heart. There is, however, a much deeper cause than this for the popular modern notion that the greatest oratory

must be extemporary, and it is one which, for
the modern world, is analogous to the origin of the
Greek requirement that speech should be artistic.
This cause is the Hebraic basis of education in
modern Christendom, especially in those countries
which have been most influenced by the Reformation. It becomes a prepossession that the true
adviser, the true warner, in all the gravest situa-
tions, on all the most momentous subjects, is one
to whom it will in that hour be given what he shall
speak, and whose inspiration, when it is loftiest,
must be communicated to him at the moment by
a Power external to himself. The ancient world
compared the orator with the poet. The modern
world compares the orator with the prophet.

It is true, indeed, that the ancient theory has *Modern ap-*
proxima-
often been partially applied in modern times, some- *tions to the*
theory of
times with great industry and with much success; *Ancient*
Oratory.
but modern conditions place necessary limits to the
application, and the great difference is this :—The
ancients required the speech to be an artistic whole;
the modern orator who composes, or verbally pre-
meditates, trusts chiefly, as a rule, to particular passages and is less solicitous for a total symmetry.
Debate, in our sense, is a modern institution; its *Influence of*
Debate.
unforeseen exigencies claim a large margin in the
most careful premeditation ; and hence, in the principal field of oratory, an insurmountable barrier is
at once placed to any real assimilation between the
ancient and the modern modes. Just so much the
more, if only for contrast, is it interesting to contemplate those modern orators who have approximated

to the classical theory in such measure as their genius and their opportunities allowed. In an inquiry of the present scope, it might be presumptuous to select living illustrations of the Pulpit, the Senate, or the Bar. It would not, indeed, be needful to go far back; but it may be better, for our purpose, to seek examples where the natural partialities of a recent memory no longer refract the steady rays of
Finished Rhetorical Prose: fame. In respect of finished rhetorical prose, which is not, either in the ancient or in the modern sense, great oratory, but which bears to it the same kind of relation that the Panegyrikos of Isokrates bears to the speech On the Crown, no one, perhaps, has
Canning's Plymouth speech. excelled Canning. The well-known passage of his speech at Plymouth in 1823 will serve as an illustration :—

'The resources created by peace are means of war. In cherishing those resources, we but accumulate those means. Our present repose is no more a proof of inability to act, than the state of inertness and inactivity in which I see those mighty masses that float in the waters above your town is a proof that they are devoid of strength and incapable of being fitted out for action. You well know, gentlemen, how soon one of those stupendous masses now reposing on their shadows in perfect stillness—how soon, upon any call of patriotism or of necessity, it would assume the likeness of an animated thing, instinct with life and motion—how soon would it ruffle, as it were, its swelling plumage—how quickly it would put forth all its beauty and its bravery, collect its scattered elements of strength, and awaken its dormant thunder. Such as is one of those magnificent machines when springing from inaction into a display of its might—such is England herself, while, apparently passive and motionless, she silently concentrates the power to be put forth on an adequate occasion.'

The ancient parallel for this is such a passage *His ana-
logue—
Isokrates.* as that in the Panegyrikos, describing the irresistible and awe-inspiring might in which the Panhellenic invasion will move through Asia—θεωρίᾳ μᾶλλον ἢ στρατείᾳ προσεοικώς [1]. But a nearer re- *Union of
rhythmical* semblance to the classical union of rhythmical finish *finish with
passion :* with living passion is afforded, in deliberative oratory, by Grattan, in forensic, by Erskine. Take the peroration of Grattan's speech in the Irish Par- *Grattan.* liament on the Declaration of Irish Rights [2]:—

'Do not suffer the arrogance of England to imagine a surviving hope in the fears of Ireland; do not send the people to their own resolves for liberty, passing by the tribunals of justice and the high court of Parliament; neither imagine that, by any formation of apology, you can palliate such a commission to your hearts, still less to your children, who will sting you with their curses in your graves, for having interposed between them and their Maker, robbing them of an immense occasion, and losing an opportunity which you did not create and never can restore.

'Hereafter, when these things shall be history, your age of thraldom and poverty, your sudden resurrection, commercial redress, and miraculous armament, shall the historian stop at liberty, and observe—that here the principal men among us fell into mimic trances of gratitude; that they were awed by a weak ministry, and bribed by an empty treasury; and, when liberty was within their grasp, and the temple opened her folding doors, and the arms of the people clanged, and the zeal of the nation urged and encouraged them on,—that they fell down and were prostituted at the threshold.

'I might, as a constituent, come to your bar and demand my liberty,—I do call upon you, by the laws of the land and their violation, by the instruction of eighteen counties,

---

[1] Isokr. Or. IV. § 182. [2] *Speeches,* Vol. I. pp. 52 f.

by the arms, inspiration, and providence of the present moment, tell us the rule by which we shall go—assert the law of Ireland—declare the liberty of the land.

'I will not be answered by a public lie in the shape of an amendment; neither, speaking for the subject's freedom, am I to hear of faction. I wish for nothing but to breathe, in this our island, in common with my fellow-subjects, the air of liberty. I have no ambition, unless it be the ambition to break your chain and contemplate your glory. I never will be satisfied so long as the meanest cottager in Ireland has a link of the British chain clanking to his rags; he may be naked, he shall not be in iron; and I do see the time is at hand, the spirit is gone forth, the declaration is planted; and though great men should apostatize, yet the cause will live; and though the public speaker should die, yet the immortal fire shall outlast the organ which conveyed it, and the breath of liberty, like the word of the holy man, will not die with the prophet, but survive him.'

Erskine.

Erskine's defence of Stockdale, the publisher of a pamphlet in defence of Warren Hastings, containing certain reflections on the Managers which the House of Commons pronounced libellous, contains a passage of which the ingenuity, no less than the finished art, recalls the best efforts of ancient forensic oratory; though this ingenuity cannot be fully appreciated without the context. At first, Erskine studiously keeps his defence of Stockdale separate from his defence of Hastings; then he gradually suggests that Hastings is entitled to indulgence on account (1) of his instructions, (2) of his situation, (3) of English and European policy abroad, (4) of the depravity to which, universally, men are liable who have vast power over a subject race,—and the last topic is illustrated thus:—

'Gentlemen, I think that I can observe that you are touched by this way of considering the subject; and I can account for it. I have not been considering it through the cold medium of books, but have been speaking of man and his nature, and of human dominion, from what I have seen of them myself among reluctant nations submitting to our authority. I know what they feel, and how such feelings can alone be repressed. I have heard them in my youth from a naked savage, in the indignant character of a prince surrounded by his subjects, addressing the governor of a British colony, holding a bundle of sticks in his hand as the notes of his unlettered eloquence; 'Who is it,' said the jealous ruler over the desert encroached upon by the restless foot of English adventure—'who is it that causes this river to rise in the high mountains and to empty itself into the ocean? Who is it that causes to blow the loud winds of winter, and that calms them again in summer? Who is it that rears up the shade of those lofty forests, and blasts them with the quick lightning at his pleasure? The same Being who gave to you a country on the other side of the waters, and gave ours to us; and by this title we will defend it!' said the warrior, throwing down his tomahawk on the ground, and raising the war-sound of his nation. These are the feelings of subjugated men all round the globe; and, depend upon it, nothing but fear will control where it is vain to look for affection[1].'

But no speaker, probably, of modern times has *Burke.* come nearer to the classical type than Burke; and this because his reasonings, his passion, his imagery, are sustained by a consummate and unfailing beauty of language. The passage in which he describes the descent of Hyder Ali upon the Carnatic is supposed to owe the suggestion of its great image, not to

[1] From a longer extract given by Brougham in his Essay on Erskine, reprinted from the Edinburgh Review in the volume of his 'Rhetorical and Literary Dissertations and Addresses,' p. 225.

Demosthenes, but to Livy's picture of Fabius hover-
ing over Hannibal; the whole passage is infinitely
more Roman, more Verrine, if the phrase may be
permitted, than Greek; but it is anything rather
than diffuse :—

'Having terminated his disputes with every enemy and
every rival, who buried their mutual animosities in their
common detestation against the creditors of the Nabob of
Arcot, he drew from every quarter whatever a savage ferocity
could add to his new rudiments in the arts of destruction;
and compounding all the materials of fury, havoc, and de-
solation into one black cloud, he hung for a while on the
declivity of the mountains. Whilst the authors of all these
evils were idly and stupidly gazing on this menacing meteor,
which darkened all their horizon, it suddenly burst, and
poured down the whole of its contents upon the plains of the
Carnatic. Then ensued a scene of woe, the like of which
no eye had seen, no heart conceived, and which no tongue
can adequately tell. All the horrors of war before known
or heard of were mercy to that new havoc. A storm of
universal fire blasted every field, consumed every house,
destroyed every temple. The miserable inhabitants, flying
from their flaming villages, in part were slaughtered; others,
without regard to sex, to age, to the respect of rank, or
sacredness of function, fathers torn from children, husbands
from wives, enveloped in a whirlwind of cavalry, and amidst
the goading spears of drivers and the trampling of pursuing
horses, were swept into captivity in an unknown and hostile
land. Those who were able to evade this tempest fled to
the walled cities. But escaping from fire, sword and exile
they fell into the jaws of famine. For months together
these creatures of sufferance, whose very excess and luxury
in their most plenteous days had fallen short of the allowance of our austerest fasts, silent, patient, resigned, without
sedition or disturbance, almost without complaint, perished
by a hundred a day in the streets of Madras or on the glacis
of Tangore, and expired of famine in the granary of India.'

Brougham[1] contrasts this passage with that in which Demosthenes says that a danger 'went by like a cloud', with that where he says, 'If the Thebans had not joined us, all this trouble would have rushed like a mountain-torrent on the city', and with that where he asks, 'If the thunder-bolt which has fallen has overpowered, not us alone, but all the Greeks, what is to be done[2]?' Brougham contends that Burke has marred the sublimity of the 'black cloud' and 'the whirlwind of cavalry' by developing and amplifying both. This, surely, is to confound the plastic with the picturesque—a point which will presently claim our attention. Demosthenes is a sculptor, Burke a painter.

Brougham on Burke compared with Demosthenes.

It might, however, have been anticipated that modern oratory would have most resembled the ancient in that branch where the conditions are most nearly similar. If Isokrates could have foreseen the splendid, the unique opportunities which in later ages would be enjoyed by the Christian preacher, what expectations would he not have formed, not merely of the heights that would be attained—past and living instances remind us that, in this respect, no estimate could well have been too sanguine—but of the average abundance in which compositions of merit would be produced! It will, of course, be recollected that no quality is here in question except that of an eloquence which, regarded as literary prose, has the finish which deserves to be called artistic. If the test, thus defined, be applied, it

Modern Eloquence of the Pulpit.

---

[1] In his *Inaugural Discourse* before the University of Glasgow.

[2] Dem. *de Corona* § 188 (νέφος), § 153 (χειμάρρους), § 194 (σκηπτός).

will be found to afford a striking confirmation of what has already been observed in regard to the effect upon oratory of that especially Protestant conception according to which the orator's function is prophetic. In the combination of argumentative power with lofty earnestness and with eloquence of the Hebraic type [1], none have surpassed, or perhaps equalled, those divines whose discourses are among the chief glories of the English language. In respect, however, of complete artistic form, of classical finish, a nearer resemblance to the antique has been presented by the great preachers of Catholic France [2].

Modern Oratory— its greatest triumphs won by sudden bursts.

The most memorable triumphs of modern oratory are connected with the tradition of thrills, of electrical shocks, given to the hearers at the moment by bursts which were extemporary, not necessarily as regards the thought, but necessarily as regards the form. It was for such bursts that the eloquence of the elder Pitt was famous; that of Mirabeau, and of Patrick Henry, owed its highest renown to the same cause. Sheil's retort, in the debate on the Irish Municipal Bill in 1837, to Lord Lyndhurst's description of the Irish (in a phrase borrowed from O'Connell), as ' aliens in blood, language and religion ', was of this kind [3]. Erskine, in his defence of Lord George

---

[1] Chatham prescribed a study of Barrow as the best foundation of a good style in speaking.

[2] In his Essay on ' Pulpit Eloquence' Brougham seems hardly to do justice to Bossuet—the more florid Isokrates of the group. Bourdaloue, with his abundant resource, his temperate pathos and his frequent harshness, may perhaps be compared with Lykurgos: Massillon, Voltaire's favourite, with his severity, rapidity, and lofty fervour, was probably the most Demosthenic.

[3] It is quoted in the excellent article on ' The British Parliament; its History and Eloquence ', Quarterly Review of April, 1872, No. cxxxii. p. 480.

Gordon, produced an astonishing effect by a pro-
testation,—which would have been violent if it had
not been solemn,—of personal belief in his client's
innocence; a daring transgression of the advocate's
province which was paralleled, with some momentary
success, in a celebrated criminal case about twenty
years ago. Now these sudden bursts, and the shock or
the transport which they may cause, were forbidden
to ancient oratory by the principal law of its being. In
nothing is the contrast more striking than in this—
that the greatest oratorical reputations of the ancient
world were chiefly made, and those of the modern
world have sometimes been endangered, by prepared
works of art. Perikles and Hypereides were renowned for no efforts of their eloquence more than
for their funeral orations. Fox's carefully composed
speech in honour of the Duke of Bedford, Chatham's
elaborate eulogy of Wolfe, were accounted among
the least happy of their respective performances.
There is, however, at least one instrument of *Use of quotation.*
sudden effect which Greek oratory and British Parliamentary oratory once had in common, but which
the latter has now almost abandoned—poetical quotation. A quotation may, of course, be highly effective
even for those to whom it is new. But the genuine
oratorical force of quotation depends on the hearers
knowing the context, having previous associations
with the passage, and thus feeling the whole felicity
of the application as, at the instant, it is flashed
upon the mind. In this respect, the opportunities
of the Greek orator were perfect. His hearers were
universally and thoroughly familiar with the great

poets. When Aeschines applies the lines from Hesiod to Demosthenes, it is as if Digby, addressing Puritans, had attempted to sum up Strafford in a verse of Isaiah. In the days when all educated Englishmen knew a good deal of Virgil and Horace, and something of the best English poets, quotation was not merely a keen, but, in skilful hands, a really powerful weapon of parliamentary debate; and its almost total disuse, however unavoidable, is perhaps a more serious deduction than is generally perceived from the rather slender resources of modern English oratory for creating a glow. Pitt's speech on the Slave Trade concluded with the expression of this hope—that 'Africa, though last of all the quarters of the globe, shall enjoy at length, in the evening of her days, those blessings which have descended so plentifully upon us in a much earlier period of the world': the first beams of the rising sun were just entering the windows of the House, and he looked upward as he said—

Nos......primus equis Oriens afflavit anhelis;
Illic sera rubens accendit lumina Vesper.

Special characteristics of Greek oratory:

Hitherto we have been seeking to bring into relief, against the modern conception, that character which is common to Greek and to Roman oratory. But Greek oratory, as compared with Roman, has a stamp of its own. It is separated from the Roman, not, indeed, by so wide an interval, yet by a line as firm as that which separates both from the modern.

all Greek art has the plastic character.

That character which, with special modifications, belongs to every artistic creation of the Greek mind, whether this be a statue, a temple, a poem, a speech, or an individual's conception of his own place in life, is usually, and rightly, called the plastic. When it is desired to describe the primary artistic aspect of Greek Tragedy, this is commonly and justly done by a comparison with Sculpture. But it is certain that *Popular misconception of what is meant by 'plastic':* comparatively few understand the real meaning of 'plastic', 'sculpturesque', in these relations; and that to a vast majority of even cultivated persons, the statement of this affinity conveys an altogether erroneous notion. The reason of this is that the place held in antiquity by Sculpture is now held jointly by Painting, Music and certain forms of Poetry; that the modern mind instinctively refers the sculptural to the standard of the picturesque; and that, consequently, while the positive and essential characteristics of Sculpture are lost sight of, its negative qualities, relatively to Painting, become most prominent. These are, the absence of colour and the exclusion of tumultuous or complex action. Hence to the popular modern conception of Sculpture there usually attaches the notion of coldness and of rigidity. When people are told that Greek Tragedy (for example) is sculpturesque, they form this idea of it—that it has grandeur, but that it is cold and rather stiff. Then, if they are convinced that somehow the Greeks really were a race with the very highest genius for art, they begin to feel a secret wish that this alleged analogy between Greek Tragedy and sculpture might turn out to be a mistake. Here is an opportunity. The ingenious step in and *A result of this misconception.* say, ' It *is* a mistake. It is pedantry and sentiment.

For our part, we have always felt that Sophokles was frigid, and that Euripides, with his pathetic humanity, his tender women, his heroes who are not ashamed to display their emotions, was the better artist; now, dismiss the prepossessions created by students who are in no sympathy with nature or men, look at the facts as they are, deign to take homely views, and say, Is it not so?'

Consequent danger to the whole study of the antique.

The question at issue here happens to be vital to the immediate subject of these pages, viz., the development, through Attic oratory, of Attic prose. It is, however, just as vital for every other department whatsoever in the study of ancient art, literature and thought, for it involves nothing less than our fundamental conception of the antique. Unless that conception is true, everything will be seen in a distorted light, and the best things that the ancient world has to teach will be neglected for the second-best.

Character of Greek thought in the best days of Greek art;

Let us take a moment of the period when, as a matter of fact, the creative activity of Greek art was abundant—say 440 B.C.—and consider what, at that moment, was the principal characteristic of Greek reflection[1]. This will be best understood by a comparison with two other characters of thought; that which has belonged, though in a multitude of special shapes, to the East, and that of mediæval Europe. Oriental thought, as interpreted by Oriental

[1] The essay on Winckelmann, in Mr W. H. Pater's 'Studies in the History of the Renaissance,' is the most perfect interpretation of the Greek spirit in art that I know. If the restatement of some of its points should gain for it fresh students, such a separation of its teaching from its beauty may deserve to be forgiven.

art, fails to define humanity or to give a clear-cut *compared with the Oriental;* form to any material which the senses offer to it. Life is conceived only generally, as pervading men, animals and vegetables, but the distinctive attributes of human life, physical or spiritual, are not pondered or appreciated. The human form, the human soul, are not, to this Eastern thought, the objects of an absorbing and analysing contemplation. To European *and with the Mediæval.* mediævalism, they are so; but the body is regarded as the prison and the shame of the soul; and mediæval art expresses the burning eagerness of the soul to escape from this prison to a higher communion. The three marks of mediæval art are individualism, desire and ecstasy; individualism, since the artist is struggling to interpret a personal intensity, and goes to grotesqueness in the effort; desire, since the perpetual longing of the Church on earth for her Master is the type of the artist's passion; ecstasy, since this passion demands the surrender of reason and has its climax in the adoration of a mystery revealed [1]. Between the Oriental and the Mediæval art stands the Greek. Greek art defines humanity, the body and the soul of man. But it has not reached the mediæval point; it has not learned to feel that the body is the prison and the shame of the soul. Rather, it regards the soul as reflecting its own divinity upon the body. 'What a piece of work is man! how noble in reason! how infinite in faculty! in form and moving how express and admirable! in action how like an angel! in

---

[1] I have not at hand an article on (I think) Mr Rossetti's poems, which appeared some years ago in the *Westminster Review*, and in which these traits of mediævalism were very finely delineated.

apprehension how like a god! the beauty of the
world! the paragon of animals!' If Hamlet could
have stopped there, he would have been a Greek;
but he could not, he was sick with a modern
distemper, abandonment to the brooding thought

*Greek re-
flection was
at a happy
pause:*

that sapped his will[1]. The Greek of the days when
art was supreme could and did stop there; he was
Narcissus, standing on the river bank, looking into
the deep, clear waters where the mirror of his image
shows the soul, too, through the eyes, Narcissus in
love with the image that he beholds,—but Narcissus
as yet master of himself,—as yet with a firm foot-hold
upon the -bank, not as yet possessed by the delirious
impulse to plunge into the depths. Here, then, was
the first condition for the possibility of a great art.
Reflection had taken the right direction, had got far
enough, but had not got too far; it was a pause.
But, in order that this pause should be joyous, and
that the mind should not, from weariness or disappointment, hasten forward, another thing was neces-

*and the
Greeks were
beautiful.*

sary—that men and women should be beautiful. By
some divine chance, the pause in reflection coincided
with the physical perfection of a race; and the result
was Greek art.

*Why Greek
art became
plastic
rather than
picturesque.*

Why, however, should this art have expressed
itself in Sculpture rather than, for instance, in Painting? Art gives pleasure by form, by colour, by
sound, or, as in poetry, by the reminiscence of all
these combined with the delight of motion. But
the mind has had a history; and the very degree in

*Series of
the arts:*

which the resources of a particular art are limited or

[1] Dowden, 'Shakspere's Mind and Art,' p. 47.

ample may give it a special affinity with an earlier
or a later stage of the mind. Architecture corresponds *Architecture:*
with the phase when man's thoughts about himself
are still indistinct; the building may hint, but it
cannot express, the artist's personality: Egyptian art
has been called a Memnon waiting for the day. Paint- *Painting, Music, Poetry;*
ing, Music and Poetry are the modern and romantic
arts, with a range of expression adequate to every
subtlety and intricacy of self-analysis. Between this
group and Architecture comes Sculpture, the art *Sculpture.*
kindred with that phase in the mind's history when
man has just attained to recognition of himself and
is observing his own typical characteristics of form
and spirit with wonder and with joy, but, as yet,
without the impulse towards analysis. In all the
greatest sculpture there breathes the unshamed and
innocent surprise of a child just waked from sleep.
But this of itself implies renouncement; the limits *The limit of expression*
of possible expression in Sculpture are severe. If, *in Sculpture not*
then, the Greek was contemplating his own soul as *irksome, but congenial,*
well as his own body, why, it might be asked, had he *to the Greek.*
recourse to a medium of interpretation for which the
spiritual subtleties of painting and poetry are impossible? The answer is,—Because he was not
observing the soul apart from the body, but as one
with the body in a godlike union; and because, to
him, any expression of spiritual subtleties was not
a gain but a loss, if it was effected at the expense
of that in which he was absorbed—the contemplation of man as man, in his totality, as the paragon
of animals. Sculpture cannot express a complex or
refined situation; but its very limitations on that

side make it the clearest interpretation of a character or a type. The Greek's attention was fixed on the typical, unchanging, divine lineaments of man, as he stood forth under the blue heaven, his outlines clear against the sunlit sea; and, for the Greek's purpose, sculpture was the more fitting just because it elimi-

The best sculpture is not cold nor vague.

nates what is restless or accidental. But he did not mean sculpture to be cold or rigid; he did not mean it to be blank or vague; and assuredly he made it none of these things. The 'Adorante' lifting up his hands in praise for victory, the cousinship of Love with Death hinted in the Genius of Eternal Slumber,—let these works and such as these be witnesses.

Mistake of conceiving Greek Tragedy as the daughter of Sculpture: They are sister forms of one tendency,

This character of Sculpture belongs also to Greek Tragedy. But this is not, as seems sometimes to be imagined, because the Greeks sought to make Tragedy like Sculpture. It is because that tendency of intellect and feeling, for which Sculpture happened to be a peculiarly apt expression, set its necessary stamp equally on every thing else that the Greek mind created. In naming this stamp 'plastic' we

which we call 'plastic'.

borrow our term from the arts of modelling; but to conceive the form of Greek Tragedy as derived from Sculpture is like conceiving the Greek language to be derived from Sanskrit. It is true that, in reference

Greek Tragedy has an alloy of trouble,

to the history of Greek thought, Tragedy is a later manifestation than Sculpture; the perfect repose is already troubled, an element of conflict has entered, man is in the presence of Nemesis, and the $\delta\rho\acute{a}\sigma a\nu\tau\iota$ $\pi a\theta\epsilon\hat{\iota}\nu$, the law that sin shall entail suffering, is

but is typical still.

the theme. But the typical character is not lost; those unchanging attributes which, on the one hand,

bring man near to the gods or, on the other, mark his
brotherhood with the dust and the limits of his mortal
destiny are presented in emphatic, untroubled lines;
and, when Retributive Justice has done its work,
that blitheness out of which the passions rose into a
storm returns subdued to the graver and deeper calm
that follows a transcendant contemplation. All honour
to those sublime voices of Titanic pain or victory that
roll, like dirges or paeans, along the spacious music of
Aeschylos; all honour to Euripides also, for no one
is capable of feeling that Sophokles is supreme who
does not feel that Euripides is admirable. Euripides *The true greatness of Euripides.*
is a great emotional dramatist; a master of the pic-
turesque; the only Greek, except Aristophanes, who
set foot in the charmed woodlands of fancy [1]. That
special claim, however, which has in recent times been
made for Euripides, and on the strength of which he
has by some been preferred to his predecessors, involves a fallacy which it is important to observe, since
what is at issue is much more than our judgment on
the relative merits of two poets, it is the principle of
appreciation relatively to all the best Greek work in
every kind. Euripides has been regarded as distinct- *Fallacy involved in calling Euripides the most 'human' of the Greek Tragedians.*
ively the human. Now if by this were meant only
that he is great in dramatising the accidents of life,
in portraying the more obvious phenomena of charac-

[1] 'An admirer of Aeschylus or Sophocles might affirm that neither Aeschylus nor Sophocles chose to use their art for the display of thrilling splendour. However that may be, Euripides, alone of Greeks, with the exception of Aristophanes, entered the fairyland of dazzling fancy which Calderon and Shakspere and Fletcher trod.' Symonds, *The Greek Poets*, p. 230. This seems to me exactly to define one of the most attractive poetical distinctions of Euripides. Compare the same writer's remarks on the lyrics of Aristophanes, p. 250.

ter, in exciting compassion for such troubles, or sympathy with such joys, as come home to us all, in establishing between the poet and the spectator not merely a vivid intelligence but something like a personal friendship, then the epithet would be perfectly just. If, however—and this is the popular notion—Euripides is to be called the 'human' poet in contrast with, for instance, Sophokles; if it is meant that Sophokles is comparatively cold, pompous, stiff, while Euripides is in a warm, flexible, fruitful sympathy with humanity—then the epithet involves a confusion of ideas than which nothing could be more fatal.

Sophokles is the most human, because he is the most Greek. Euripides is human, but Sophokles is more human; Sophokles is so in the only way in which a Greek could be so, by being more Greek. When the best Greek mind was truest to the law of its own nature, it looked at man and man's life in the manner of Sophokles—fixing its regard on the permanent, divine characteristics of the human type, and not suffering minor accidents or unrulinesses or griefs so to thrust themselves forward as to mar the symmetry of the larger view. True simplicity is not the avoidance, but the control, of detail. In Sophokles, as in great sculpture, a thousand fine touches go to that which, as the greatest living creator in fiction has proved, he can still help to teach—the delineation of *Sophokles the most perfect type of the Greek intellect.* the great primary emotions. Sophokles is the purest type of the Greek intellect at its best. Euripides is a very different thing, a highly gifted son of his day. Rhetorical Dialectic has broken into Tragedy, and the religious basis, the doctrine of Nemesis, has been abandoned in favour of such other interests as the poet can devise. Euripides was brilliantly fertile in plots. This is what Aristotle means by τραγικώτατος, alluding especially to sudden and pathetic reversals of situation; for, before Alexander's time, 'tragic' had already come near to 'sensational'[1]. No woman in Greek Tragedy is either so human, or so true a woman, as the Antigone of Sophokles[2].

Since, as has been seen, Oratory was for the Greeks a fine art, it follows that Greek Oratory must have, after its own kind, that same typical character which belongs to Greek Sculpture and to Greek Tragedy. Wherein, then, does it manifest this character? We must here be on our guard against the great stumblingblock of such inquiries, the attempt to find the analogy in the particulars and not in the whole. It might be possible to take a speech of Demosthenes and to work out the details of a correspondence with a tragedy of Sophokles or a work of Pheidias; but such refinements have usually a perilous neighbourhood to fantasy, and, even when they are legitimate, are apt to be more curious than instructive. How truly and universally Greek Oratory bears the plastic stamp, can be seen only when it is regarded in its largest aspects. The

The plastic character as manifested in Greek oratory.

---

[1] The gradual degradation of the words τραγωδεῖν, τραγῳδία, etc., is a painful hint of this. Perhaps the nadir has been reached when a contemporary of Aristotle's, a master, too, of all Attic refinements, can use τραγῳδίαι of the menaces with which a Macedonion queen intimidated Athens: Hypereides ὑπὲρ 'Ευξενίππου col. 37, τὰς τραγῳδίας αὐτῆς (*i.e.* 'Ολυμ-

πιάδος) καὶ τὰς κατηγορίας ἀφῃρηκό-τες ἐσόμεθα.

[2] To Sophokles, hardly less than to Plato, apply the words of Professor Jowett (Introduction to the Phaedros, 2nd edit. II. 102), 'We do not immediately recognize that under the marble exterior of Greek literature was concealed a soul thrilling with spiritual emotion.'

*A series of
types is
developed
by a series
of artists.* first point to be observed is that, in Greek Oratory,
we have a series of types developed by a series of
artists, each of whom seeks to give to his own type
the utmost clearness and distinction that he is
capable of reaching. The same thing is true of
Tragedy, but not in the same degree; for, in Tragedy,
the element of consecrated convention was more per-
sistent; and, besides, Oratory stood in such manifold
and intimate relations with the practical life that the
artist, in expressing his oratorical theory, could express his entire civic personality. Hence the men
who moulded Attic Oratory, whether statesmen or
not, are good examples of conscious obedience to that
law of Greek nature which constrained every man to
make himself a living work of art. 'In its poets and
orators', says Hegel [1], 'its historians and philosophers, Greece cannot be conceived from a central
point unless one brings, as a key to the understanding of it, an insight into the ideal forms of sculpture,
and regards the images of statesmen and philosophers
as well as epic and dramatic heroes from the artistic
point of view; for those who act, as well as those
who create and think, have, in those beautiful days
of Greece, this plastic character. They are great
and free, and have grown up on the soil of their own
individuality, creating themselves out of themselves,
and moulding themselves to what they were and
willed to be. The age of Perikles was rich in such
characters: Perikles himself, Pheidias, Plato, above
all Sophokles, Thucydides also, Xenophon and Sokrates, each in his own order, without the perfection

---

[1] Aesthetik, Part III. Section 2, ch. 1, quoted by Pater, p. 192.

of one being diminished by that of the others. They are ideal artists of themselves, cast each in one flawless mould—works of art which stand before us as an immortal presentment of the gods.'

The plastic character of Greek oratory,—thus seen, first of all, in the finished distinction of successive types, clearly modelled as the nature that wrought them,—is further seen in the individual oration. Take it whence we will, from the age of *In the individual oration,* Antiphon or of Demosthenes, from the forensic, from the deliberative or from the epideictic class, two great characteristics will be found. First, however little *the main lines of the theme are unperplexed,* of sustained reasoning there may be, however much the argument may be mingled with appeals, reminiscences or invectives, everything bears on the matter in hand. It is an exertion of art, but of art strictly pertinent to its scope. No Greek orator could have written such a speech as that of Cicero For Archias or For Publius Sextus. In a Greek speech the main lines of the subject are ever firm; they are never lost amid the flowers of a picturesque luxuriance. Secondly, wherever pity, terror, anger, *and the unity is sealed by a final calm.* or any passionate feeling is uttered or invited, this tumult is resolved in a final calm; and where such tumult has place in the peroration, it subsides before the last sentences of all. The ending of the speech On the Crown—which will be noticed hereafter[1]—is exceptional and unique. As a rule, the very end is calm; not so much because the speaker feels this to be necessary if he is to leave an impression of personal dignity, but rather because the sense of an ideal

---

[1] Vol. II. p 415.

beauty in humanity and in human speech governs
his effort as a whole, and makes him desire that,
where this effort is most distinctly viewed as a whole
—namely, at the close—it should have the serenity

Attic pero-
rations in
Cicero and
Erskine.

of a completed harmony. Cicero has now and then
an Attic peroration, as in the Second Philippic and
the Pro Milone; more often he breaks off in a burst
of eloquence—as in the First Catilinarian, the Pro
Flacco and the Pro Cluentio. Erskine's concluding
sentences in his defence of Lord George Gordon
are Attic :—'Such topics might be useful in the
balance of a doubtful case ; yet, even then, I should
have trusted to the honest hearts of Englishmen to
have felt them without excitation. At present the
plain and rigid rules of justice are sufficient to entitle
me to your verdict[1].'

The person-
alities of
ancient
oratory.

This seems the fitting place to touch for a moment
on a trait of ancient forensic oratory which has sometimes been noticed with rather exaggerated emphasis,
and which, it might be objected, is strangely discord-
ant with the character just described—the disposition
of Greek as well as Roman orators to indulge in
personalities of a nature which would be deemed
highly indecorous in modern times. Their case is
scarcely, perhaps, mended by the observation that

---

[1] This calmness of the Greek
peroration is noticed by Brougham
in his *Dissertation* (p. 25), but is
more fully discussed in his essay
on *Demosthenes*, pp. 184 f. He does
not, however, penetrate to the true
Greek feeling when he says, 'The
same chastened sense of beauty
which forbade a statue to speak
the language of the passions, required that both the whole oration
and each highly impassioned portion of it, should close *with a*
calmness approaching to indiffe-
rence, and tameness.' There comes
in the popular modern notion of
the sculpturesque.

the point of honour did not then exist. A more important circumstance to observe is that the language in question, however strong, is seldom redundant. It finds its place ; but it does not overflow; nor does it destroy that self-mastery in the speaker on which the unity of his utterance depends. From the artistic point of view—and from this alone it is now being regarded—it is a distressing blemish; yet not, even here, of the order to which it is referred by those whose estimate of it is purely modern, since it is not permitted to disturb the symmetry or the repose of the whole. Unquestionably, the scale of life in the Greek republics, and the dialect of the aristocracy at Rome, often imparted to the mutual criticisms of their orators a parochial character which is comparatively rare in the public discussions of the present day. Apart from this accident, however, modern analogies are, unfortunately, not wanting[1]. The speech against Ktesiphon and the speech against Piso certainly contain exceedingly strong phrases. Catullus, who used the ordinary language of society in his day[2], is less euphemistic than Byron. But scurrility is not the measure of vituperation. Ancient invective concentrated the former. Modern invective prefers to diffuse, without diluting, the latter.

[1] Specimens of the language addressed by Coke, then Attorney-General, to Raleigh, whose prosecution he was conducting, will be found in a note to Mr Forsyth's *Hortensius*, p. 45. The phrases are surpassed by nothing in Aeschines. Chatham's most effective retorts were personalities which might have satisfied Cicero. One or two of them will be found in the *Quarterly Review*, No. 132, p. 470. Those who desire further illustrations may read, or recall, the debates in the House of Commons of May 15 and June 8, 1846.

[2] See H. A. J. Munro on Catullus' 29th Poem in the *Journal of Philology*, II. 1—34 (1869).

*Superiority
of Greek to
Roman
oratory.*

*Brougham
on Cicero.*

The superiority of Greek oratory to Roman, in the deliberative and forensic branches alike, has been recognised by the best critics as well as by the most competent practical judges. Brougham, who speaks with the authority of both characters, brings this out with great force and clearness. He says:— 'In all his (Cicero's) orations that were spoken (for, singular as it may seem, the remark applies less to those which were only written, as all the Verrine, except the first, all the Philippics, except the first and ninth, and the Pro Milone), hardly two pages can be found which a modern assembly would bear. Some admirable arguments on evidence, and the credit of witnesses, might be urged to a jury; several passages, given by him on the merits of the case, and in defence against the charge, might be spoken in mitigation of punishment after a conviction or confession of guilt; but, whether we regard the political or forensic orations, the style, both in respect

*Cicero's
orations
utterly unfit
for the
modern
Senate or
Bar:
whereas
almost all
the Greek
orations
could be
adapted.*

of the reasoning and the ornaments, is wholly unfit for the more severe and less trifling nature of modern affairs in the senate or at the bar. Now, it is altogether otherwise with the Greek masters; changing a few phrases, which the difference of religion and of manners might render objectionable,—moderating, in some degree, the virulence of invective, especially against private character, to suit the chivalrous courtesy of modern hostility,—there is hardly one of the political or forensic orations of the Greeks that might not be delivered in similar circumstances before our senate or tribunals[1].'

---

[1] *Inaugural Discourse*, pp. 122 f. Hume, again, observing that Cicero

The main reason of this decided advantage on the *Reasons of this superiority: Greek oratory is always to the point:* part of Greek practical oratory—and the epideictic oratory has a corresponding excellence relatively to that of the French Pulpit—is the business-like character already noticed. If everything is not logical, everything is at least relevant. Cicero, with all his ingenuity, brilliancy and wit, is so apt to wander into mere display, and this display is so openly artificial, that, as Brougham says, 'nothing can be less adapted to the genius of modern elocution'. The style of modern debate comes far nearer to the Greek than to the Latin. But there are two other causes which should be remarked, one especially influential in Deliberative, the other in Forensic, oratory. The first is that, in the days of *the political inspirations of Greek oratory are nobler:* the great Roman eloquence, Rome had no political rival. Her discipline and her manners contributed with her civic security to exempt her citizens from sudden or violent emotion. What Claudian[1] afterwards happily called the *vitae Romana quies* already prevailed. If the paradox of Quintilian[2] be true, that Demosthenes has *plus curae*, Cicero *plus naturae*, it is true in this sense alone, that Cicero is an inferior artist, and indulges more freely the taste of the natural man for ornament. But that Roman oratory should be on the whole more artificial than the Greek, and more limited in its range of subjects, was inevitable. Athens, the antagonist of Sparta or

---

is 'too florid and rhetorical,' and that Greek oratory is 'more chaste and austere,' adds:—'could it be copied, its success would be infallible over a modern assembly.'

(ESSAY XII., *Of Eloquence*, p. 60.)

[1] *De sexto consulatu Honorii Augusti* (404 A.D.) v. 150.

[2] x. 1 § 106.

Thebes, Athens vigilant against Persia or threatened by Macedon, was a city in which the inspirations of eloquence were not only personal but national.

and the forensic motive is more genuine.
Secondly: the Roman *patronus*, who pleaded his client's cause gratuitously, rewarded by the fact that all the higher paths of ambition opened directly from the forum, had, doubtless, an incentive to eloquent declamation which his Attic brother, the professional *logographos*, did not possess. But he had not anything like the same inducement to handle his case scientifically. He was a political aspirant, not a man settled to a calling; and, from a forensic point of view, the element of unreality in his position had a strong tendency to vitiate his performance by making it, before all things, a display.

Early History of Greek Oratory.
The least gifted people, in the earliest stage of intellectual or political growth, will always or usually have the idea, however rude, of a natural oratory. But oratory first begins to have a history, of which the development can be traced, when two conditions have been fulfilled. First, that oratory should be conceived, no longer subjectively, but objectively also, and from having been a mere faculty, should have become an art. Secondly, that an oration should have been written in accordance with the theory of that art. The history of Greek oratory begins with Gorgias. The history of Attic oratory, properly so called, begins with Antiphon.

Two conditions for the possibility of any such history.

The special attributes and endowments of the

Greeks would lead us to expect, before the beginnings of an oratorical art, a singularly rich and various manifestation of natural eloquence, and also an early moment of origin for the art itself. Now, as a *Late appearance of Greek oratory as an Art.* matter of fact, the origin of the art was singularly late, relatively to the gifts and to the general artistic tendency of the race ; but the causes of this delay were external and political. On the other hand, *Extraordinary brilliancy of the pre-theoretic Oratory.* no documents of any early society can show an exuberance, a brilliancy, a diversified perfection of natural eloquence comparable to that which makes one of the chief glories of the Homeric poems. By ' natural' is meant, not necessarily unstudied, but unsystematic, or antecedent to a theory of Rhetoric. The man to whom the gods had given *Homeric estimate of Eloquence.* ἀγορητύς, the power of discourse,—that which, with beautiful strength, φυή, and good sense, φρένες, makes the Homeric triad of human excellences,— might cultivate it; but so long as this cultivation is empirical, not theoretic, the eloquence which it achieves is still natural. From Achilles to Thersites, the orators of the Iliad and the Odyssey are indi- *Homeric illustrations of Eloquence.* vidual. If Achilles alone is a Demosthenes, who had no defects to conquer and no mysteries to learn, Nestor is an Isokrates unaided or unembarrassed by his system, Telemachos an ingenuous youth who has no need of prompting by a Lysias, Odysseus a speaker in whom the logical terseness of Isaeos is joined to something like the unscrupulous smartness, though to nothing like the theatrical splendour, of Aeschines. Nor does any oratory that the ancient *Modern character of the great Homeric speeches:* world has left approach so nearly as the Homeric to the modern ideal. The reason of this is that the great orations of the Iliad are made in debate, and the greatest of all are replies,—as the answer of Achilles to the envoys in the First Book. Condensed statement, lucid argument, repartee, sarcasm, irony, overwhelming invective, profound and irresistible pathos,—all these resources are absolutely commanded by the orators of the Iliad, and all these must have belonged to him, or to those, by whom the Iliad was created. As Mr Gladstone has said[1], 'Paradise Lost' does not represent the time of Charles the Second, nor the 'Excursion' the first decades of this century, but 'as, when we find these speeches in Homer, we know that there must have been men who could speak them, so, from the existence of units who could speak them, we know that there must have been crowds who could feel them.'

Their historical significance.

The Homeric ideal, to shine in eloquence as in action, to be at once 'a speaker of words and a doer of deeds,' 'good in counsel, and mighty in war,' had ample scope, as far as kings and nobles were concerned, in the council and the agora. But the eloquence of the commons does not appear to have been particularly encouraged by the chiefs, and the consummate individuality of an Achilles or an Odysseus was no real step towards the development of a popular oratory based upon a theory communicable to all. In the presence of these great debaters of the Iliad, the Homeric *tis*, when present at all, is essentially a layman, confined strictly to the critical function and uttering his criticisms, when

The Homeric eloquence is still aristocratic, not civil.

[1] *Studies on Homer,* III. 107.

they find utterance, in the fewest and plainest words. Democracy, with its principle of ἰσηγορία,— the principle that every citizen has an equal right to speak his mind about the concerns of the city,— was necessary before a truly civil eloquence could be even possible. But, after Democracy had arisen, a further condition was needed,—the cultivation of the popular intelligence. What is so strikingly characteristic of Greek Democracy in the period before an artistic oratory is this,—that the power of public speaking now exists, indeed, as a political weapon, but, instead of being the great organ by which the people wield the commonwealth, is constantly used by designing individuals against the people. It is employed as a lever for changing the democracy into a tyranny. Such names as Arista-goras, Evagoras, Protagoras, Peisistratos, frequent especially in the Ionian colonies, indicate, not the growth of a popular oratory, but the ascendancy which exceptionally gifted speakers were able to acquire, especially in democracies, before oratory was yet an accomplishment studied according to a method.

The intellectual turning-point came when Poetry ceased to have a sway of which the exclusiveness rested on the presumption that no thought can be expressed artistically which is not expressed metrically. So soon as it had been apprehended that to forsake poetical form was not necessarily to renounce beauty of expression, an obstacle to clear reflection had been overcome. Mythology and cosmical speculation began to have a rival,—a curiosity withdrawn from the cloud-regions of the past or of the infinite to the things of practical life. And this life itself was growing more complex. The present, with its problems which must be solved under penalties, was becoming ever more importunate, and would no longer suffer men's thoughts to wander in mazes where they could find no end:—

> The riddling Sphinx put dim things from our minds,
> And set us to the questions at our doors.

Political turning-point— opening of secure intercourse between the cities:

The political turning-point came with the Persian Wars. Greek freedom was secured against the barbarian. A maritime career was opened to commerce. The Greek cities everywhere came into more

and the new primacy of Athens.

active intercourse; and the centre of the Greek world was Athens. The Dorian States, Sparta and Argos, had never been favourable to the artistic treatment of language. This, like all art and science, was especially the province of the Ionians; and, for the future of oratory, it was of the highest importance that the central city of Hellas should be Ionian. But, though Athens perfected the art, and soon became almost its sole possessor, the first elements

External influences which prepared Attic Oratory.

were prepared elsewhere. The two principal forces which moulded Attic oratory came from the East and the West. One was the Practical Culture of Ionia; the other was the Rhetoric of Sicily.

I. The Practical culture of Ionia.

The theories of the Ionian physicists had not been able to interest more than a few, still less had they been able to draw away the mass of the people from the old poetical faith; nor had the Ionian chroniclers made any but the rudest approaches to a

written prose. But the national Wars of Liberation
had quickened all the pulses of civic life. Freedom
once secured, the new intellectual tendency took
a definite shape. Men arose who, in contrast
with the speculative philosophers, undertook to
give a practical culture. This culture had representatives in every part of Greece. But, while
in Sicily and Magna Graecia it was engrossed with
Rhetoric, in Asiatic, and especially Ionian, Hellas
it was more comprehensive. There, its essence was
Dialectic, in connexion with a training sometimes
encyclopaedic, sometimes directed especially to grammar or to literary criticism. These more comprehensive teachers were known by the general name
of Sophists[1]. Those who, like the Sicilians, had a
narrower scope were sometimes called Sophists, but
were especially and properly called Rhetors.

Protagoras of Abdera, the earliest of the Sophists *Protagoras.*
proper, was born about 485 B.C., and travelled
throughout Greece, teaching, for about 40 years, from
455 to 415. The two things by which he is significant for artistic oratory are, his Dialectic, and the

---

[1] It does not fall within my province to enter on the 'Sophist' controversy, to which, in this country,
eminent scholars have lately given
a new life. But I would invite the
reader's attention to a note, on
p. 130 of my second volume, as to
the use of the word by Isokrates.
And I would record my general
agreement with the reasoned development of Grote's view by Mr
H. Sidgwick, in the 'Journal of
Philology,' Vol. IV. No. 8 (1872).

For the details given here re-
specting particular Sophists or
Rhetors, I have used chiefly :—(1)
Cope's papers on the Sophists and
the Sophistical Rhetoric, in the
*Journal of Classical and Sacred
Philology*, I. 145—188, II. 129—169,
III. 34—80 : (2) Westermann, *Gesch.
der Beredsamkeit*, pp. 36—48 :
(3) Blass, *die Attische Beredsamkeit von Gorgias bis zu Lysias*,
pp. 1—78.

Commonplaces which he made his pupils commit to memory. His Dialectic is famous for its undertaking to make the weaker cause the stronger. One of the uses of Rhetoric, as Aristotle says, is to succour truth when truth is imperilled by the weakness of its champion; but this is not the place to inquire whether Protagoras intended, or how far he was bound to foresee, an immoral application. As a mental discipline, his Dialectic was important to oratory, not merely by its subtlety, but by its treatment of the rhetorical syllogism. The prepared topics which his pupils learned seem to mark a stage when public speaking in general was no longer purely extemporary, but when, on the other hand, the speech was not, as in Antiphon's time, wholly written. In regard to language, Protagoras insisted on ὀρθοέπεια—*i. e.* a correct accidence : but there is no proof that he sought to make a style ; both the Ionic fragment in Plutarch[1] and the myth in Plato[2] are, for the prose of the time, simple, and they are free from the Gorgian figures.

Prodikos.   Prodikos of Keos—the junior by many years of Protagoras—was neither, like the latter, a dialectician nor a rhetor of the Siceliot type, but rather, like Hippias, the teacher of an encyclopaedic culture. There is no reason to think that he, any more than Protagoras or Hippias, concerned himself with the artistic oratory of Gorgias. Xenophon gives in the *Memorabilia*[3] a paraphrase of the 'Choice of Hera-

---

[1] Plut. παραμυθητικὸς πρὸς Ἀπολ-λώνιον, c. 33 (*Moral.* p. 118), τῶν γὰρ υἱέων νεηνιῶν—ἀμηχανίην.

[2] Plat. *Protag.* pp. 320 D—328 C.

[3] II. i. §§ 21—33. Xen. calls it τὸ σύγγραμμα τὸ περὶ Ἡρακλέους.

kles' as related by Prodikos in his fable called
Ὧραι. When Philostratos[1] says that he need not
describe the style of Prodikos because Xenophon
has sketched it, he is refuted by Xenophon himself,
who observes that the diction of Prodikos was
more ambitious than that of his paraphrase[2]. There
are certainly confusions of synonyms which the
Platonic Prodikos distinguishes[3]; and the only
safe inference appears to be that, however faithful
Xenophon may have been to the matter of the
fable, he is a witness of no authority for its form.
The true point of contact between Prodikos and the
early Rhetoric is his effort to discriminate words
which express slight modifications of the same idea,
and which, therefore, were not ordinarily distinguished by poets or in the idiom of daily life. However unscientific his effort may have been, it at least
represented a scientific tendency, which soon set its
mark on literature as well as on thought. Two men
who are said to have been pupils of Prodikos—
Euripides and Isokrates—show clear traces of it;
but, for reasons which will appear further on, it is
especially distinct in the earliest phase of artistic
oratory—in Antiphon, and above all in Thucydides.

Hippias of Elis is of no immediate significance *Hippias.*

---

[1] *Vit. Sophist.* p. 16 (Kayser),
καὶ τί ἂν χαρακτηρίζοιμεν τὴν τοῦ
Προδίκου γλῶτταν, Ξενοφῶντος αὐτὴν ἱκανῶς ὑπογράφοντος;

[2] *Mem.* II. i. § 34, οὕτω πως
διώκει (διῴκει?) Πρόδικος τὴν ὑπ᾿
Ἀρετῆς Ἡρακλέους παίδευσιν, ἐκίσ-
ιησε μέντοι τὰς γνώμας ἔτι μεγα-
λειοτέροις ῥήμασιν ἢ ἐγὼ νῦν.

[3] As Blass points out (*l. c.*),
Xenophon (*Mem.* II. i. § 24) makes
Prodikos use τέρπεσθαι, ἥδεσθαι,
εὐφραίνεσθαι, indistinguishably:
whereas Plato (*Prot.* 337 c) makes
Prodikos appropriate εὐφραίνεσθαι
to intellectual, ἥδεσθαι to sensuous
pleasure.

for our subject.   Neither Dialectic nor Rhetoric
was included, or at least prominent, in the large
circle of arts and sciences which he professed to
teach.   Economics, Ethics and Politics—'the faculty
of managing public affairs along with his own[1]'—
formed his especial province.   Like all the other
Sophists, he touched, of course, the domain of
grammar and prosody ; his Τρωικὸς λόγος[2], a dialogue
between Nestor and Neoptolemos, made pretensions
to elegance of style, but probably not of a poetical
or Gorgian cast[3] ; and, in Plato, Hippias assigns,
not his oratory, but his political insight, as the
ground of his selection as an ambassador by the
Eleans[4].

Thrasymachos of Chalkedon stands in a far
riper and more definite relation to Attic rhetorical
prose, and will more properly be noticed in connexion with the progress from Antiphon to Lysias,
when we come to look back on the development
as a whole[5].

Summary:
influence
of the
Ionian
Practical
culture.

These, then, were the two things by which the
Eastern or Ionian school of practical culture prepared the ground for Attic oratory : first and chiefly,
popular Dialectic ; secondly, in the phrase of Protagoras, orthoepy—attention to correctness in speaking or writing.   In contrast with the Eastern

---

[1] Plat. *Hipp. Mai.* 282 B, τὸ
καὶ τὰ δημόσια πράττειν δύνασθαι
μετὰ τῶν ἰδίων. ·Cf. Cope in *Journ.
Class. and Sacr. Phil.* III. 63.

[2] Plat. *l. c.* p. 286 A.

[3] Philostratos, at least, says of
Hippias that he wrote 'powerfully
and naturally,' εἰς ὀλίγα καταφεύ-

γων τῶν ἐκ ποιητικῆς ὀνόματα, *Vit.
Sophist.* p. 15 (Kayser).

[4] Plat. *l. c.* p. 281 (*ad init.*)   He
is a δικαστὴς καὶ ἄγγελος τῶν λόγων
οἳ ἂν παρὰ τῶν πόλεων ἑκάστων
λέγωνται.

[5] See Vol. II. ch. xxiii.

Dialectic stands the Western Rhetoric. In contrast with the Ionian study of correct diction, ὀρθοέπεια, stands the Sicilian study of beautiful diction, εὐέπεια.

Deeper causes than a political crisis fitted Sicily to become the birthplace of Rhetoric. The first cause was the general character of the Sicilian Greeks. Thucydides remarks that the quick and adventurous Athenians, who were often benefited by Lacedaemonian slowness or caution, found most formidable adversaries in the Syracusans just because the Syracusans were so like themselves[1]; and this resemblance, we have good reason to suppose, included the taste for lively controversy and the passion for lawsuits described by Aristophanes in the *Wasps*. 'An acute people, with an inborn love of disputation', is the description of the Sicilians which Cicero quotes from Aristotle[2]: 'Sicilians are never so miserable', he says in one of the Verrine speeches, 'that they cannot make a happy joke[3]'. The population thus gifted had, further, gone through the same political phases as Athens; through aristocracy they had arrived at tyranny, and through tyranny at a democracy. The flourishing age of the Sicilian Tyrants—the early part of the fifth century B.C.— was illustrated by art and literature, by the lyric poetry which, native to Ionia, found its most splendid theme in the glory of these Dorian princes of the West, and by a home-growth of Comedy, the creation of Phormis and Epicharmos. It was in 466

II. The Sicilian Rhetoric.

Character of the Sicilian Greeks.

Political development of the Sicilian cities.

The Age of the Sicilian Tyrants.

The Democratic Revolution.

---

[1] μάλιστα ὁμοιότροποι, Thuc. VIII. 96.

[2] Cic. *Brut.* xii. § 46.

[3] Cic. *In Verr.* IV. 43 *ad fin.* Cf. Quint. VI. 3 § 41.

that Thrasybulos, last of the Gelonian dynasty, was expelled and that a democracy was established at Syracuse. Somewhat later, a democracy arose at

Agrigentum also. Popular life was now as exuberant in Sicily as it was at Athens after the Persian Wars; but, with its mixture of races, it was less fortunately tempered; its vigour, instead of glowing with the sense of national welfare secured against aliens, had the feverish vehemence of a domestic reaction; and hence we should be prepared to find these younger democracies showing almost at once some features which do not appear in the elder Athenian democracy until the time of the Peloponnesian War. But it was neither by the turbulent rivalries of the popular assembly, nor by

the natural growth of συκοφαντική or pettifogging, that the formulation of Rhetoric as an Art was immediately caused. The absolute princes of Sicily had done as they listed. They had banished, they had confiscated,—like Dionysios I. in later times,

they had effaced towns and transferred populations,—they had turned all things upside-down. When they were driven out, and when governments arose based on the equality of citizens before the law, a

crowd of aggrieved claimants presented themselves wherever that law had a seat. 'Ten years ago', this one would say, 'Hieron banished me from Syracuse because I was too much a democrat, and gave my house on the Epipolae to Agathokles, who still lives among you; I ask the people to restore it to me.' 'When Gelon razed our city', another would say, 'and divided the lands among his friends, we were commanded to dwell at Selinus, where I have lived many years; my father's land was given to a favourite of the tyrant's, whose first cousin still holds it; I ask you to insist on this man making restitution.' Claims of this kind would be innumerable. And, besides those which were founded in justice, a vast number of false claims would be encouraged by the general presumption that the rights of property had been universally deranged. If, twenty years after the Cromwellian Settlement of Ireland, a government had arisen of such a nature as to make it worth people's while to dispute every possession taken under that settlement in the Ten Counties, the state of things which would have ensued would have borne some resemblance to that which prevailed throughout Sicily, but especially at Syracuse, in 466 B.C.[1]

Now, if we consider what would be, as a rule, *General features of such claims.* the characteristics of claims to property made under such conditions, we shall find that they throw a significant light on the little which is expressly recorded in regard to the first artists of Rhetoric. First, such claims would, as a rule, go several years back, and would often require for their elucidation that a complicated mass of details should be stated or arranged. Secondly, such claims would often lack documentary support; the tablets proving a purchase, a sale, or a contract, would, in many or most cases, have been lost or destroyed, and the

---

[1] Those who wish to test the accuracy of this illustration are referred to the History of the Cromwellian Settlement by Mr J. P. Prendergast. (Longmans, 1865.)

claimant would have to rely chiefly on inferences
from other facts which he could substantiate.
Best aids for such claimants : If, then, we imagine a man conceiving the idea
that these innumerable claimants want help, and
that the occupation of helping them may be a
way to notoriety or gain, in what particular forms
is it probable that he would have tried to render
1. Skill in marshalling facts : this help? He would have seen, first, that people
must be assisted to deal with an array of complex
facts; they must be taught method. He would
have seen, secondly, that they must be assisted
to dispense with documentary or circumstantial
2. Skill in arguing probabilities. evidence; they must be given hints as to the best
mode of arguing from general probabilities.

Empedokles. Diogenes Laertios quotes a statement of Aristotle
that Empedokles was the inventor of Rhetoric, as
Zenon of Dialectic[1]. The more cautious phrase of
Sextus Empiricus[2] (also from Aristotle), which
Quintilian translates, is that Empedokles *broke
ground* (κεκινηκέναι, *aliqua movisse*) in Rhetoric.
Assuredly the poet and philosopher of Agrigentum
created, at least, no rhetorical system. His oratory—
which, after the fall of Thrasydaeos in 472, found
political scope in resistance to a restoration of the
tyranny—however brilliant, was practical only; and
his analogy—so far as the wanderings of his later

---

[1] Diog. VIII. 57, Ἀριστοτέλης
δ᾽ ἐν τῷ σοφιστῇ φησι πρῶτον Ἐμ-
πεδοκλέα ῥητορικὴν εὑρεῖν, Ζήνωνα
δὲ διαλεκτικήν. In his lost work
περὶ ποιητῶν, Arist. (as quoted by
Diog. *l. c.*) said that Empedokles
was δεινὸς περὶ τὴν φράσιν and
μεταφορικός, as well as generally

Ὁμηρικός. Twining notices (Vol. I. p.
249) the apparent discrepancy between this statement and that in
the *Poetics* c. 1.—that Empedokles
and Homer have οὐδὲν κοινὸν πλὴν
τὸ μέτρον.

[2] VII. 6 : Quint. III. 1 § 8.

years and the union of care for studied expression
with a doctrine give the semblance of such—is, at
least, more with the Sophists of proper Greece than
with the Sicilian Rhetors.

The founder of Rhetoric as an Art was Korax *Korax.*
of Syracuse. He had enjoyed some political consideration in the reign of Hieron (478—467 B.C.),
and was probably several years older than Empedokles. The law-suits which followed the establishment of the democracy are said to have given
him the idea of drawing up, and committing to
writing, a system of rules for forensic speaking.
This was his τέχνη or Art of Rhetoric—the earliest
theoretical Greek book, not merely on Rhetoric, but in
any branch of art. There is no mention of speeches
composed by him either for himself or for others.
Nor, except the story of his law-suit with Tisias, is
there any evidence that he taught Rhetoric for pay.
In regard to the contents of his 'Art' two facts *Treatise of Korax on Rhetoric:*
are known which are of interest. They are pre-
cisely those which, as has been shown, we should
have expected to find. First, he gave rules for
arrangement—dividing the speech into five parts— *Arrangement.*
proem, narrative, arguments (ἀγῶνες), subsidiary re-
marks (παρέκβασις) and peroration[1]. Secondly, he *The topic of εἰκός.*
illustrated the topic of *general probability*, bringing
out its two-edged application : *e. g.* if a physically
weak man is accused of an assault, he is to ask,
'Is it probable that *I* should have attacked *him?*';
if a strong man is accused, he is to ask, 'Is it

---

[1] The ἀγῶνες and παρέκβασις are
thus explained in the Greek pro-
legomena to Hermogenes, Spengel, συναγωγὴ τεχνῶν, p. 25.

probable that I should have committed an assault
in a case where there was sure to be a presumption against me?'. Nothing could be more suggestive of the special circumstances in which the art
of Rhetoric had its birth. The same topic of
Probability holds its place in the Tetralogies of
Antiphon[1]. But its original prominence was, in
truth, a Sicilian accident[2].

Tisias.
Tisias, the pupil of Korax, must have been born
about 485 B.C. We hear that he was the master of
Lysias at the colony of Thurii (founded in 443 B.C.),
and of the young Isokrates at Athens—about 418 B.C.;
Pausanias makes him accompany Gorgias to Athens
in 427 B.C.; and speaks of him as having been
banished from Syracuse[3]. Whatever may be the
worth of these details, the main facts about Tisias
are clear. He led the wandering life of a Sophist.

*The 'Rhe-
toric' of
Tisias.
The topic
of εἰκός
further
developed.*
And in his Art of Rhetoric—the only work of his
which antiquity possessed—he followed his master
in further developing the topic of Probability[4].

Those who bring a scientific spirit to the study
of Attic oratory need not be cautioned against
allowing what is ignoble, puerile, or even immoral in
the earliest Greek Rhetoric to prejudice their esti-

[1] See below, pp. 47 ff.

[2] This topic of εἰκός—the great weapon of the early Rhetoric—stands ninth among those topics of the fallacious enthymeme which Aristotle enumerates in *Rhet.* II. 24—a chapter which, for his *Rhetoric*, is what the περὶ σοφιστικῶν ἐλέγχων is for the *Topica*. The fallacy arises from the omission to distinguish between abstract and particular probability. Arist. illustrates it by the verses of Agathon:—'Perhaps one might call this very thing a probability,—that many improbable things will happen to men.' 'Of this topic' says Aristotle (*Rh.* II. 24 § 9) 'the Treatise of Korax is made up.' Cf. Spengel, συναγωγὴ τεχνῶν pp. 30 f.

[3] Pausan. VI. 17 § 8.

[4] Plat. *Phaedr.* 267 A, 273 A—C.

mate of the real services afterwards rendered both
to language and to thought by the conception of
expression as an art. Popular sentiment is universally against new subtleties. To gauge the morality
of the early Rhetoric by the feeling of the people
would be as unreasonable as to judge Sokrates on
the testimony of the *Clouds*. The real meaning of *Real mean-ing of the lawsuit story.*
the story about the lawsuit between Korax and
Tisias lies in its illustration of the people's feeling.
Korax, suing Tisias for a fee, argued that it must be
paid whether he gained or lost his cause; if he
gained, under the verdict; if he lost, because the
success of his pupil proved the fee to have been
earned; Tisias inverted the dilemma; and the judges
dismissed them both with the comment, 'bad crow,
bad eggs.' What this really expresses is not the
character of the earliest Rhetoric, but its grotesque
unpopularity.

Gorgias is a man of whose powers and merits *Gorgias.*
it is extremely difficult for us now to form a
clear or impartial notion. This is not, however,
because the portrait of him in Plato is so vivid.
Nothing more distinguishes Plato from later sati-
rists of like keenness than his manner of hinting the
redeeming points of the person under dissection;
and, whenever Gorgias comes in—whether in the
dialogue that bears his name or elsewhere—it may
be discerned (I venture to think) that Plato's purpose was to bring out an aspect of the man—that
aspect which he considered most important—but
that he allowed, and was writing for those who
knew, that there was another side to the picture.

This other side is suggested by the fact that Gorgias had at least some influence on a man of such intellectual power as Thucydides, on one so highly cultivated as the tragic poet Agathon, and on so shrewd a judge of practical ability as Jason of Pherae. The difficulty of now estimating Gorgias comes from this,—that he was an inventor whose originality it is hard for us to realise, but an artist whose faults are to us peculiarly glaring. Gorgias of Leontini was born about 485 B. C. Tradition made him the pupil of Empedokles; but their nearness in age makes this unlikely. That they knew each other is probable enough. Gorgias, like Protagoras, began with natural philosophy; and, after employing Eleatic methods to combat Eleatic conclusions, turned from a field of which he held himself to have

The province of Gorgias, neither Dialectic nor Rhetoric,

proved the barrenness. The practical culture to which he next addressed himself differed both from that of the Eastern Sophists and from that of the Sicilian Rhetors. It was founded neither upon Dialec-

but Oratory. tic nor upon a systematic Rhetoric. Its basis was Oratory considered as a faculty to be developed empirically. Whether Gorgias left a written Art or not, is doubtful; it seems more probable that he did not[1]; and his method of teaching—which reappears a century and a half later with the beginnings of Asianism[2]—rested on the commission to memory of prepared passages. These passages were especially such as might serve to magnify the speaker's theme (αὔξησις) or to bring out the enormity of a wrong (δείνωσις). Beautiful and effective expression (λέξις)

---

[1] On this point see Blass, p. 53.   [2] See Vol. II. ch. xxiv.

was the one great object. Gorgias seems to have
given little or no heed to the treatment of subject-
matter,—to invention or management; or even to
that special topic of Probability which was already
engaging so much of the attention of Rhetoric. He
was himself a man with a brilliant gift for language.
His general conception was simple enough, but, for
his own day and world, both bold and original.
If the faculty of expression is cultivated to the right
point, and is combined with a certain amount of
general information, it will carry all before it. Just
in the spirit in which Vivian Grey is described as
saying to himself 'knowledge is power', Gorgias said
to himself, 'expression is power.' He considered
the gift in its relation to victory, and this victory not to be such narrow and painful success
as was prepared by the pedantries of the rhetors,
but dazzling and world-wide. Everything recorded
of the man suggests his immense self-confidence, his
capacity for sustained work, his exuberant vitality,
and, above all, his power of doing what a new style
would not have done without other gifts—setting
the fashion to the ambitious among the rising generation, or even exciting a popular enthusiasm. In *His first
visit to
Athens.*
427 b. c. the Leontines sent an embassy to Athens,
praying for help in their war with Syracuse. 'At
the head of the envoys,' says Diodoros[1], 'was
Gorgias the rhetor, a man who far surpassed all his

---

[1] XII. 53, τῷ ξενίζοντι τῆς λέξεως ἐξέπληξε τοὺς Ἀθηναίους
ὄντας εὐφυεῖς καὶ φιλολόγους, δια-
φέρουσιν ἀντιθέτοις καὶ ἰσοκώλοις
καὶ παρίσοις καὶ ὁμοιοτελεύτοις καὶ
ἑτέροις τοιούτοις. On these, see
Vol. II. pp. 64 f.

τὸ ξενίζον
in his
speaking,

contemporaries in oratorical force. He astonished
the Athenians, with their quick minds and their
love of eloquence, by the foreign fashion (τῷ ξενίζοντι) of his language'—and by figures which the
historian proceeds to enumerate. Now Gorgias
appears to have always spoken and written in the
Attic dialect—not in the ordinary Sicilian Doric,
nor in the Ionic of Leontini[1]. The τὸ ξενίζον of
Diodoros is that 'foreign' air which Aristotle in his
Rhetoric calls τὸ ξενικόν[2], and which, for Athenians
at least, was capable, when rightly used, of being
a charm in oratory. There is no word which will
exactly translate it, but it is nearly akin to what
we mean by 'distinction.' That which was, to the
Athenians, τὸ ξενίζον, or the element of distinction,

its poetical
character.

in the Sicilian's speaking, was its poetical character ;
and this depended on two things—the use of poetical words, and the use of symmetry or assonance
between clauses in such a way as to give a strongly
marked prose-rhythm and to reproduce, as far as
possible, the metres of verse. The only considerable
fragment of Gorgias extant is that from the Funeral
Oration—for the *Palamedes* and the *Helen* are now
generally admitted to be later imitations. A few

Specimen
from his
Epitaphios.

sentences from this will give the best idea of his
manner :—

μαρτυρίας δὲ τούτων τρόπαια ἐστήσαντο τῶν πολε-
μίων, Διὸς μὲν ἀγάλματα, τούτων δὲ ἀναθήματα, οὐκ

---

[1] Blass, p. 52.

[2] (*e.g.*) Arist. *Rhet.* III. 2 § 3, διὸ
δεῖ ποιεῖν ξένην τὴν διάλεκτον·
θαυμασταὶ γὰρ τῶν ἀπόντων εἰσίν·
ἡδὺ δὲ τὸ θαυμαστόν. So *ib.* § 8,

τὸ σαφὲς καὶ τὸ ἡδὺ καὶ τὸ ξενικὸν
ἔχει μάλιστα ἡ μεταφορά. And III.
7 § 11, τὰ ξένα μάλιστα ἁρμόττει
λέγοντι παθητικῶς.

ἄπειροι οὔτε ἐμφύτου Ἄρεος οὔτε νομίμων ἐρώτων οὔτε
ἐνοπλίου ἔριδος οὔτε φιλοκάλου εἰρήνης, σεμνοὶ μὲν
πρὸς τοὺς θεοὺς τῷ δικαίῳ, ὅσιοι δὲ πρὸς τοὺς τοκέας
τῇ θεραπείᾳ, δίκαιοι πρὸς τοὺς ἀστοὺς τῷ ἴσῳ, εὐσεβεῖς
δὲ πρὸς τοὺς φίλους τῇ πίστει. τοιγαροῦν αὐτῶν ἀποθανόντων ὁ πόθος οὐ συναπέθανεν, ἀλλ' ἀθάνατος ἐν
οὐκ ἀσωμάτοις σώμασι ζῇ οὐ ζώντων[1].

It may be hard now to understand how such *His great*
popularity
a style can have moved to transports of delight men *at Athens—*
how it is to
who lived among the works of Pheidias and Iktinos, *be under-*
stood.
who knew the prose of Herodotos, and whose ears
were familiar with Homer, with Aeschylos and with
Sophokles. It is more difficult still, perhaps, to
realize that the invention of this style was a proof
of genius. Gorgias was the first man who definitely
conceived how literary prose might be artistic. That
he should instinctively compare it with the only
other form of literature which was already artistic,
namely poetry, was inevitable. Early prose necessarily begins by comparing itself with poetry. Gorgias was a man of glowing and eager power; he
carried the assimilation to a length which seems
incredibly tasteless now. But let it be remembered
that the interval between Gorgias and Thucydides,
in some passages of the historian's speeches, is not
so very wide. And if the enthusiasm of the Ekklesia still seems incomprehensible, let it be remembered that they felt vividly the whole originality of
the man, and did not at all see that his particular
tendency was mistaken. It was only by and by,
and after several compromises, that men found out

[1] Sauppe, *Or. Att.* II. 130.

the difference between τὸ ἔρρυθμον and τὸ εὔρυθμον, between verse and rhythmical prose; namely, that rhythm is the framework of the former but only the fluent outline of the latter.   If a style is new and forcible, extravagances will not hinder it from being received with immense applause at its first appearance.   Then it is imitated until its originality is forgotten and its defects brought into relief.   In the maturity of his genius, Lord Macaulay pronounced the Essay on Milton to be 'disfigured by much gaudy and ungraceful ornament.'   Gorgias was the founder of artistic prose; and his faults are the more excusable because they were extravagant.   Granting the natural assumption that prose was to be a kind of poetry, then Gorgias was brilliantly logical; and, as the event proved, his excesses did good service by calling earlier attention to the fallacy in his theory.   Allowing, however, all that has been advanced above, it might still seem strange that Gorgias should have had this reception from the Assembly which, within three years, had been listen-

Perikles.

Was his oratory artistic in form?

ing to Perikles.   But the true question is whether Perikles had aimed at giving to his eloquence the finish of a literary form.   Suidas says that Perikles was the first who composed a forensic speech before delivering it; his predecessors had extemporised[1]. Cicero says that Perikles and Alkibiades are the most ancient authors who have left authentic writings[2].   Quintilian, however, thinks that the com-

---

[1] Suidas *s. v.* Περικλῆς; ῥήτωρ καὶ δημαγωγός, ὅστις πρῶτος γραπτὸν λόγον ἐν δικαστηρίῳ εἶπε, τῶν πρὸ αὐτοῦ σχεδιαζόντων.

[2] Cic. *De Orat.* II. § 93, *antiquissimi fere sunt, quorum quidem scripta constent:* where the 'constent' seems to imply that the

positions extant under the name of Perikles are not
worthy of his reputation, and that, as others had
conjectured, they were spurious[1]. Plutarch says *Statement of Plutarch.*
positively that Perikles has left nothing written
(ἔγγραφον) except decrees[2]. The antithesis meant
by ἔγγραφον is with those sayings of Perikles which
tradition had preserved; especially those bold similes
from nature and life to which reference will be made
in considering the style of Antiphon[3]. The speeches *Thucydidean Speeches of Perikles.*
in Thucydides doubtless give the general ideas of
Perikles with essential fidelity; it is possible, further, that they may contain recorded sayings of his
like those in Aristotle: but it is certain that they
cannot be taken as giving the form of the statesman's
oratory. Like the other speeches, they bear the
stamp of a manner which was not so fully developed
until after his death. Perikles as an orator is best *Notices of his oratory.*
known to us from the brief but emphatic notices of
the impression which he made. 'This man,' says
Eupolis, 'whenever he came forward, proved himself the greatest orator among men: like a good
runner, he could give the other speakers ten feet
start, and win.......Rapid you call him; but, besides
his swiftness, a certain persuasion sat upon his lips
—such was his spell: and, alone of the speakers,

question of authenticity had been
examined. But in *Brut.* § 27
he says, more doubtfully, *Ante
Periclem, cuius. scripta quaedam
feruntur, littera nulla est quae
quidem ornatum aliquem habeat.*

[1] Quint. III. 1 § 12, *Equidem
non reperio quicquam tanta elo-
quentiae fama dignum; ideoque*

*minus miror esse qui nihil ab
eo scriptum putent, haec autem
quae feruntur ab aliis esse com-
posita.*

[2] Plut. *Pericl.* c. 8, ἔγγραφον
μὲν οὐδὲν ἀπολέλοιπε πλὴν τῶν ψη-
φισμάτων· ἀπομνημονεύεται δὲ
ὀλίγα παντάπασιν.

[3] Below, pp. 27 f.

Its distinctive conditions.

he ever left his sting in the hearers[1].' When Aristophanes is describing the outbreak of the Peloponnesian War, 'Perikles the Olympian,' he says, 'was thundering and lightening and putting Greece in a tumult[2].' Unique as an Athenian statesman, Perikles must have been in two respects unique also as an Athenian orator;—first, because he occupied such a position of personal ascendancy as no man before or after him attained; secondly, because his thoughts and his moral force won him such renown for eloquence as no one else ever got from Athenians without the further aid of artistic expression. His manner of speaking seems to have been tranquil, stately to a degree which Plutarch seems inclined to satirize[3], but varied by occasional bursts having the character of lofty poetry[4].

---

[1] A. κράτιστος οὗτος ἐγένετ' ἀνθρώπων λέγειν | ὁπότε παρέλθοι, χὥσπερ ἀγαθοὶ δρομῆς | ἐκ δέκα ποδῶν ᾕρει λέγων τοὺς ῥήτορας. B. ταχὺν λέγεις μέν πρὸς δέ γ' αὑτοῦ τῷ τάχει | πειθώ τις ἐπεκάθιζεν ἐπὶ τοῖς χείλεσιν· | οὕτως ἐκήλει· καὶ μόνος τῶν ῥητόρων | τὸ κέντρον ἐγκατέλειπε τοῖς ἀκροωμένοις. Eupolis, Δῆμοι, Bothe *Frag. Com.* I. 162, where the ancient citations of this famous passage are brought together. See (*e.g.*) Cic. Quint. XII. 10. *Brut.* § 38.

[2] Ar. *Ach.* 530.

[3] Plut. *Per.* c. 5.

[4] Cf. Mr Watkiss Lloyd's 'Age of Perikles' I. 159 (speaking of the sweetness of voice and facile swiftness which distinguished the elocution of Perikles):—'The combination of power, rapidity, and fascination that is thus avouched, is probably not so much explained by, as it explains, the tradition of his obligations to such varied instructors as Anaxagoras, Damon, and Aspasia...To Plato, Perikles was still, though only by traditional reputation, the most accomplished of all orators' (*Phaedr.* p. 269 E, πάντων τελεώτατος εἰς τὴν ῥητορικήν.)—As Mr Lloyd says, Plato seems inclined *there* to connect this excellence of Perikles with a study of psychology under Anaxagoras: though the *Phaedo* p. 97 B implies that Anaxagoras did not enter on such inquiries. Undoubtedly *psychology* is what Plato in the *Phaedros* is recommending, first of all, to Isokrates; see on this, Blass, *Isokrates und Isaios*, p. 29.

The earliest of those Athenian orators who have History of Athenian oratory begins with Antiphon: left writings is not the disciple of him who most represented the new art of oratory. Antiphon was chiefly formed, not by the new Oratory, but by the a disciple, not of Gorgias, but of the Sicilian Rhetoric. new Rhetoric, not by Gorgias but by Tisias. The influence of Gorgias meets us somewhat, of course, even in Antiphon, but far more decidedly in Thucydides, and then, chastened to a form of which its beginnings had little promise, in Isokrates. The Rhetoric and Popular Dialectic at Athens from 450 B.C. second half of the fifth century at Athens had already given a place in the popular life to the new culture. While Comedy set itself against that culture, Tragedy had been more compliant. No con- Tragedy. trast could be more significant than that between the singular barrenness of the trial-scene in the *Eumenides,* or the measured controversies of the *Ajax,* and the truly forensic subtleties of the *Orestes.* Nor was the exercise only mimic. Already the public advocates (συνηγόροι) formed a class. The Forensic Advocacy. private advocate was forbidden to take money. Hence he usually begins by defining the personal interest which has led him to appear. In the next century, at least, the law was not strictly observed[1]; private advocacy was often paid; and it is not rash

---

[1] Lykurgos thus speaks of the mercenary advocacy which in his time had become a tolerated practice, κατὰ Λεωκράτους § 138 (circ. 330 B.C.):—'I am astonished if you do not see that your extreme indignation is well deserved by men who, *although they have no tie whatever either of kinship or of friendship with the accused persons, continually help in defending*

them for pay' —μισθοῦ συναπολο- γουμένοις ἀεὶ τοῖς κρινομένοις.—But the real error both of Greece and of Rome (until, at some time before Justinian, Trajan's renewal of the Lex Cincia was repealed), lay in their refusal to recognise Advocacy as a profession. See, on the theory, Forsyth, *Hortensius,* pp. 377 ff.

to suppose that this practice was as old as the frequency of litigation.

Athens the chief seat of Civil Oratory.

But while literary fashion or private need thus lent their aid, greater and older causes than these had prepared Athens to be the home of Civil Oratory.

Political morality of the Greeks.

The chief importance of Grecian history depends on this, that the Greeks are the first people from whom we can learn any lessons in the art of ruling men according to law[1]. While all the nations with which the Greeks came in contact were governed more or less despotically, the Greek cities alone were governed politically. No Persian or Egyptian had any conception of the principle that both sides of a public question should be fairly heard, that it should be decided by the opinion of the civic majority, and that the minority should be bound by this decision. Every Greek city, be it planted where it might, at the Pillars of Herakles or on the shores of the Inhospitable Sea, was perfectly familiar with this doctrine. Sometimes a tyrant forcibly suspended its operation, sometimes an oligarchy capriciously narrowed its scope, but it was known wherever the Greek tongue

This morality most practical at Athens.

was spoken. In democratic Athens, more than in any other Greek city, this doctrine was no speculative opinion, no occasional motive, but the present and perpetual spring of public action; nor did any goddess of the pantheon receive a tribute more fitting or more sincere than that which Athenians

Relation of Athenian to Greek Oratory.

annually laid on the altar of Persuasion[2]. It has

---

[1] Freeman, 'General 'Sketch of European History,' ch. II. § 3: and the essay on 'The Athenian Democracy' (Second Series, no. IV.).

[2] Isokr. *Antid.* (Or. xv.) § 249, τὴν μὲν γὰρ Πειθὼ μίαν τῶν θεῶν

sometimes been said that Greek Oratory means
Athenian Oratory. This is far from being true in
the sense that all the considerable masters of oratorical prose were either natives of Attica or permanent residents at Athens. Gorgias of Leontini,
Theodoros of Byzantium, Thrasymachos of Chalkedon, Anaximenes of Lampsakos, Naukrates of
Erythrae, Philiskos of Miletos, Ephoros of Cumae,
Theopompos of Chios, Theodektes of Phaselis, and
many more, might be adduced. But there is another
sense in which the statement is true. Athens was
the home, though Attica was not the birth-place,
of all the very greatest men in this branch of art,
of all the men whose works had wide and lasting
acceptance as canons. Athens was, further, the edu-
cator of all those men, whether first-rate or not,
who, after about 400 B.C., won a Panhellenic name
for eloquence. The relation of Athenian to Greek
oratory is accurately stated by Isokrates when, in
353 B.C., he is defending his theory of culture
against supposed objections—objections which, as
the very history of his school shows, had never
really taken hold of the Athenian mind, but were
restricted to a much narrower circle than his rather
morbid sensibility imagined[1]. 'You must not
forget that our city is regarded as the established[2]
teacher of all who can speak or teach others to speak.
And naturally so, since men see that our city offers

νομίζουσιν εἶναι, καὶ τὴν πόλιν
ὁρῶσι καθ᾽ ἕκαστον τὸν ἐνιαυτὸν
θυσίαν αὐτῇ ποιουμένην.

[1] Isokr. *Antid.* (Or. xv.) §§ 295—
298.

[2] δοκεῖ γεγενῆσθαι διδάσκαλος:
note the tense,—expressing a
position thoroughly won and generally recognised.

the greatest prizes to those who possess this faculty,
—provides the most numerous and most various
schools for those who, having resolved to enter the
real contests, desire a preparatory discipline,—and,
further, affords to all men that experience which
is the main secret of success in speaking. Besides, men hold that the general diffusion and the
happy temperament of Attic speech, the Attic
flexibility of intelligence and taste for letters, contribute not a little to literary culture ; and hence
they not unjustly deem that all masters of expression
are disciples of Athens. See, then, lest it be folly
indeed to cast a slur on this name which you have
among the Greeks... ; that unjust judgment will
be nothing else than your open condemnation of
yourselves. You will have done as the Lacedaemonians would do if they introduced a penalty for
attention to military exercises, or the Thessalians,
if they instituted proceedings at law against men
who seek to make themselves good riders.'

Political aspect of Athenian Oratory. Athenian oratory has two great aspects, the
artistic and the political. The artistic aspect will
necessarily be most prominent in the following pages,
since their special object is to trace the development
of Attic oratory in relation to the development
of Attic prose. When, however, Attic oratory is
considered, not relatively to Attic prose, but in
itself, the artistic aspect is not more important than
the political; and, if even the literary value of the
Attic orations is to be fully understood, their political significance must not for a moment be left out of
sight. This significance resides not merely in the

matter or form of each discourse, but also in the *Political training of the Greek citizen,* training which had been received by the public to which it is addressed. We must ask ourselves, not merely, 'Is this subject well treated?' but also, 'What manner of a multitude can it have been for which the speaker thought this treatment adapted?' The common life of every Greek city, not suppressed by tyranny or too much warped by oligarchy, was a political education for the citizens. The reason is manifest from the very fact that the society *was* a city, and neither a village nor a nation. On the one hand there was the instinct which demanded the highest attainable organisation under laws. On the other, there was the inability to conceive parliament except as a primary assembly. At Athens this political education of the citizens *and especially of the Athenian.* was more thorough than elsewhere, because at Athens the tendency of a commonwealth to deposit all power in an assembly was worked out with most logical completeness[1]. All the powers of the State, legislative, executive and judicial were concentrated in the absolute Demos: the law-courts were committees of the Ekklesia, as the archons or generals were its officers. The world has seen nothing like this. The Italian Republics of the middle age were *Civic sentiment in the Greek and in the Italian Republics.* fragments of the Roman Empire and the Kingdom of Italy. It was from their prosperity as municipalities that they had derived their independence as States. They grew up among traditions of feudal privilege, represented here and there by a noble who

---

[1] Freeman, *Historical Essays* (Second Series), pp. 128 f.

could openly violate the order of the city within
whose walls he lived[1]. A Florentine, like an Athenian, was a citizen with his share in the government
of the city: Florence, like Athens, recognised the
right of the assembled People to decide questions of
State. But Florence, until its latest days, had
nothing truly corresponding to the Ekklesia. The
citizens were occasionally called together, but there
was no popular Assembly with an organised and
continual superintendence of all affairs. Nor was
the civic sentiment so vivid or so direct for the
Florentine as for the Athenian. The Florentine acted
in politics primarily as member of a commercial
guild[2] and only secondarily as a citizen. The Greek
Republics far more than the Italian, Athens far more
than Florence, afforded the proper atmosphere for
such an oratory as alone, in strictness, can take the
lofty name of Civil; that is, which is addressed by a
citizen, educated both in ruling and in obeying, to
the whole body of fellow-citizens who have had the
same twofold training as himself. The glory of Attic
oratory, as such, consists not solely in its intrinsic
excellence, but also in its revelation of the corporate
political intelligence to which it appealed: for it
spoke sometimes to an Assembly debating an issue
of peace or war, sometimes to a law-court occupied

*Athens and
Florence.*

*Civil
Oratory
defined.*

*Attic
Oratory
fulfils this
definition.*

---

[1] In the Essay on 'Ancient
Greece and Mediæval Italy' (*Historical Essays*, Second Series), Mr
Freeman has worked out the likeness and unlikeness which here
are barely touched on.

[2] The Florentine burgher was
qualified for the franchise by belonging to one of the incorporated
arts: Symonds, 'Renaissance in
Italy: Age of the Despots,' p.
128. On the mercantile character
of the Italian republics as in-
fluencing the political, *ib.* 173 f.

with a private plaint, sometimes to Athenians mingled with strangers at a festival, but everywhere and always to the Athenian Demos, everywhere and always to a paramount People, taught by life itself to reason and to judge.

CHAPTER I.

ANTIPHON.

LIFE.

IN describing the Revolution of the Four Hundred at Athens, Thucydides lays stress upon the fact that the measures which had effected it owed their unity and their success to the control of a single mind. The figure of Peisandros is most conspicuous in the foreground. 'But he who contrived the whole matter, and the means by which it was brought to pass, and who had given his mind to it longest, was Antiphon; a man second to no Athenian of his day in virtue; a proved master of device and of expression; who did not come forward in the assembly, nor, by choice, in any scene of debate, since he lay under the suspicion of the people through a repute for cleverness; but who was better able than any other individual to assist, when consulted, those who were fighting a cause in a law-court or in the assembly. In his own case, too—when the Four Hundred in their later reverses were being roughly used by the people, and he was accused of having aided in setting up this same government—he is

known to have delivered the greatest defence made
in the memory of my age by a man on trial for his
life[1].'

This passage gives in outline nearly all that is
known of the life of Antiphon. Other sources supply details, and make it possible to work up the
sketch into something like a picture; but they add
nothing which enlarges its framework. The Revolution of the Four Hundred is still the one great
scene presented to our view.

Birth of Antiphon.   Antiphon was born about the year 480 B.C.[2],
being thus rather younger than Gorgias, and some
eight or nine years older than the historian Thucydides. He was of the tribe of Aiantis and of the
deme of Rhamnus[3]; of a family which cannot have

---

[1] Thuc. VIII. 68.

[2] [Plut.] *Vitt. X. Oratt.* γέγονε
κατὰ τὰ Περσικὰ καὶ Γοργίαν τὸν
σοφιστὴν, ὀλίγῳ νεώτερος αὐτοῦ.
Gorgias can scarcely have been
more than seventy in 411 B.C.
Blass would place the birth of Gorgias 'a few years' below 496 (*Att.
Bereds.* p. 45). Clinton suggests
485 (sub ann. 427).

[3] He is often distinguished as
the 'Rhamnusian' from namesakes.
Of these there are especially three
with whom his ancient biographers
—the pseudo-Plutarch, Philostratos, Photios (cod. 259), and the
anonymous author of the γένος Ἀν-
τιφῶντος—frequently confuse him.
I. *The Antiphon who was put to
death by the Thirty Tyrants,* seven
years after the orator's death:
Xen. *Hellen.* III. 40. He had furnished two triremes at his own
cost during the war: and of him

Philostratos is probably thinking
when he says of the *orator,* ἐστρα-
τήγησε πλεῖστα, ἐνίκησε πλεῖστα,
ἑξήκοντα τριήρεσι πεπληρωμέναις
ηὔξησεν Ἀθηναίοις τὸ ναυτικόν. The
speech of Lysias περὶ τῆς Ἀντιφῶν-
τος θυγατρός (pseudo-Plut. *Vitt. X.
Oratt.*) referred to his daughter.
II. *Antiphon the tragedian,* put
to death by Dionysios the elder,
towards the end of his reign, i.e.
about 370 B.C.: Arist. *Rhet.* II. 6.
The anonymous biographer says of
the *orator,* τραγῳδίας ἐποίει: and
Philostratos describes him as put
to death by Dionysios for criticising his tragedies. III. *Antiphon the Sophist,* introduced by
Xenophon as disputing with Sokrates, *Memor.* I. 6. 1. Diogenes
calls him τερατοσκόπος (soothsayer),
Suidas, ὀνειροκριτής—by which title
he is often referred to. Hermogenes expressly distinguishes him

been altogether obscure, since it was made a reproach to him on his trial that his grandfather had
been a partisan of the Peisistratidae[1]. The tradition
that his father Sophilos was a sophist antedates by
a generation the appearance of that class of teachers[2],
and may have been suggested simply by the jingle of
the words[3]. Antiphon himself, as the style of his
composition indicates, must have felt the sophistic
influence; but there is no evidence for his having
been the pupil of any particular sophist. He is
allowed by general consent to have been the first
representative at Athens of a profession for which
the new conditions of the time had just begun to
make a place,—the first λογογράφος, or writer of
speeches for money[4]. With the recent growth of
Rhetoric as a definite art, the inequality, for purposes
of pleading or debating, between men who had and
who had not mastered the newly-invented weapons
of speech had become seriously felt. A rogue skilled
in the latest subtleties of argument and graces of
style was now more than ever formidable to the
plain man whom he chose to drag before a court or
to attack in the ekklesia : and those who had no
leisure or taste to become rhetoricians now began to
find it worth while to buy their rhetoric ready-made.
Forensic speeches were, no doubt, those with which
Antiphon most frequently supplied his clients.   But

*Antiphon
the first
λογογράφος.*

from the orator (περὶ ἰδεῶν, II.
497); but they are confused by the
pseudo-Plut. and by Photios.

[1] Harpokration s. v. στασιώτης.

[2] K. O. Müller, *Hist. Gr. Lit.*
c. XXXIII.,Vol. II. p. 105, ed. Donaldson.

[3] Donalds., note, *ibid.*

[4] [Plut.] *Vitt. X. Oratt.* λόγους
συνέγραψε πρῶτος ἐπὶ τοῦτο τραπεὶς,
ὥσπερ τινές φασι. Diod. *ap.* Clem.
Alex. *Strom.* I. 365, πρῶτον δικανι-
κὸν λόγον εἰς ἔκδοσιν γραψάμενον.

Hermogenes[1] describes him as 'the inventor and founder of the political style',—a phrase including deliberative as well as forensic oratory : and this exactly agrees with the statement of Thucydides that Antiphon was practised in aiding, not only those who had lawsuits, but debaters in the ekklesia[2]. Besides being a speech-writer, he was also a teacher of rhetoric, and, as the allusion in the Menexenos[3] implies, the most fashionable master of Plato's time at Athens. The tradition that Thucydides was the pupil of Antiphon may have been suggested by the warmth and emphasis of the passage in which the orator is mentioned by the historian[4]; a passage which, in its sudden glow of a personal admiration, recalls two others in the History—the tribute to the genius of Themistokles, and the character of Perikles. In the tradition itself there is nothing improbable, but it wants the support of evidence. The special relation of master to pupil need not be assumed to

Antiphon and Thucydides.

---

[1] Hermog. περὶ ἰδ. II. p. 415, λέγεται.. εὑρετὴς καὶ ἀρχηγὸς γενέσθαι τοῦ τύπου τοῦ πολιτικοῦ. By πολιτικοὶ λόγοι, as distinguished from διαλεκτική, were meant both συμβουλευτικοί and δικανικοί : see Isokr. κατὰ σοφ. § 20.

[2] Thuc. VIII. 68, τοὺς ἀγωνιζομένους καὶ ἐν δικαστηρίῳ καὶ ἐν δήμῳ...δυνάμενος ὠφελεῖν.

[3] Plat. *Menex.* p. 236 A.

[4] [Plut.] *Vitt. X. Oratt.* Καικίλιος δὲ (Caecilius of Calacte, the Greek rhetorician of the time of Augustus) ἐν τῷ περὶ αὐτοῦ συντάγματι Θουκυδίδου τοῦ συγγραφέως (VIII. 68.) μαθητὴν τεκμαίρεται γεγονέναι, ἐξ ὧν ἐπαινεῖται παρ' αὐτῷ ὁ Ἀντιφῶν. Ruhnken (*Disp. de Ant.*) says that some mss. have διδάσκαλον instead of μαθητήν here : Blass suggests καθηγητήν. Hermogenes (περὶ ἰδ. II. 497) refers to the tradition as one which 'many' receive ; but rejects it for the inadequate reason that the style of Thucydides resembles that of Antiphon *the Sophist* (see note above) rather than that of Antiphon the orator. In Bishop Thirlwall's remarks (c. XXVIII. Vol. IV. p. 23 *note*, ed. 1855) I entirely concur. Ruhnken's 'satis, ni fallor, *demonstravimus* Thucydidem ab Antiphonte esse eruditum,' is surely not justified by his reasonings.

account for a tone which congeniality of literary
taste[1], common sufferings at the hands of the democracy, or perhaps personal friendship, would sufficiently explain.

Nothing is directly known of Antiphon's political *Antiphon's*
relations before the year 411 B.C.; but there are *life to 411*
slight indications which agree well with his later *B.C.*
hostility to the democracy. Harpokration has preserved the names of two speeches written by him,
one for the people of Samothrace, on the subject of
the tribute which they paid to Athens; another,
on the same subject, for the people of Lindos in
Rhodes[2]. The oppression of the subject-allies by the
demagogues, who extorted from them large sums on
any pretence or threat, was a commonplace of complaint with oligarchs[3]. The employment of Antiphon, afterwards so staunch an oligarch, by aggrieved
allies, preparing to represent their grievances at the
imperial city, was perhaps more than an accident of
professional routine. The hostility of Antiphon to
Alkibiades[4], again, need not have had any political

[1] See below, ch. II. pp. 23 ff., on
the affinity between the styles of
Antiphon and Thucydides.

[2] Harpokration quotes five times
a speech of Antiphon περὶ τοῦ
Σαμοθρᾴκων φόρου, spoken, as the
fragments show, by their ambassador; and in ten places refers to
another περὶ τοῦ Λινδίων φόρου.

[3] See, e. g., Ar. *Vesp.* 669 ff.

[4] Plutarch (*Alk.* c. 3) quotes
Antiphon as the authority for a
discreditable story about Alkibiades; and goes on to say that it
must be received with caution, on

account of Antiphon's avowed enmity towards him: ἐν δὲ ταῖς Ἀν-
τιφῶντος λοιδορίαις γέγραπται.
These λοιδορίαι would seem to have
fo med a sort of polemical pamphlet. But Athenaeos, on the other
hand, quotes a statement made by
Antiphon, ἐν τῷ κατ' Ἀλκιβιάδου
λοιδορίας (Athen. XII 525 B). This
would seem to have been a speech
in a δίκη κακηγορίας (Dem. *Konon.*
§ 18), for which λοιδορία is used
as a convertible term: cf. Ar.
Vesp. 1207, εἷλον διώκων λοιδορίας.
Sauppe thinks that the mistake is

meaning; but it would have been especially natural
in one who had shared the views, and who mourned
the fate, of Nikias. At all events, the words of
Thucydides give a vivid idea of the position held at
Athens by Antiphon just before the Revolution of the
Four Hundred. His abilities were acknowledged,
but they were exerted only for others; he himself
came forward neither in the assembly, nor—'when
he could help it[1]'—in the law-courts; he lay under
the suspicion of the people for 'cleverness.' The
nature of the 'cleverness' (δεινότης) for which Antiphon was distrusted and disliked is sufficiently illustrated by his Tetralogies. It was the art of fighting
a cause which could hardly be defended on any
broad ground by raising in succession a number of
more or less fine points. The indignant bewilder-
ment expressed by the imaginary prosecutor in the
Second Tetralogy[2] on finding the common-sense view
of the case turned upside-down represents what
many a citizen of the old school must have felt when
he encountered, in the ekklesia or the law-court, a
client of the ingenious 'speech-writer.' Antiphon
was a cautious, patient man. The comic poets could
ridicule him for his poverty or his avarice[3]; they
could say that the speeches which he sold for great
sums were 'framed to defeat justice[4];' but a care-

with Athenaeos, not with Plutarch.
See Blass, *Att. Bereds.* p. 95.

[1] Thuc. VIII. 68, οὐδ' ἐς ἄλλον
ἀγῶνα ἑκούσιος οὐδένα.

[2] Tetr. II. Γ *ad init.*

[3] [Plut.] *Vitt. X. Oratt.* κεκω-
μῴδηται δ' εἰς φιλαργυρίαν ὑπὸ Πλά-

τωνος ἐν Πεισάνδρῳ.

[4] Philostratos p. 17, καθάπτεται ἡ
κωμῳδία τοῦ 'Αντιφῶντος ὡς δεινοῦ
τὰ δικανικὰ καὶ λόγους κατὰ τοῦ δι-
καίου ξυγκειμένους ἀποδιδομέ-
νου πολλῶν χρημάτων αὐτοῖς μάλιστα τοῖς κινδυνεύουσιν.

fully obscure life probably offered no hold to any
more definite attack.   Meanwhile he was quietly
at work with the oligarchic clubs.   According to
Thucydides he was not merely the arch-plotter of
the Revolution.   He was the man who 'had thought
about it longest.'

In the spring of 411 B.C. the opportunity for *The Revo-*
which Antiphon had been waiting at last came. *lution.*
Alkibiades, by promises of Persian aid, induced the
oligarchs in the army at Samos to commence a movement for the overthrow of the Athenian democracy.
Peisandros, as their representative, came to Athens,
and, by insisting on the hopelessness of the war
without such help as Alkibiades covenanted to bring,
extorted from the ekklesia a vote for that change of
constitution which the exile demanded.   Having
visited the various oligarchical clubs in the city
and urged them to combine in favour of the project,
Peisandros went back to confer with Alkibiades.
When he presently returned to Athens,—with the
knowledge that his hopes from Persia were idle, but
that, on the other hand, the Revolution must go on,—
he found a state of things very different from that
which he had left.   He had left the people just conscious that an oligarchy was proposed, and consenting,
in sheer despair, to entertain the idea; but, at the
same time, openly and strongly averse to it, and in
a temper which showed that the real difficulties of
the undertaking were to come.   He now finds that,
in the brief interval of his absence, every difficulty
has already vanished.   Not a trace of open opposition remains in the senate or in the ekklesia; not a

murmur is heard in the conversation of the citizens[1].
It is a fair inference from the words of Thucydides
that the principal agent in producing this rapid and
wonderful change had been Antiphon[2]. A brief consideration of the task which he had to do, and of
the manner in which it was done, will supply the
best criterion of his capacity. He had, first, to
bring into united and disciplined action those oligarchical clubs to which Peisandros had appealed.
These are described as ' leagues with a view to lawsuits and to offices[3];' that is, associations of which
the members were pledged by oath to support, personally and with funds, any one of their body who
brought, or defended, a civil action, or who sought
one of the offices of the State. When, with the
steady advance of democracy from the Persian wars
onwards, the oligarchs found themselves more and
more in a minority, such associations became their
means of concentrating and economising their one
great power—wealth. The tone of such clubs would
always be, in a general way, antipopular. But
they were unaccustomed to systematic action for
great ends; and, in regard to those smaller ends
which they ordinarily pursued, their interests would,
from the nature of the case, frequently conflict.
Antiphon need not have had much difficulty in
proving to them that, on this occasion, they had a
common interest. But to make them effective as
well as unanimous; to restrain, without discourag-

---

[1] Thuc. VIII. 65, 66.

[2] Cf. Grote, ch. LX.I; Curtius,
Hist. Gr. Vol. III. p. 435 (Ward's

transl.).

[3] ξυνωμοσίας ἐπὶ δίκαις καὶ ἀρ-
χαῖς, Thuc. VIII. 54.

ing, the zeal of novices in a political campaign, and
to make of these a compact and temperate force,
loyally taking the word from the best men among
them, and so executing the prescribed manœuvres
that in a short time they were completely ascendant
over an enormous and hostile, but ill-organised majority,—this, assuredly, was the achievement of no
ordinary leader.   The absence of overt, and the skilful use of secret, violence was the characteristic of
the Revolution.   Adverse speakers were not menaced,
but they disappeared ; until apparent unanimity,
and real terror, had silenced every objection.   Antiphon had seen clearly how the Athenian instinct
of reverence for constitutional forms might be used
against the constitution.   His too, on the showing of
Thucydides, must have been that clever invention,
the imaginary body of Five Thousand to whom the
franchise was to be left ; a fiction which, to the
end, did service to the oligarchs by giving them
a vague prestige for strength.

The Council of the Four Hundred comprised *The two parties in the Council.*
two distinct elements, — those thorough oligarchs
who had been the core of the conspiracy; and a
number of other men, more or less indifferent to
the ideas of oligarchy, who had accepted the Revolution because they believed that it alone could save
Athens.   Had the new Government been able to
conciliate or to frighten the army at Samos, both
sorts of men would have been satisfied, and the
Council would have gone on working, for a time
at least, as a seemingly harmonious whole.   But
the resolute hostility of the army, which at once

made the case of the Four Hundred really hopeless,
brought the discord to light forthwith. The Council
was thenceforth divided into an Extreme and a
Moderate party. Among the leaders of the Extreme party were Peisandros, Phrynichos, Aristarchos, Archeptolemos, Onomakles and Antiphon.
The Moderates were led by Theramenes and
Aristokrates. Two chief questions were in dispute
between the parties. The Moderates wished to
call into political life the nominal civic body of
Five Thousand; the ultra-oligarchs objected that
it was better, at such a crisis, to avoid all chance
of a popular rising. The ultra-oligarchs were fortifying Eëtioneia, alleging the danger of an attack
from Samos; the Moderates accused them of wish-
ing to receive Peloponnesian troops.

The Extreme party was soon driven, in May
411 B.C., to the last resource of an embassy to
Sparta. Phrynichos, Antiphon, Archeptolemos,
Onomakles and eight others[1] were sent 'to make
terms with the Lacedaemonians in any way that
could at all be borne[2].' Thucydides does not say
what the envoys offered at Sparta or what answer
they got; but he states plainly the length which
he conceives that their party was ready to go.
'They wished, if possible, having their oligarchy,
at the same time to rule the allies; if that could
not be, to keep their ships, their walls, and their

---

[1] Thuc. VIII. 90, Ἀντιφῶντα καὶ
Φρύνιχον καὶ ἄλλους δέκα. That
Archeptolemos and Onomakles
were on the embassy appears from

[Plut.] *Vitt. X. Oratt.*
[2] Thuc. *ib.* παντὶ τρόπῳ ὅστις
καὶ ὁπωσοῦν ἀνεκτός ξυναλλα-
γῆναι πρὸς τοὺς Λακεδαιμονίους.

independence; or, if shut out even from this, at
all events not to have their own lives taken first
and foremost by the people on its restoration;
sooner would they bring in the enemy and covenant
to keep the city on any terms, without wall or
ships, if only their persons should be safe[1].'

This embassy brought the unpopularity of the *Fall of the Four Hundred.*
Extreme party to a crisis. Immediately upon his
return Phrynichos was assassinated. The revolt
of the citizens employed in fortifying Eëtioneia
quickly followed. The assembly in the Anakeion,
broken up by the sudden appearance of the Peloponnesian fleet, met again on the Pnyx soon after
the Peloponnesian victory at Oropos; and the Four
Hundred, who had taken office in March, were
deposed about the middle of June.

The leading ultra-oligarchs hastened to save
themselves by flight. Peisandros, Alexikles and
others went to Dekeleia; Aristarchos, taking with
him a body of bowmen, contrived to betray Oenoe
on the Athenian frontier into the hands of the
Boeotians who were besieging it. But, of the
twelve who had formed the embassy, and who now,
before all others, were in peril, three remained at
Athens—Antiphon, Archeptolemos and Onomakles.
An information against these three men was laid
before the ekklesia by the Generals. The eisangelia charged them with having gone on an embassy
to Sparta for mischief to Athens, sailing, on their
way thither, in an enemy's ship, and traversing the

---

[1] Thuc. VIII. 91.

enemy's camp at Dekeleia. A psephism was passed by the ekklesia directing the arrest of the accused that they might be tried by a dikastery, and instructing the Thesmothetae to serve each of them, on the day following the issue of the decree, with a formal summons. On the day fixed by the summons the Thesmothetae were to bring the cases into court; and the Generals, assisted by such Synegori, not more than ten in number, as they might choose from the Council of the Five Hundred, were to prosecute for treason[1].

Trial and condemnation of Antiphon.

Onomakles seems to have escaped or died before the day. Archeptolemos and Antiphon were brought to trial. The scanty fragments of the speech made by Antiphon in his own defence reveal only one item of its contents. One of the prosecutors, Apolexis, having asserted that Antiphon's grandfather had been a partisan of the Peisistratidae, Antiphon. replied that his grandfather had not been punished after the expulsion of the tyrants, and could scarcely, therefore, have been one of their 'body-guard[2].'

---

[1] [Plut.] *Vitt. X. Oratt.*

[2] Harpokr. s.v. στασιώτης (Sauppe, *Or. Att.* II. p. 138.) ᾿Αντιφῶν ἐν τῷ περὶ τῆς μεταστάσεως· περὶ τοίνυν ὧν ᾿Απόληξις κατηγόρηκεν ὡς στασιώτης ἦν ἐγὼ καὶ ὁ πάππος ὁ ἐμός· ἔοικε νῦν ὁ ῥήτωρ ἰδίως ἐπὶ τοῦ δορυφόρου κεχρῆσθαι τῷ ὀνόματι· ἐν γοῦν τοῖς ἑξῆς φησιν ὅτι· οὐκ ἂν τοὺς μὲν τυραννοῦντας ἠδυνήθησαν οἱ πρόγονοι κολάσαι, τοὺς δὲ δορυφόρους ἠδυνάτησαν. Curtius (*Hist. Gr.* Vol. III. p. 460, transl. Ward) infers from this frag-

ment that Antiphon in his speech argued 'that the Four Hundred had acted as one equally responsible body, and that, therefore, either all ought to be punished or all acquitted.' He observes that 'reference seems to be made to an unjustifiable separation of the parties involved: this is indicated by the distinction drawn between the τύραννοι and the δορυφόροι.' It is very likely that Antiphon may have used this argument: but I do not see how it is to be inferred from the fragments of the speech

The other special topics are unknown; but their range, at least, is shown by the title under which the speech was extant. It was inscribed περὶ μετα-στάσεως, On the Change of Government. It dealt, then, not merely with the matter specified in the eisangelia—the embassy to Sparta—but with the whole question of the Revolution. It is described by Thucydides as the greatest defence made in the memory of that age by a man on trial for his life. The story in the Eudemian Ethics[1], whether true or not, seems at any rate characteristic. Agathon, the tragic poet, praised the speech; and Antiphon—on whom sentence of death had passed—answered that a man who respects himself must care more what one good man thinks than what is thought by many nobodies.

The sentence ran thus :—

'Found guilty of treason—Archeptolemos son of Hippodamos, of Agryle, being present : Antiphon son of Sophilos, of Rhamnus, being present. The award on these two men was—That they be delivered to the Eleven : that their property be confiscated and the goddess have the tithe : that their houses be razed and boundary-stones put on the sites, with the inscription, 'the houses of Archeptolemos and Antiphon the traitors :' that the two demarchs [of Agryle and Rhamnus] shall point out

περὶ τῆς μεταστάσεως that he used it. The distinction between the τύραν-νοι and the δορυφόροι is made, as a perusal of the fragment will show, solely in reference to the Peisistratidae.

[1] *Eth. Eudem.* III. 5, καὶ μᾶλλον ἂν φροντίσειεν ἀνὴρ μεγαλόψυχος τί δοκεῖ ἐνὶ σπουδαίῳ ἢ πολλοῖς τοῖς τυγχάνουσιν, ὥσπερ Ἀντιφῶν ἔφη πρὸς Ἀγάθωνα κατεψηφισμένος τὴν ἀπολογίαν ἐπαινέσαντα.

their houses. That it shall not be lawful to bury
Archeptolemos and Antiphon at Athens or in any
land of which the Athenians are masters. That
Archeptolemos and Antiphon and their descendants,
bastard or true-born, shall be infamous; and if a
man adopt any one of the race of Archeptolemos
or Antiphon, let the adopter be infamous. That this
decree be written on a brazen column and put in the
same place where the decrees about Phrynichos are
set up[1].'

Character of Anti- phon's poli- tical life. The distinctive feature in the life of Antiphon is
the suddenness of his appearance, at an advanced
age, in the very front of Athenian politics. Unlike
nearly all the men associated with him, he had neither made his mark in the public service nor come
forward in the ekklesia; yet all at once he becomes
the chief, though not the most conspicuous, organiser
of an enterprise requiring in the highest degree
trained political tact; does more than any other
individual to set up a new government; and acts
to the last as one of its foremost members. The
reputation and the power which enabled him to take
this part were mainly literary. Yet it would not
probably be accurate to conceive Antiphon as a
merely literary man who suddenly emerged and
succeeded as a politician. It would have been a
marvel, indeed, if any one had become a leader on
the popular side in Athenian politics who had not
already been prominent in the ekklesia. But the
accomplishments most needed in a leader of the
oligarchic party might be learned elsewhere than in

[1] [Plut.] *Vitt. X. Oratt.*

the ekklesia. The member of a ἑταιρεία, though a
stranger to the bema, might gain practice in the
working of those secret and rapid combinations upon
which his party had come to rely most in its unequal
struggle with democracy. As fame and years by
degrees brought Antiphon more and more weight in
the internal management of the oligarchic clubs,
he would acquire more and more insight into the
tactics of which at last he proved himself a master[1].
He need not, then, be taken as an example of instinct supplying the want of training : he had probably had precisely the training which could serve
him best. The real significance of his late and
sudden prominence lies in its suggestion of previous
self-control. No desire of place, no consciousness of
growing power, had tempted him to stir until in his
old age he knew that the time had come and that all
the threads were in his hand.

The ability which Antiphon brought to the *Character of his ability.*
service of his party is defined as the power ἐνθυμηθῆναι καὶ ἃ γνοίη εἰπεῖν. It was the power
of a subtle and quick mind backed by a thorough
command of the new rhetoric. He was masterly
in device and in utterance. Fertility of expedient,

---

[1] 'By far the larger number of
the members of the party belonged
to the sophistically-trained younger
generation...who greedily imbibed
the political teaching communicated to them at the meetings of
the party by Antiphon, *the Nestor
of his party, as it was the fashion
to call him.*' (Curtius, *Hist. Gr.*
III. p. 435, transl. Ward.)
The only authority for this
'fashion' which I have been able
to find is [Plut.] *Vitt. X. Oratt.:*
πρῶτος δὲ καὶ ῥητορικὰς τέχνας
ἐξήνεγκε, γενόμενος ἀγχίνους· διὸ
καὶ Νέστωρ ἐπεκαλεῖτο. As this
notice makes the name 'Nestor'
refer simply to rhetorical skill, not
to political sagacity, I have hesi-
tated to follow Curtius in his picturesque application of it.

ingenuity in making points in debate, were the qualities which the oligarchs most needed; and it was in these that the strength of Antiphon lay. In promptness of invention where difficulties were to be met on the instant he probably bore some likeness to Themistokles; but there is no reason for crediting him with that largeness of view, or with any share of that wonderful foresight, which made Themistokles a statesman as well as a diplomatist.

His ἀρετή. Thucydides praises Antiphon not only for his ability but, with equal emphasis, for his ἀρετή, his virtue. The praise may be interpreted by what Thucydides himself says elsewhere about the moral results of the intense conflicts between oligarchy and democracy[1]. The ἀρετή, precious as rare, of a public man was to be a loyal partisan; to postpone personal selfishness to the selfishness of party; to be proof against bribes; and at the worst not to flinch, or at least not to desert. Thucydides means that of the men who brought about the Revolution Antiphon was perhaps the most disinterested and the most constant. He had taken previously no active part in public affairs, and was therefore less involved than such men as Peisandros and Phrynichos in personal relations: his life had been to some extent that of a student: he had never put himself forward for office: he seems, to judge from his writings, to have really believed and felt that old Attic religion which at least the older school of oligarchs professed to cherish: and thus altogether

[1] Thuc. III. 82.

might be considered as the most unselfishly earnest
member of his party, the man who cared most for its
ideas. In this measure he was disinterested: he was
also constant. When the Council fell, he could, no
doubt, have escaped with Peisandros and the rest.
Considering his long unpopularity, and the fact that
he would be assumed to have been the chief spokesman of the odious embassy to Sparta, his condemnation was perhaps more certain than that of any other
person. But he stood his ground: and for the last
time put out all his strength in a great defence of
the fallen Government.

In a general view of Antiphon's career there is *The new power of Rhetoric.*
one aspect which ought not to be missed—that aspect
in which it bears striking evidence to the growing
importance in Athenian public life of the newly-
developed art of Rhetoric. Antiphon's first and
strongest claim to eminence was his mastery over
the weapons now indispensable in the ekklesia and
the law-courts; it was this accomplishment, no less
fashionable than useful, which recommended him to
the young men of his party whom he had no other
pretension to influence; it was this rhetorical δεινότης
to which he owed his efficiency in the Revolution.
In his person the practical branch of the new culture
for the first time takes a distinct place among the
qualifications for political rank. The Art of Words
had its definite share in bringing in the Four Hundred: it was a curious nemesis when seven years
later it was banished from Athens by the Thirty.

CHAPTER II.

ANTIPHON.

STYLE.

Antiphon the most antique of the orators. ANTIPHON stands first among the orators of the Attic canon; and he claims this place not merely because he was born a few years earlier than any one of the rest. A broad difference separates him from those who were nearly his contemporaries hardly less than from men of the next century, from Andokides and Lysias as well as from Demosthenes and Hypereides. He represents older ideas and an older conception of the manner in which these ideas are to find expression. His successors, taken collectively, are moderns; compared with them, he is ancient.

The beginnings of Greek Prose. The outburst of intellectual life in Hellas during the fifth century before Christ had for one of its results the creation of Greek prose. Before that age no Greek had conceived artistic composition except in the form of poetry. The Ionians who had already recorded myths or stated philosophies in prose had either made no effort to rise above the ease of daily talk, or had clothed their meaning in a poetical diction of the most ambitious kind. As the mental horizon of Greece was widened, as subtler ideas and more various combinations began to ask for closer and more flexible expression, the desire grew for something more precise than poetry, firmer and more compact than the idiom of conversation. Two special causes aided this general tendency. The development of democratic life, making the faculty of speech before popular assemblies and popular law-courts a necessity, hastened the formation of an oratorical prose. The Persian Wars, by changing Hellenic unity from a sentiment into a fact, and reminding men that there was a corporate life, higher and grander than that of the individual city, of which the story might be told, supplied a new motive to historical prose. Athens under Perikles became the focus of all the feelings which demanded this new utterance, and of all the capabilities which could make the utterance artistic. The Athenian mind, with its vigour, its sense of measure, its desire for clearness, was fitted to achieve the special excellences of prose[1], and moulded that Attic dialect in which the prose-writer at last found his most perfect instrument. But the process of maturing the new kind of composition was necessarily slow; for it required, as its first condition, little less than the creation of a new language, of an idiom neither poetical nor mean. Herodotos, at the middle point of the fifth century, shows the poetical element still preponderant. The close of that century may be taken as the end of the first great stage in the growth of a prose literature. If a line is drawn there, Lysias will be perhaps the first representative name below it: Antiphon and Thucydides will be among the last names above it.

[1] See Curtius, *Hist. Gr.* Vol. II. p. 517, transl. Ward.

Character of the early Prose.

The leading characteristic of the earlier prose is dignity. The newly created art has the continual consciousness of being an art. It is always on its guard against sliding into the levity of a conversational style. The composer feels above all things that his written language must be so chosen as to produce a greater effect than would be produced by an equivalent amount of extemporary speaking. Every word is to be pointed and pregnant; every phrase is to be the condensed expression of his thought in its ultimate shape, however difficult this may be to the reader or hearer who meets it in that shape for the first time; the movement of the whole is to be slow and majestic, impressing by its weight and grandeur, not charming by its life and flow. The prose-writer of this epoch instinctively compares himself with the poet. The poet is a craftsman, the possessor of a mystery revealed to the many only in the spell which it exerts over their fancies; just so, in the beginnings of a literary prose, its shaper likes to think that he belongs to a guild. He does not care to be simply right and clear : rather he desires to have the whole advantage which his skill gives him over ordinary men; he is eager to bring his thoughts down upon them with a splendid and irresistible force. In Greece this character, natural to immature prose, was intensified by a special cause —the influence of the Sophists. In so far as these teachers dealt with the form of language, they tended to confirm that view of the prose-writer in which he is a professional expert dazzling and overawing laymen. The Sophists of Hellas Proper dwelt especially

on the minute proprieties of language, as Protagoras
on correct grammatical forms[1] and Prodikos on the
accurate use of synonyms[2]; the Sophists of Sicily
taught its technical graces[3].   In this last respect the
teaching of Gorgias was thoroughly reactionary, and
was calculated to hinder the growth of a good prose
just at the critical point.   At the moment when prose
was striving to disengage itself from the diction of
poetry, Gorgias gave currency to the notion that
poetical ornament of the most florid type was its
true charm.   When, indeed, he went further, and
sought to imitate the rhythm as well as the phrase
of poetry, this very extravagance had a useful result.
Prose has a rhythm, though not of the kind at which
Gorgias aimed ; and the mere fact of the Greek ear
becoming accustomed to look for a certain proportion
between the parts of a sentence hastened the transition from the old running style to the periodic.

Dionysios has described vividly the character-   *Dionysios
istics of that elder school of composition to which   'austere'
Antiphon belonged.   He distinguishes three prin-   style.*
cipal styles, the austere, the smooth and the
middle[4].   He cites poets, historians and orators who

---

[1] ὀρθοέπεια,Plat.*Phaedr*.p.267 c.
[2] ὀρθότης ὀνομάτων, Plat. *Eu-
thyd.* p. 277 E.   On the work of
Protagoras and Prodikos in these
departments, see Mr Cope in the
*Journal of Classical and Sacred
Philology*, vol. III. pp. 48—57.
[3] Spengel, Συναγ. τεχνῶν, p. 63:
'Omnino Graeci sophistae, et quos
diximus, et alii minus noti, recte et
dilucide eloqui studebant; et si uno
vocabulo omnia comprehendamus,

Graeci ὀρθοέπειαν, Siculi εὐέπειαν
elaborabant.'

[4] αὐστηρά, γλαφυρά and κοινὴ (or
μέση) ἁρμονία: Dionys. περὶ συνθ.
ὀνομ. cc. 22, 23, 24.   The three
ἁρμονίαι, or styles of *composition*,
distinguished by Dionysios, must
not be confused with the three
λέξεις, or styles of *diction*, which he
distinguishes in his essay on Demosthenes, cc. 1—3.   The ἁρμονίαι refer, of course, to the putting to-

are examples of each. Among orators Antiphon is
his representative of the austere style, Isokrates of
the smooth, Demosthenes of the middle. The austere
style is thus described[1] :

'It wishes its separate words to be planted
firmly and to have strong positions, so that each
word may be seen conspicuously; it wishes its
several clauses to be well divided from each other
by sensible pauses. It is willing to admit frequently
rough and direct clashings of sounds, meeting like
the bases of stones in loose wall-work, which have
not been squared or smoothed to fit each other, but
which show a certain negligence and absence of
forethought. It loves, as a rule, to prolong itself
by large words of portly breadth. Compression by
short syllables is a thing which it shuns when not
absolutely driven to it.

'As regards separate words, these are the objects
of its pursuit and craving. In whole clauses it
shows these tendencies no less strongly; especially
it chooses the most dignified and majestic rhythms.
It does not wish the clauses to be like each other
in length of structure, or enslaved to a severe syn-

gether of words; the λέξεις, to the
choice of words. As to λέξεις, Dionysios recognises (1) an *elaborate
diction*, which employs farfetched
and unusual words, ἐξηλλαγμένη,
περιττὴ λέξις, of which Thucydides
is the great example: (2) a *smooth
and plain diction*, λιτή, ἀφελὴς
λέξις, best represented by Lysias:
(3) a *mixed diction*, μικτὴ καὶ σύν-
θετος λέξις, of which the type is

Isokrates. Of Antiphon and Isaeos,
in respect to λέξις, he says merely
that there was nothing 'novel' or
'striking' in their choice of words.
(*Demosth.* c. 8.) Probably he would
have regarded them as intermediate in λέξις between Thucydides
and Lysias, but as representing the
compromise in a less mature and
finished form than Isokrates.

[1] Dionys. περὶ συνθ. ὀνομ. c. 22.

tax, but noble, simple, free.   It wishes them to bear
the stamp of nature rather than that of art, and to
stir feeling rather than to reflect character.   It does
not usually aim at composing periods as a compact
framework for its thought; but, if it should ever
drift undesignedly into the periodic style, it desires
to set on this the mark of spontaneity and plainness.
It does not employ, in order to round a sentence,
supplementary words which do not help the sense;
it does not care that the march of its phrase should
have stage-glitter or an artificial smoothness; nor
that the clauses should be separately adapted to the
length of the speaker's breath.   No indeed.   Of all
such industry it is innocent...   It is fanciful in
imagery, sparing of copulas, anything but florid; it
is haughty, straightforward, disdainful of prettiness,
with its antique air and its negligence for its beauty.'

It is important to remember that this description
is applied to a certain kind of poetry as well as of
prose, to Pindar and Aeschylos as well as to Thucydides and Antiphon; and that, taken in reference
to prose alone, it needs modification.   It is not
true, for instance, of the older prose that it always
shrank from the *display* of artificialism.   Negligent
it often was; but at other times it was consciously,
ostentatiously artificial.   Its general characteristics,
however, are admirably given by Dionysios.   It is
dignified; it relies much on the weight of single
words; it is bold but not florid; it aims at moving
the hearer rather than at reflecting the character of
the speaker. Antiphon, his representative orator,
exemplifies these points clearly,—as' will be seen

better if he is compared from time to time with the
critic's representative historian, Thucydides.

In the first place, then, Antiphon is preeminently
dignified and noble. He is to his successors generally as Aeschylos to Euripides. The elder tragedy
held its gods and heroes above the level of men by
a colossal majesty of repose, by the passionless
utterance of kingly thoughts; and the same feeling
to which these things seemed divine conceived its
ideal orator as one who controls a restless crowd by
the royalty of his calm power, by a temperate and
stately eloquence. The speaker who wins his hearers
by blandishments, who surprises them by adroit
turns, who hurries them away on a torrent of
declamation, belonged to a generation for which
gods also and heroes declaimed or quibbled on the
stage. Plutarch has described, not without a tinge
of sarcasm, the language and demeanour by which
Perikles commanded the veneration of his age[1].
'His thoughts were awe-inspiring[2], his language
lofty, untainted by the ribaldry of the rascal crowd.
His calm features, never breaking into laughter;
his measured step; the ample robe which flowed
around him and which nothing deranged; his moving
eloquence; the tranquil modulation of his voice;
these things, and such as these, had over all men a
marvellous spell.' The biographer goes on to relate
how Perikles was once abused by a coarse fellow
in the market-place, bore it in silence until he had

---

[1] Plut. *Per.* c. 5.

[2] σοβαρόν. The word is openly
sarcastic, and is meant by Plutarch
to describe a pompous tone which

Perikles took from 'his sublime
speculations' (μετεωρολογία) and
'supramundane talk' (μεταρσιολε-
σχία) with Anaxagoras.

finished his business there, and when his persecutor followed him home, merely desired a slave to take a lantern and see the man home[1]. It is not probable that the receiver of the escort felt all the severity of the moral defeat which he had sustained; and he is perhaps no bad representative of the Athenian democracy in its relations to the superb decorum[2] of the old school. Much of this decorum survives in Antiphon, who, in a literary as in a political sense, clung to traditions which were fading. Yet even in him the influence of the age is seen. The Tetralogies, written for practice, and in which he had to please no one but himself, are the most stately of his compositions. The speech On the Murder of Herodes is less so, even in its elaborate proem; while part of the speech On the Choreutes, doubtless the latest of his extant works, shows a marked advance towards the freedom and vivacity of a newer style. It was in the hands of Antiphon that rhetoric first became thoroughly practical; and for this very reason, conservative as he was, he could not maintain a rigid conservatism. The public position which he had taken for his art could be held only by concessions to the public taste.

Antiphon relies much on the full, intense significance of single words. This is, indeed, a cardinal *Reliance on single words.*

---

[1] *loc. cit.*

[2] εὐκοσμία. Aeschines says that Solon made regulations περὶ τῆς τῶν ῥητόρων εὐκοσμίας. The oldest citizen was to speak first in the assembly—σωφρόνως ἐπὶ τὸ βῆμα παρελθὼν ἄνευ θορύβου καὶ ταραχῆς. (*In Ctes.* § 2.) Cf. Dem. *de F. L.* § 251: 'He said that the sobriety (σωφροσύνη) of the popular speakers of that day is illustrated by the statue of Solon with his cloak drawn round him and his hand within the folds.'

point in the older prose. Its movement was slow; each word was dropped with deliberation; and now and then some important word, heavy with concentrated meaning, came down like a sledge-hammer. Take, for instance, the chapter in which Thucydides shows how party strife, like that in Corcyra, had the effect of confusing moral distinctions. Blow on blow the nicely-balanced terms beat out the contrasts, until the ear is weary as with the clangour of an anvil. 'Reckless daring was esteemed loyal courage,—prudent delay, specious cowardice; temperance seemed a cloak for pusillanimity; comprehensive sagacity was called universal indifference[1].' 'Remonstrance is for friends who err; accusation for enemies who have done wrong[2].' In Antiphon's speech On the Murder of Herodes, the accused says (reminding the court that his case ought not to be decided until it has been heard before the Areiopagos):—'Be now, therefore, surveyors of the cause, but then, judges of the evidence,—now surmisers, but then deciders, of the truth[3].' And in the Second Tetralogy:—'Those who fail to do what they mean are agents of a mischance; those who hurt, or are hurt, voluntarily, are authors of suffering[4].' Ex-

---

[1] Thuc. III. 82. Hermogenes (περὶ ἰδεῶν I. cap. VI.) remarks that σεμνότης is a matter of ὀνόματα, phrases, not of ῥήματα, single words; and that the attempt to achieve σεμνότης by ῥήματα is a mistake. Thucydides, however, he says, is constantly doing this : καταφανῶς δὲ αὐτὸ ἐν τῇ τῆς στάσεως ἐκφράσει τῶν Κερκυραίων πεποίηκε.

[2] Thuc. I. 69. Another good in-

stance is II. 62, αὔχημα μὲν γὰρ καὶ ἀπὸ ἀμαθίας εὐτυχοῦς καὶ δειλῷ τινὶ ἐγγίγνεται, καταφρόνησις δὲ ὃς ἂν καὶ γνώμῃ πιστεύῃ τῶν ἐναντίων προέχειν.

[3] *de caed. Herod.* § 94 νῦν μὲν οὖν γνωρισταὶ γίνεσθε τῆς δίκης, τότε δὲ δικασταὶ τῶν μαρτύρων· νῦν μὲν δοξασταί, τότε δὲ κριταὶ τῶν ἀληθῶν.

[4] *Tetral.* II. B. § 6, οἵ τε γὰρ ἁμαρτάνοντες ὧν ἂν ἐπινοήσωσί τι

amples of this eagerness to press the exact meaning
of words are frequent in Antiphon, though far less
frequent than in Thucydides. It is evidently natural to that early phase of prose composition in which,
newly conscious of itself as an art, it struggles to
wring out of language a force strange to the ordinary idiom; and in Greece this tendency must have
been further strengthened by the stress which Gorgias laid on antithesis, and Prodikos on the discriminating of terms nearly synonymous. Only so long as
slow and measured declamation remained in fashion
could the orator attempt thus to put a whole train
of thought into a single weighty word. What the old
school sought to effect by one powerful word, the later
school did by the free, rapid, brilliant development
of a thought in all its fulness and with all the variety of contrasts which it pressed upon the mind.

A further characteristic of the older style—that *Antiphon is imaginative but not florid.*
it is 'fanciful in imagery, but by no means florid'—
is exemplified in Antiphon. The meaning of the
antithesis is sufficiently clear in reference to Aeschylos and Pindar, the poets chosen by Dionysios as his
instances.   In reference to prose also it means a
choice of images like theirs, bold, rugged, grand; and
a scorn, on the other hand, for small prettinesses, for
showy colouring, for maudlin sentiment. The great
representative in oratory of this special trait must
have been Perikles. A few of his recorded expressions bear just this stamp of a vigorous and daring
fancy;—his description of Aegina as the 'eyesore' of

δρᾶσαι, οὗτοι πράκτορες τῶν ἀκου-   ἢ πάσχοντες, οὗτοι τῶν παθημάτων
σίων εἰσίν· οἱ δὲ ἑκούσιόν τι δρῶντες   αἴτιοι γίγνονται.

the Peiraeus[1]; his saying that, in the. slain youth of
Athens, the year had lost its spring[2]; his declaration,
over the bodies of those who fell at Samos, that
they had become even as 'the gods; 'for the gods
themselves we see not, but infer their immortality
from the honours paid to them and from the blessings which they bestow[3].' The same imaginative
boldness is found in Antiphon, though but rarely,
and under severe control. 'Adversity herself is
wronged by the accused,' he makes a prosecutor
exclaim, 'when he puts her forward to screen a
crime and to withdraw his own villainy from view[4].'
A father, threatened with the condemnation of
his son, cries to the judges:—'I shall be buried
with my son—in the living tomb of my childless-
ness[5].' But in Antiphon, as in Thucydides, the
haughty[6], careless freedom of the old style is shown
oftener in the employment of new or unusual words
or phrases[7]. The orator could not, indeed, go so far
as the historian, who is expressly censured on this
score by his Greek critic[8] ; but they have some expressions of the same character in common[9].   While

---

[1] Arist. *Rhet.* III. 10.

[2] *ib.*, and I. 7.

[3] Plut. *Per.* c. 8.

[4] *Tetr.* I. Γ. § 1.

[5] *Tetr.* II. B. § 10: cf. II. Γ. § 12.

[6] μεγαλόφρων—αὐθέκαστος : Dionys. περὶ συνθ. ὀνομ. c. 22.

[7] E.g. *Tetr.* I. Γ. § 10 τὰ ἴχνη τῆς
ὑποψίας : *Tetr.* I. Δ. § 10 τὰ ἴχνη τοῦ
φόνου : *Tetr.* II. B. § 2 ἀνατροπεὺς
τοῦ οἴκου ἐγένετο : *Tetr.* IV. Γ. § 2
φιλοθύτης : *Herod.* § 78 χωροφιλεῖν
(=φιλοχωρεῖν.)

[8] Dionysios speaks of τὸ κατά-
γλωσσον τῆς λέξεως καὶ ξένον in
Thucydides (*de Thuc.* c. 53), and
remarks (*ib.* 51) that it was not a
general fashion of the time, but a
characteristic distinctive of him.

[9] The Thucydidean style may be
recognised, for instance, in *Tetr.*
I. Γ. § 3, ἡ αἰσχύνη—ἀρκοῦσα ἦν σω-
φρονίσαι τὸ θυμούμενον τῆς γνώμης :
Herod. § 73 κρεῖσσον δὲ χρὴ ἀεὶ
γίγνεσθαι τὸ ὑμέτερον δυνάμενον
ἐμὲ δικαίως σώζειν ἢ τὸ τῶν ἐχθρῶν

Antiphon is sparing of imagery, he is equally moderate in the use of the technical figures of rhetoric.
These have been well distinguished as 'figures of
language' (σχήματα λέξεως) and 'figures of thought'
(σχήματα διανοίας)—the first class including various
forms of assonance and of artificial symmetry between
clauses; the second including irony, abrupt pauses,
feigned perplexity, rhetorical question and so forth.
Caecilius of Calacte, the author of this distinction,
was a student of Antiphon, and observed that the
'figures of thought' are seldom or never used by
him[1]. The figures of language all occur, but rarely[2].
Blass[3] and K. O. Müller[4] agree in referring this
marked difference between the older and later schools
of oratory—the absence, in the former, of those
lively figures so abundant in the latter—to an essential change which passed upon Greek character in
the interval. It was only when fierce passion and
dishonesty had become strong traits of a degenerate
national character that vehemence and trickiness
came into oratory. This seems a harsh and scarcely
accurate judgment. It appears simpler to suppose
that the conventional stateliness of the old eloquence
altogether precluded such vivacity as marked the
later; and that the mainspring of this new vivacity
was merely the natural impulse, set free from the
restraints of the older style, to give arguments their
most spirited and effective form.

βουλόμενον ἀδίκως με ἀπολλύναι:
ib. § 84 οἱ μὲν ἄλλοι ἄνθρωποι τοῖς
ἔργοις τοὺς λόγους ἐλέγχουσιν, οὗτοι
δὲ τοῖς λόγοις ζητοῦσι τὰ ἔργα ἄπι-
στα καθιστάναι.
    [1] Caecilius *ap.* Phot. *Cod.* 259,

p. 485, Bekker.
    [2] See Blass, *Att. Bereds.* pp.
130—134.
    [3] *Att. Bereds.* p. 134.
    [4] *Hist. Gk. Lit.* c. xxxiii. § 5.

*Pathos and
Éthos in
Antiphon.*

Nothing in the criticism of Dionysios on the 'austere' style is more appreciative than his remark, that it aims rather at pathos than at êthos. That is, it addresses itself directly to the feelings; but does not care to give a subtle persuasiveness to its words by artistically adjusting them to the character and position of the person who is supposed to speak them. It is tragic; yet it is not dramatic. There has never, perhaps, been a greater master of stern and solemn pathos than Thucydides. The pleading of the Plataeans before their Theban judges, the dialogue between the Athenians and the Melians, the whole history of the Sicilian Expedition and especially its terrible closing scene, have a wonderful power over the feelings; and this power is in a great degree due to a certain irony. The reader feels throughout the restrained emotion of the historian; he is conscious that the crisis described was an agonising one, and that he is hearing the least that could be said of it from one who felt, and could have said, far more. On the other hand, a characteristic colouring, in the literary sense, is scarcely attempted by Thucydides. No writer is more consummate in making personal or national character appear in the history of actions. And when his characters speak, they always speak from the general point of view which he conceived to be appropriate to them. But in the form and language of their speeches there is little discrimination. Athenians and Lacedaemonians, Perikles and Brasidas, Kleon and Diodotos[1] speak much in the same style; it is

---

[1] Thuc. III. 42.

the ideas which they represent by which alone they
are broadly distinguished[1]. The case is nearly the
same with Antiphon. His extant works present
no subject so great as those of Thucydides, and his
pathos is necessarily inferior in degree to that of the
historian; but it resembles it in its stern solemnity,
and also in this, that it owes much of its impressiveness to its self-control. The second[2] and fourth[3]
speeches of the First Tetralogy, and the second[4] and
third[5] of the Second, furnish perhaps the best examples. In êthos, on the contrary, Antiphon is
weak; and this, in a writer of speeches for persons
of all ages and conditions, must be considered a
defect. In the Herodes case the defendant is a
young Mytilenean, who frequently pleads his inexperience of affairs and his want of practice as a
speaker. The speech On the Choreutes is delivered
by an Athenian citizen of mature age and eminent
public services. But the two persons speak nearly
in the same strain and with the same measure of
self-confidence. Had Lysias been the composer,
greater deference to the judges and a more decided
avoidance of rhetoric would have distinguished the
appeal of the young alien to an unfriendly court
from the address of the statesman to his fellow-
citizens.

The place of Antiphon in the history of his art is *The style of Antiphon how far periodic.*

---

[1] One exception may possibly
be noted. It seems as if the
unique personality of Alkibiades
were sometimes indicated by a
characteristic insolence and vehemence of language: *e. g.* VI. 18
§ 3 καὶ οὐκ ἔστιν ἡμῖν ταμιεύεσθαι

εἰς ὅσον βουλόμεθα ἄρχειν : *ib.* § 4
ἵνα Πελοποννησίων στορέσωμεν τὸ
φρόνημα.

[2] Esp. §§ 1—4, 9.

[3] Esp. §§ 1—3.

[4] §§ 1—3, 10—12.

[5] §§ 3, 4.

further marked by the degree in which he had attained a periodic style. It is perhaps impossible to
find English terms which shall give all the clearness
of the Greek contrast between περιοδική and εἰρομένη
λέξις¹. The 'running' style, as εἰρομένη expresses, is
that in which the ideas are merely strung together,
like beads, in the order in which they naturally present themselves to the mind. Its characteristic is
simple continuity. The characteristic of the 'periodic' style is that each sentence 'comes round' upon
itself, so as to form a separate, symmetrical whole².
The running style may be represented by a straight
line which may be cut short at any point or prolonged
to any point : the periodic style is a system of independent circles. The period may be formed either,
so to say, in one piece, or of several members (κῶλα,
membra), as a hoop may be made either of a single
lath bent round, or of segments fitted together. It
was a maxim of the later Greek rhetoric that, for
the sake of simplicity and strength, a period should
not consist of more than four³ of these members or
segments ; Roman rhetoric allowed a greater num-
ber⁴.

Aristotle⁵ takes as his example of the 'running'

---

¹ λέξις εἰρομένη (Arist. *Rhet.* III.
9). Demetrios (ἑρμ. περὶ περιόδων
§ 12) calls it διηρημένη, 'disjointed,'
διαλελυμένη 'loose,' διερριμμένη
'sprawling'—in contrast to the
close, compact system of the periodic style. It is also called by Dionysios *de Demosth.* c. 39, κομμα-
τική, 'commatic,' as consisting of
short clauses (κόμματα) following

each other without pause. Aristotle (l. c.) calls the periodic style
κατεστραμμένη, 'compact.'
² Cicero calls the period *circui-
tum et quasi orbem verborum* (*de
Orat.* III. 51. 198).
³ Hermogenes περὶ εὑρεσ. II. p.
240, Spengel.
⁴ Quint. IX. 4. 124.
⁵ *Rhet.* III. 9.

style the opening words of the History of Herodotos;
and, speaking generally, it may be said that this was
the style in which Herodotos and the earlier Ionian
logographers wrote.   But it ought to be remembered
that neither Herodotos, nor any writer in a language
which has passed beyond the rudest stage, exhibits the
'running' style in an ideal simplicity.   In its purest
and simplest form, the running style is incompatible
with the very idea of a literature[1].   Wherever a literature exists, it contains the germ, however immature, of the periodic style ; which, if the literature is
developed, is necessarily developed along with it.
For every effort to grasp and limit an idea naturally
finds expression more or less in the periodic manner,
the very nature of a period being to comprehend and
define.   In Herodotos, the running style, so congenial to his direct narrative, is dominant; but
when he pauses and braces himself to state some
theory, some general result of his observations, he
tends to become periodic just because he is striving
to be precise[2].   From the time of Herodotos onward
the periodic style is seen gradually more and more
matured, according as men felt more and more the
stimulus to find vigorous utterance for clear conceptions.   Antiphon represents a moment at which this
stimulus had become stronger than it had ever before

---

[1] Blass, *Att. Bereds.* p. 124 :
Eine gewisse Periodik hat natür-
lich die griechische und jede Lit-
teratur von Anfang an gehabt : eine
ganz reine λέξις εἰρομένη ist in der
Wirklichkeit nie vorhanden.

[2] See (for instance) the passage
in which Herodotos speculates

on the causes of the overflowing
of the Nile, II. 24, 25. It begins
in a thoroughly periodic style :—
εἰ δὲ δεῖ, | μεμψάμενον γνώμας τὰς
προκειμένας, | αὐτὸν περὶ τῶν ἀ-
φανέων ἀποδέξασθαι, | φράσω διότι
μοι δοκέει πληθύεσθαι ὁ Νεῖλος τοῦ
θέρεος.

been in the Greek world. His activity as a writer
of speeches may be placed between the years 421
and 411 B.C.[1]. The effects of the Peloponnesian war
in sharpening political animosities had made themselves fully felt; that phase of Athenian democracy
in which the contests of the ekklesia and of the law-
courts were keenest and most frequent had set in;
the teaching of the Sophists had thrown a new light
upon language considered as a weapon. Every man
felt the desire, the urgent necessity, of being able
in all cases to express his opinions with the most
trenchant force; at any moment his life might depend upon it. The new intensity of the age is
reflected in the speeches of Antiphon. Wherever
the feeling rises highest, as in the appeals to the
judges, he strives to use a language which shall
'pack the thoughts closely and bring them out
roundly[2].' But it is striking to observe how far
this periodic style still is from the ease of Lysias or
the smooth completeness of Isokrates. The harshness of the old rugged writing refuses to blend with
it harmoniously,—either taking it up with marked
transitions, or suddenly breaking out in the midst of
the most elaborate passages[3]. It is everywhere plain
that the desire to be compact is greater than the

[1] The speech On the Murder of
Herodes must probably be placed
between 421 and 416 B.C.; the
speech On the Choreutes about 413.

[2] Dionys. *de Lys.* c. 6 (in reference to Lysias) ἡ συστρέφουσα τὰ
νοήματα καὶ στρογγύλως ἐκφέρουσα
λέξις,—a good description of the
periodic style generally as opposed

to the εἰρομένη.

[3] *E. g.,* in the speech On the
Murder of Herodes, sections 1, 2
show thoroughly artistic periods :
§ 20, again, is almost pure εἰρομένη:
in Tetral. II. Γ. 7 (ἀξιῶν δὲ διὰ τὸ
φανερὰν εἶναι τὴν ὑποψίαν...ἐπέθετο
αὐτῷ) the κατεστραμμένη and εἰρομένη are combined.

power. Antitheses and parallelisms[1] are abundantly employed, giving a rigid and monotonous effect to the periods which they form. That more artistic period of which the several parts resemble the mutually-supporting stones of a vaulted roof[2], and which leads the ear by a smooth curve to a happy finish, has not yet been found. An imperfect sense of rhythm, or a habit of composition to which rhythmical restraint is intolerable except for a very short space, is everywhere manifest. The vinegar and the oil refuse to mingle. Thucydides presents the same phenomenon, but with some curious differences. It may perhaps be said that, while Antiphon has more technical skill (incomplete as that skill is) in periodic writing, Thucydides has infinitely more of its spirit. He is always at high pressure, always nervous, intense. He struggles to bring a large, complex idea into a framework in which the whole can be seen at once. Aristotle says that a period must be of 'a size to be taken in at a glance[3];' and this is what Thucydides wishes the *thought* of each sentence to be, though he is sometimes clumsy in the mechanism of the sentence itself. Dionysios mentions among the excellences which Demosthenes borrowed from the historian, 'his rapid movement, his terseness, his intensity, his sting[4];' excellences, he adds, which

---

[1] *E.g. Accus. Venen.* § 5 τοῦ μὲν ἐκ προβουλῆς ἀκουσίως ἀποθανόντος τῆς δὲ ἑκουσίως ἐκ προνοίας ἀποκτεινάσης.

[2] περιφερὴς στέγη, Demetrios περὶ ἑρμ. § 12, where this comparison is made.

[3] μέγεθος εὐσύνοπτον: *Rhet.* III.9.

[4] τὰ τάχη—τὰς συστροφάς—τοὺς τόνους—τὸ πικρόν : Dionys. *De Thuc.* 53. He adds τὸ στρυφνόν (which seems to be a metaphor of the same kind as αὐστηρόν, and to mean 'his biting flavour'); and τὴν ἐξεγείρουσαν τὰ πάθη δεινότητα.

neither Antiphon nor Lysias nor Isokrates possessed. This intensity, due primarily to genius, next to the absorbing interest of a great subject, does, in truth, place Thucydides, with all his roughness, far nearer than Antiphon to the ideal of a compact and masterly prose. Technically speaking, Thucydides as well as Antiphon must be placed in the border-land between the old running style and finished periodic writing. But the essential merits of the latter, though in a rude shape, have already been reached by the native vigour of the historian; while to the orator a period is still something which must be constructed with painful effort, and on a model admitting of little variety.

Antiphon's treatment of subject-matter.

These seem to be the leading characteristics of Antiphon as regards form: it remains to consider his treatment of subject-matter. The arrangement of his speeches, so far as the extant specimens warrant a judgment, was usually simple. First a proem (προοίμιον) explanatory or appealing; next an introduction (technically προκατασκευή) dealing with the circumstances under which the case had been brought into court, and noticing any informalities of procedure: then a narrative of the facts (διήγησις): then arguments and proofs (πίστεις), the strongest first: finally an epilogue or peroration (ἐπίλογος). The Tetralogies, being merely sketches for practice, have only proem, arguments and epilogue, not the 'introduction' or the narrative. The speech On the Murder of Herodes and the speech On the Choreutes (in the latter of which the epilogue seems to have been lost) are the best examples of Antiphon's

method. It is noticeable that in neither of these
are the facts of the particular case dealt with closely
or searchingly; and consequently in both instances
the narrative of the facts falls into the background.
Narrative was the forte of Andokides and Lysias;
it appears to have been the weak side of Antiphon,
who was strongest in general argument. General
presumptions,—those afforded, for instance, by the
refusal of the prosecutors to give up their slaves
for examination, or by the respective characters of
prosecutor and prisoner and by their former relations—are most insisted upon. The First Tetralogy
is a good example of Antiphon's ingenuity in
dealing with abstract probabilities (εἰκότα); and the
same preference for proofs external to the immediate circumstances of the case is traceable in all
his extant work. The adroitness of the sophistical
rhetoric shows itself, not merely in the variety of
forms given to the same argument, but sometimes
in sophistry of a more glaring kind[1].

The rhetorician of the school is further seen in
the great number of commonplaces, evidently ela-
borated beforehand and without reference to any
special occasion, which are brought in as opportunity
offers. The same panegyric on the laws for homicide
occurs, in the same words, both in the speech On the
Choreutes and in that On the Murder of Herodes.
In the last-named speech the reflections on the
strength of a good conscience[2], and the defendant's
contention that he deserves pity, not punishment[3],

---

[1] See *e.g.* the argument in a circle
in Tetr. I. A. § 6.

[2] *de Choreut.* § 93.

[3] *ib.* § 73.

are palpably commonplaces prepared for general use. Such patches, unless introduced with consummate skill, are doubly a blemish; they break the coherence of the argument and they destroy everything like fresh and uniform colouring; the speech becomes, as an old critic says, uneven[1]. But the crudities inseparable from a new art do not affect Antiphon's claim to be considered, for his day, a great and powerful orator. In two things, says Thucydides, he was masterly,—in power of conception and in power of expression[2]. These were the two supreme qualifications for a speaker at a time when the mere faculty of lucid and continuous exposition was rare, and when the refinements of literary eloquence were as yet unknown. If the speaker could invent a sufficient number of telling points, and could put them clearly, this was everything. Antiphon, with his ingenuity in hypothesis and his stately rhetoric, fulfilled both requirements. Remembering the style of his oratory and his place in the history of the art, no one need be perplexed to reconcile the high praise of Thucydides with what is at first sight the startling judgment of Dionysios. That critic, speaking of the eloquence which aims at close reasoning and at victory in discussion, gives the foremost place in it to Lysias. He then mentions others who have practised it,—Antiphon among the rest. 'Antiphon, however,' he says, 'has nothing but his antique and stern dignity; a fighter of causes (ἀγωνιστής) he is

---

[1] ἀνώμαλον: Alkidamas Περὶ Σοφιστ. §§ 24, 25.

[2] Thuc. VIII. 68: κράτιστος ἐνθυμηθῆναι γενόμενος καὶ ἃ γνοίη εἰπεῖν. Comp. [Plut.] Vitt. X. Oratt. 8: ἔστι δὲ ἐν τοῖς λόγοις ἀκριβὴς καὶ πιθανὸς καὶ δεινὸς περὶ τὴν εὕρεσιν.

not, either in debate or in lawsuits[1].' If, as Thucydides tells us, no one could help so well as Antiphon
those who were fighting causes (ἀγωνιζομένους)[2] in
the ekklesia or the lawcourts; if, on his own trial, he
delivered a defence of unprecedented brilliancy; in
what sense is Dionysios to be understood? The explanation lies probably in the notion which the critic
attached to the word 'agonist.' He had before his
mind the finished pleader or debater of a time when
combative oratory considered as an art had reached
its acme; when every discussion was a conflict in
which the liveliest and supplest energy must be put
forth in support of practised skill; when the successful speaker must grapple at close quarters with his
adversary, and be in truth an 'agonist,' an athlete
straining every nerve for victory. Already Kleon
could describe the 'agonistic' eloquence which was
becoming the fashion in the ekklesia as characterized
by swift surprises, by rapid thrust and parry[3];
already Strepsiades conceives the 'agonist' of the
lawcourts as 'bold, glib, audacious, headlong[4].' This
was not the character of Antiphon. He was a subtle
reasoner, a master of expression, and furnished others
with arguments and words; but he was not himself

---

[1] Dionys. *de Isaeo* c. 20: 'Αντι-
φῶν γε μὴν τὸ αὐστηρὸν ἔχει μόνον
καὶ ἀρχαῖον, ἀγωνιστὴς δὲ λόγων
οὔτε συμβουλευτικῶν οὔτε δικανικῶν
ἐστί.

[2] Thuc. VIII. 68.

[3] It is remarkable how strongly
this image of debate in the ekklesia
as an ἀγών is brought out in Kleon's
speech, Thuc. III. 37, 38: ἀγωνισταί

—ξυνέσεως ἀγῶνι ἐπαιρομένους—ὡς
οὐκ ἔγνωσται ἀγωνίσαιτ' ἄν—ἐκ τῶν
τοιῶνδε ἀγώνων—αἴτιοι δ' ὑμεῖς κα-
κῶς ἀγωνοθετοῦντες—ἀνταγωνιζόμε-
νοι. The characteristics of the
ἀγωνιστής are τὸ εὐπρεπὲς τοῦ λόγου ἐκπονῆσαι—καινότης λόγου—ὀ-
ξέως λέγειν (*ib.*)

[4] Ar. *Nub.* 445 θρασὺς, εὔγλωτ-
τος, τολμηρὸς, ἴτης.

a man of the arena. He never descended into it
when he could help; he had nothing of its spirit.
He did not grapple with his adversary, but in the
statelier manner of the old orators attacked him (as
it were) from an opposite platform. Opposed in
court to such a speaker as Isaeos, he would have
had as little chance with the judges as Burke with
one of those juries which Curran used to take by
storm. Perhaps it was precisely because he was not
in this sense an 'agonist' that he found his most
congenial sphere in the calm and grave procedure of
the Areiopagos.

*Religious
feeling of
Antiphon.*

Nor was it by the stamp of his eloquence alone
that he was fitted to command the attention of that
Court. In politics Antiphon was aristocratic; in
religion, an upholder of those ancient ideas and
conceptions, bound up with the primitive traditions of Attica, of which the Areiopagos was the
embodiment and the guardian. For most minds
of his day these ideas were losing their awful
prestige,—fading, in the light of science, before newer
beliefs, as oligarchy had yielded to democracy, as
Kronos to the dynasty of Zeus. But, as Athene,
speaking in the name of that dynasty, had reserved
to the Eumenides a perpetual altar in her land[1], so
Antiphon had embraced the new culture without
parting from a belief in gods who visit national
defilement[2], in spirits who hear the curse of

[1] Aesch. *Eum.* 804.

[2] See, for instance, the close of
the accuser's first speech in the
First Tetralogy (I. A. § 10)...'It is
also harmful for you that this man,

vile and polluted as he is, should
enter the precincts of the gods to
defile them, or should poison with
his infection the guiltless persons
whom he meets at the same table.

dying men[1] and avenge blood crying from the ground. In the recent history of his own city he had seen a great impiety followed by a tremendous disaster[2]. The prominence which he always gives to the theological view of homicide means more than that this was the tone of the Court to which his speeches were most frequently addressed : it points to a real and earnest feeling in his own mind. There is no better instance of this feeling than the opening of the Third Tetralogy—a mere exercise, in which the elaborate simulation of a religious sentiment would have had no motive :—

'The god, when it was his will to create mankind, begat the earliest of our race and gave us for nourishers the earth and sea, that we might not die, for want of needful sustenance, before the term of old age. Whoever, then, having been deemed worthy of these things by the god, lawlessly robs any one among us of life, is impious towards heaven and confounds the ordinances of men. The dead man,

From such causes spring plagues of barrenness (αἱ ἀφορίαι) *and reverses in men's fortunes. You must therefore remember that vengeance is yours : you must impute to this man his own crimes : you must bring their penalty home to him, and purity back to Athens.'* Again, in *Tetr.* II. Γ. § 8, he speaks of θεία κηλίς. Compare the passage in which the Erinyes threaten Attica with λιχὴν ἄφυλλος, ἄτεκνος, *Eum.* 815; and Soph. *O. T.* 25, 101.

[1] οἱ ἀλιτήριοι (which Antiphon uses in the sense of ἀλάστορες : and so Andok. *de Myst.* § 131)—οἱ τῶν

ἀποθανόντων προστρόπαιοι : *Tetr.* III. A. § 4. He uses ἐνθύμιος (*Tetr.* II. A. 2 &c.), just as the older poets do, of a sin which lies heavy on the soul, bringing a presage of avenging Furies; and the poetical ποινή (*Tetr.* I. Δ. § 11), of atonement for blood.

[2] Timaeos, writing early in the 3rd century B.C., directly connected the defeat of the Athenians in Sicily with the mutilation of the Hermae—noticing that the Syracusan Hermokrates was a descendant of the god Hermes : Tim. *frag.* 103—4, referred to by Grote, vol. VII. p. 230.

robbed of the god's gift, necessarily bequeaths, as
that god's punishment, the anger of avenging spirits
—anger which unjust judges or false witnesses,
becoming partners in the impiety of the murderer,
bring, as a self-sought defilement, into their own
houses.　We, the champions of the murdered, if for
any collateral enmity we prosecute innocent persons,
shall find, by our failure to vindicate the dead, dread
avengers in the spirits which hear his curse; while,
by putting the pure to a wrongful death, we become
liable to the penalties of murder, and, in persuading
you to violate the law, responsible for your sin also[1].'

Aeschylean tone in Antiphon.

The analogy of Antiphon to Aeschylos in regard
to general style has once already been noticed; it
forces itself upon the mind in a special aspect here,
where the threat of judgment from the grave on
blood is wrapt round with the very terror and dark-
ness of the *Eumenides*.　In another place, where
Antiphon is speaking of the signs by which the gods
point out the guilty, the Aeschylean tone is still
more striking.　No passage, perhaps, in Aeschylos
is more expressive of the poet's deepest feeling about
life than that in which Eteokles forebodes that the
personal goodness of Amphiaraos will not deliver
him :—

> Alas that doom which mingles in the world
> A just man with the scorners of the gods !
> *　　*　　*　　*　　*　　*　　*　　*
> Aye, for a pure man going on the sea
> With men fierce-blooded and their secret sin
> Dies in a moment with the loathed of heaven[2].

---

[1] *Tetr.* III. A. §§ 2 f.　　　　[2] Aesch. *Theb.* 593 ff.

In the Herodes trial the defendant appeals to the silent witness which the gods have borne in his behalf:—'You know doubtless that often ere now men red-handed or otherwise polluted have, by entering the same ship, destroyed with themselves those who were pure towards the gods; and that others, escaping death, have incurred the extremity of danger through such men. Many again, on standing beside the sacrifice, have been discovered to be impure and hinderers of the solemn rites. Now in all such cases an opposite fortune has been mine. First, all who have sailed with me have had excellent voyages: then, whenever I have assisted at a sacrifice it has in every instance been most favourable. These facts I claim as strong evidence touching the present charge and the falsity of the prosecutor's accusations[1].'

Coincidences of thought and tone such as these deserve notice just because they are general coincidences. There is no warrant for assuming a resemblance in any special features between the mind of Antiphon and the mind of Aeschylos: all the more that which the two minds have in common illustrates the broadest aspect of each. By pursuits and calling Antiphon belonged to a new Athenian democracy antagonistic to the old ideas and beliefs: by the bent of his intellect and of his sympathies he belonged, like Aeschylos, to the elder democracy. It is this which gives to his extant work a special interest over and above its strictly literary interest. All the other men whose writings

[1] *De caed. Herod.* §§ 82 ff.

remain to show the development of oratorical Attic prose have around them the atmosphere of eager debate or litigation; Antiphon, in language and in thought alike, stands apart from them as the representative of a graver public life. Theirs is the spirit of the ekklesia or the dikastery; his is the spirit of the Areiopagos.

CHAPTER III.

ANTIPHON.

WORKS.

SIXTY speeches ascribed to Antiphon were known *The φονικοὶ λόγοι alone extant.* in the reign of Augustus; but of these Caecilius pronounced twenty-five spurious[1]. Fifteen, including the twelve speeches of the Tetralogies, are now extant. All these relate to causes of homicide. The titles of lost speeches prove that Antiphon's activity was not confined to this province; but it was in this province that he excelled; and as the orations of Isaeos are now represented by one class only, the κληρικοί, so the orations of Antiphon are represented by one class only, the φονικοί.

The Tetralogies have this special interest, that *The Tetralogies.* they represent rhetoric in its transition from the technical to the practical stage, from the schools to the law-courts and the ekklesia. Antiphon stood between the sophists who preceded and the orators who followed him as the first Athenian who was at once a theorist of rhetoric and a master of practical eloquence. The Tetralogies hold a corresponding place between merely ornamental exercises and real

---

[1] [Plut.] *Vitt. X. Oratt.*

orations. Each of them forms a set of four speeches, supposed to be spoken in a trial for homicide. The accuser states his charge, and the defendant replies; the accuser then speaks again, and the defendant follows with a second reply. The imaginary case is in each instance sketched as lightly as possible; details are dispensed with; only the essential framework for discussion is supplied. Hence, in these skeleton-speeches, the structure and anatomy of the argument stand forth in naked clearness, stripped of everything accidental, and showing in bold relief the organic lines of a rhetorical pleader's thought. It was the essence of the technical rhetoric that it taught a man to be equally ready to defend either side of a question. Here we have the same man— Antiphon himself—arguing both sides, with tolerably well-balanced force; and it must be allowed that much of the reasoning—especially in the Second Tetralogy—is, in the modern sense, sophistical. In reference, however, to this general characteristic one thing ought to be borne in mind. The Athenian law of homicide was precise, but it was not scientific. The distinctions which it drew between various degrees of guilt in various sets of circumstances depended rather on minute tradition than on clear principle. A captious or even frivolous style of argument was invited by a code which employed vague conceptions in the elaborate classification of accidental details. Thus far the Tetralogies bear the necessary mark of the age which produced them. But in all else they are distinguished as widely as possible from the essays of a

merely artificial rhetoric ; not less from the ' displays '
of the elder sophists than from the ' declamations '
of the Augustan age[1]. They are not only thoroughly
real and practical, but they show Antiphon, in one
sense, at his best. He argues in them with more
than the subtlety of the speeches which he composed for others, for here he has no less an antagonist than himself : he speaks with more than
the elevation of his ordinary style,—for in the
privacy of the school he owed less concession to an
altered public taste.

The First Tetralogy supposes the following case. *First Tetralogy.*
A citizen, coming home at night from a dinner-party,
has been murdered. His slave, found mortally
wounded on the same spot, deposes that he recognised one of the assassins. This was an old enemy
of his master, against whom the latter was about to
bring a lawsuit which might be ruinous. The accused
denies the charge : the case comes before the court
of the Areiopagos. The speeches of accuser and defendant comprise a number of separate arguments,
each of which is carefully, though very briefly, stated,
but which are not systematised or woven into a
whole. An enumeration of the points raised on either
side in this case will give a fair general idea of the
scope of the Tetralogies generally.

---

[1] 'Antiphon is a sophist,' (says
Reiske (*Orat. Att.* VII. p. 849)—
'nay, in a manner the father of
that *pedantic* (*umbratici*), hair-
splitting, empty, affected kind of
speaking with which the schools
of the ancients were rife.' The
very phrase ' scholae veterum '
shows the vagueness of this assertion. Precisely that which
distinguished Antiphon from the
earlier sophists was his practical
bent. No man could be less fairly
called ' umbraticus.'

I. *First Speech of Accuser.*

1. §§ 1—3. (*Proem.*) The accused is so crafty that even an imperfect proof against him ought to be accepted: a proof complete in all its parts is hardly to be looked for.—It is not to be supposed that the accuser would have deliberately incurred the guilt of prosecuting an innocent person.

[Here a narrative of the facts would naturally follow; but as this is a mere practice-speech, it is left out, and the speaker comes at once to the proofs—first, those derived from argument on the circumstances themselves (the ἔντεχνοι πίστεις)—then, the testimony of the slave (which represents the ἄτεχνοι.)]

2. § 4. The deceased cannot have been murdered by robbers; for he was not plundered.

3. Nor in a drunken brawl; for the time and place are against it.

4. Nor by mistake for some one else; for, in that case, the slave would not have been attacked too.

5. §§ 5—8. It was therefore a premeditated crime; and this must have been prompted by a motive of revenge or fear.

6. Now the accused had both motives. He had lost much property in actions brought by the deceased, and was threatened with the loss of more. The murder was the only means by which he could evade the lawsuit hanging over him. [Here follows a curious argument in a circle.] And he must have felt that he was going to lose the lawsuit, or he would not have braved a trial for murder.

7. § 9. The slave identifies him.

8. §§ 9—11. (*Epilogue.*) If such proofs do not suffice, no murderer can ever be brought to justice, and the State will be left to bear the wrath of the gods for an unexpiated pollution.

II. *First Speech of the Defendant.*

1. §§ 1—4. (*Proem.*) The accuser deserves the pity of the judge, for he is the most unlucky of men. In death, as

in life, his enemy hurts him still. It is not enough if he
can prove his own innocence ; he is expected to point out
the real culprit. The accuser credits him with craft. If he
was so crafty, is it likely that he would have exposed himself to such obvious suspicion ?

2. §§ 5—6. The deceased may have been murdered by
robbers, who were scared off by people coming up before
they had stripped him.

3. Or he may have been murdered because he had been
witness of some crime.

4. Or by some other of his numerous enemies ; who
would have felt safe, knowing that the suspicion was sure to
fall on the accused, his great enemy.

5. § 7. The testimony of the slave is untrustworthy,
since, in the terror of the moment, he may have been mistaken ; or he may have been ordered by his present masters
to speak against the accused. Generally, the evidence of
slaves is held untrustworthy ; else they would not be racked.

6. § 8. Even if mere *probabilities* are to decide the
case, it is more *probable* that the accused should have employed some one else to do the murder, than that the slave
should, at such a time, have been accurate in his recognition.

7. § 9. The danger of losing money in the impending
lawsuit could not have seemed more serious to the accused
than the danger, which he runs in the present trial, of losing
his life.

8. §§ 10—13. (*Epilogue.*) Though he be deemed the
probable murderer, he ought not to be condemned unless he
is proved to be the actual murderer.—It is his adversary
who, by accusing the innocent, is really answerable for the
consequences of a crime remaining unexpiated.—The whole
life and character of the accused are in his favour, as much
as those of the accuser are against *him.*—The judges must
succour the illfortune of a slandered man.

III.   *Second Speech of the Accuser.*

1. § 1. (*Proem.*) The defendant has no right to speak
of his 'misfortune:' it is his fault. The first speech for

the prosecutor proved his guilt; this shall overthrow his defence.

2. § 2. Had the robbers been scared off by people coming up, these persons would have questioned the slave about the assassins, and given information which would have exculpated the accused.

3. Had the deceased been murdered because he had been witness of a crime, this crime itself would have been heard of.

4. § 3. His other enemies, being in less danger from him than the accused was, had so much less motive for the crime.

5. § 4. It is contended that the slave's testimony is untrustworthy because it was wrung from him by the rack. But, in such cases as these, the rack is not used at all. [Nothing is said about the hypothesis that the slave may have been suborned by his masters.]

6. § 5. The accused is not likely to have got the deed done by other hands, since *he* would have been suspected all the same, and could not have been so sure of the work being done thoroughly.

7. § 6. The lawsuit hanging over him—a certainty—would have seemed more formidable to him than the doubtful chance of a trial for murder.

8. §§ 7—8. (Notice of a few topics touched on by the defendant at the beginning and end of his speech.)—The fear of discovery is not likely to have deterred such a man from crime: whereas the prospect of losing his wealth—the instrument of his boasted services to the State—is very likely to have driven him to it.—When the certain murderer cannot be found, the presumptive must be punished.

9. §§ 9—11. (*Epilogue.*) The judges must not acquit the accused—condemned alike by probabilities and by proofs—and thereby bring bloodguiltiness on themselves. By punishing him, they can take the stain of murder off the State.

IV. *Second Speech of the Defendant.*

1. §§ 1—3. (*Proem.*) He is the victim of cruel ma-

lignity. Though bound only to clear himself, it is demanded
of him that he shall account for the crime.

2. §§ 4—5. Suppose that robbers did the murder, but
were scared, before they had taken their booty, by people
coming up. Would these persons, as it is contended, have
remained to make inquiries? Coming on a bloody corpse
and a dying man at dead of night, would they not rather
have fled in terror from the spot?

3. § 6. Suppose that the deceased was slain because he
had been witness of a crime :—the fact of such crime not having been heard of, does not prove that it did not take place.

4. § 7. The slave, with death from his wounds close at
hand, had nothing to fear if he bore false testimony.

5. § 8. But the accused can prove a distinct *alibi.* All
his own slaves can testify that on the night in question—
the night of the Diïpolia—he did not leave his own house.

[The assertion of the *alibi* has been reserved till this
point, because now the prosecutor cannot reply.]

6. § 9. It is suggested that he may have committed
the crime to protect his wealth. But desperate deeds, such
as this, are not done by prosperous men. They are more
natural to men who have nothing to lose.

7. § 10. Even if he were the presumptive murderer, he
would not have been proved the actual: but, as it is, the
probabilities also are for him. On all grounds, therefore,
he must be acquitted, or there is no more safety for any
accused man.

8. §§ 11—12. (*Epilogue.*) The judges are entreated not
to condemn him wrongfully, and so leave the murder un-
atoned for, while they bring a new stain of bloodguiltiness
on the State.

A tolerably full analysis of this First Tetralogy
has been given, because it is curious as showing the
general line of argument which a clever Athenian
reasoner, accustomed to writing for the courts, thought
most likely to succeed on either side of such a case.
It will be seen that, though other kinds of evidence

come into discussion, the contest turns largely on general probabilities (εἰκότα)—a province for which Antiphon had the relish of a trained rhetorician, and on which he enlarges in the speech On the Murder of Herodes[1]. As regards style, in this as in the other Tetralogies the language is noble throughout, rising, in parts of the speeches of the accused, to an austere pathos[2]; it is always concise without baldness, but somewhat over-stiff and antique. There is also too little of oratorical life; at which, however, in short speeches written for practice, the author perhaps did not aim.

Second Tetralogy. The subject of the Second Tetralogy is the death of a boy accidentally struck by a javelin while watching a youth practising at the gymnasium. The boy's father accuses the youth—whose father defends him—of accidental homicide; and the case comes before the court of the Palladion. In order to understand the issues raised, it is necessary to keep in mind the Greek view of accidental homicide. This view was mainly a religious one. The death was a pollution. Some person, or thing, must be answerable for that pollution, and must be banished from the State, which would else remain defiled[3]. In a case like the supposed one, three hypotheses were possible:—that the cause of the impurity had been the thrower, the person struck, or the missile. Pe-

---

[1] See esp. *de caed. Herod.* §§ 57—63.

[2] Esp. B. §§ 1—4 : Δ §§ 1—3.

[3] This feeling about homicide comes out strongly in the custom of trying cases of φόνος in the open air : ἵνα τοῦτο μὲν οἱ δικασταὶ μὴ ἴωσιν εἰς τὸ αὐτὸ τοῖς μὴ καθαροῖς τὰς χεῖρας, τοῦτο δὲ ὁ διώκων τὴν δίκην τοῦ φόνου ἵνα μὴ ὁμωρόφιος γένηται τῷ αὐθέντῃ. Cf. supra, p. 40, *note* 2; and Dem. *Aristocr.* §§ 65—79.

rikles and Protagoras spent a whole day in discussing a similar question. Epitimos, an athlete, had chanced to hit and kill a certain Pharsalian : did the guilt lie, they inquired, with Epitimos, with the man killed, or with the javelin[1] ? There was a special court—that held at the Prutaneion—for the trial of inanimate things which had caused death. Here, however, the question is only of living agents. The judges have nothing whatever to do with the question as to how far either was morally to blame. The question is simply which of them is to be considered as, in fact, the author or cause of the death.

The accused, in his first speech, assumes that the case *Analysis.* admits of no doubt; states it briefly; and concludes with an appeal to the judges (A. §§ 1—2). The father of the accused, after bespeaking patience for an apparently strange defence (B. §§ 1—2)—argues that the error, the ἁμαρτία, was all on the boy's side (§§ 3—5). The thrower was standing in his appointed place; the boy was not obliged to place himself where he did. The thrower knew what he was about; the boy did not—he chose the wrong moment for running across. He was struck; and so *punished himself for his own fault* (§§ 6—8).—The accuser answers in the tone of a plain man bewildered by the shamelessness of the defence, (Γ. §§ 1—4). It is absurd, he says, to pretend that the boy killed himself with a weapon which he had not touched. On the showing of the defence itself, the blame is divided: if the boy ran, the youth threw: neither was passive (§§ 5—10).—The youth's father answers that his meaning has been perverted (A. §§ 1—2): he did not mean, of course, that the boy pierced himself, but that he became the *first cause* of his own death (§§ 3—5). The youth did no more than the other throwers, who did not hit the boy only because he did not

---

[1] Plut. *Perikl.* 36.

cross their aim (§§ 6—8). Involuntary homicide is, doubtless, punishable by law; but, in this instance, the involuntary
slayer—the deceased himself—has been punished already.
To condemn the accused would be only to incur a new
pollution (§§ 9—10).

The striking point of the whole Tetralogy is the
ingenuity with which the defender inverts the
natural view of the case. The guilt of blood is, he
says, with the deceased alone, who has taken satisfaction for it from himself. 'Destroyed by his own
errors, he was punished by himself in the same
instant that he sinned.' (Δ. § 8.)

*Third
Tetralogy.*

Another peculiarity of the Athenian law of
homicide is illustrated by the third and last Tetralogy. An elderly man had been beaten by a younger
man so severely that in a few days he died. The
young man is tried for murder before the Areiopagos.

Analysis.

The accuser, in a short speech, appeals chiefly to the
indignation of the judges, dwelling, in a striking passage
on the sin of robbing a fellow-mortal of the god's gift
(A. §§ 1—4).—The defendant argues in reply that, if the
homicide is to be regarded as *accidental*, then it rests
with the surgeon, under whose unskilful treatment the man
died; but, if it is to be regarded as *deliberate*, then the
murderer is the deceased himself, since he struck the first
blow, which set the train of events in motion (B. §§ 3—5).—
The accuser answers that the elder man is not likely to have
first struck the younger (Γ. § 2); and that to blame the surgeon is idle; it would not be more absurd to inculpate the
persons who called in his aid (§ 5).—[Here the second
speech of the accused could naturally follow. But the accused has, in the meantime, taken advantage of the Athenian law by withdrawing into voluntary exile. The judges
have no longer any power to punish him. A friend, however,

who was a bystander of the quarrel, comes forward to defend
the innocence of the accused.]   The guilt, he maintains, lies
with the old man; he, as can be proved, gave the first blow
(Δ. §§ 2—5); he is at once the murdered and the murderer
(§ 8).

The line thus taken by the defence is remarkable.
It relies chiefly on the provocation alleged to have
been given by the deceased.   But it does not insist
upon this provocation as mitigating the guilt of the
accused.   It insists upon it as transferring the whole
guilt from the accused to the dead man.   Athenian
law recognised only two kinds of homicide; that
which was purely accidental, and that which resulted
from some deliberate act.   In the latter case, whether
there had been an intent to kill or not, some one
must be a murderer.   Thus, here, it would not have
been enough for the defence to show that the accused
had, without intent to kill, and under provocation,
done a fatal injury.   It is necessary to go on to
argue that the deceased was guilty of his own
murder.

The literary form of the Third Tetralogy deserves
notice in two respects; for the solemnity and
majesty of the language in the accuser's first address; and for the vivacity lent by rhetorical question and answer to part of the first speech of the
defendant[1]—a vivacity which distinguishes it, as
regards style, from everything else in these studies.

Of extant speeches written by Antiphon for real
causes, by far the most important is that On the   *Speech On
the Murder
Murder of Herodes.   The facts of the case were as   *of Herodes.*

---

[1] Tetral. III. B. §§ 2, 3.

follows. Herodes, an Athenian citizen, had settled at Mytilene in 427 B.C. after the revolt and reduction of that town. He was one of the kleruchs among whom its territory was apportioned, but not otherwise wealthy[1]. Having occasion to make a voyage to Aenos on the coast of Thrace, to receive the ransom of some Thracian captives who were in his hands, he sailed from Mytilene with the accused,—a young man whose father, a citizen of Mytilene, lived chiefly at Aenos[2]. Herodes and his companion were driven by a storm to put in at Methymna on the north-west coast of Lesbos; and there, as the weather was wet, exchanged their open vessel for another which was decked. After they had been drinking on board together, Herodes went ashore at night, and was never seen again. The accused, after making every inquiry for him, went on to Aenos in the open vessel; while the decked vessel, into which they had moved at Methymna, returned to Mytilene[3]. On reaching the latter place again, the defendant was charged by the relatives of Herodes with having murdered him at the instigation of Lykînos, an Athenian[4] living at Mytilene, who had been on bad terms with the deceased. They rested their charge principally on three grounds. First, that the sole companion of the missing man must naturally be considered accountable for his disappearance. Secondly, that a slave had confessed under torture to having assisted the defendant in the murder. Thirdly, that

[1] § 58.   [2] § 78.
[3] Compare § 28 with § 23.
[4] See § 61; and also § 62, ἀπεσ-τέρει μὲν ἐμὲ τῆς πατρίδος, ἀπεσ-τέρει δὲ αὐτὸν ἱερῶν, which implies, as Blass points out, that Lesbos was not the πατρίς of Lykînos, as it was of the defendant.

on board the vessel which returned from Methymna
had been found a letter in which the defendant
announced to Lykînos the accomplishment of the
murder.

It was necessary that the trial should take place *Mode of*
legal
at Athens, whither all subject-allies were compelled *procedure.*
to bring their criminal causes. The ordinary course
would have been to have laid an indictment for
murder (γραφὴ φόνου) before the Areiopagos. Instead, however, of doing this the relatives of Herodes
laid an information against the accused as a 'malefactor'[1]. He was accordingly to be tried by an ordinary dikastery under the presidency of the Eleven.
'Malefactor,' at Athens, ordinarily meant a thief,
a housebreaker, a kidnapper, or criminal of the like
class; but the term was, of course, applicable to
murder, especially if accompanied by robbery. Instances of persons accused of murder being proceeded against, not by an indictment, but by an
information, and being summarily arrested without previous inquiry, occur only a few years later
than the probable date of this speech[2]. When,

---

[1] ἔνδειξις κακουργίας: cf. § 9
κακοῦργος ἐνδεδειγμένος. When the
accused arrived in Athens, he was,
on the strength of the ἔνδειξις,
arrested by the Eleven : § 85 ἀπή-
χθην. Hence in § 9 he speaks of
ταύτην τὴν ἀπαγωγήν. The terms
ἔνδειξις κακουργίας and ἀπαγωγὴ
κακουργίας do not denote two different processes, but two parts of
the same process. Ἔνδειξις was the
laying of information against a
person not yet apprehended : ἀπ-

αγωγή was the act of apprehending
him.

[2] The two murderers of Phrynichos in 411 were 'seized and put
in prison' by his friends (ληφθέντων
καὶ ἐς τὸ δεσμωτήριον ἀποτεθέντων),
—that is, were proceeded against
by ἀπαγωγή: Lykurgos *in Leokr.*
§ 12. The procedure in the case
of Agoratos (391 B.C.), again, was
by an ἔνδειξις, not by a γραφὴ
φόνου, and there was an ἀπαγωγή
of the accused (Lys. *in Agorat.*

therefore, the accused contends that the form of the
procedure was unprecedented and illegal, this is probably to be understood as an exaggeration of the fact
that it was unusual. In two ways it must have
been distasteful to the prisoner; first, as an indig-
nity; secondly, as a positive disadvantage. Trial
before the Areiopagos left to the prisoner the option
of withdrawing from the country before sentences;
and imposed upon the accuser a peculiarly solemn
oath[1]. In this case, moreover, the unusual (though
not illegal) procedure was accompanied by unjust
rigours. When the accused arrived in Athens,
although he offered the three sureties required by
law, his bail was refused; he was imprisoned. This
treatment, of which he reasonably complains[2], may
have been due in part to the unpopularity of Mytileneans at Athens, and to the fact that Herodes had
been an Athenian citizen.

Date of the speech. The date of the speech must lie between the
capture of Mytilene in 427[3] B.C. and the revolt of
Lesbos in 412 B.C. The accused says that in 427 B.C.

---

§ 85). Strictly speaking the ἔνδειξις
and ἀπαγωγή were applicable only
to those cases in which the accused
was taken ἐπ᾽ αὐτοφώρῳ: that is,
in which no further proof of his
guilt was required. Thus Pollux
defines ἔνδειξις as ὁμολογουμένου
ἀδικήματος μήνυσις, οὐ κρίσεως ἀλλὰ
τιμωρίας δεομένου. Agoratos appears to have raised this very point:
Lys. *in Agor.* § 85. But, since the
procedure of the Areiopagos was
so highly favourable to the accused,
a prosecutor would generally prefer the procedure by ἔνδειξις if

there was any decent pretence for
it. And the condition of *manifest*
guilt does not seem to have been
rigorously insisted upon by the
authorities. There was, probably,
a feeling that the forms of the
Areiopagos would be in a manner
profaned by application to crimi-
nals of the vilest class.

[1] *De caed. Herod.* § 12, δέον σε
διομόσασθαι ὅρκον τὸν μέγιστον καὶ
ἰσχυρότατον, ἐξώλειαν αὑτῷ καὶ γέ-
νει καὶ οἰκίᾳ τῇ σῇ ἐπαρώμενον.

[2] § 17.

[3] § 76.

he was too young[1] to understand the events which
were passing, and that he knows them only by
hearsay. On the other hand, he can hardly have
been less than twenty at the time of the trial.
Kirchner[2] and Blass are inclined to place the speech
about 421 B.C.; it would perhaps be better to put
it three or four years later, about 417 or 416 B.C.
On the other hand, a slight indication—which seems
to have escaped notice—appears to show that it was
at least earlier than the spring of 415 B.C. The
accused brings together several instances in which
great crimes had never been explained[3]. If the
mutilation of the Hermae had then taken place, he
could scarcely have failed to notice so striking an
example.

The speech opens with a proem in which the defendant *Analysis.*
pleads his youth and inexperience (§§ 1—7) ; and which is
followed by a preliminary argument (προκατασκευή) on the
informality of the procedure (§§ 8—18). The defendant
then gives a narrative of the facts up to his arrival at Aenos
(§§ 19—24) ; and shows that the probabilities, as depending
upon the facts thus far stated, are against the story of the
prosecutors (§§ 25—28). The second part of the narrative
describes how the vessel into which Herodes and the defendant had moved at Methymna returned to Mytilene ; how
the slave was tortured, and under torture accused the defendant of murder (§§ 29—30).

The defendant now concentrates his force upon proving
the testimony of the slave to be worthless (§§ 31—51). He
next discusses the statement of the prosecutors that a letter,
in which he announced the murder to Lykînos, had been
found on board the returning vessel (§§ 52—56). He shows

---

[1] § 75.
[2] Kirchner *De temporibus ora-*
tionum Antiphont. pp. 2 ff., quoted

by Blass, *Attisch. Bereds.* p. 166.
[3] §§ 67—70.

that he could have had no motive for the murder (§§ 57—63).
He maintains that he cannot justly be required to suggest
a solution of the mystery. It is enough if he establishes his
own innocence. Many crimes have finally baffled investi-
gation (§§ 64—73). He notices the reproaches brought
against his father as having taken part in the revolt of
Mytilene and having been generally disloyal to Athens
(§§ 74—80).

Besides all the other proofs, the innocence of the prisoner
is vindicated by the absence of signs of the divine anger.
Voyages and sacrifices in which he has taken part have
always been prosperous (§§ 81—84). In a concluding appeal
the judges are reminded that, in any case, justice cannot
be frustrated by his acquittal, since it will still be possible
to bring him before the Areiopagos (§§ 85—95).

Remarks.   In reviewing the whole speech as an argument,
the first thing which strikes us is the notable contrast between the line of defence taken here and that
traced for a case essentially similar in the model-
speeches of the First Tetralogy. There, the defendant employs all his ingenuity in suggesting ex-
planations of the mysterious crime which shall make
the hypothesis of his own guilt unnecessary. Here,
the defendant pointedly refuses to do any thing of
the kind. It is enough if he can show that he was
not the murderer; it is not his business to show who
was or might have been. On this broad, plain
ground the defence takes a firm stand. The arguments are presented in a natural order, as they arise
out of the facts narrated, and are drawn out at a
length proportionate to their consequence,—by far
the greatest stress being laid on the worthlessness
of the slave's evidence; in discussing which, indeed,

the speaker is not very consistent[1]. One apparent omission is curious. The prisoner incidentally says that he never left the vessel on the night when Herodes went on shore and disappeared[2]; but he does not dwell upon, or attempt to prove, this all-essential *alibi*. If the numerous commonplaces and general sentiments seem to us a source of weakness rather than strength, allowance must be made for the taste and fashion of the time; and every one must recognise the effectiveness of the appeal to divine signs in which the argument finds its rhetorical climax.

As a composition, the speech has great merits. The êthos, indeed, is not artistic; a style so dignified and so sententious is scarcely suitable to a speaker who is continually apologising for his youth and inexperience. Nor, except in the passage which touches on the ruin of Mytilene[3], is there even an attempt at pathos. But there is variety and versatility; the opening passage is artistically elaborate, the concluding, impressive in a higher way; while the purely argumentative part of the speech is not encumbered with any stiff dignity, but is clear,

---

[1] In § 39 it is contended that the slave cannot have represented himself as taking part in the murder, but only as helping to dispose of the corpse. In § 54, on the contrary, it is assumed that the slave represented himself as the actual murderer. Lastly, in § 68, the view taken in § 39 is not only reasserted, but is ascribed to the adversaries as their own.

[2] § 26 λέγουσι δὲ ὡς ἐν μὲν τῇ γῇ ἀπέθανεν ὁ ἀνήρ, κἀγὼ λίθον ἐπέβαλον αὐτῷ εἰς τὴν κεφαλήν, ὃς οὐκ ἐξέβην τὸ παράπαν ἐκ τοῦ πλοίου.

[3] § 79 : 'For all Mytileneans, the memory of their past error has been made indelible; they exchanged great prosperity for great misery ; they beheld their country made desolate.'

simple, and sufficiently animated. Altogether the
style has less sustained elevation, but shows more
flexibility, greater maturity and mastery, than that
of the Tetralogies.

Speech On the Choreutes.   The speech On the Choreutes relates to the death
of Diodotos, a boy who was in training as member of
a chorus to be produced at the Thargelia, and who
was poisoned by a draught given to him to improve
his voice[1]. The accused is the choregus, an Athenian
citizen, who discharged that office for his own and
another tribe, and at whose house the chorus received
their lessons. The accuser, Philokrates, brother of the
deceased Diodotos, laid an information for poisoning
before the Archon Basileus; and after some delay,
the case came before the Areiopagos[2]. It was not
contended that the accused had intended to murder
the boy, but only that he had ordered to be ad-

---

[1] The object with which the
draught was given is not stated in
the speech itself: but the argument says εὐφωνίας χάριν ἔπιε φάρ-
μακον καὶ πιὼν τέθνηκεν. Compare
the passage in which Plutarch
speaks of the pains taken to train
the voices of the chorus (*De glor.
Athen.* c. 6): οἱ δὲ χορηγοὶ τοῖς
χορευταῖς ἐγχέλια καὶ θριδάκια καὶ
σκελλίδας καὶ μυελὸν παρατιθέντες
εὐώχουν ἐπὶ πολὺν χρόνον φωνασ-
κουμένους καὶ τρυφῶντας.

[2] That the Areiopagos was the
court which tried the case appears
certain (1) because that court alone
had jurisdiction in γραφαὶ φαρμά-
κων: (2) because the special compliment to the court as 'the most
conscientious and upright in Greece'
(§ 51) points to the Areiopagos

Some have supposed that this case
came before court at the Palladion,
because, in § 16, the accused is
spoken of as βουλεύσας τὸν θάνατον,
and, according to Harpokration,
cases of βούλευσις were tried at
the Palladion by the Ephetae. But
the βούλευσις of Harpokration is a
technical term, = ἐπιβούλευσις, and
denotes the intent to kill in cases
in which death had not actually
followed. On the other hand, the
accused here is said βουλεῦσαι τὸν
θάνατον merely in the sense that it
was *by his order* that the draught
was given to the boy, though he
did not hand the cup to him. No
intent to murder was imputed to
him: see § 19 οἱ κατήγοροι ὁμολο-
γοῦσι μὴ ἐκ προνοίας μηδ᾽ ἐκ παρα-
σκευῆς γενέσθαι τὸν θάνατον.

ministered to him the draught which caused his
death. According to Athenian law this was, however, a capital offence. The present speech is the
second made by the defendant, and the last, therefore, of the trial. Its date may probably be placed
soon after the Sicilian disaster [1].

In a long proem, the accused dwells on the advantage *Analysis.*
of a good conscience—on the excellence of the court of the
Areiopagos—and on the weight of a judicial decision in
such a case (§§ 1—6). He goes on to complain of the manner
in which the adversaries have mixed up irrelevant charges
with the true issue; he will address himself to the latter, and
then refute the former (§§ 7—10). A narrative of the facts
is then begun; but he breaks it off with the remark that
it would be easy to expose the falsehoods contained in the
adversary's second speech, and that he will now bring proofs
(§§ 11—15). The testimony of witnesses is adduced and
commented upon (§§ 16—19). The defendant goes on to
contrast his own conduct in the matter with that of the
accuser; dwells on the refusal of his challenge to an examination of slaves; and urges the strength in all points of
his case (§§ 20—32). The evidence closed, he digresses

---

[1] In §§ 12, 21, 55 the choregus
speaks of having brought an action
for embezzlement of public monies
against Philînos and two other
persons. Now Antiphon wrote a
speech κατὰ Φιλίνου,—very probably, as Sauppe conjectures, a-
gainst this same Philînos when
prosecuted by the choregus: and
from the speech κατὰ Φιλίνου are
quoted the words, τούς τε θῆτας
ἅπαντας ὁπλίτας ποιῆσαι. Sauppe
thinks this points to a time just
after the Sicilian disaster: 'in
illis enim rerum angustiis videntur
Athenienses thetes ad arma vo-
casse.' (*Or. Att.* vol. II. p. 144.)

This is quite possible: but Sauppe's
other argument that the fact of
the choregus representing *two*
tribes (§ 11) points to a contrac-
tion of public expenses in a time of
distress, is not worth much, since
we do not know that this may not
have been the usual custom at the
Thargelia. At any rate the decidedly modern character of the
speech as compared with the *De
caed. Herodis* warrants us in placing it some years after the latter,
which (as has been said above)
was probably spoken between 421
and 416 B. C.

into a full review of the adversaries' conduct from the first, in order to illustrate their malice and dishonesty. 'What judges,' he asks in conclusion, 'would they not deceive, if they have dared to trifle with the awful oath under which they came before this court?' (§§ 33—51.)

Remarks.　　It seems probable that the end of the speech has been lost. Standing last in the MSS. of Antiphon, it would thus be the more liable to mutilation; and in the concluding speech of a trial the orator would scarcely have broken the rule, which he observes in every other instance, of finishing with an appeal to the judges. The fact that a rhetorical promise made in the speech[1] is not literally fulfilled need not be insisted upon to strengthen this view.

In the speech On the Murder of Herodes, Antiphon had to rely mainly on his skill in argument; here, witnesses were available, the case against the accusers was strong, and little was needed but a judicious marshalling of proofs. This is ably managed; but, as a display of power, the speech is necessarily of inferior interest. The Mytilenean defendant in the Herodes case and the choregus here speak in the same general tone—with a certain directness and earnestness; but the common êthos is more strongly marked here, as the personality of the speaker comes more decidedly forward. In other points of style there is a striking contrast between

---

[1] In § 8 the speaker says that he will first deal with the matter at issue, and then meet certain other charges which the adversaries have brought against him, but which he feels sure that he can turn to their own discomfiture. The promise, however, is conditional — ἐὰν ὑμῖν ἡδομένοις ᾖ: and is, in effect, if not literally, fulfilled by the digression (§§ 33—51) in which he brings out the malicious character of their whole conduct towards him.

the earlier and the later oration. The proem here is, indeed, as measured and as elaborate as any thing in the earlier work. But it stands alone; in the rest of the speech there is no stiffness. The language is that of ordinary life; the sentences are more flowing, if not always clear; the style is enlivened by question and exclamation, instead of being ornamented with antitheses and parallelisms; and already the beginning of a transition to the easier, more practical style of the later eloquence is well-marked.

The short speech entitled 'Against a Step-mother, on a Charge of Poisoning,' treats of a case which, like the preceding, belonged to the jurisdiction of the Areiopagos. The speaker, a young man, is the son of the deceased. He charges his step-mother with having poisoned his father several years before[1], by the instrumentality of a woman who was her dupe. The deceased and a friend, Philoneos, the woman's lover, had been dining together; and she was persuaded to administer a philtre to both, in hope of recovering her lover's affection. Both the men died; and the woman—a slave—was put to death forthwith. The accuser now asks that the real criminal, —the true Klytaemnestra[2] of this tragedy,—shall suffer punishment. *Speech Against a Stepmother.*

After deprecating in a proem (§§ 1—4) the odium to which his position exposes him, and commenting on the refusal of the adversaries to give up their slaves for examination (§§ 5—13), the speaker states the facts of the case. (§§ 14—20.) He goes on to contrast his own part as his father's avenger with that of his brother, the champion of *Analysis.*

[1] § 30. [2] § 7.

the murderess (§§ 21—25); appeals for sympathy and re-tribution (§§ 26—27); denies that his brother's oath to the innocence of the accused can have any good ground, whereas his own oath to the justice of his cause is supported by his father's dying declaration (§§ 28—30); and concludes by saying that he has discharged his solemn duty, and that it now remains for the judges to do theirs. (§ 31.)

Remarks.

Two questions have been raised in connexion with this speech; whether it was written merely for practice; and whether it was the work of Antiphon. I. It has been urged that stories of this kind were often chosen as subjects by the rhetoricians of the schools; that the designation of the ac-cused as Klytaemnestra is melodramatic; that the name Philoneos (Φιλόνεως) seems fictitious; that the address to the Areiopagites as ὦ δικάζοντες in § 7 is strange; and that the speech stands in the mss. before the Tetralogies[1]. The last ob-

---

[1] Spengel rejects the speech, but without assigning reasons (συν. τεχνῶν, p. 118). The special ob-jections mentioned above were advanced by Maetzner, an editor of Antiphon, and are examined by Dr. P. G. Ottsen in a tract *De rerum inventione ac dispositione quae est in Lysiae atque Anti-phontis orationibus* (Flensburg, 1847). If the speech was written as a mere exercise, then it cer-tainly is not the work of Antiphon, who would have treated the subject as he treats the subjects of the Te-tralogies—in outline merely, with-out needless details of name or place. But there is no good ground for assuming that the speech was

not spoken in a real cause. The story has some melodramatic fea-tures, but contains nothing which might not have occurred in ordi-nary Greek life. With the de-signation of the accused as Kly-taemnestra, compare Andok. *de Myst.* § 129, τίς ἂν εἴη οὗτος; Οἰδί-πους ἢ Αἴγισθος; ἢ τί χρὴ αὐτὸν ὀνομόσαι; Isaeos mentions Διοκλέα τὸν Φλυέα, τὸν Ὀρέστην ἐπικαλού-μενον: *de Cirrh. hered.* (Or. VIII.) § 3. Maetzner derived the name Φιλόνεως from φίλος and ναῦς, and thought it suspicious that such a name should be given to a resi-dent in the Peiraeus. Ottsen ac-cepts the etymology, but does not share the suspicion. Even if Φιλό-

jection alone requires notice. The place of the
speech in the mss. is, as Blass observes, due to
the fact that it is the only accusatory speech;
the Tetralogies comprise both accusation and defence; then come the defensive orations[1]. On the
other hand the prominence of narrative and the
entire absence of argument in this speech—in direct
contrast to the Tetralogies, which are all argument
and no narrative—and the unfitness of the subject
for practising the ingenuity of an advocate, seem
conclusive against the view that this was a mere
exercise. II. The question of authenticity is more
difficult. As regards matter, nothing can be weaker
than the speech. There is no argument. An un-
supported assertion that the accused had attempted
the same crime before; the belief of the deceased
that his wife was guilty; the refusal of the adversaries to give up their slaves; these are the only
proofs. As regards style, there is much clumsy
verbiage[2]. On the other hand, the narrative (§§
14—20) shows real tragic power, especially in the

νεως could be equivalent to Φιλόναυς
(cf. λιπόναυς, μυριόναυς, &c.), the fact
of a person so called living at a sea-
port would be about as strange as
the fact of a person called Philip living at Ἄργος ἱππόβοτον. Lastly, as
to the ὦ δικάζοντες in § 7, the great
variety of forms used by Greek
orators in addressing the judges
would forbid us to pronounce this
one inadmissible because it is unusual. But the genuineness of
the words is not above suspicion.
Blass, in his edition of Antiphon,

brackets as spurious the words in
§ 7, πῶς οὖν περὶ τούτων, ὦ δικάζοντες—οὐκ εἴληφε. One good ms.
omits them; and they seem like a
scholium on what immediately pre-
cedes.

[1] *Attisch. Bereds.* p. 180.

[2] e. g. § 21 τῷ τεθνεῶτι ὑμᾶς κε-
λεύω καὶ τῷ ἠδικημένῳ .. τιμω-
ροὺς γενέσθαι...ἄξιος καὶ ἐλέου καὶ
βοηθείας καὶ τιμωρίας παρ᾽ ὑμῶν
τυχεῖν...§ 22 ἀθέμιτα καὶ ἀτέλεστα
καὶ ἀνήκουστα...§ 23 δικασταὶ ἐγέν-
εσθε καὶ ἐκλήθητε.

contrast drawn between the unconsciousness of the
miserable dupe and the craft of the instigator;
throughout there is a pathos of the same kind as
that of the Tetralogies, but higher; and lastly there
is a strong resemblance to a particular passage in the
speech On the Choreutes[1]. The conclusion to which
Blass comes appears sensible[2]. Our knowledge of
Antiphon's style is not so complete as to justify this
rejection of the speech; but it must in any case be
assigned to a period when both his argumentative
skill and his power as a composer were still in a
rude stage of their development.

Lost works.   Besides the extant compositions, twenty-four
others, bearing the name of Antiphon, are known
by their titles. Among these three deserve especial
notice, because their titles have occasioned different
inferences as to their contents, and because it is now
tolerably certain that they belong, not to Antiphon

Authorship of the treatises On Truth, On Concord, On Statesmanship. the orator, but to Antiphon the sophist[3]. These
are the 'speeches' (or rather essays) On Truth, On
Concord, On Statesmanship[4]. As regards the first of
these, indeed, the testimony of Hermogenes[5] that it

---

[1] Compare § 1 with *de Choreuta* § 27.

[2] *Att. Bereds.* p. 184.

[3] See p. 2, note 3.

[4] ἀληθείας λόγοι Β:—περὶ ὁμονοίας:—πολιτικός. The fragments are given in Sauppe's *Fragm.Oratt. Att.* pp. 145 ff. printed in Baiter and Sauppe's *Oratores Attici*, and in the edition of Antiphon by Blass, pp. 124—143 (Teubner, 1871).

[5] Hermog. περὶ ἰδεῶν. II. c. 11. p. 414. There were two Antiphons, he says, ὧν εἷς μέν ἐστιν ὁ ῥήτωρ, οὖπερ

οἱ φονικοὶ φέρονται λόγοι καὶ δημηγορικοὶ καὶ ὅσοι τούτοις ὅμοιοι. ἕτερος δὲ ὁ καὶ τερατοσκόπος καὶ ὀνειροκρίτης λεγόμενος γενέσθαι, οὗπερ οἵ τε περὶ τῆς ἀληθείας λέγονται λόγοι καὶ ὁ περὶ ὁμονοίας καὶ οἱ δημηγορικοὶ καὶ ὁ πολιτικός. Spengel proposed to detach the words καὶ ὁ περὶ ὁμονοίας καὶ οἱ δημηγορικοὶ καὶ ὁ πολιτικός from the last clause, and to insert them in the first clause after φέρονται λόγοι, (omitting, of course, the καὶ δημηγ. which already stands there, and

was the work of the Sophist has scarcely been
questioned. But the treatise On Concord has often
been given to the orator on the assumption that it
was a speech, enforcing the importance of harmony,
which he delivered in some political crisis, perhaps
at the moment when the Four Hundred were
threatened with ruin by internal dissensions[1]. The
treatise on Statesmanship, again, might, as far as
the title witnesses, have been a practical exposition of oligarchical principles by the eloquent
colleague of Peisandros. An examination of the
fragments leads, however, to the almost certain
conclusion that all these three works must be
ascribed to the Sophist. The essay On Truth was
a physical treatise, in which cosmic phenomena
were explained mechanically in the fashion of the
Ionic School[2]. The essay On Concord was an ethical

the τε in οἵ τε περὶ τῆς ἀληθείας).
He would thus make Hermogenes
ascribe the περὶ ὁμονοίας and the
πολιτικός to Antiphon the orator,
and the ἀληθείας λόγοι *only* to
Antiphon the sophist. But this is
an arbitrary and violent treatment
of the text. Sauppe is no doubt
right in thinking that its only cor-
ruption is the recurrence of οἱ
δημηγορικοί in the second clause.
The article had been accidentally
left out where the word first occurs,
and a corrector wrote οἱ δημηγορικοί
at full length in the margin, whence
it crept into the text a second
time.

[1] In reference to the meeting of
the Four Hundred on the day after
the mutiny of the hoplites in the
Peiraeus (Thuc. VIII. 92, 93), Mr

Grote says—'It may probably have
been in this meeting of the Four
Hundred that Antiphon delivered
his oration strongly recommending
concord.' (*Hist. Gr.* c. 62, vol. VIII.
p. 94 *n.*) 'In hoc autem libro,'
(says Blass, *Antiphon* p. 130)
'sicut fragmenta docent, de mori-
bus sophista disserebat deque
vitae brevitate et aerumnis: rem-
publicam vero civiumque concor-
diam nusquam attigit.'

[2] Protagoras called his Treatise
of Natural Philosophy ἀλήθεια, ἢ
περὶ τοῦ ὄντος. The most suggestive fragment of the ἀληθείας λόγοι
is no. 13 in Sauppe's list (*fragm.
Or. Graec.* p. 149). Galen ad
Hippokr. *epidem.* I. 3. vol. 17, 1.
p. 681 (Kühn) says:—οὕτω δὲ καὶ
παρ' Ἀντιφῶντι κατὰ τὸ δεύτερον,

treatise, exhorting all men to live in harmony and friendship, instead of embittering their short lives by strife[1]. The essay on Statesmanship was no party-pamphlet, but a discussion of the training required to produce a capable citizen[2]. Besides the speeches known to the ancients, a work on the Art

The Rhetoric. of Rhetoric[3], and a collection of Proems and Epilogues[4], were current under Antiphon's name.

The collection of Proems and Epilogues. Sauppe and Spengel[5] believe the Tetralogies to be examples taken from the Rhetoric; the latter, however, is expressly condemned as spurious by Pollux[6]. The collection of Proems and Epilogues may, as Blass[7] suggests, have furnished the opening and concluding passages of the Speech On the Murder of Herodes, and the opening passage of that On the Choreutes. In the latter case the difference of style between the proem and all that follows it is certainly striking.

τῆς 'Αληθείας ἔστιν εὑρεῖν γεγραμμένην τὴν προσηγορίαν ἐν τῇδε τῇ ῥήσει· ὅταν οὖν γένωνται ἐν τῷ ἀέρι ὄμβροι τε καὶ πνεύματα ὑπενάντια ἀλλήλοις, τότε συστρέφεται τὸ ὕδωρ καὶ πυκνοῦται κατὰ πολλά, κ. τ. λ.

[1] See, for instance, fragments 1 and 4 of the περὶ ὁμονοίας in Sauppe:—ἀναθέσθαι δὲ ὥσπερ πεττὸν τὸν βίον οὐκ ἔστιν...πολλοὶ δ' ἔχοντες φίλους οὐ γιγνώσκουσιν, ἀλλ' ἑταίρους ποιοῦνται θῶπας, πλούτου καὶ τύχης κόλακας.

[2] For instance, in fragment 2 of the πολιτικός we have a precept on the value of a character for steady business habits—μήτε φιλοπότην κληθῆναι καὶ δοκεῖν τὰ πράγματα

καταμελεῖν ὑπ' οἴνου ἡσσώμενον.

[3] ῥητορικαὶ τέχναι.

[4] προοίμια καὶ ἐπίλογοι.

[5] Sauppe, *Fragm. Oratt. Gr.* p. 145.

[6] Pollux (VI. 143) quotes a word as used by Antiphon ἐν ταῖς ῥητορικαῖς τέχναις: but adds—δοκοῦσι δ' οὐ γνήσιαι.

[7] *Attisch. Bereds.* p. 103, where he quotes (note 7) Cic. *Brut.* 47 for the statement of Aristotle—*huic (Gorgiae) Antiphontem Rhamnusium similia quaedam habuisse conscripta:* — where *conscripta* seems to mean a collection of *communes loci* stored up to be used as they might be wanted.

CHAPTER IV.

ANDOKIDES.

LIFE.

THE life of Andokides has, in one broad aspect, a striking analogy to the life of Antiphon. Each man stands forth for a moment a conspicuous actor in one great scene, while the rest of his history is but dimly known; and each, at that moment, appears as an oligarch exposed to the suspicion and dislike of the democracy. The Revolution of the Four Hundred is the decisive and final event in the life of Antiphon. The mutilation of the Hermae is the first, but hardly less decisive event, in the known life of Andokides; the event which, for thirteen years afterwards, absolutely determined his fortunes, and which throws its shadow over all that is known of their sequel.

Andokides was born probably about 440 B.C.[1] Birth of Andokides. The deme Kydathene, of which he was a member, was included in the Pandionian tribe. His family was traced by Hellanikos the genealogist through

---

[1] According to [Lys.] *in Andok.* § 46, he was in 399 B.C. πλέον ἢ τετταράκοντα ἔτη γεγονώς. He speaks of his 'youthfulness' in 415 B.C.: *de Red.* § 7. His father, Leogoras II., may have been born about 470: Andokides I. about 500: Leogoras I. about 540. The pseudo-Plutarch puts his birth in the archonship of Theagenides, Ol. 78. 1, 468 B.C.: probably on the assumption that the orator was the Andokides of Thuc. I. 51.

Odysseus up to the god Hermes[1], and had been known in Athenian history for at least three generations. Leogoras, his great grandfather, had fought against the Peisistratidae[2]. Andokides the elder, his grandfather, was one of ten envoys who negotiated the Thirty Years' Truce with Sparta in 445[3]; and had commanded with Perikles at Samos in 440[4], and with Glaukon at Corcyra in 435[5]. Leogoras, father of the orator, was, to judge from Aristophanes, famous chiefly for his dinners and his pheasants[6].

The only glimpse of the life of Andokides before 415 B. C. is afforded by himself. He belonged to a set or club, of which one Euphiletos was a leading member[7], and with which his address ' To His Associates ' (πρὸς τοὺς ἑταίρους), mentioned by Plutarch, has sometimes been con-

---

[1] [Plut.] *Vit. Andok.* γένους Εὐπατριδῶν, ὡς δὲ Ἑλλάνικος, καὶ ἀπὸ Ἑρμοῦ· καθήκει γὰρ εἰς αὐτὸν τὸ Κηρύκων γένος. The pseudo-Plutarch seems to have inferred from the fact that the descent of Andokides was traced from Hermes, that he belonged to the priestly family of the Κήρυκες, who represented their ancestor Κῆρυξ as the son of Hermes (Paus. I. 38. 3). But Plutarch (*Alkib.* c. 21) tells us that Hellanikos traced Andokides up to Odysseus; the line from Hermes, then, was not through Kēryx, but through Autolykos, whose daughter Antikleia was mother of Odysseus.

[2] Andok. *de Myst.* § 106. In *de Red.* § 26 Valckenär and Sauppe read ὁ τοῦ ἐμοῦ πατρὸς πάππος instead of ὁ τοῦ ἐμοῦ πατρὸς πρόπαππος.

[3] Andok. *de Pace* § 6.

[4] Schol. Aristid. III. 485, ap. Blass *Att. Bereds.* p. 270.

[5] Thuc. I. 51.

[6] Ar. *Vesp.* 1269: *Nub.* 109 τοὺς φασιανοὺς οὓς τρέφει Λεωγόρας. Athen. IX. p. 387 A κωμωδεῖται γὰρ ὁ Λεωγόρας ὡς γαστρίμαργος ὑπὸ Πλάτωνος ἐν Περιαλγεῖ. Besides his son Andokides, Leogoras had a daughter who married Kallias a son of Telekles: *de Myst.* § 117: cf. §§ 42, 50.

[7] *De Myst.* §§ 61—63. Euphiletos is there described as proposing the sacrilege at a convivial meeting of the club (εἰσηγήσατο... πινόντων ἡμῶν § 61). Its members were intimate associates (ἐπιτήδειοι § 63: cf. οἷς ἐχρῶ καὶ οἷς συνῆσθα § 49). There is nothing to show that this club of young men was anything so serious as a political ἑταιρεία.

nected[1]. It was in May, 415, when he was about *Affair of the Hermae.*
twenty-five, when the Peiraeus was alive with pre-
parations for the sailing of the fleet to Sicily, and
all men were full of dreams of a new empire opening
to the city, that Athens was astonished by a sacrilege,
of which it is hard now to realise the precise effect
upon the Athenian mind. When it appeared that
the images of Hermes throughout the town—in the
marketplace, before the doors of houses, before the
temples—had been mutilated in the night, the sense
of a horrible impiety was joined to a sense of helpless-
ness against revolution[2]; for to an Athenian it would
occur instinctively that the motive of the mutilators
had been not simply to insult, but to estrange, the
tutelar gods of the city. This terror, while still
fresh, was intensified by the rumoured travesties in
private houses of the innermost sacrament of Greek
religion, the Mysteries of Eleusis. In order to
understand the position of Andokides, it is necessary to keep these two affairs distinct. There is
nothing to shew that he was in any way concerned,
as accomplice or as informer, with the profanation
of the Mysteries. As a matter of course, the author
of the speech against him asserts it[3]; but his own
denial is emphatic and clear[4], and agrees with what
is known from other sources. It was in the affair

---

[1] Plut. *Them.* c. 32. See ch. VI.
ad fin.

[2] Thuc. VI. 27 καὶ τὸ πρᾶγμα
μειζόνως ἐλάμβανον· τοῦ τε γὰρ
ἔκπλου οἰωνὸς ἐδόκει εἶναι καὶ ἐπὶ
ξυνωμοσίᾳ ἅμα νεωτέρων πραγμάτων καὶ δήμου καταλύσεως γεγενῆσθαι. Cf. Isokr. *de Bigis* § 6.

[3] [Lys.] *in Andok.* § 51 μιμού-
μενος τὰ ἱερὰ ἐπεδείκνυε τοῖς ἀμυή-
τοις, κ.τ.λ.

[4] Andok. *de Myst.* § 29 περὶ
μὲν τῶν μυστηρίων...ἀποδέδεικταί
μοι ὡς οὔτε ἠσέβηκα οὔτε μεμή-
νυκα, κ.τ.λ.

of the Hermae alone that he was implicated. The
first important evidence in this matter was given by
Teukros, a resident-alien, who had fled to Megara,
and who was brought back to give information under
a promise of impunity. This man denounced twelve
persons as guilty in regard to the Mysteries, and
eighteen as mutilators of the Hermae. Among the
eighteen were Euphiletos and other members of the
club to which Andokides belonged; of whom some
were at once put to death, and others fled[1].

But there was a very general belief that the
bottom of the matter had not been reached, and
that the conspiracy had been far more widely spread;
a belief which the commissioners of enquiry, especially Peisandros, seem to have encouraged. As
usual in such cases, the demand for discoveries
created the supply. Diokleides, the Titus Oates of
this plot, came forward to state that the conspiracy
included no less than three hundred persons. Forty-
two of these were denounced, among whom were
Andokides, his father, his brother-in-law and ten
other of his relatives. They were imprisoned at
once; Diokleides was feasted as a public benefactor
at the Prytaneion; and the whole town spent the
night under arms, panic-stricken by the extent of
the conspiracy,—not knowing whence, when, or in
what strength they might be attacked by the
enemies of gods and men[2]. Andokides has described
the first night in prison. Wives, sisters, children,
who had been allowed to come to their friends, joined
in their tears and cries of despair. Then it was that

---

[1] *De Myst.* § 35.   [2] *De Myst.* § 45.

Charmides, one of his cousins, besought him to tell all that he knew, and to save his father, his relations and all the innocent citizens who were threatened with an infamous death. Andokides yielded. He was brought before the Council, and stated that the story of Teukros was true. The eighteen who had died or fled were indeed guilty. But there were four more whom Teukros had left out, and whom Andokides now named. These four fled[1].

The deposition of Andokides, confirming as it did the testimony of Teukros, and at the same time supplementing that testimony, was accepted, at least at the time, as the true and complete account. The affair of the Hermae was dropped, and attention was fixed once more upon the affair of the Mysteries[2]. At some time not much later, Leogoras, the father of Andokides, gained an action which he brought against the senator Speusippos, who had illegally committed for trial Leogoras and the other persons accused by the slave Lydos of having profaned the Mysteries in the house of his master Pherekles[3]. Andokides himself was less fortunate. He had given his information under a promise of personal indemnity guaranteed by a decree of the ekklesia. After his disclosures, however, a new decree, proposed by Isotimides, cancelled the former. It pro- *Decree of Isotimides.* vided that those who had committed impiety and confessed it should be excluded from the marketplace and from the temples; a form of ‘disgrace’ (atimia)

---

[1] *De Myst.* § 68.

[2] Thuc. VI. 61 ἐπειδὴ τὸ τῶν Ἑρμῶν ᾤοντο σαφὲς ἔχειν, πολὺ δὴ μᾶλλον καὶ τὰ μυστικὰ ὧν ἐπαίτιος ἦν μετὰ τοῦ αὐτοῦ λόγου καὶ τῆς ξυνωμοσίας ἐπὶ τῷ δήμῳ ἀπ’ ἐκείνου (τοῦ Ἀλκιβιάδου) ἐδόκει πραχθῆναι.

[3] *De Myst.* § 17.

virtually equivalent to banishment. Andokides was considered as falling under this decree, and was accordingly driven to leave Athens.

This closes the first chapter of his life. Two questions directly arising out of it suggest themselves for consideration here.

*The speech
on the
Mysteries.*
First—Does the speech On the Mysteries give the story which he really told before the Council at Athens in 415? In that speech, he represents himself as having stated that the mutilation of the Hermae had been proposed by Euphiletos at a convivial meeting of their club; that he had strenuously opposed it; and that, while he was confined to his house by illness, Euphiletos had seized the opportunity of executing the scheme, telling the others that Andokides had become favourable to it. Now it is a suspicious fact that in the speech On his Return, spoken in 410—that is, eleven years before the speech On the Mysteries—Andokides distinctly pleads guilty to certain offences committed in 415, and excuses them by his youth, his folly, his madness at the time[1]. It is suspicious, also, that not merely the author of the speech against him[2], but also Thucydides in terms which can hardly be explained away[3], and Plutarch still more explicitly[4], represent him as having accused

---

[1] *De Red.* §§ 7, 25.

[2] [Lys.] *in Andok.* §§ 36, 51.

[3] Thuc. VI. 60 καὶ ὁ μὲν αὐτός τε καθ' ἑαυτοῦ καὶ κατ' ἄλλων μηνύει τὸ τῶν Ἑρμῶν. Bishop Thirlwall thinks that this need not mean more than that Andokides confessed privity to the fact (*Hist.*

Gr. vol. III. Appendix III. p. 500). But the words would naturally mean that he confessed participation in the fact. And so Mr Grote understands them, vol. VII. p. 279.

[4] Plut. *Alk.* 21 οὗτος (Τίμαιος) ἀναπείθει τὸν Ἀνδοκίδην ἑαυτοῦ κα-

himself along with the rest. It can hardly be
doubted that, in 415, he told the Council that the
mutilation of the Hermae had been a mad freak
committed by the club of young men to which he
belonged, and by himself among the number. Probably he felt that it would be useless to make
a reservation of his own innocence. No one would
believe him; and at the same time it would
seriously damage the plausibility of his alleged
acquaintance with the plans of the conspirators.
It is very likely, however, that he did make excuses
for himself, such as that his active part in the
affair had been small, or that he had been drawn
into it against his will, or in a moment of excitement.
At the distance of sixteen years such excuses might
easily grow into a denial of his having been concerned
at all.

It is a further question whether, supposing that
the story which he told at the time inculpated himself, this story was true. Was he really guilty? It
ought to be remembered that the eighth book of
Thucydides was probably written before the speech
On the Mysteries had been delivered, or the exiles
of 415 had returned; and that, therefore, we have
perhaps larger materials than Thucydides himself
had for forming a judgment on an affair which (as
he says) had never been cleared up[1]. Great weight
ought surely to be allowed to the circumstance that.

τήγορον καὶ τινῶν ἄλλων γενέσθαι
μὴ πολλῶν ... ὁ Ἀνδοκίδης ἐπείσθη
καὶ γενόμενος μηνυτὴς καθ᾽ αὑτοῦ καὶ
καθ᾽ ἑτέρων ἔσχε τὴν ἐκ τοῦ ψηφίσματος ἄδειαν αὐτός· οὓς δ᾽ ὠνό-
μασε, κ. τ. λ.

[1] Thuc. VI. 60.

the Hermes before the house of Andokides was one
of the very few[1] which had not been mutilated. The
explanation of this given by Andokides himself in 399
is at least plausible. Euphiletos, he says, had told
the other conspirators that Andokides had himself
undertaken the mutilation of this particular image ;
and so it escaped, Andokides being ill and ignorant
of the whole matter. Now if Euphiletos had a spite
against Andokides for having condemned his proposal, he could not, in fact, have taken a more
effectual revenge. The sparing of this Hermes was
just the circumstance, which, in the event, turned
suspicion most strongly upon Andokides. Had he
been out himself that night and engaged in the
sacrilege, he could scarcely have failed to think of a
danger so evident, and would have taken care that
his own house should not be marked out by its
immunity. If the number of mutilators was as
small as he states, the neglect of such a precaution
is altogether inconceivable. The conjecture to which
we should incline is that the Hermae were mutilated
by the small club of young men to which Andokides
belonged, but that, for some reason or other, he had
no hand in it ; that, however, when he gave his
evidence at the time, he accused himself of having
been actively concerned, thinking that otherwise the
rest of his story would be disbelieved. It would follow
that the version of the matter given in his speech

---

[1] The *only* one—μόνος τῶν Ἑρμῶν
τῶν Ἀθήνησιν, according to Andokides himself, *de Myst.* § 62. But
Plut. *Alk.* 21 says ἐν ὀλίγοις πάνυ
τῶν ἐπιφανῶν μόνος σχεδὸν ἀκέραιος
ἔμεινε : and Thuc. VI. 27 says only
οἱ πλεῖστοι περιεκόπησαν.

On the Mysteries is, on the whole, true in itself, but
is untrue as a representation of what he stated in 415.

The second chapter in the life of Andokides *Life of Andokides from 415 to 402.*
covers the years from 415 to 402. It is the history
of his exile.

On leaving Athens in 415 he appears to have
adopted a merchant's life. Archelaos, king of
Macedonia, a friend of his family, gave him the
right of cutting timber and exporting it[1]. In
Cyprus, according to the author of the speech
against him, he was imprisoned by the king of
Citium on account of some treachery[2]; a story
from which it would be unsafe to infer more than
that Andokides had visited. the island. When,
after the Sicilian disaster, Samos became the head-
quarters of the Athenian fleet, he endeavoured to
conciliate his countrymen there by supplies of corn
and cargoes of oar-spars and of bronze, which his
mercantile connexion enabled him to get for them
at a cheap rate[3]. In the spring of 411 he made *His first return to Athens.*
his first attempt to re-establish himself at Athens.
He was unaware, at the moment of his return, that
the revolution of the Four Hundred had taken place.
The hatred of the oligarchical clubs, incurred by his
denunciation of his own associates, and the enmity
of Peisandros, whose desire to keep up a panic had
been thwarted by his reassuring disclosures, would
have been enough to have prevented him from ex-
pecting any other reception than that which he

---

[1] Andok. *de Red.* § 11. Cf.
Theophr. *Char.* XXIII., where the
ἀλαζών boasts of having received,
as a special honour from Antipatros,
the ἐξαγωγὴ ξύλων ἀτελής.
[2] [Lys.] *in Andok.* § 26.
[3] *De Red.* § 11.

actually experienced[1]. He was instantly denounced
to the Council by Peisandros for supplying oars to
the hostile democracy at Samos, and was thrown
into prison[2]. Released by the downfall of the oligarchy, he again visited Cyprus,—where, according
to his accuser he was once more imprisoned 'for a
misdeed'—this time by Evagoras king of Salamis[3];
but we may hesitate whether to recognise here the
monotony of fate or of invention.

In Cyprus Andokides found a new opportunity
to serve the interests of Athens. The loss of her
power in the Propontis had cut off her corn-trade
with the Euxine; and Andokides procured the de-
spatch of corn-ships from Cyprus to the Peiraeus.
His second return to Athens. It must have been in the spring or summer of 410,
before the results of the victory at Kyzikos had re-
moved all fear of famine[4], that Andokides was again
at Athens, and in a speech in the ekklesia pleaded
for the removal of the disabilities under which the
decree of Isotimides was held to have placed him.
He expresses penitence for his errors in 415; and
lays stress upon certain information which he had
given to the Senate, as well as upon his services in
procuring a supply of corn[5]. His application was

[1] He says (*de Red.* § 13) κατέ-
πλευσα ὡς ἐπαινεθησόμενος ὑπὸ τῶν
ἐνθάδε: and he would hardly have
expected the 'praise' of the Four
Hundred for having ministered to
the army at Samos. Earlier in the
narrative, indeed, (§ 11) he says that
he brought the supplies to Samos
'when the Four Hundred had already seized the government;' but

this is a way of fixing the date.
It does not follow that the tidings
from Athens had then reached
Samos.

[2] *De Red.* § 15.

[3] [Lys.] *in Andok.* § 28.

[4] For a discussion of the date of
the speech On his Return, see
Chap. VI.

[5] *De Red.* §§ 19 ff.

rejected; and for the third time he went into exile.
During the next eight years he is said to have visited
Sicily, Italy, the Peloponnesus, Thessaly, the Hellespont, Ionia and Cyprus[1]. In Cyprus he had received,
perhaps from Evagoras, a grant of land[2]; and the
fortune which afterwards enabled him to discharge
costly offices at Athens, although his patrimony had
been wrecked[3], appears to show that he had been
active and successful as a merchant.

The general amnesty of 403 at last gave him the
opportunity which he had so long sought in vain.
He returned to Athens from Cyprus[4], probably about
the beginning of 402[5]; and for three years was not
only unmolested, but was readmitted to the employ-
ments and honours of an active citizen. He was
a choregus, and dedicated in the Street of Tripods
the prize which he had won with a cyclic chorus[6];
he was gymnasiarch at the Hephaestia—head of
sacred missions to the Isthmian and Olympian
games—and steward of the sacred treasure[7]; he is
heard of as speaking in the Senate and preferring
accusations in the law-courts[8]. At length, in 399[9],

---

[1] [Lys.] *in Andok.* § 6.

[2] In *De Myst.* § 4 he supposes his
enemies saying of him—ἔστι πλεύ-
σαντι εἰς Κύπρον, ὅθενπερ ἧκει, γῆ
πολλὴ καὶ ἀγαθὴ διδομένη καὶ δωρεὰ
ὑπάρχουσα.

[3] ib. § 144.   [4] ib. § 4.

[5] The contest between the exiles
at the Peiraeus and the town party
was not finally concluded till Boedromion (Sept. — Oct.) 403 B.C.
See Clinton, *F. H.* At the time
when the amnesty was sworn, Andokides was absent from Athens:

[Lys.] *in Andok.* § 39. It seems
safe, then, to conclude that he did
not return to Athens before the
early part of 402.

[6] [Plut.] *Vit. Andok.*

[7] *De Myst.* § 132.

[8] [Lys.] *in Andok.* § 33 παρασκευ-
άζεται τὰ πολιτικὰ πράττειν καὶ ἤδη
δημηγορεῖ. Cf. ib. § 11, where mention is made of a γραφὴ ἀσεβείας
brought by Andokides against one
Archippos.

[9] Three years after his return to
Athens: *de Myst.* § 132. The date

the zeal of his enemies—stimulated, perhaps, by his prosperity—appears to have revived. After one attempt which seems to have been abortive[1], he was brought to trial, in the autumn of 399, on a charge of impiety. He had attended the Greater Mysteries at Eleusis; and his enemies contended that he had thereby violated the decree of Isotimides, by which he was excluded from all temples. Before the Eleusinian festival was over[2], an information to this effect was laid before the Archon Basileus. The accusers were Kephisios, Epichares and Meletos, supported by Kallias and Agyrrhios. The fact that Andokides was supported in court by Anytos and Kephalos[3], two popular public men, as well as by advocates chosen by his tribe, shows that his assiduous services to the State, and perhaps the persevering malice of his adversaries, had at last produced their effect upon the general feeling towards him. He speaks like a man tolerably confident of a verdict; and he was acquitted.

Little is known of the life of Andokides after 399. From the speech On the Mysteries it appears

---

399 is confirmed by another consideration. In *de Myst.* § 132 the offices which he had held are enumerated in apparently chronological order:—πρῶτον μὲν γυμνασίαρχον Ἡφαιστίοις, ἔπειτα ἀρχιθεωρὸν εἰς Ἰσθμὸν καὶ Ὀλυμπίαζε, εἶτα δὲ ταμίαν ἐν πόλει τῶν ἱερῶν χρημάτων. Now the Olympic festival at which he was ἀρχιθεωρός must have been that of Ol. 95. 1, 400 B.C. After this architheoria he had been tamias; but clearly was so no longer at the time when the speech On

the Mysteries was spoken.

[1] [Lys.] *in Andok.* § 30 ἀφικόμενος εἰς τὴν πόλιν δὶς ἐν τῷ αὐτῷ [ἐνιαυτῷ ?] ἐνδέδεικται. Neither Andokides nor his accuser say anything about the result of the earlier ἔνδειξις: probably, then, it never came to a trial.

[2] The great Eleusinia fell in the last half of Boedromion (end of Sept. and beginning of Oct.). The ἔνδειξις was laid ταῖς εἰκάσι, τοῖς μυστηρίοις τούτοις, *de Myst.* § 121.

[3] *De Myst.* § 150.

that he was at that time unmarried and childless[1].
His uncle Epilykos had died leaving two daughters,
whom Andokides and Leagros, as the nearest kinsmen, had claimed in marriage before the Archon.
The girl claimed by Andokides had died before the
claim was heard ; the other was now claimed by
Kallias, who had induced Leagros to retire in his
favour, and Andokides, to defeat this intrigue, had
entered a counter-claim ; but in 399 the case was
still undecided[2]. If Andokides died without legitimate issue, his family became extinct[3].

The first reappearance of Andokides in public life
is marked by the speech On the Peace with Lacedaemon, which belongs to 390, the fourth year of
the Corinthian War[4]. Athens, Boeotia, Corinth and
Argos were at this time allied against Sparta. The
success of Agesilaos in 391 had led the Athenians,
probably in the winter of 391—90, to send plenipotentiaries, among whom was Andokides, to treat
for peace at Sparta. According to the terms proposed by the Lacedaemonians, Athens was to retain
her Long Walls—rebuilt three years before by Konon

---

[1] *De Myst.* § 148.
[2] *ib.* §§ 117—123.
[3] *ib.* § 146.
[4] From the speech itself it appears that (1) the Boeotians had
been now four years at war, § 20 :
(2) Lechaeum had been taken by
the Lacedaemonians, § 18 : (3) The
Lacedaemonians are spoken of as
having been already thrice vic-
torious—at Corinth, Coronea, and
Lechaeum ; and nothing is said of
any check which they had received :
§ 18. The destruction of the mora by

Iphikrates—so tremendous a blow
to the Spartan arms—can hardly,
then, have taken place. Grote puts
the victory of Iphikrates in 390 :
see his note, vol. ix. p. 455, which
discusses Clinton's view that it occurred in 393.

Krüger places the speech of Andokides in 393 : Grote and Kirchner in 391 ; but the data above
mentioned seem in favour of 390 :
which is the year for which Blass
decides (*Att. Bereds.* pp. 282 f.).

—and her fleet; she was also to recover Lemnos, Imbros and Skyros : and Boeotia was to be gratified by the withdrawal of the Spartan garrison from Orchomenos. The plenipotentiaries did not use their powers, but requested that the Athenian ekklesia might have forty days in which to consider these proposals; and returned, accompanied by Spartan envoys, to Athens[1]. It was in the ensuing debate —early in the year 390—that the speech of Andokides was made.

This, his only recorded utterance on a public question, is temperate and sensible. He points out that it is idle to wait either for the prospect of crushing Sparta in war, or for the prospect of recovering by diplomacy all the possessions abroad which Athens had lost in 405 ; her ships and walls are now, as they always were, her true strength, and she ought to accept thankfully the secured possession of these. The soundness of this view was proved in the sequel. By the Peace of Antalkidas three years later Athens got only what she was offered in 390 ; and she got it, not by treaty on equal terms with a Hellenic power, but as part of the price paid by the Persian king for the disgraceful surrender of Asiatic Hellas. The advice of Andokides probably lost something of its effect through the suspicion of 'laconism' attaching to all statesmen of oligarchical

---

[1] Xenophon and Diodoros say nothing about such an embassy from Sparta to Athens. But, according to the author of the Argument to the Speech, Φιλόχορος μὲν οὖν λέγει καὶ ἐλθεῖν τοὺς πρέσβεις ἐκ Λακεδαιμονίας καὶ ἀπράκτους ἀνελθεῖν μὴ πείσαντος τοῦ Ἀνδοκίδου. Philochoros, writing circ. 300—260 B.C., is a trustworthy witness for the fact of the embassy.

antecedents; and, though he had long cast in his
lot with the democracy, a certain odour of oligarchy
must have clung to him still.   At any rate his advice was not taken.   The story that he was not only
disobeyed, but banished[1], probably represents merely
the desire to add one disaster more to a history so
full of repulses.

A fair estimate of Andokides is made difficult by
the fact that he was first brought into notice by a
scandal, and that the memory of this scandal runs
through nearly all that is known of his after-life.
At the age of twenty-five he is banished for the
Hermae affair; he is defeated, on the same ground,
in two attempts to return; at the end of sixteen
years he is brought to trial for impiety; and his
acquittal is the last thing recorded about him.   At
that time he was only forty-one; already, since his
return in 402, he had discharged public services;
and now, formally acquitted of the charges which
had so long hung over him, he might hope for a
new career.   His speech On the Peace shows that in
390 he was sufficiently trusted by his fellow-citizens
to have been sent as a plenipotentiary to Sparta;
and proves also, by its statesmanlike good sense, his
fitness for such a trust.   But, except in this speech,
nothing is recorded of his later and probably brighter
years.   History knows him only under a cloud.   It
was, moreover, his misfortune that while the informations which he laid in 415 made him hateful
to the oligarchs, his hereditary connexion with oli-

Character of Ando- kides.

---

[1] [Plut.] *Vit. Andok.* πεμφθεὶς καὶ δόξας ἀδικεῖν ἔφυγε.
δὲ περὶ τῆς εἰρήνης εἰς Λακεδαίμονα.

garchy exposed him to the continual suspicion of the democrats. One year he is imprisoned by the Four Hundred; the next he is repulsed by the ekklesia. It would be an easy inference that there must have been something palpably bad and false in the man to whom both parties were harsh, did not a closer view show that one party may have been influenced by spite and the other by prejudice. Many of those who believed that Andokides was concerned in the mutilation of the Hermae must have regarded him with sincere horror. But on the other hand it should be remembered that such horror is never so loudly expressed, and is never so useful to personal enmity, as at a time when a popular religion, still generally professed, is beginning to be widely disbelieved. Diagoras and Sokrates were accused of impiety with the more effect because the views ascribed to them resembled the real views of many who seemed orthodox. Besides those who hated Andokides as an informer, as an oligarch, or as an iconoclast, there were probably many who regarded him with that special kind of dislike which attaches to a person who drives the world into professing angry conviction on matters to which it is secretly indifferent. Viewed apart from the feelings which worked on his contemporaries, the facts of his life seem to warrant severe blame as little as they warrant high praise. His youthful associates were dissolute; through them he was involved, rightly or wrongly, in the suspicion of a great impiety; and this suspicion clung to him for years. But it was never proved; and when he was at last brought

to trial, he was acquitted.   As an exile he conferred
on Athens services which, if not disinterested, were
at all events valuable ; after his return he discharged
costly public services, and represented the State on
an important mission.

To judge from his extant works he had not
genius, but he was energetic and able.   Hard and
various experiences had sharpened his shrewdness ;
he had a quick insight into character, and especially
the triumphant skill of a consciously unpopular man
in exposing malignant motives.   There was no noble-
ness in his nature, except such as is bred by self-
reliance under long adversity ; but he had practical
good sense, which his merchant's life in exile must
have trained and strengthened.   If the counsel which
he gives to Athens in his speech On the Peace with
Lacedaemon may be taken as a sample of his statesmanship, he was an adviser of the kind rarest in the
ekklesia ; not only clearsighted in the interests of
the city, but bold enough to recommend to Athenians
a safe rather than a brilliant course.

CHAPTER V.

ANDOKIDES.

STYLE.

ANDOKIDES differs in one important respect from all
the other Attic orators of the canon. He is not an
artist. Each of the rest represents some theory,
more or less definite, of eloquence as an art; and is
distinguished, not merely by a faculty, but by certain technical merits, the result of labour directed
to certain points in accordance with that theory.
Among these experts Andokides is an amateur.
In the course of an eventful life he spoke with ability and success on some occasions of great moment
and great difficulty. But he brought to these efforts
the minimum of rhetorical training. He relied almost
wholly on his native wit and on a rough, but shrewd,
knowledge of men.

This accounts for the comparatively slight attention paid to Andokides by the ancient rhetoricians
and critics. Dionysios mentions him only twice;
once, where he remarks that Thucydides used a
peculiar dialect, which is not employed by 'Andokides, Antiphon, or Lysias[1];' again, where he says

---

[1] Dionys. *de Thuc.* c. 51.

that Lysias is the standard for contemporary Attic,
'as may be judged from the speeches of Andokides,
Kritias and many others[1].' Both these notices recognise Andokides as an authority for the idiom of
his own day; and it is evident that he had a
philological interest for the critic. On the other
hand it is clear that Dionysios discovered in him no
striking power; for Andokides does not occur in his
long list of men foremost in the various departments of oratory[2]. Quintilian names him only in
one slighting allusion. Who, he asks, is to be our
model of Attic eloquence? 'Let it be Lysias; for his
is the style in which the lovers of 'Atticism' delight.
At this rate we shall not be sent back all the way
to Andokides and Kokkos[3].' It has been thought
that Quintilian refers to the Kokkos mentioned by
Suidas as a pupil of Isokrates; but, however this
may be, the context is enough to show that he
means to mark, not the antiquity, but the inferi-
ority (in his view) of the two men. When Herodes
Atticus was told by his Greek admirers that he deserved to be numbered with the Attic Ten, he turned
off the compliment, with an adroitness which his biographer commends, by saying—'At all events I am
better than Andokides[4].' More definite censure is
expressed in the compact criticism of Hermogenes :—

---

[1] *de Lys.* c. 2.

[2] *de Isaeo* cc. 19 ff.

[3] Quint. XII. 10. § 21. *Nam quis
erit hic Atticus? Sit Lysias; hunc
enim amplectuntur amatores is-
tius nominis modum. Non igitur
iam usque ad Coccum et Ando-
cidem remittemur.*

[4] Philostratos, *Vit. Her. Att.* II. 1.
§ 14, p. 564 ed. Kayser. βοώσης δὲ
ἐπ᾽ αὐτὸν τῆς Ἑλλάδος καὶ καλούσης
αὐτὸν ἕνα τῶν δέκα, οὐχ ἡττήθη τοῦ
ἐπαίνου, μεγάλου δοκοῦντος, ἀλλ᾽
ἀστειότατα πρὸς τοὺς ἐπαινέσαντας,
Ἀνδοκίδου μὲν, ἔφη, βελτίων εἰμί.

'Andokides aims at being a political orator, but
does not quite achieve it. His figures want clear
articulation; his arrangement is not lucid; he constantly tacks on clause to clause, or amplifies in an
irregular fashion, using parentheses to the loss of a
distinct order. On these accounts he has seemed to
some a frivolous and generally obscure speaker. Of
finish and ornament his share is small; he is equally
deficient in fiery earnestness. Again, he has little,
or rather very little, of that oratorical power which
is shown in method; general oratorical power he
has almost none [1].'

The phrase 'political oratory' as used by Hermogenes has two senses, a larger and a narrower.
In the larger sense it denotes all public speaking
as opposed to scholastic declamation, and comprises
the deliberative, the forensic, the panegyric styles.
In the narrower sense it denotes practical oratory,
deliberative or forensic, as opposed not only to scholastic declamation but also to that species of panegyric speaking in which no definite political question
is discussed [2]. Here, the narrower sense is intended.

---

[1] Hermog. περὶ ἰδεῶν B. c. XI.
(vol. II. p. 416 Spengel *Rhet. Gr.*):—
ὁ δὲ Ἀνδοκίδης πολιτικὸς μὲν εἶναι
προαιρεῖται, οὐ μὴν πάνυ γε ἐπιτυγ-
χάνει τούτου· ἀδιάρθρωτος γάρ ἐστιν
ἐν τοῖς σχήμασι καὶ ἀδιευκρίνητος καὶ
τὰ πολλὰ ἐπισυνάπτει τε καὶ περιβάλλει ἀτάκτως διὰ τὸ ταῖς ἐπεμβολαῖς
χωρὶς εὐκρινείας χρῆσθαι, ὅθεν ἔδοξέ
τισι φλύαρος καὶ ἄλλως ἀσαφὴς εἶναι·
ἐπιμελείας δὲ αὐτῷ καὶ κόσμου πάνυ
βραχὺ μέτεστι, γοργότητός τε ὡσαύ-
τως. καὶ μέντοι καὶ τῆς κατὰ μέθοδον δεινότητος ὀλίγον ἀλλὰ καὶ σφό-

δρα ὀλίγον ἔχει, τῆς δ' ἄλλης σχεδὸν
οὐδ' ὅλως.

[2] For the larger sense, see περὶ
ἰδεῶν B. c. X. περὶ τοῦ πολιτικοῦ
λόγου: in which chapter he says,
τούτου δὲ τοῦ λόγου τοῦ πολιτικοῦ ὁ
μέν ἐστι συμβουλευτικὸς ὁ δὲ δικανι-
κὸς ὁ δὲ πανηγυρικός. For the narrower sense, see c. XI. περὶ τοῦ ἁ-
πλῶς πολιτικοῦ λόγου: and c. XII.
περὶ τοῦ ἁπλῶς πανηγυρικοῦ. It is
in the narrower sense—that is, as
including deliberative and forensic
speaking only, and excluding all

When Hermogenes says that Andokides does not
succeed in being a 'political' speaker, he means
that Andokides does not exhibit—for instance, in
the speech On his Return and in the speech On the
Peace—the characteristic excellences of deliberative speaking; nor—for instance in the speech On the
Mysteries—the characteristic excellences of forensic
speaking. What Hermogenes took these excellences
to be, he explains at length in another place; the
chief of them are these three;—clearness; the stamp
of truth; fiery earnestness [1].

The first and general remark of Hermogenes
upon Andokides implies, then, that he is wanting
in these qualities. The special remarks which follow
develop it. They refer partly to his arrangement of
subject-matter, partly to his style of diction. He
is said to have little 'power' (or 'cleverness') 'of
method'; that is, little tact in seeing where, and
how, each topic should be brought in[2]; he 'amplifies'[3]

---

epideiktic speaking, on whatever
subject—that πολιτικὸς λόγος is
generally used : see *e.g.* the Ῥητορι-
κὴ πρὸς Ἀλέξανδρον, c. I. (Spengel),
δύο γένη τῶν πολιτικῶν εἰσὶ λόγων,
τὸ μὲν δημηγορικὸν τὸ δὲ δικανικόν.
Cf. Isok. κατὰ σοφ. § 19.

[1] See περὶ ἰδ. B. c. x. passim : esp.
ad init. φημὶ τοίνυν δεῖν ἐν τῷ τοι-
ούτῳ λόγῳ πλεονάζειν μὲν ἀεὶ τόν τε
τὴν σαφήνειαν ποιοῦντα τύπον καὶ
τὸν ἠθικόν τε καὶ ἀληθῆ καὶ μετὰ τού-
τους τὸν γοργόν.

[2] The distinction drawn by Hermogenes in his criticism upon Andokides between ἡ κατὰ μέθοδον δεινότης and what he calls ἡ ἄλλη δεινότης is explained by his own wri-

tings. His treatise Περὶ μεθόδου
δεινότητος discusses the proper occasion (καιρὸς ἴδιος c. I.) for using
the various figures and arts of rhetoric. It is a treatise upon Rhetorical Tact. By ἡ ἄλλη δεινότης
he means simply what he speaks
of in περὶ ἰδ. B. c. XI., περὶ δεινότητος:—oratorical power in the largest and most general sense, including all particular excellences whatsoever.

[3] περιβάλλει. Hermogenes uses
the terms περιβολή, περιβάλλειν in
a special technical sense, for which
it is difficult to find any precise
English equivalent. 'Amplifica-
tion' perhaps comes nearest. There

unnecessarily, by detailing circumstances unnecessary
for his point ; he obscures the order of his ideas by
frequent parentheses, or by adding, as an afterthought, something which ought to have come earlier.
As regards diction, in the first place his ' figures ' are
said to be 'wanting in clear articulation' (ἀδιάρθρωτα).
Hermogenes elsewhere[1] enumerates thirteen 'figures'
of rhetoric, which are either certain fixed modes of
framing sentences, such as the antithesis and the
period; or (in the phrase of Caecilius) ' figures of
thought,' such as irony and dilemma[2]. Hermogenes
means that Andokides does not use 'figures' of
either sort with precision ; he does not work them
out to an incisive distinctness ; he leaves them ' in-
articulate '—still in the rough, and with their outlines dull. Again Andokides has little 'finish' (ἐπιμέλεια)—a term by which his critic means refinement
and smoothness in composition[3]. Lastly, Andokides
is said to be wanting in ' fiery earnestness.' The
word γοργότης, which we have attempted thus to
paraphrase, plays a very important point in the
rhetorical terminology of Hermogenes: it describes
one of the three cardinal excellences of ' political '

---

are two sorts of περιβολή : (1) κατ'
ἔννοιαν—when some special statement is prefaced by a general
statement : *e.g.* πονηρὸν ὁ συκα-
φάντης ἀεί· τοῦτο δὲ καὶ φύσει κίναδος
τἀνθρώπιόν ἐστι : (2) κατὰ λέξιν,
when a fact is related with all
its attendant circumstances : *e.g.*
ὑπεσχόμην χορηγήσειν· πότε; τρίτον
ἔτος τουτί· ποῦ; ἐν τῇ ἐκκλησίᾳ. διὰ
τί; οὐ καθεστηκότος χορηγοῦ, κ.τ.λ.
See Herm. περὶ ἰδ. A. c. XI.

[1] Hermog. περὶ εὑρέσεως Δ.—
Ch. I. is περὶ λόγου σχημάτων in
genera : cc. II.—XIV. discuss the
several σχήματα.

[2] See supra, p. 29.

[3] See the chapter περὶ ἐπιμελείας
καὶ κάλλους, Hermog. περὶ ἰδ. A. c. XII,
where he opposes κάλλος τι καὶ εὐ-
ρυθμία to τὸ ἀμελὲς καὶ ἄρρυθμον:
and observes, πλεῖον δέ τι τῆς ἐπιμελείας καὶ τοῦ κάλλους ἔχουσιν αἱ
μικραὶ τῶν λέξεων καὶ δι' ὀλίγων

oratory[1]. Perhaps no simple English equivalent can
be found for it. But Hermogenes has explained
clearly what he means by it. He means earnest
feeling, especially indignation, uttered in terse, intense, sometimes abrupt language. It is to a strong
and noble emotion what 'keenness' (ὀξύτης) and
'tartness' (δριμύτης) are to a lower kind of eagerness.
The lofty invectives of Demosthenes against Philip
supply Hermogenes with his best examples of it[2].

We have now seen the worst that can be said
of Andokides from the point of view of the technical
Rhetoric; and it must be allowed that, from that
point of view, the condemnation is tolerably complete. Now the canon of the Ten Attic Orators was
probably drawn up at the time when scholastic
rhetoric was most flourishing, and when, therefore,
the standard of criticism used by Hermogenes and
Herodes was the common one. It may seem surprising, then, that Andokides was numbered in the
decad at all. Kritias, his contemporary, whom so
many ancient writers praise highly, might be supposed to have had stronger claims; and the fact
that the memory of Kritias as a statesman was hateful, is not enough in itself to explain his exclusion

---

συγκείμεναι συλλαβῶν· οἷον, περὶ
τοῦ πῶς ἀκούειν ὑμᾶς ἐμοῦ δεῖ
(from Dem. *de Coron.* § 2). So
the use of short, simple words
may be a mark of ἐπιμέλεια—showing how the notion of *refinement*
comes into it.

[1] περὶ ἰδ. B. c. X. *ad init.*

[2] See the chapter περὶ γοργότη-
τος (περὶ ἰδ. B. c. I.). He there
says that γοργότης is the opposite

of slackness and languor (τὸ ἀνει-
μένον καὶ ὕπτιον):—that it usually
expresses itself in the trenchant
style (διὰ τοῦ τμητικοῦ γίνεται τύπου).
He cites as examples of γοργότης
the opening of the Third Philippic:
also *de Coron.* § 10, ἔστι τοίνυν οὗτος
ὁ πρῶτος: κ.τ.λ., and several other
passages from the same speech;
de falsa Legat. § 24, τί γὰρ καὶ
βουλόμενοι κ.τ.λ.

from a literary group[1]. Probably one reason, at least, for the preference given to Andokides was the great interest of the subjects upon which he spoke. The speech on the Mysteries, supplying, as it does, the picturesque details of a memorable event, had an intrinsic value quite apart from its merits as a composition. The speech On the Peace with Lacedaemon, again, gives a clear picture of a crisis in the Corinthian War; and is an illustration, almost unique in its way, of Athenian history at the time just after the rebuilding of the walls by Konon, when, for the first time since Aegospotami, Athenian visions of empire were beginning to revive. As Lykurgos seems to have owed his place among the Ten chiefly to his prominence as a patriot, so Andokides may have been recommended partly by his worth as an indirect historian. Again, Dionysios, as we have seen, recognised at least the philological value of Andokides. It is further possible that even rhetoricians of the schools may have found him interesting as an example of merely natural eloquence coming between two opposite styles of art; between the formal grandeur of Antiphon and the studied ease of Lysias.

General tendency of ancient criticism upon oratory. Unjust to Andokides.

It is a result of the precision with which the art of rhetoric was systematized in the Greek and Roman schools that much of the ancient criticism upon oratory is taintéd by a radical vice. The ancient critics too often confound literary merit with oratori-

[1] K. O. Müller says (*Hist. Gr. Lit.* c. XXXIII. Vol. II. p. 115 *n.*, ed. Donaldson) 'It is surprising that Kritias was not rather enrolled among the Ten; but perhaps his having been one of the Thirty stood in his way.'

cal merit. They judge too much from the standpoint
of the reader, and too little from the standpoint of
the hearer. They analyse special features of language and of method; they determine with nicety
the rank of each man as a composer; but they too
often forget that, for the just estimation of his rank
as a speaker, the first thing necessary is an effort
of imaginative sympathy. We must not merely
analyse his style; we must try to realise the effect
which some one of his speeches, as a whole, would
have made on a given audience in given circumstances. As nearly all the great orators of antiquity
had been trained in the rudiments of the technical
rhetoric, the judgment upon their relative merits
is not, as a rule, much disturbed by this tendency
in their critics. It may often, indeed, be felt that
the judgment, however fair in itself, is based too
much upon literary grounds. But, in most cases,
so far as we can judge, no great injustice is done.
Criticism of this kind may, however, happen to be
unjust; and it has certainly been unjust in the
case of Andokides. Others far excel him in finish
of style, in clearness of arrangement, in force
and in fire; but no one can read the speech
On the Mysteries (for instance) without feeling
that Andokides was a real orator. The striking
thing in that speech is a certain undefinable
tone which assures even the modern reader that
Andokides was saying the right things to the
judges, and knew himself to be saying the right
things. He is, in places, obscure or diffuse; he
sometimes wanders from the issue, once or twice

into trivial gossip; but throughout there is this glow of a conscious sympathy with his hearers. He may not absolutely satisfy the critics; but he was persuading, and he felt with triumph that he was persuading, the judges.

It is somewhat difficult to analyse the style of a speaker whose real strength lay in a natural vigour directed by a rough tact; and who, in comparison with other Greek orators, cared little for literary form. An attempt at such an analysis may, however, start from the four epithets given to Andokides in the Plutarchic Life[1]. He is there said to be 'simple' (ἁπλοῦς); 'inartificial in arrangement' (ἀκατάσκευος); 'plain' (ἀφελής); and 'sparing of figures' (ἀσχημάτιστος). The first two epithets apparently refer to the order in which his thoughts are marshalled; the last two, to the manner in which they are expressed. We will first speak of the latter, and then come back to the former.

The sense in which the diction of Andokides is 'plain' will be best understood by a comparison with Antiphon and Lysias. Antiphon consciously strives to rise above the language of daily life; he seeks to impress by a display of art. Lysias carefully confines himself to the language of daily life; he seeks to persuade by the use of hidden art. Andokides usually employs the language of daily life; he is free, or almost free, from the archaisms of Antiphon, and writes in the new-Attic dialect, the dialect of Lysias and his successors[2]. On the

---

[1] [Plut.] *vit. Andok.* § 15, ἔστι δὲ ἁπλοῦς καὶ ἀκατάσκευος ἐν τοῖς

λόγοις, ἀφελής τε καὶ ἀσχημάτιστος. [2] As exceptions may be noted

other hand, he does not confine himself to a rigid
simplicity. In his warmer or more vigorous passages, especially of invective or of intreaty, he often
employs phrases or expressions borrowed from the
idiom of Tragedy[1]. These, being of too decidedly
poetical a colour, have a tawdry effect; yet it is
evident that they have come straight from the
memory to the lips; they are quite unlike prepared fine things; and they remind us, in fact, how
really natural a speaker was Andokides,—neither
aiming, as a rule, at ornament, nor avoiding it on
principle when it came to him. The 'plainness'
of Lysias is an even, subtle, concise plainness, so
scrupulous to imitate nature that nature is never
suffered to break out; the 'plainness' of Andokides
is that of a man who, with little rhetorical or

the frequent use of the formula
τοῦτο μέν.. τοῦτο δέ (*e. g. de Myst.*
§ 103: *de Red.* § 16: *de Pace* § 40):
and of the dative οἱ—avoided, as a
rule, by the other orators: *e.g. de
Myst.* §§ 15, 38, 40, 41, 42, etc.

[1] *E.g. De Myst.* § 29, οἱ λόγοι
τῶν κατηγόρων ταῦτα τὰ δεινὰ καὶ
φρικώδη ἀνωρθίαζον: (cf. Aesch.
Choeph. 271, ἐξορθιάζων πολλά.)
Ib. § 67, πίστιν τῶν ἐν ἀνθρώποις
ἀπιστοτάτην. *Ib.* § 68, ὁρῶσι τοῦ
ἡλίου τὸ φῶς—a phrase which,
however, occurs also in the fragment of the speech of Lykurgos
against Lysikles. *Ib.* § 99, ὦ συκο-
φάντα καὶ ἐπίτριπτον κίναδος: (cf.
Soph. *Ai.* 104, τοὐπίτριπτον κίναδος.) *Ib.* § 146 (γένος) οἴχεται πᾶν
πρόρριζον: (cf. Soph. *El.* 765 πρόρριζον...ἔφθαρται γένος.) *De Pace*,
§ 34, εἰρήνης πέρι: cf. Arist. *Poet.*

c. 22, where the collocation Ἀχίλλεως πέρι instead of περὶ Ἀχίλλεως
is specially instanced as a violation
of the idiom (διάλεκτος) of ordinary
life. Add to these examples the
use of the poetical φρενῶν in
De Red. § 7, τοιαύτην συμφορὰν
τῶν φρενῶν: which, however, occurs also in the peroration of Demosth. *de Corona*, § 324, τούτοις
βελτίω τινὰ νοῦν καὶ φρένας ἐνθεί-
ητε. Both instances, perhaps, come
under the principle of Aristotle
(*Rhet.* III. 7. § 11) that unusual or
poetical words μάλιστα ἁρμόττει
λέγοντι παθητικῶς. The writer of
the speech κατ''Αλκιβιάδου has imitated the tragic vein which appears
in the genuine speeches of Andokides: § 22, παρανομώτερος Αἰγί-
σθου γέγονεν. Cf. § 23.

literary culture, followed chiefly his own instinct in
speaking. Lysias had at his command all the resources of technical rhetoric, but so used them
towards producing a sober, uniform effect that his
art is scarcely felt at any particular point; it is
felt only in the impression made by the whole.
Andokides had few of such resources. As his biographer says, he is 'sparing of figures.' Here the
distinction already noticed between 'figures of language' and 'figures of thought' must be kept in
mind. Andokides uses scarcely at all the 'figures
of language': that is, he seldom employs antitheses
—aims at parallelism between the forms of two
sentences—or studies the niceties of assonance [1].
His neglect of such refinements —which, in his day,
constituted the essence of oratorical art, and which
must have been more or less cultivated by nearly
all public speakers—has one noticeable effect on his
composition. There is no necessary connection between an antithetical and a periodic style. But,
in the time of Andokides, almost the only period
in use was that which is formed by the antithesis

*and
sparing of
figures
(ἀσχημά-
τιστος.)*

---

[1] In technical language, he
seldom attempts, (1) ἀντίθεσις,
the opposition of words, or of
ideas, or of both, in the two corresponding clauses of a sentence :
(2) παρίσωσις, a general correspondence between the *forms* of two sentences or clauses : (3) παρομοίωσις,
correspondence of sound between
words in the same sentence. See
on these, Mr Sandys's ed. of Isokr.
Ad Demonicum, and *Panegyricus*,
p. xiv. One special form of παρομοίωσις, viz. ὁμοιοτέλευτον, occurs
e.g. in Andok. *De Pace*, § 2, διά
τε τὴν ἀπειρίαν τοῦ ἔργου διά τε τὴν
ἐκείνων ἀπιστίαν : another special
form, viz. παρήχησις, e.g. in *De
Red.* § 24, εἰ γὰρ ὅσα οἱ ἄνθρωποι
τῇ γνώμῃ ἁμαρτάνουσι, τὸ σῶμα αὐτῶν μὴ αἴτιόν ἐστι, κ.τ.λ.: where
there is a general resemblance of
sound between γνώμη and σῶμα.
But such artifices, so common in
the other orators, are rare and
exceptional in Andokides.

or parallelism of clauses. Hence, since he rarely
uses antitheses or parallelisms, Andokides composes
far less in a periodic style than Thucydides or
Antiphon or even Lysias. His sentences, in the
absence of that framework, are constantly sprawling
to a clumsy length; they are confused by parentheses, or deformed by supplementary clauses, till
the main thread of the sense is often almost lost[1].
But while he thus dispenses with the ornamental
'figures of language,' Andokides uses largely those
so-called 'figures of thought" which give life to a
speech ;—irony—indignant question, and the like[2].

[1] See *e.g. De Myst.* § 57: εἰ μὲν
γὰρ ἦν δυοῖν τὸ ἕτερον ἐλέσθαι, ἢ
καλῶς ἀπολέσθαι ἢ αἰσχρῶς σωθῆναι,
ἔχοι ἄν τις εἰπεῖν κακίαν εἶναι τὰ γε-
νόμενα· | καίτοι πυλλοὶ ἂν καὶ τοῦτο-
εἵλοντο, τὸ ζῆν περὶ πλείονος ποιη-
σάμενοι τοῦ καλῶς ἀποθανεῖν· | ὅπου
δὲ τούτων τὸ ἐναντιώτατον ἦν, | σιω-
πήσαντι μὲν αὐτῷ τε αἴσχιστα ἀπολέσθαι μηδὲν ἀσεβήσαντι, ἔτι δὲ τὸν
πατέρα περιιδεῖν ἀπολόμενον καὶ τὸν
κηδεστὴν καὶ τοὺς συγγενεῖς καὶ ἀνε-
ψιοὺς τοσούτους, οὓς οὐδεὶς ἀπωλ-
λυεν ἢ ἐγὼ μὴ εἰπὼν ὡς ἕτεροι ἥμαρ-
τον· | Διοκλείδης μὲν γὰρ ψευσάμε-
νος ἔδησεν αὐτούς, σωτηρία δὲ αὐτῶν
ἄλλη οὐδεμία ἦν ἢ πυθέσθαι ᾿Αθηναί-
ους πάντα τὰ πραχθέντα· | φονεὺς
οὖν αὐτῶν ἐγιγνόμην ἐγὼ μὴ εἰπὼν
ὑμῖν ἃ ἤκουσα.

Here the parenthesis, καίτοι πολ-
λοί...τοῦ καλῶς ἀποθανεῖν, first of
all disturbs the original plan of the
antithesis; this plan is resumed by
the words ὅπου δὲ τὸ ἐναντιώτατον
ἦν: but then the speaker goes off
into a new antithesis, σιωπήσαντι
μέν, κ.τ.λ., which is never com-

pleted; for the clause οὓς οὐδεὶς
ἀπώλλυεν ἢ ἐγώ, κ.τ.λ. leads to a
new parenthesis in explanation,
Διοκλείδης μὲν γάρ...τὰ πραχθέντα:
and the final clause, φονεὺς οὖν αὐτῶν ἐγιγνόμην, κ.τ.λ., is a conclusion
drawn from this parenthesis, not
the proper completion of that second member of the original antithesis which the words ὅπου δὲ τὸ
ἐναντιώτατον ἦν commenced.

This is a strong example; but it
is typical of the perplexity in which
many passages of Andokides are
involved through the same cause—
imperfect or careless structure of
antithesis.

[2] Among the minor σχήματα διανοίας used by Andokides, asyndeton is one of the most frequent.
It often adds life and vigour to
his style: see *e.g. De Myst.* §
16:—τρίτη μήνυσις ἐγένετο. ἡ γυνὴ
᾿Αλκμαιονίδου, γενομένη δὲ καὶ Δάμω-
νος—᾿Αγαρίστη ὄνομα αὐτῇ—αὕτη
ἐμήνυσεν, κ.τ.λ.: cf. §§ 33, 115, 127.
He also uses the figure called ἀναφορά—*i.e.* the emphatic repetition

This animation is indeed one of the points which most distinguish his style from the ordinary style of Antiphon, and which best mark his relative modernism.

The method of Andokides is simple (ἁπλοῦς) and inartificial (ἀκατάσκευος.) As Andokides is 'plain' in diction and avoids ornamental figures, so he is also 'simple' in treatment of subject-matter, and avoids an artificial arrangement[1]. His two speeches before the ekklesia—that On his Return and that On the Peace—shew, indeed, no distinct or systematic partition. In his speech On the Mysteries he follows, with one difference, the arrangement usually observed by Antiphon and more strictly by Lysias. There is a

of a word at the beginning of successive clauses: and ὑποφορά—the 'suggestion' of some argument or objection which is then refuted. In *De Myst.* § 148, ἀναφορά and ὑποφορά occur together:—τίνα γὰρ καὶ ἀναβιβάσομαι δεησόμενον ὑπὲρ ἐμαυτοῦ; τὸν πατέρα; ἀλλὰ τέθνηκεν. ἀλλὰ τοὺς ἀδελφούς; ἀλλ' οὐκ εἰσίν. ἀλλὰ τοὺς παῖδας; ἀλλ' οὔπω γεγένηνται. ὑμεῖς τοίνυν καὶ ἀντὶ πατρὸς ἐμοὶ καὶ ἀντὶ ἀδελφῶν καὶ ἀντὶ παίδων γένεσθε· εἰς ὑμᾶς καταφεύγω καὶ ἀντιβολῶ καὶ ἱκετεύω· ὑμεῖς με παρ' ὑμῶν αὐτῶν αἰτησάμενοι σώσατε.

[1] As he is ἀφελής and ἀσχημάτιστος, so he is also ἁπλοῦς and ἀκατάσκευος. The word ἀκατάσκευος is, indeed, often closely synonymous with ἀφελής and ἁπλοῦς: e.g. Dionys. *Isae.* c. 7, ἀκατάσκευον φαίνεται εἶναι καὶ ὡς ἂν ἰδιώτης τις εἰπεῖν δύναιτο τὸ εἰρημένον: cf. Ernesti *Lex. Tech. Gr. Rhet.* s.v., who quotes from Menander διαιρ. ἐπιδ. p. 624, εἶδος ἀπαγγελίας ἁπλοῦν ἀφελὲς καὶ ἀκατάσκευον. But in one

or two places the usage of Dionysios seems to confirm the view that the author of the Plutarchic Life of Andokides meant ἁπλοῦς and ἀκατάσκευος to refer mainly to arrangement of subject-matter, as the other two epithets refer mainly to diction. Contrasting the method of Lysias with the method of Isaeos, Dionysios says (*Isae.* c. 3): παρὰ Λυσίᾳ μὲν οὐ πολλὴν τὴν ἐπιτέχνησιν οὔτ' ἐν μερισμοῖς τῶν πραγμάτων οὔτ' ἐν τῇ τάξει τῶν ἐνθυμημάτων οὔτ' ἐν ταῖς ἐξεργασίαις αὐτῶν (τις) ὄψεται· ἁπλοῦς γὰρ ὁ ἀνήρ. Again, he says (*ib.*) that Isaeos 'in proportion as he falls short of the other's grace, excels him in cleverness of artificial arrangement'—ὅσον ἀπολείπεται τῆς χάριτος ἐκείνης, τοσοῦτον ὑπερέχῃ τῇ δεινότητι τῆς κατασκευῆς. In the essay of Dionysios on Thucydides, again, (c. 27) τὸ φορτικὸν τῆς λέξεως καὶ σκολιὸν καὶ δυσπαρακολούθητον are opposed to τὸ ἀγενὲς καὶ χαμαιπετὲς καὶ ἀκατάσκευον.

proem, followed by a short prothesis or general statement of the case; then narrative and argument; lastly epilogue[1]. But the narrative as a whole is not kept distinct from the argument as a whole. Each section of the narrative is followed by the corresponding section of the argument. Dionysios notices such interfusion as a special mark of art in Isaeos[2]. In Andokides it is rather a mark of art-lessness. He had a long story to tell, and was unable, or did not try, to tell it concisely. The very length of his narrative compelled him to break it up into pieces and to comment upon each piece separately. He has not effected this without some loss of clearness, and one division of the speech is thoroughly confused[3]. But it should be remembered that a defective ordering of topics, though a grave fault, was less serious for Andokides than it would have been for a speaker in a different style. The main object of Andokides was to be in sympathy with his audience—amusing them with stories, however irrelevant—putting all his arguments in the most vivid shape—and using abundant illustration. Lucid arrangement, though always important, was not of firstrate importance for him. His speeches were meant to carry hearers along with them, rather than to be read and analysed at leisure.

---

[1] Proem, §§ 1—7: prothesis, §§ 8—10: narrative and argument, §§ 11—139: epilogue, §§ 140—150.

[2] Dionys. *Isae.* § 14: τοτὲ δὲ μερίσας αὐτὰς (τὰς διηγήσεις) εἰς τὰ κεφάλαια, καὶ παρ' ἕκαστον αὐτῶν τὰς πίστεις παρατιθείς, ἐκμηκύνει τε μᾶλλον καὶ ἐκβαίνει τὸ τῆς διηγήσεως σχῆμα, τῷ συμφέροντι χρώμε-νος: 'sometimes he divides his statement under heads; and, presenting the proofs under the several heads, adds somewhat to the length of the narrative, while he departs, as may be expedient, from its strict form.'

[3] §§ 92—150.

*Andokides
has little
skill in the
common-
places of
rhetorical
argument.*   But it is not merely in special features of diction
or of arrangement that Andokides is seen to be no
technical rhetorician.   A disciple of the sophistical
rhetoric learned to deal copiously and skilfully with
those commonplaces of argument which would be
available in almost any case.   His education taught
him to prefer general argument to argument from
particular circumstances, unless these were especially
easy to manipulate.   We see this in Antiphon's
First Tetralogy : it is a model exercise in making
the utmost of abstract probabilities as inferred from
facts which are very slightly sketched.   In the
speech On the Murder of Herodes the statement of
the facts is hurried over, and there is no attempt at
a close and searching analysis of them.   But for a
speaker unskilled in rhetorical commonplace the
particulars of any given subject would be everything.
Picturesque narration, shrewd inference from small
circumstances, lively illustration of character would
naturally be his chief resources.   And so it is with
Andokides.   His strength is in narrative, as the
strength of Antiphon is in argument.   Andokides
relies on his case, Antiphon on his science ; it is only
Lysias who hits the masterly mean, who makes his
science the close interpreter of his case, who can
both recount and analyse.   But, although the narrative element in Andokides exceeds the just proportion always observed by Lysias, it is, from a
*Strength
of Ando-
kides in
narrative.* literary point of view, a great charm.   The speech
On the Mysteries is full of good bits of description,
lively without set effort to be graphic.   For instance,
the scene in the prison, when Andokides was per-

suaded to denounce the •real mutilators of the
Hermae :—

'When we had all been imprisoned in the same
place; when night had come, and the gaol had been
closed; there came, to one his mother, his sister to
another, to another his wife and children; and there
arose a piteous sound of weeping and lamentation
for the troubles of the hour. Then Charmides (he
was my cousin, of my own age, and had been brought
up with me in our house from childhood) said to
me :—'Andokides, you see how serious our present
dangers are; and though hitherto I have always
shrunk from saying anything to annoy you, I am
forced by our present misfortune to speak now.
All your intimates and companions except us your
relations have either been put to death on the
charges which threaten us with destruction, or have
taken to flight and pronounced themselves guilty.
If you have heard anything about this affair which
has occurred, speak it out, and save our lives—save
yourself in the first place, then your father, whom
you ought to love very dearly, then your brother-in-
law, the husband of your only sister,—your other
kinsmen, too, and near friends, so many of them;
and me also, who have never given you any annoyance in all my life, but am most zealous for you and
for your interests, whenever anything is to be done.'
When Charmides said this, judges, and when the
others besought and entreated me severally, I
thought to myself,—'most miserable and unfortunate of men, am I to see my own kinsfolk perish
undeservedly—to see their lives sacrificed and their

property confiscated, and in addition to this their
names written up on tablets as sinners against the
gods,—men who are wholly innocent of the matter,—
am I to see moreover three hundred Athenians
doomed to undeserved destruction and the State
involved in the most serious calamities, and men
nourishing suspicion against each other,—or shall I
tell the Athenians just what I heard from Euphiletos himself, the real culprit [1]?'

Another passage in the same speech illustrates
the skill of Andokides in dramatising his narrative.
He delighted to bring in persons speaking. Epichares, one of his accusers in this case, had been an
agent of the Thirty Tyrants. He turns upon him.

'Speak, slanderer, accursed knave—is this law
valid or not valid? Invalid, I imagine, only for this
reason,—that the operation of the laws must be
dated from the archonship of Eukleides. So you
live, and walk about this city, as you little deserve
to do; you who, under the democracy, lived by
pettifogging, and under the oligarchy—lest you
should be forced to give back all the profits of that
trade—became the instrument of the Thirty.

'The truth is, judges, that as I sat here, while he
accused me, and as I looked at him, I fancied myself
nothing else than a prisoner at the bar of the Thirty.
Had this trial been in their time, who would have
been accusing me? Was not this man ready to

[1] *De Myst.* §§ 48—51. Compare,
as another graphic passage, the
account in §§ 38—40 of the story
told by Diokleides—how he had
seen by moonlight the conspirators
meeting in the orchestra of the
theatre of Dionysos.

accuse, if I had not given him money? He has
done it now. And who but Charikles would have
been cross-examining me? 'Tell me, Andokides,
did you go to Dekeleia, and enforce the hostile
garrison on your country's soil?'—'Not I.'—'How
then? You ravaged the territory, and plundered
your fellow-citizens by land or sea?'—'Certainly not.'
—'And you did not serve in the enemy's fleet, or
help to level the Long Walls, or to abolish the democracy?'—'None of these things have I done.'—
'None? Do you think, then, that you will enjoy
impunity, or escape the death suffered by many
others?'

'Can you suppose, judges, that my fate, as your
champion, would have been other than this, if I had
been caught by the Tyrants? I should have been
destroyed by them, as they destroyed many others,
for having done no wrong to Athens[1].'

References of Ando-kides to the early his-tory of Attica.

The love of Andokides for narrative, wherever it
can be introduced, is strikingly seen in his mode of
handling his legal argument in the speech On the
Mysteries. Instead of simply citing and interpret-
ing the enactments upon which he relies, he reviews
in order the events which led to the enactments being
made[2]. The same tendency appears in his habit of
drawing illustrations from the early history of
Attica. These references are in many points loose
and confused[3]. Andokides, however, is hardly

---

[1] *De Myst.* §§ 99—102.
[2] *De Myst.* §§ 70—91.
[3] Remarks on the historical references in *De Myst.* §§ 106—108

and in *De Pace* §§ 3—7 will be
found in ch. VI., in connexion with
these speeches respectively.

a worse offender in this respect than (for instance)
Aeschines[1]; and has more excuse. In the time of
Andokides written history was a comparatively new
invention, and most men knew the events even of
their grandfathers' days only from hearsay. Nor does
the apparent inaccuracy of Andokides in regard to
earlier history affect his authority as a witness for
events with which he was contemporary. The
value of his testimony for the years 415—390 is
unquestioned.

Love of Andokides for gossip.   Andokides sometimes shows his taste for narrative in a special form which deserves notice. He
is a master of shrewd and telling gossip. He di-
verges from the main thread of his argument into
anecdotes which will amuse his hearers, and either
directly damage the adversary, or at least strike
some chord favourable to himself. A part of the
speech On the Mysteries is, in fact, made up of
such stories (§§ 110—136.) Speaking, for instance,
of the son of his accuser Kallias, he reminds the
judges that there was once a certain Hipponikos
at Athens whose house was haunted by an avenging
spirit—so said the children and the women: and
the saying came true, for the man's son proved a
very demon to him. Well, the house of Kallias is
haunted by a fiend of the same kind (§§ 130—131).
In this trait Andokides resembles one, and one only,
of the other Greek orators : it is precisely the im-
pudent, unscrupulous cleverness of Aeschines. There

---

[1] See, *e.g.* Aeschin. *De Falsa
Legat.* § 172, where Miltiades is
spoken of as alive after Salamis:
and *ib.* § 174, where the 1000 talents
set apart in 431 B.C. against special
need (Thuc. II. 24) are represented
as the total sum then in the Athenian treasury.

is the same shrewd perception of what will raise
a laugh or a sneer; the same adroitness, unchecked
by self-respect, in making a point of this kind whenever the opportunity offers; the same command of
coarse but telling abuse; the same ability and
resolution to follow the workings, and profit by the
prejudices, of low minds.   Akin to this taste for *Proneness of Andok-*
gossip is a certain proneness to sink into low comedy. *ides to low comedy.*
There is a fragment of Andokides, describing the
influx of country-people into Athens in 431 B.C.,
which will illustrate this.   It has exactly the tone
of the *Acharnians:*—

'Never again may we see the colliers coming in
from the hills to the town — the sheep and oxen
and the waggons — the poor women and old men —
the labourers arming themselves!   Never more may
we eat wild greens and chervil[1]!'

In passing judgment upon Andokides, it must *Summary.*
be allowed that he possesses neither literary merit
nor properly oratorical merit which can entitle him
to rank with the greatest masters of Greek rhetorical prose.   His language has neither splendour
nor a refined simplicity; he is not remarkably acute
in argument; and, compared with his contemporaries,
he is singularly without precision in the arrangement
of his ideas.   His extant works present no passage
conceived in the highest strain of eloquence; he

---

[1] μὴ γὰρ ἴδοιμέν ποτε πάλιν ἐκ
τῶν ὀρέων τοὺς ἀνθρακευτὰς ἥκοντας
καὶ πρόβατα καὶ βοῦς καὶ τὰς ἁμάξας
εἰς τὸ ἄστυ, καὶ γύναια καὶ πρεσβυ-
τέρους ἄνδρας καὶ ἐργάτας ἐξοπλιζο-
μένους· μηδὲ ἄγρια λάχανα καὶ σκάν-
δικας ἔτι φάγοιμεν.   Quoted by Suidas, p. 3327 B, from a scholium on
Ar. *Acharn.* 477: Sauppe, *Fragm.
Oratt. Gr.* p. 166: Blass, *Andoc.*
(Teubner) p. 97.

never rises to an impassioned earnestness. On the
other hand, his naturalness, though not charming,
is genuine; he has no mannerisms or affectations;
and his speeches have a certain impetus, a certain
confident vigour, which assure readers that they must
have been still more effective for hearers. The chief
value of Andokides is historical. But he has also
real literary value of a certain kind: he excels in
graphic description. A few of those pictures into
which he has put all the force of a quick mind—
the picture of Athens panicstricken by the sacrilege[1]—the scene of miserable perplexity in the
prison[2]—the patriotic citizen arraigned before the
Thirty Tyrants[3]—have a vividness which no artist
could easily surpass, combined with a freshness
which a better artist might possibly have lost[4].

[1] *De Myst.* §§ 43—45.
[2] *De Myst.* §§ 48—51.
[3] *Ib.* §§ 70—91.
[4] Sluiter's judgment (*Lectiones
Andocideae,* p. 3) does not show
much discrimination:—'At equidem, quanquam Andocidi orationem
non tribuam ratione et arte excul-
tam et politam; subtilitatem tamen,
impetum atque *gravitatem* illius
sum admiratus. Arte Lysiae cedit,
nervos plures habet et lacertos:
vehemens imprimis in reprehen-
dendo, in defendendo se gravis, ad
misericordiam erga se movendam
odiumque in adversarios excitan-
dum plane compositus, *in propo-
nendis diiudicandisque argumentis subtilis et acutus, dictione purus
et elegans, plenus Attici saporis:*
ut iure a Grammaticis in numerum
sit relatus et inter decem collocatus
principes.'

CHAPTER VI.

ANDOKIDES.

WORKS.

FOUR speeches ascribed to Andokides are extant, bearing the titles 'On the Mysteries:'
'On his Return:' 'On the Peace with the Lacedaemonians:' 'Against Alkibiades.' The speech On the
Mysteries, as the chief extant work of its author,
stands first in the manuscripts and the editions.
But the second oration relates to an earlier passage
in the life of Andokides, and may conveniently be
considered first.

The speech of Andokides 'On his Return' affords *Speech 'On his Return.'*
no further internal evidence of its own date than
that it was spoken later than 411 and earlier than
405 B. C.[1] Blass places it in 409[2]. But a circumstance which he has not noticed seems to us to make
it almost certain that the speech cannot have been
delivered later than the summer of 410. Andokides
lays stress upon the service which he has rendered
to Athens by securing a supply of corn from Cyprus.

---

[1] Later than 411—as being a
considerable time after the fall of
the Four Hundred in June, 411,
§§ 13—16, &c.: and obviously earlier than Aegospotami—since (*e.g.*)
the Peiraeus is open to corn-ships,
§ 21. — The notice in [*Lys.*] *in
Andok.* § 29 gives no help towards fixing the date.

[2] *Attisch. Bereds.* p. 278.

There had been a disappointment about this supply ; but he states that he has overcome the difficulty,— that fourteen corn ships will be in the Peiraeus almost immediately, and that others are to follow[1]. Now the event which had made this supply a matter of anxiety to Athens was the stoppage of the usual importations from the south coast of the Euxine. In 411 she had lost the command of the Bosphorus by the revolt of Chalkedon, and the command of the Hellespont by the revolt of Abydos[2]. But, in 410, the battle of Kyzikos was followed by the re-establishment of Athenian power in the Propontis and in its adjacent straits. The corn-trade of the Euxine once more flowed towards Athens ; and, in the autumn of 410, Agis, from his station at Deke-leia, saw with despair the multitude of corn-ships which were running into the Peiraeus[3]. The benefit, therefore, for which Andokides claims so much credit, would have been no great benefit, had it been conferred later than the middle of the year 410. The Four Hundred were deposed about the middle of June, 411 ; and it would have been natural that Andokides should have endeavoured to return at least in the course of the following year.

As a speech on a private matter before the public assembly, this oration belongs to the same class as that which Demosthenes is said to have written for Diphilos in support of his claim to be

---

[1] §§ 20—21.

[2] See Grote, VIII. pp. 171 ff.

[3] Xen. *Hellen.* I. i. 35, Ἄγις δὲ ἐκ τῆς Δεκελείας ἰδὼν πλοῖα πολλὰ σίτου εἰς Πειραιᾶ καταθέοντα οὐδὲν ὄφελος ἔφη εἶναι τοὺς μετ᾽ αὐτοῦ πολὺν ἤδη χρόνον Ἀθηναίους εἴργειν τῆς γῆς, εἰ μή τις σχήσοι καὶ ὅθεν ὁ κατὰ θάλατταν σῖτος φοιτᾷ.

rewarded by the State[1]. Andokides is charged, in
the speech of the pseudo-Lysias, with having gained
admittance to the ekklesia by bribing its presidents[2].
It is unnecessary to believe this story. But the
emphasis which he himself lays on the valuable
information which he had previously given to the
Senate[3] suggests that, without some such recommendation, he would have found it difficult to obtain a
hearing from the people.

The object of the speech is to procure the removal of certain disabilities under which he was
alleged to lie. His disclosures in 415 were made
under a guarantee of immunity from all consequences.
But the decree of Isotimides, passed soon afterwards,
excluded from the marketplace and from temples all
'who had committed impiety and who had confessed
it;' and his enemies maintained that this decree applied to him.

In the proem he points out the malice or stupidity of *Analysis.*
the men who persist in rejecting the good offices which he
is anxious to render to Athens; and refers to the importance

---

[1] That is to say, it is a δημηγορία,
but not properly a *deliberative*
speech; not a true συμβουλευτικὸς
λόγος. Dionysios mentions (*De
Deinarcho,* c. 11) a δημηγορικὸς λόγος written for Diphilos, in which
the latter urged before the ekklesia his own claim to certain public
honours (δωρεαί). Dionysios thinks
that this must have been written by
Demosthenes, not by Deinarchos.
Cf. Sauppe, *Fragm. Oratt. Gr.*
p. 251.

[2] [Lys.] *in Andok.* § 29, καταπλεύσας δὲ ἐκεῖθεν δεῦρο εἰς δημο-

κρατίαν εἰς τὴν ἑαυτοῦ πόλιν τοῖς μὲν
πρυτάνεσιν ἔδωκε χρήματα ἵνα αὐτὸν
προσαγάγοιεν ἐνθάδε, ὑμεῖς δ᾽ αὐτὸν
ἐξηλάσατε ἐκ τῆς πόλεως.

[3] Andok. *De Red.* § 19, ἐμοὶ τοίνυν τὰ μὲν ἤδη πεπραγμένα σχεδόν τι
ἅπαντες ἂν εἰδείητε, τὰ δὲ μέλλοντά
τε καὶ ἤδη πραττόμενα ἄνδρες ὑμῶν
πεντακόσιοι ἐν ἀπορρήτῳ ἴσασιν, ἡ
βουλή. The words ἄνδρες πεντακόσιοι deserve notice as a clever rhetorical touch: they imply a con-
gratulation on the recent abolition
of the Senate of *Four* Hundred.

of the communications which he has made in confidence to
the Senate. (§§ 1—4.) His so-called crimes—committed in
'youth' and 'folly'—are, he contends, his misfortunes. .For the
disclosures which he was driven to make five years before he
deserves pity—nay, gratitude—rather than hatred (§§ 5—9).

He then speaks of his life in exile; of his services
to the army at Samos in 411; of his return to Athens in
the time of the Four Hundred; and of his imprisonment
at the instance of Peisandros, who denounced him as the
friend of the democracy (§§ 10—16). Statesmen and generals serve the State at the State's expense; he has served
it at his own charge. Nor has the end of these services
been yet seen. The people will be soon in possession of the
secrets which he has imparted to the Senate; and will soon
see supplies of corn, procured by his intercession, enter the
Peiraeus. (§§ 17—21.) In return for so much, he asks but
one small boon—the observance of the promise of impunity
under which he originally laid his information, but which
was afterwards withdrawn through the influence of his
enemies. (§§ 22—23.)

The peroration opens with a singular argument. When
a man makes a mistake, it is not his body's fault: the
blame rests with his mind. But he, since he made his
mistake, has got a new mind. All that remains, therefore,
of the old Andokides is his unoffending body. (§ 24.) As
he was condemned on account of his former deeds, he ought
now to be welcomed for his recent deeds. His family has
ever been patriotic; his great-grandfather fought against the
Peisistratidae; he, too, is a friend of the people. The people, he well knows, are not to blame for the breach of faith
with him; they were persuaded to it by the same advisers
who persuaded them to tolerate an oligarchy. They have
repented of the oligarchy; let them repent also of the unjust sentence. (§§ 25—28.)

Remarks. There is a striking contrast between this defence
before the ekklesia and that which Andokides made
on the same charges. some eleven years later, before a

law-court. There he flatly denies that he is in any
degree guilty; he turns upon his adversaries with
invective and ridicule; he carries the whole matter
with a high hand, speaking in a thoroughly confident
tone, and giving free play to his lively powers of
narration. Here it is quite otherwise. He speaks
with humility and remorse of the 'folly'—the 'madness' of his youth; he complains feelingly of the
persecution which he has suffered; he implores, in
return for constant devotion to the interests of
Athens, just one favour—a little favour, which will
give his countrymen no trouble, but which will be
to him a great joy. In 399 he is defiant; in 410
he is almost abject. In 410 the traces of guilt to
which his enemies pointed were still fresh. Before
his next speech was spoken, they had been dimmed,
not by lapse of time only, but by that great wave
of trouble which swept over Athens in 405, and
which left all older memories faint in comparison
with the memory of the Thirty Tyrants. Andokides the wealthy choregus, the president of the
sacred mission, the steward of the sacred treasure,
supported on his trial by popular politicians and by
advocates chosen from his tribe, was a different
person from the anxious suitor who, in the speech
On his Return, implored, but could not obtain
tolerance.

In the style of the speech there is little to remark except that its difference from that of the
speech On the Mysteries exactly corresponds with
the difference of tone. There the orator is diffuse,
careless, lively; here he is more compact—for he

dared not treat a hostile assembly to long stories—
more artificial—and decidedly more dull. Once only
does the dramatic force of his natural style flash
out—where he describes his appearance before the
Council of the Four Hundred. 'Some of the Four
Hundred learned that I had arrived; sought me at
once; seized me; and brought me before the Council.
In an instant Peisandros was at my side:—'Senators,
I impeach this man for bringing corn and oar-spars
to the enemy'' (§ 14.)

Speech On the Mysteries. The events with which the speech On the Mysteries is connected have been related in the life of
Andokides. After his return to Athens, (probably
early in 402 B. C.,) under favour of the general
amnesty which followed the overthrow of the
Thirty Tyrants, he had spent three years in the
discharge of various public offices. At length, in
399 B. C., his enemies renewed their attack. During
the festival of the Great Mysteries, which Andokides
attended, in the autumn of that year, Kephisios
laid an information against him before the Archon
Basileus.

Mode of legal procedure. Some obscurity hangs over the form of the accusation; we will give the account of it which ap-
pears most probable. When, in 415 B.C., Andokides
made his disclosures, he did so on the guarantee of
impunity (ἄδεια) which a special decree of the ekklesia
had given to all who should inform. Subsequently,
however, Isotimides proposed and carried a decree
that all *who had committed impiety and had confessed it* should be excluded from the marketplace
and from the temples. The enemies of Andokides

maintained that he came under this decree. This
was the immediate cause of his quitting Athens in
415. In 409 he was unsuccessful in applying to have
the sentence of disfranchisement cancelled. On his
return in 402, however, nothing had been said at
first about his disabilities.

His accusers now contended that he had broken
the decree of Isotimides by attending the Mysteries
and entering the Eleusinian Temple. To attend the
festival or enter the temple unlawfully would, of
course, be an impiety. The information which they
laid against him charged him, therefore, on this
ground, with impiety. It was an ἔνδειξις ἀσεβείας.
But, in order to prove it, it was necessary to show
that he came under the decree of Isotimides. It was
necessary to show that he had committed impiety,
as well as given information, in 415 B.C.

His defence is therefore directed to showing,
in the first place, that he had not committed impiety
at that time either by profaning the Mysteries or
by mutilating the Hermae. The speech takes its
ordinary title from the fact that the Mysteries form
one of its prominent topics. But a more general
title would have better described the range of its
contents. It might have been more fitly called a
Defence on a Charge of Impiety.

This view of the matter explains some difficulties.
Andokides says (*de Myst.* § 71), 'Kephisios has
informed against me according to the existing law,
but bases his accusation on the decree of Isotimides.'
That is, Kephisios laid against Andokides an ordinary ἔνδειξις ἀσεβείας. But the charge of ἀσέβεια

rested on the assumption that he had broken the decree of Isotimides. He was not *directly* charged either with profaning the Mysteries or with mutilating the Hermae; his guilt in one or both of these matters was assumed. He proceeds to prove that this assumption is groundless; and that, therefore, the decree does not apply to him[1].

The charge, like all connected with religion, was brought into court by the Archon Basileus. Since details connected with the Mysteries might be put in evidence, the judges were chosen exclusively from the initiated of the higher grade[2]. Kephisios, the chief accuser[3], was assisted by Melêtos, who had been implicated in the murder of Leon under the Thirty[4], and by Epichares, who had been a member of their government[5]. On the same side were Kallias[6] and Agyrrhios[7], each of whom had a private quarrel with the accused. Andokides was supported by Anytos and Kephalos, both politicians of mark, and both popular for the part which they had taken

---

[1] Blass says: 'Kephisios, der als Hauptkläger auch die Hauptrede hielt, hatte nach Andokides seine Anklage gegründet auf das Psephisma des Isotimides.' (*Att. Bereds.* p. 300.) This statement, though substantially true, is not calculated to convey a clear idea of the *form* in which the accusation was preferred. Andokides was not simply accused of usurping certain rights which the decree of Isotimides had taken from him. That would have been an ἔνδειξις ἀτιμίας. He was accused specifi-

cally of *impiety*—the result of usurping such rights: it was an ἔνδειξις ἀσεβείας. Thus alone can we understand why the cause was brought into court by the Archon Basileus; and why death was the penalty. (Cf. *de Myst.* § 146: [Lys.] *in Andok.* § 55.)

[2] § 29 οἱ μεμυημένοι: § 31 μεμύησθε καὶ ἑωράκατε τοῖν θεοῖν τὰ ἱερά.

[3] § 71.

[4] § 94.

[5] § 95.

[6] §§ 110—131.

[7] §§ 132—136.

in the restoration of the democracy[1]. Advocates chosen for him by his tribesmen were also in court. It is remarkable if, as there is reason to believe, two men engaged on different sides in this trial were, in the same year, united in preferring a more famous charge of impiety. Anytos undoubtedly, Meletos[2] probably, was the accuser of Sokrates.

The speech On the Mysteries falls into three main divisions. In the first, Andokides shows his innocence in regard to the events of 415 B.C. In the second he shows that, in any case, the decree of Isotimides is now obsolete. In the third he deals with a number of minor topics.

I. §§ 1—69.

1. (*Proem.*) §§ 1—7. Andokides dwells on the rancour *Analysis.* of his enemies; insists on the fact of his having remained to stand his trial—instead of withdrawing to his property in Cyprus—as a proof of a good conscience; and appeals to the judges[3].

---

[1] § 150. For Anytos, see Xen. *Hellen.* II. 3 §§ 42, 44: for Kephalos, Demosth. *de Cor.* § 219.

[2] Meletos is mentioned in §§ 12 f., 35, 63, 94. He was a partisan of the Thirty (§ 94), and is clearly identical with the Meletos who went to Sparta as one of the envoys of the Town Party in 403 to discuss the terms of peace between the Town and the Peiraeus (Xen. *Hellen.* II. 4. § 36). All this agrees with what is known about the age of the Meletos who accused Sokrates. See the article by Mr Philip Smith in the Dict. of Greek and Roman Biography.

[3] Parts of this proem, viz. § 1 to the words πολλοὺς λόγους ποιεῖσθαι, and §§ 6, 7 αἰτοῦμαι οὖν—ἀκούσητε ἀπολογουμένου occur, slightly varied, in Lysias *de bonis Aristophanis* §§ 2—5. Spengel and Blass believe that both Andokides and Lysias used a proem written by some third person; Andokides interpolating in it some matter of his own. It is true that the transition from § 5 to § 6 in the speech of Andokides is harsh,

2. §§ 8—10. He is perplexed as to what topic of his defence he shall first approach. After a fresh appeal to the judges he resolves to begin with the facts relating to the Mysteries.

3. §§ 11—33. *The Mysteries Case.* He neither profaned them himself, nor informed against others as having profaned them. Four persons, on four distinct occasions, did, in fact, so inform: viz.:—(i) Pythonikos, who produced the slave Andromachos, § 11: (ii) Teukros, § 15: (iii) Agariste, § 16: (iv) Lydos, § 17. Lydos implicated Leogoras the father of Andokides. Leogoras, however, not only cleared himself, but got a verdict in an action which he brought against the senator Speusippos, §§ 17, 18. (This occasions a parenthesis, in which Andokides defends himself against the imputation of having denounced his father and relations: §§ 19—24.) The largest reward for information (μήνυτρα) was adjudged to Andromachos; the second, to Teukros: §§ 27, 28. Andokides calls upon the judges to recognise his innocence as regards the Mysteries: §§ 29—33.

4. §§ 34—69. *The Hermae Case.* In this matter the chief informants were (i) Teukros: §§ 34—35: (ii) Diokleides, whose allegations caused a general panic: §§ 36—46: (iii) Andokides himself. The circumstances, motives and results of his disclosure are stated at length: §§ 47—69.

II. §§ 70—91.

It is argued that the decree of Isotimides is now void, because it has been cancelled by subsequent decrees, laws and oaths, §§ 70—72. These are next enumerated, as follows.

1. §§ 73—79. During the siege of Athens by the

as if a patch had been made; but the transition from § 3 to § 4 is hardly less harsh, as Blass himself observes; indeed he suggests that a *second* borrowed proem may have been used there; but this is improbable. I should prefer to suppose that the whole proem is the work of Andokides himself, and that Lysias (whose speech belongs to 387 B.C.) abridged it.

Lacedaemonians in 405 B.C. the decree of Patrokleides was passed, reinstating all the disfranchised.

2. § 80. After the truce with Sparta in 404, when the Thirty Tyrants were established, all exiles received free permission to return.

3. § 81. After the expulsion of the Thirty in 403 a general amnesty was proclaimed.

4. §§ 82—89. At the same time, in accordance with the decree of Tisamenos, a revision of the laws was ordered. This revision having been completed, four new general laws (νόμοι) were passed:—viz. (i) That no 'unwritten' law should have force: (ii) That no decree (ψήφισμα) of ekklesia or senate should overrule a law (νόμος): (iii) That no law should be made against an individual (ἐπ' ἀνδρί, § 87): (iv) That decisions of judges or arbiters, pronounced under the former democracy, should remain valid; but that, in future, all decisions should be based on the code as revised in the archonship of Eukleides in 403 B.C. [This is expressed by the phrase χρῆσθαι νόμοις ἀπ' Εὐκλείδου ἄρχοντος, § 87.]

5. §§ 90, 91. Returning to the subject of § 81, Andokides recalls the terms of the oath of amnesty taken in 403 B.C. He then quotes the official oath of Senators and the official oath of Judges.

III. §§ 92—150 (end).

1. §§ 92—105. He shows that, if the amnesty is to be violated in his case, it may be violated to the cost of others also. The accusers, Kephisios, Meletus and Epichares, as well as others, would, in various ways, be liable to punishment.

2. §§ 106—109. He illustrates the good effect of general amnesties by two examples from the history of Athens: (i) the moderation shown after the expulsion of the Peisistratidae: (ii) an amnesty in the time of the Persian Wars.

3. §§ 110—136. He answers a charge made against
him by Kallias. Kallias asserted that Andokides, terrified
by the accusation hanging over him, had laid a suppliant's
bough (ἱκετηρία) on the altar in the temple at Eleusis during
the festival of the Great Mysteries. To take sanctuary, or
to place a symbol of supplication, in that temple at that
season, was a capital offence (as implying the approach
of guilt to the temple at a holy season). Andokides explains the motive of this false charge. Kallias was seeking
for his son an heiress whose hand was claimed by Andokides
(§§ 110—123). This leads to a digression about a scandal
connected with the birth of this son (§§ 124—131). He
then attacks the abettors of Kallias in this slander—especially Agyrrhios, a fraudulent tax-farmer who had a grudge
against Andokides (§§ 132—136).

4. §§ 137—139. He ridicules the assertion made by
the accuser, that the gods must have preserved so great
a traveller from the dangers of the sea because they reserved
him for the hemlock.

5. §§ 140—150. Peroration, on three topics chiefly:—
(i) the credit which Athens has gained by her policy of
amnesties—credit which the judges are bound to sustain:
(ii) the public services of the ancestors of Andokides: (iii)
his own opportunities for usefulness to the State hereafter, if
he is acquitted.

Andokides was acquitted. Before speaking of
the method and style of his speech, it is due to its
great historical interest to notice some of the disputed statements of fact which it contains.

*Historical
matter in
the Speech.*   1. Does the speech represent that account of
his own conduct which Andokides gave in 415 when
he made his disclosures before the Council of Four
Hundred? Next—had he, as a matter of fact, taken
part in the mutilation of the Hermae? These two

questions have been shortly discussed in Chapter IV.[1]
Some reasons are there suggested for believing (1)
that, in 415, Andokides had criminated himself as
well as others : (2) that he was, in fact, innocent.

2.   In § 11 Pythonikos, who brought forward
the evidence of the slave Andromachos, is named as
the first denouncer of Alkibiades. ' Some resident-
aliens and slaves in attendance on their masters'
(ἀκολούθων) are said by Thucydides (VI. 28) to
have been the first accusers ; and Plutarch adds
that these were brought forward by Androkles.
Androkles is mentioned by Andokides only in § 27,
as claiming the reward (μήνυτρα) from the Senate.
In order to reconcile Andokides with Thucydides, it
must be supposed either (1) that the 'resident-aliens
and slaves' of Thucydides (VI. 28) were the witnesses
of Pythonikos, and not, as Plutarch states (*Alkib.* 19),
of Androkles : or (2) that they were the witnesses,
some of Pythonikos, some of Androkles ; and that
those brought forward by Androkles did not crimi-
nate Alkibiades, although Androkles *afterwards* found
witnesses who did so. The former supposition, which
makes Plutarch inaccurate, seems the most likely.

3.   In § 13 it is stated that, on Pythonikos making his accusations, Polystratos was at once arrested
and executed, and that the other accused persons fled.
It is certain, as Grote[2] observes, that Alkibiades
was accused, but neither fled nor was brought to
trial ; and it would seem more probable, therefore,
that the charge was dropped, for the time, in reference to the others also. On this point, however, it

[1] p. 76.   [2] *Hist. Gr.* III p. 243.

does not seem necessary to assume inaccuracy in Andokides.   The position of Alkibiades, as a commander
of the expedition on which the hopes of the people
were set and which was about to sail, was wholly
exceptional.   The evidence against him may also
have been of a different nature.

4.   In § 13 there is an oversight.   Among those
denounced by Pythonikos was Panaetios.   And it is
said that all persons so denounced—except Polystratos, who was put to death—fled.   But in § 68
Panaetios appears as leaving Athens in consequence
of the later denunciation of Andokides.   As thê list
in § 13 contains ten names in all, the speaker might
easily have made a mistake about one of the number.
Or the evidence against Panaetios—who is named
last of the ten—may have been so weak that he
was acquitted upon this first charge.

5.   In § 34 it is said that some of the persons
accused by Teukros were put to death.   To this Mr
Grote[1] opposes the fact that Thucydides (VI. 60)
names as having suffered death only some of those
who were denounced by Andokides.   It seems unsafe, however, to conclude that the orator has made
a wrong statement.   The language of Thuc. VI. 53,
ξυλλαμβάνοντες κατέδουν, hardly warrants the inference that imprisonment was the utmost rigour
used in other cases.   The statement of Andokides
in § 34 is incidentally confirmed by the words which
he ascribes to Charmides in § 49.

6.   In § 38 Andokides quotes, without comment,
the statement of Diokleides that he had seen the

[1] *Hist. Gr.* VII. p. 268.

faces of some of the conspirators by the light of a full moon. Now Plutarch says that one of the informers (he does not give the name), being asked how he had recognised the faces of the mutilators, answered, 'by the light of the moon;' and was thus convicted of falsehood, it having been new moon on the night in question [1]. Diodoros (XIII. 2) tells the same story, without mentioning any name; but his account does not apply to Diokleides. Mr Grote is unquestionably right in treating the new-moon story as a later fiction [2]. Andokides would not have failed to notice so fatal a slip on the part of Diokleides; nor is it likely that the informer would have made it.

7. In § 17 the action brought by Leogoras against Speusippos is mentioned directly after the evidence of Lydos. But it should be observed that it is mentioned parenthetically; and that the indefinite κἄπειτα does not fix its date at all. Leogoras was in the prison with his son (§ 50); and the action was doubtless not brought until after the disclosures of Andokides.

8. In § 45 the panic, during which the citizens kept watch under arms through the night, is placed in immediate connection with the informations of Diokleides, who caused this panic by representing the plot as widely spread. It is said, also, that the Boeotians took advantage of the alarm at Athens to march to the frontier. Now Thucydides (VI. 60)

---

[1] Plut. *Alk.* c. 20 εἰς δ' αὐτῶν ἐρωτώμενος ὅπως τὰ πρόσωπα τῶν ἑρμοκοπιδῶν γνωρίσειε, καὶ ἀποκρινά- μενος ὅτι πρὸς τὴν σελήνην, ἐσφάλη τοῦ παντός, ἕνης καὶ νέας οὔσης ὅτε ταῦτ' ἐδρᾶτο.

[2] *Hist. Gr.* VII. p. 271.

states that, during one night an armed body of
citizens garrisoned the Theseion ; but he puts this
after the disclosures of Andokides, and connects
it with the appearance of a Spartan force at the
isthmus. Bishop Thirlwall justly remarks that, unless there were two or more occasions on which the
citizens kept armed watch, Andokides, who goes
into minute detail, is more likely than Thucydides
to be right about the time of it[1].

9. In § 106 the expulsion from Athens of the
tyrants—that is, Hippias and his adherents—is described as following upon a battle fought ἐπὶ Παλληνίῳ, which seems to mean 'at the Pallenion,' the
temple of Athene Pallenis at Pallene, about 10 miles
E.N.E. of Athens[2]. Now it was near this temple
that Peisistratos, on his third return, won the victory
which led to the final establishment of his tyranny,
probably in 545 B.C.[3] But no battle at the same
spot, or anywhere near it, is mentioned by any
other authority in connexion with the expulsion of
of the Peisistratidae. According to Herodotos, the
Lacedaemonians sent, in 510, an expedition under
Kleomenes. Kleomenes, on entering Attica from

---

[1] *Hist. Gr.* III. p. 499 (appendix
III. to ch. xxv.)

[2] Professor Rawlinson, in the
Journal of Philology, Vol. I. No. 2,
p. 25, questions whether the Παλλήνιον of Andokides means the
temple of Athene at Pallene. The
proper name of that temple was,
he thinks, 'the Pallenis.' It appears to me as I have endeavoured
to show (*Journ. Philol.* Vol. II.

No. 3, p. 48) that Παλληνίς is always
the epithet of the goddess, not the
name of the temple. I believe
Παλλήνιον to be identical with what
Herodotos (I. 62) calls Παλληνίδος
Ἀθηναίης ἱρόν.

[3] This is the date fixed on by
Curtius (*Hist. Gr.* Vol. I. p 359
tr. Ward). Clinton (*F. H.* II. p.
202) thinks 537 more probable.

the isthmus, met and routed the Thessalian cavalry of Hippias; advanced to Athens; and besieged the Peisistratidae, who presently capitulated[1]. Herodotos and Andokides can be reconciled only by supposing that the account of Herodotos is incomplete[2]. It seems more probable, however, that Andokides has confused the scene of a battle won by Peisistratos with the scene of a battle lost by the Peisistratidae[3].

10.　In § 107 it is said that when, later, the Persian king made an expedition against Greece, the Athenians recalled those who had been banished, and reinstated those who had been disfranchised, when the tyrants were expelled. No such amnesty is recorded in connection with the first Persian invasion in 490; but Plutarch mentions such a measure as having been passed shortly before the battle of Salamis in 480[4]. Now the Persian invasion in 490 was undertaken for the purpose of restoring Hippias; and the invasion in 480 was undertaken partly at the instance of his family. Men (or their descendants) who had been banished or disfranchised in 510 would certainly not have been restored to Athenian citizenship in 490 or 480. Andokides seems, then,

---

[1] Her. v. 64.

[2] Professor Rawlinson thinks that there was a second battle, (after that won by Kleomenes on entering Attica), in which the Alkmaeonidae and the other exiles fought on the Spartan side; and this battle, he suggests, may have been fought near Pallene (*Journ. Phil.* I. 2. pp. 25 ff.).

[3] The view that the battle described by Andokides as fought ἐπὶ Παλληνίῳ is identical with that mentioned in Herod. v. 64 is held by Sluiter, *Lect. Andoc.* p. 6: Wordsworth, *Athens and Attica,* p. 198 *note:* Thirlwall, *Hist. Gr.* II. p. 80 *note:* Grote, *Hist. Gr.* IV. p. 165 *note.*

[4] Plut. *Them.* c. 11.

to have remembered vaguely that an act of amnesty was passed at Athens on some occasion during the Persian wars; to have placed this act in 490 instead of 480; and to have represented it as passed in favour of the very persons who would probably have been excluded from it.

11.   In § 107 it is said of the Athenians;— 'They resolved to meet the barbarians at Marathon... They fought and conquered; they freed Greece and saved their country.   And having done so great a deed, they thought it not meet to bear malice against any one for the past.   Therefore, although through these things *they entered upon their city desolate, their temples in ashes, their walls and houses in ruins*, yet by concord they achieved the empire of Greece,' &c.   From this passage Valckenär[1], Sluiter and Grote infer that Andokides has transferred the burning of Athens by Xerxes in 480 to the first invasion in 490.   This is hardly a necessary inference.   Andokides is speaking of the struggle with Persia—extending from 490 to 479—as a whole. He names Marathon: he does not name Salamis or Plataea.   He merely says that, after the Athenians had 'freed Greece,' they came back to find their city in ruins[2].

Arrangement and Style of the Speech.

It is impossible to read the speech On the

---

[1] See Valckenär's note, quoted and endorsed by Sluiter, *Lect. Andoc.* p. 48, and by Grote, IV. p. 165 n.:—'Confundere videtur Andokides diversissima: Persica sub Miltiade et Dario et victoriam Marathoniam, quaeque evenere sub Themistocle, Xerxis gesta. Hic urbem incendio delevit, non ille. Nihil magis est manifestum quam diversa ab oratore confundi.'

[2] See the *Journal of Philology*, Vol. I. No. 1, p. 165, for a discussion of this passage.

Mysteries without feeling that, as a whole, it is
powerful, in spite of some evident defects. The
arrangement is best in what we have called the first
division (§§ 1—69), which deals with two distinct
groups of facts, those relating to the Mysteries case
and those relating to the Hermae case. These facts
are stated in an order which is, on the whole,
clear and natural, though not free from the parentheses of which Andokides was so fond, and of which
sections 19—24 form an example. Less praise is
due to the second part of the speech (§§ 70—91),
devoted to the various enactments which had made
the decree of Isotimides obsolete. It is at once full
and obscure, giving needless, and withholding necessary, details. The third part (§§ 92—end) is a mere
string of topics, unconnected with each other, and
but slightly connected with the case. This confused
appendix to the real defence is, however, significant.
It shows the anxiety of Andokides to make the
judges understand the rancorous personal feeling of
his enemies; an anxiety natural in a man who for
sixteen years had been pursued by unproved accusations. The passages about Kallias and Agyrrhios probably had a stronger effect upon the court
than any conventional appeal to compassion would
have produced.

As regards style, the language of the speech is
thoroughly unaffected and easy, plain without studied avoidance of ornament, and rising at the right
places—as when he speaks of the old victories of
freedom (§§ 106—109), and in the peroration (§§ 140
—150). But the great merit of the composition is

its picturesqueness, its variety and life. The scene in the prison (§§ 48—53) and the description of the panic at Athens (§§ 43—45) are perhaps the best passages in this respect. If Andokides had not many rhetorical accomplishments, he certainly had perception of character, and the knack of describing it. Diokleides bargaining with Euphemos (§ 40)—Charmides exhorting Andokides to save the prisoners (§§ 49, 50)—Peisandros urging that Mantitheos and Aphepsion should be put on the rack (§ 43)—are well given in a few vivid touches.

Speech On the Peace with the Lacedaemonians. The speech On the Peace with the Lacedaemonians belongs, as has been noticed in a former chapter [1], to the year 390. Athens, Thebes, Corinth and Argos had then been four years at war with Sparta. Andokides had just returned from an embassy to Sparta with a view to peace. The terms proposed by the Lacedaemonians were, as regarded Athens, permission to retain her walls and ships, and the restoration of Lemnos, Imbros and Skyros. The orator, speaking in debate in the ekklesia, urges that these terms should be accepted.

Analysis. The opponents of peace contend that peace with Lacedaemon is fraught with danger to the democracy (§§ 1—2). He meets this objection by instancing a number of cases in which peace with Sparta, so far from injuring the Athenian democracy, was productive of the greatest advantage to it. He cites (1) a peace with Sparta negotiated by Miltiades during a war in Euboea: §§ 3—5. (2) The Thirty Years' Truce, 445 B.C. §§ 6—7. (3) The Peace of Nikias,

---

[1] Ch. IV. p. 83.

421 B.C.: §§ 8, 9.—The compulsory truce with Sparta in 404, followed by the establishment of the Thirty Tyrants, was not, properly speaking, a peace at all; and is therefore no exception to the rule that peace with Sparta has always been found salutary (§§ 10—12).

There is no good reason for continuing the war. The claims of Athens have now been recognised; the Boeotians desire peace; the hope of finally crushing Sparta is idle (§§ 13—16). Athens is the power which gains most by the peace now proposed (§§ 17—23). If Boeotia makes peace, Athens will be left with one weak ally, Corinth, and another who is a positive encumbrance—selfish Argos (§§ 24—27). Athens must not, here, prefer weak friends, as formerly she preferred Amorges to Xerxes II.; Egesta to Syracuse; Argos to Sparta (§§ 28—32). The speaker goes on to notice a variety of objections to the peace. Some say that walls and ships are not money, and wish to recover their property abroad [τὰ σφέτερ' αὐτῶν τῆς ὑπεροπίας, § 36] which was lost when the Athenian empire fell. But such men ought to remember that walls and ships were just the means by which the empire was won in the first instance (§§ 33—39).

In a peroration the assembly is reminded that the decision rests wholly with it; Argive and Corinthian envoys have come urging war; Spartan envoys, offering peace. The true plenipotentiaries are not the ambassadors, but those who vote in the ekklesia (§§ 40, 41 [1]).

According to the author of the Argument, the *Question of authenticity.* speech On the Peace was judged spurious by Dionysios[2], and Harpokration also doubted its authenticity[3]. Among modern critics, Taylor[4] and Markland[5] are the chief who have taken the same view; but they have a majority of opinions against

---

[1] πρεσβευτὰς οὖν πάντας ὑμᾶς ἡμεῖς οἱ πρέσβεις ποιοῦμεν.

[2] Auct. Argum. *ad fin.* ὁ δὲ Διονύσιος νόθον εἶναι λέγει τὸν λόγον.

[3] He quotes it thrice, but always

with the addition εἰ γνήσιος.

[4] *Lectiones Lysiacae,* c. VI. (Vol. II. p. 260, ed. Reiske.)

[5] *Ad* Aeschin. *De Falsa Legat.* p. 302.

them[1]. Probably the suspicions of Dionysios, like
those of Taylor, arose mainly from the difficulties of
the historical passage (§§ 3—6); and from the fact
that this passage is found, slightly modified, in the
speech of Aeschines On the Embassy.

*Historical
Difficulties.*

It is said in §§ 3—5 that, when the Athenians
'had the war in Euboea'—being then masters of
Megara, Troezen and Pegae—Miltiades, son of Kimon, who had been ostracised, was recalled, and was
sent to treat for peace at Sparta. A peace was
concluded between Athens and Sparta for fifty
years[2]; and was observed on both sides for thirteen
years. During this peace the Peiraeus was fortified
(478 B.C.), and the Northern Long Wall was built
(457 B.C.). Now (1) the only recorded war of
Athens in which Euboea was concerned, during the
life of Miltiades, was in 507, when the Chalkidians
were defeated and their territory given to the first
kleruchs. (2) Megara, Troezen and Pegae were not
included in the Athenian alliance until long after
478 B.C. (3) Miltiades was never ostracised; having
been sent to the Chersonese before the invention of
ostracism by Kleisthenes. (4) No such peace as that
spoken of is known; though in 491, an Athenian
embassy went to Sparta with a different object—to
denounce the medism of the Aeginetans[3]. Most
critics have assumed that Andokides refers to the Five

[1] Sluiter, *Lect. Andoc.* c. x. p.
205, and Valckenär quoted there:
Ruhnken, *Hist. Crit. Or. Graec.*
(Opusc. Vol. i. p, 325); Wesseler
ad Diod. Sic. xii. c. 8; and Blass,
Att. Bereds. p. 322, are among
the defenders of the speech as au-

thentic.

[2] Taylor, correcting Andokides
from Aeschin. *De Fals. Legat.*
§ 172, reads πεντήκοντα for πέντε:
and so Blass.

[3] Her. vi. 49.

Years' Truce between Athens and Sparta, concluded
in 450 B.C., mainly through the influence of Kimon,
son of Miltiades; and that he names the father instead of the son[1]. But all agree that the passage
as it stands is full of inaccuracies, and can be reconciled with history only by conjectural emendation[2].

Again, in § 6 it is said that Athens having been
plunged into war by the Aeginetans, and having
done and suffered much evil, at last concluded the
Thirty Years' Peace with Sparta (445 B.C.). The
impression conveyed by this statement is wrong.
The war between Athens and Aegina began about
458, and ended in 455 with the reduction of Aegina.
In 450 Athens and Sparta made a truce for five
years. A new train of events began with the revolution in Boeotia in 447, followed by the revolt of
Megara and Euboea ; and it was this which led up
to the peace of 445 B.C.

These inaccuracies are in regard only to the
earlier history of Athens : and the undoubtedly genuine speech On the Mysteries contains allusions
which are no less inaccurate. In regard to contemporary events the speaker makes no statement
which can be shown to be incorrect : and on one
point—the position of Argos at the time—he is
incidentally confirmed in a striking manner by
Xenophon[3]. A forger would have studied the early

---

[1] This view, briefly stated by
Sluiter, *Lectiones Andocideae*, c. x.
p. 135, is discussed and approved
by Clinton, *Fasti Hellen.* Vol. II.
Append. c. 8. p. 257; and adopted
by Grote, v. p. 453, *note* 3. For
the Five Years' Truce Clinton gives
the date 450, which I take : Grote,
452 : Curtius (*Hist. Gr.* II. p. 402 tr.
Ward) 451—450.

[2] Cf. Curtius, *Hist. Gr.* Vol. II.
p. 412 (tr. Ward): Grote, v. pp.
455—464.

[3] The speech On the Peace

Passage
common to
Andokides
and
Aeschines.

history with more care, and would not have known
the details of the particular situation so well. But
how does it happen that the whole historical passage
(§§ 3—12) reappears, with modifications, in the
speech of Aeschines On the Embassy [1]? Either Aeschines copied this speech, or a later writer copied
the speech of Aeschines. There can be little doubt
that the former was the case. Andokides, grandfather of the orator, is mentioned in the speech On
the Peace [2] as a member of the embassy to Sparta in
445 B.C. In the speech of Aeschines [3] he is named
as chief of that embassy. This Andokides—an obscure

speaks of the Argives as having
'made a peace on their own account'
which protected their territory:
§ 27 αὐτοὶ δ' ἰδίᾳ εἰρήνην ποιήσαντες
τὴν χώραν οὐ παρέχουσιν ἐμπολε-
μεῖν. Now Xenophon tells us that
in 392 the Corinthian government
had formed a close alliance with
Argos. The boundary-stones between the territories were taken
up; an Argive garrison held the
citadel of Corinth; and the very
name of Corinth was changed to
Argos (Hellen. IV. 4—6). In 391
Agesilaos had ravaged the Argive
territory before taking Lechaeum
(Hell. IV. 4—19). The next year,
399, Ol. 97. 3, was the year of the
Isthmia. The Argives assumed
the presidency of the festival, and
offered the sacrifice to Poseidon,
on the ground that 'Argos was
Corinth'—ὡς Ἄργους τῆς Κορίνθου
ὄντος (Hell. IV. 5. 1). Consequently
they claimed the privilege of the
Sacred Month (ἱερομηνία) for Argolis. And so, precisely in the
year 390, to which we saw that the

speech On the Peace belongs, it
was true that the Argive territory
enjoyed a special immunity. This
had not been the case in 391; nor
was it any longer the case in 388
(the next Isthmian year), when
Agesipolis asked Zeus at Olympia
and Apollo at Delphi whether he
was bound to respect this fictitious
extension of the ἱερομηνία—was
absolved by the gods from respect-
ing it—and ravaged Argolis (H. IV.
7. 2).

[1] Aeschin. De Fals. Legat. § 172,
συνταραχθέντες δέ... to § 176, ἠναγ-
κασμένοι. The topics are the same
as those of Andok. De Pace, §§
3—12: the language is coincident
in several points, yet, on the whole,
much altered.

[2] § 6 ᾑρέθησαν δέκα ἄνδρες ἐξ
Ἀθηναίων ἁπάντων πρέσβεις ἐς Λα-
κεδαίμονα αὐτοκράτορες, ὧν ἦν καὶ
Ἀνδοκίδης ὁ πάππος ὁ ἡμέτερος.

[3] Aesch. De Fals. Legat. § 174,
Ἀνδοκίδην ἐκπέμψαντες καὶ τοὺς
συμπρέσβεις.

member, if he was a member, of the embassy which, according to Diodoros[1], was led by Kallias and Chares —would not have been named at all except by his own grandson. Again, there are traces in Aeschines of condensation—not always intelligent —from the speech On the Peace. Thus the latter[2] says (referring to the years before the Peloponnesian war)—'we laid up 1000 talents in the acropolis, *and set them apart by law for the use of the people at special need'*: Aeschines, leaving out the qualifying clause, makes it appear that the sum of 1000 talents was the total sum laid up in the Athenian treasury[3] during the years of peace.

The treatment of the subject certainly affords no argument against the authenticity of the speech. Andokides gave little care to arrangement, and here there is no apparent attempt to treat the question methodically. On the other hand, the remarks about Corinth and Argos[4], and the answer to those who demanded the restoration of lands abroad[5], are both acute and sensible. In this, as in his other speech before the ekklesia, the descriptive talent of Andokides had little scope; but, as in the speech On the Mysteries, the style is spirited and vigorous. *Remarks on the Speech.*

The speech against Alkibiades is certainly spurious. It discusses the question whether the speaker, or Nikias or Alkibiades is to be ostracised. The *Speech against Alkibiades.*

---

[1] XII. 7.

[2] Andok. *De Pace*, § 7 πρῶτον μέν...ἀνηνέγκαμεν χίλια τάλαντα εἰς τὴν ἀκρόπολιν καὶ νόμῳ κατεκλείσαμεν ἐξαίρετα εἶναι τῷ δήμῳ· τοῦτο δὲ τριήρεις ἄλλας ἑκατόν, κ.τ.λ.

[3] Aeschin. *De Fals. Legat.* § 174 χίλια μὲν γὰρ τάλαντα ἀνηνέγκαμεν νομίσματος εἰς τὴν ἀκρόπολιν, ἑκατὸν δὲ τριήρεις ἑτέρας, κ.τ.λ.

[4] §§ 24—27.

[5] §§ 36—39.

situation resembles one which is mentioned by Plutarch. Alkibiades, Nikias and Phaeax were rivals for power, and it had become plain that one of the three would incur ostracism[1]. They therefore made common cause against Hyperbolos, who was ostracised, probably in 417 B. C.[2]

The supposed date of this speech is fixed by a reference in § 22 to the capture of Melos. Melos was taken in the winter of 416—415 B. C. Nikias left Athens, never to return, in the spring of 415. Therefore the speech could have been spoken only in the early part of 415 B. C.

Analysis. The orator, after stating the point at issue, and censuring the institution of ostracism (§§ 1—6), enters upon an elaborate invective against Alkibiades (§§ 10—40). The latter is attacked for having doubled the tribute of the allies (§§ 10—12); for having ill-used his wife (§§ 13—15); for contempt of the law (§§ 16—19); for beating a choregus (§§ 20, 21); for insolence after his Olympian victory (§§ 24—33). He is then contrasted with the speaker (§§ 34—40), who concludes with a notice of his own public services (§§ 41, 42).

The Speech not by Andokides. The speech is twice cited without suspicion by Harpokration: it is also named as genuine by Photios[3]. The biographer of Andokides does not men-

---

[1] Plut. *Alk.* c. 13. In *Aristid.* c. 7 and in *Nik.* c. 11 Plutarch names only Alkibiades and Nikias as the rivals; adding, in *Nik.* c. 11, that Theophrastos substitutes Phaeax for Nikias.

[2] The Schol. on Ar. *Vesp.* 1007 quotes Theopompos for the statement ἐξωστράκισαν τὸν Ὑπέρβολον ἐξ ἔτη. ὁ δὲ καταπλεύσας εἰς Σάμον

...ἀπέθανε. The death of Hyperbolos is fixed by Thuc. VIII. 73 to 411 B.C. Blass, with Cobet and others, thinks that the 'six years' of Theopompos represent simply the number of years which intervened between the banishment of Hyperbolos and his death. This brings the ostracism to 417 B.C.

[3] Phot. *Cod.* 261.

tion it; but, in its place, mentions a Defence in reply to Phaeax[1]. There are traces of its ascription in antiquity both to Lysias[2] and to Aeschines[3]. But an examination of the speech will show that it cannot have been spoken by Andokides, or written by him for the use of another; that it was probably not written by any one who lived at the time of which it treats; and that there is good reason for believing it to be the work of a late sophist.

That Andokides spoke this speech is inconceivable. The speaker says (§ 8) that he has been four times tried; and (§ 41) that he has been ambassador to Molossia, Thesprotia, Italy and Sicily. But elsewhere, excusing himself for acts committed in the very year in which this speech is supposed to have been delivered—in 415—Andokides pleads that he was young and foolish at the time[4]. Moreover, no writer mentions Andokides as having been in danger of ostracism at the same time as Nikias and Alkibiades.

Nor is it credible that Andokides wrote the speech for another person—Phaeax, for instance, as Valckenär[5] suggests. The style is strongly against this. It is far more artificial than anything by Andokides which we possess; it approaches, indeed, more nearly to the style of Isokrates. The formal

---

[1] [Plut.] *Vit. Andoc.* ἀπολογία πρὸς Φαίακα.

[2] Athenaeos (IX. p. 408 C.) quotes some words from § 29 of the speech, as from Λυσίας κατ᾽ ᾽Αλκιβιάδου.

[3] This may be surmised from Diogenes Laertios, II. 63, who says, speaking of Aeschines *the Sokratic*,

ἦν δὲ καὶ ἐν τοῖς ῥητορικοῖς ἱκανῶς γεγυμνασμένος, ὡς δῆλον ἔκ τε τῆς ἀπολογίας [τοῦ πατρός—Blass ὑπὲρ] Φαίακος τοῦ στρατηγοῦ καὶ Δίωνος.

[4] *De Reditu,* § 7.

[5] See Valckenär's dissertation, given at the end of Chap. I. of Sluiter's *Lect. Andoc.*

antitheses in the proem (§§ 1—2) are a striking example of this character[1].

Was
Phaeax the
author?
Taylor[2] and others have ascribed the speech to Phaeax himself. Plutarch names Phaeax, Alkibiades and Nikias as the three men over whom ostracism was hanging at the same time; and quotes from a speech against Alkibiades, with which the name of Phaeax is connected, a story which appears (in a different form) in our speech[3]. Then it is known from Thucydides that Phaeax went on an embassy at least to Sicily and Italy[4]. Valckenär's and Ruhnken's[5] arguments against Taylor are inconclusive. If the speech was really written at the time of which it treats, it cannot be disproved, any more than it can be proved, that Phaeax was the author.

---

[1] Compare also § 21 ἀλλ' ὑμεῖς ἐν μὲν ταῖς τραγῳδίαις τοιαῦτα θεωροῦντες δεινὰ νομίζετε, γιγνόμενα δὲ ἐν τῇ πόλει ὁρῶντες οὐδὲν φροντίζετε, with Isokr. Panegyr. § 168 ἐπὶ μὲν ταῖς συμφοραῖς ταῖς ὑπὸ τῶν ποιητῶν συγκειμέναις δακρύειν ἀξιοῦσιν, ἀληθινὰ δὲ πάθη πολλὰ καὶ δεινὰ γιγνόμενα διὰ τὸν πόλεμον ἐφορῶντες τοσούτου δέουσιν ἐλεεῖν, κ.τ.λ.

[2] Lect. Lysiac. c. VI.

[3] Plut. Alk. c. 13 φέρεται δὲ καὶ λόγος τις κατ' Ἀλκιβιάδου καὶ Φαίακος γεγραμμένος ἐν ᾧ μετὰ τῶν ἄλλων γέγραπται καὶ ὅτι τῆς πόλεως πολλὰ πομπεῖα χρυσᾶ καὶ ἀργυρᾶ κεκτημένης Ἀλκιβιάδης ἐχρῆτο πᾶσιν αὐτοῖς ὥσπερ ἰδίοις πρὸς τὴν καθ' ἡμέραν δίαιταν. For καὶ Φαίακος Taylor (l. c.) and Vater (Rerum Andocidearum cap. IV.) propose ὑπὸ Φαίακος: Blass (Att. Bereds. 330)

ὑπὲρ Φαίακος. Blass thinks that, whoever the author of the speech was, the person meant to be defended was Phaeax; and that the ἀπολογία πρὸς Φαίακα in [Plut.] Vit. Andoc. may have come from an original ἀπολογία Φαίακι, i.e. ὑπὲρ Φαίακος.

The story of the sacred vessels can hardly have been taken by Plutarch only from § 29 of the speech, where it runs:—τὰ πομπεῖα παρὰ τῶν ἀρχιθεωρῶν αἰτησάμενος ὡς εἰς τἀπινίκια τῇ προτεραίᾳ τῆς θυσίας χρησόμενος ἐξηπάτησε καὶ ἀποδοῦναι οὐκ ἤθελε.

[4] Thuc. v. 4.

[5] Ruhnken, Historia Crit. Oratt. Graec. (Opusc. I. p. 326). Ruhnken, as Sluiter points out, borrows largely from Valckenär's dissertation (see above), which had appeared 12 years before.

But an overwhelming amount of evidence tends *The Speech probably by a late sophist.* to show that the speech is the work of a later sophist. First stand two general reasons; the supposed occasion of the speech, and the style of its composition.

As far as the nature of ostracism is known to us, *Ostracism misconceived.* the whole speech involves a thorough misconception of it : it assumes a situation which could never have existed. Once every year the ekklesia was formally asked by its presidents whether, in that year, an ostracism should be held. If it voted affirmatively, a day was fixed. The market-place was railed in for voting, every citizen might write any name he pleased on the shell which he dropped into the urn ; and if against any one name there were six thousand votes, the person so indicated was banished for ten— in later times, for five—years. The characteristic feature of the whole proceeding was the absence of everything like an open contest between definite rivals. The very object of ostracism was to get rid of a dangerous man in the quietest and least invidious way. No names were mentioned; far less was discussion dreamed of. The idea of a man rising in the ekklesia or other public gathering, and stating that he was one of three persons who were in danger of ostracism; then inveighing at great length and with extraordinary bitterness against one of the other two ; and concluding with a vindication of his own consequence—would have probably seemed to Athenians of the days of ostracism incredibly indecent and absurd. In the first place, they would have been offended by his open assumption—whether true or not—that *he* was one of the citizens who had rendered the resort to ostracism necessary; secondly, they would have resented his attempt to prejudice the ballot; and if, in the end, he had escaped, his escape would probably have been due to their conviction that, as the poet Plato said of Hyperbolos, 'it was not for such fellows that shells were invented[1].' But the speaker against Alkibiades does not only himself speak thus; he asserts that Alkibiades is about to address the house next, and to endeavour to move it by his tears[2].

Style.

If the nature of the situation supposed were not enough, the style of the composition would in itself be almost decisive. The speaker begins with a formal statement of the matter in hand, evidently meant for a reader; and then goes on to string together all the tritest stories about Alkibiades. This —the body of the speech—has the unmistakable air of a compilation.

Particular errors.

The arguments from the supposed occasion and from the style are confirmed by the evidence of particular misstatements. In §§ 22, 23 Alkibiades is said to have had a child by a Melian woman who came into his power after the capture of Melos; but the speech, as has been shown, can refer only to the spring of 415: and Melos was taken only in the winter of 416—415. In § 33 Kimon is said to have been banished because he had married his own sister. In § 13 the commander at Delium—a battle fought but nine years before the supposed date of the speech

---

[1] *Ap.* Plut. *Alk.* c. 13 οὐ γὰρ τοιούτων εἵνεκ᾽ ὄστραχ᾽ εὑρέθη.

[2] § 39. Grote (IV. p. 202, *note*) remarks on the erroneous conception of ostracism involved in the speaker complaining that he is going to be ostracised *without* any secret voting—as if by a show of hands. But in § 2 the οὔτε before διαψηφισαμένων κρύβδην is now omitted by Schleiermacher and Blass.

—is called Hipponikos instead of Hippokrates. The two last blunders would have been impossible for an Athenian of that age. On the whole there can be little doubt that in this speech we must recognize the work of a late rhetorician who saw, in the juxtaposition of Alkibiades, Nikias and Andokides, a dramatic subject; who had only an indistinct notion of how ostracism was managed in olden times; and who believed himself sufficiently prepared for his task when he had read in Plutarch all the scandalous stories relating to Alkibiades.

Beside the extant speeches of Andokides, the titles of four others have been preserved. (1) Plutarch quotes an address ' To the Associates,' or members of the oligarchical clubs, as authority for a statement that the remains of Themistokles had been dishonoured at Athens; but adds that the statement was made by Andokides merely for the purpose of exasperating the oligarchs against the people[1]. Ruhnken[2], with whom Sauppe[3] agrees, thought that this Address was a letter written by Andokides, then in exile, to the fellow-conspirators of Peisandros in 411. But the breach of Andokides with the oligarchical party, after his informations in 415, was decisive and final; when he returned to Athens in 411 he was at once denounced by Peisandros and imprisoned. It seems better, then, with Kirchhoff[4] and Blass[5], to refer this Address to an earlier time than 415 : perhaps to the years 420—418, a period

Lost Works.

Address to the Associates.

---

[1] Plut. *Themist.* c. 32.
[2] *Hist. Crit. Or. Gr.* (Opusc. I. p. 326).
[3] *Or. Att.* II. p. 165.
[4] *Andocidea,* Hermes I. pp. 1—20.
[5] *Att. Bereds.* p. 286; and *Andoc.* (Teubner) p. 96.

of keen struggle between the oligarchical and popular

Delibera-
tive Speech. parties at Athens[1]. (2) The 'Deliberative Speech'
quoted by the lexicographers[2] is identified by Kirchhoff with the last-mentioned. Its title seems, however, to show plainly that it was of a different kind,
and was either spoken, or supposed to be spoken, in

Speech On
the Infor- debate in the ekklesia. (3) Harpokration once
mation. quotes a ' Speech On the Information' ($\pi\epsilon\rho\grave{\iota}$ $\tau\hat{\eta}s$ $\grave{\epsilon}\nu$-
$\delta\epsilon\acute{\iota}\xi\epsilon\omega s$) for the word $\zeta\eta\tau\eta\tau\acute{\eta}s$, which occurs twice in
the speech On the Mysteries[3]. Hence the two
speeches have sometimes been identified. But the
pseudo-Plutarch expressly distinguishes them[4]. And
the author of the speech against Andokides states
that two informations had been laid against him in
the same year[5]. It is true that there is no proof
of the earlier information having resulted in a trial ;
and that the title of the lost speech, if really distinct
from the *De Mysteriis*, was ill-chosen. But it is
difficult to suppose that the biographer could have
made such a blunder as to quote the same speech by
two different titles in the same sentence. On the
whole, Sauppe's[6] view, that the speech On the Mysteries and the speech On the Information were
distinct, appears most probable. If the lost speech
referred, like the *De Mysteriis*, to the Hermae case,
it must have contained the word which Harpokration
quotes ; and it would have been natural for him to

---

[1] Cf. Plut. *Alk.* c. 13.

[2] Antiatticista, Bekker *Anecd.*
vol. I. p. 94, v. 25. Photios, p. 288,
23.

[3] §§ 36, 40.

[4] [Plut.] *Vit. Andoc.* mentions
first the speeches On the Myste-

ries and On his Return; and then
adds, $\sigma\acute{\omega}\zeta\epsilon\tau\alpha\iota$ $\delta\grave{\epsilon}$ $\alpha\grave{\upsilon}\tau o\hat{\upsilon}$ $\kappa\alpha\grave{\iota}$ $\acute{o}$ $\pi\epsilon\rho\grave{\iota}$
$\tau\hat{\eta}s$ $\grave{\epsilon}\nu\delta\epsilon\acute{\iota}\xi\epsilon\omega s$ $\lambda\acute{o}\gamma os$ $\kappa\alpha\grave{\iota}$ $\grave{\alpha}\pi o\lambda o\gamma\acute{\iota}\alpha$
$\pi\rho\grave{o}s$ $\Phi\alpha\acute{\iota}\alpha\kappa\alpha$ $\kappa\alpha\grave{\iota}$ $\acute{o}$ $\pi\epsilon\rho\grave{\iota}$ $\tau\hat{\eta}s$ $\epsilon\grave{\iota}\rho\acute{\eta}\nu\eta s$.

[5] [Lys.] *in Andoc.* § 30.

[6] *O. A.* II. p. 165.

quote it from the earlier of the two compositions in
which it occurred.   (4) The 'Reply to Phaeax' is *Reply to Phaeax.*
known only from the pseudo-Plutarch, who does not
name the speech 'Against Alkibiades'[1].   It has been
shown that the latter is probably the work of a late
sophist; and it is likely that Phaeax, rather than
Andokides, was intended to be the speaker.   If,
then, it could be assumed that 'Reply to Phaeax'
is an inaccurate quotation of the title, which ought
to have been cited as ' Reply *for* Phaeax,' there is no
difficulty in supposing the identity of this work with
the extant speech Against Alkibiades.

Besides the names of these four speeches, two *Doubtful fragments.*
fragments of unknown context have been preserved[2].
One of them expresses the hope that Athens may
not 'again' see the country people thronging in
to seek shelter within the walls.   This seems to refer
to the invasion by Archidamos in 431.   If this be so,
the speech to which the fragment belonged was
probably older than 413, when Agis occupied Dekeleia, and when the scenes of 431 must have been to
some extent repeated.   Such a passage might have
found place either in the address To the Associates
or in the Deliberative Speech[3].   The other fragment speaks of Hyperbolos as then at Athens; and
is therefore older, at least, than 417[4].

---

[1] [Plut.] *Vit. Andoc.* l. c.

[2] Sauppe, *O. A.* II. p. 166: Blass
Andoc. (Teubner) p. 97.

[3] Sauppe refers the fragment to
the πρὸς τοὺς ἑταίρους. So, also,
does Kirchhoff, identifying the
πρὸς τοὺς ἑταίρους with the συμ-

βουλευτικός.   If these, however,
were distinct, the fragment may
belong just as well to the συμβου-
λευτικός.

[4] On the date of the ostracism
of Hyperbolos, see above, p. 134,
note 1.

CHAPTER VII.

LYSIAS,

LIFE.

LYSIAS, though he passed most of his years at Athens, did not possess the citizenship, and, except in the impeachment of Eratosthenes, appears to have had no personal contact with the affairs of the city. Yet, as in literary style he is the representative of Atticism, so in his fortunes he is closely associated with the Athenian democracy. He suffered with it in its two greatest calamities—the overthrow in Sicily and the tyranny of the Thirty; he took part in its restoration; and afterwards, in his speeches for the law-courts, he became perhaps the best, because the soberest, exponent of its spirit—the most graceful and most versatile interpreter of ordinary Athenian life.

Kephalos, the father of Lysias, was a Syracusan, who settled at Athens as a resident alien on the invitation of Perikles[1]. Such an invitation would scarcely have carried much weight before Perikles had begun to be a leading citizen,—*i.e.* before about

---

[1] Lys. *in Eratosth.* § 4.

460 B.C.; and the story which represented Kephalos
as having been driven from Syracuse when the democracy was overthrown by Gelon (485 B.C.) is
therefore not very probable[1].

Lysias was born at Athens after his father had
come to live there. The year of his birth cannot
be determined. Dionysios assumes the same year
as the pseudo-Plutarch—Ol. 80. 2., 459 B.C.; but
admits, what the latter does not, that it is a
mere assumption[2]. And the ground upon which
the assumption rested is evident. Lysias was known
to have gone to Thurii when he was fifteen. Thurii
was founded Ol. 84. 1., 444 B.C.: it was inferred,
then, that Lysias was born in 459 B.C. But there is
nothing to prove that Lysias went to Thurii in the
year of its foundation. The date 459 B.C. must be
regarded, therefore, as a mere guess. It is the guess,
however, which had the approval of the ancients;
and it is confirmed by this circumstance—that Lysias
was reported to have died at about eighty[3], and
that, in fact, his genuine works, so far as they are
extant, cease at about 380 B.C.[4] In the absence

---

[1] [Plut.] *Vit. Lys.* ὡς δέ τινες,
ἐκπεσόντα τῶν Συρακουσῶν ἡνίκα
ὑπὸ Γέλωνος ἐτυραννοῦντο.

[2] Dionys. *Lys.* c. 1 says that in
the archonship of Kallias (412 B.C.)
Lysias was forty-seven, *as one
might conjecture*—ὡς ἄν τις εἰκά-
σειεν. Again in c. 12 he *supposes*
that Lysias may have died in 379
at the age of 80. The pseudo-Plutarch *Vit. Lys.* says boldly:—γενόμενος Ἀθήνησιν ἐπὶ Φιλοκλέους
ἄρχοντος τοῦ μετὰ Φρασικλῆ, κατὰ

τὸ δεύτερον ἔτος τῆς ὀγδοηκοστῆς
Ὀλυμπιάδος.

[3] Dionys. *Lys.* c. 12 : [Plut.] *Vit.
Lys.*

[4] The speech *Against Evandros*
(382 B.C.), and that *For Pherenikos*,
of which a fragment remains, (381
or 380 B.C.)—are his latest known
works. The two lost speeches *For
Iphikrates* (Sauppe, *Frag.* XVIII.
and LXV, *Att. Or.* II. pp. 178, 190)
belonged respectively to the years
371 and 354; but the judgment of

of certainty, then, it seems probable that the date 459 is not far wrong.

This is not, however, the prevalent modern view. Lysias was said to have gone to Italy after his father's death[1]; and this fact is the criterion for the date of his birth on which C. F. Hermann[2] and Baur[3] rely, as the ancient writers relied on the foundation-year of Thurii. Kephalos is introduced in Plato's *Republic*, of which the scene is laid (C. F. Hermann thinks) in 430 B.C. Lysias, then, it is agreed, cannot have gone to Thurii before 429, or have been born before 444. Blass justly objects to a dialogue of Plato being used as an authority for a date of this kind; but he himself arrives at the same conclusion on another ground— viz. because Kephalos cannot have come to Athens earlier than 460, and had lived there (as his son says[4]) thirty years. Again, Lysias was certainly older than Isokrates[5], who was born in 436. The birth of Lysias must therefore be put (Blass thinks) between 444 and 436.

Dionysios in rejecting them (*Lys.* c. 12) has been generally confirmed by modern writers.

[1] τοῦ πατρὸς ἤδη τετελευτηκότος : pseudo-Plut. *Vit. Lys.*

[2] *Gesammelte Abhandlungen*, p. 15.

[3] *Uebersetzung d. Reden d. Lys.* pp. 5 ff.—Blass, *Attisch. Bereds.* p. 333.

[4] Lys. *in Eratosth.* § 4.

[5] A dialogue of Plato can seldom be safely cited to prove that one of the persons of the imaginary conversation was, or was not, alive at a given time long before. But when, in such a dialogue, one of two persons contemporary with Plato is represented as very decidedly older than the other, it must be assumed that this was the case. To infer from the *Republic* that Kephalos was alive in 430 B.C. would be rash. But it is perfectly safe to infer from the *Phaedros* (p. 278 E, &c.) that Lysias was an orator of matured powers when Isokrates was a boy.

This view depends altogether on the statement that Lysias remained at Athens till his father's death—a statement vouched for only by the Plutarchic biographer, who is surely untrustworthy on such a point. Further, it assumes both the date and the literal biographical accuracy of the *Republic;* or else—what is at least doubtful—that Kephalos could not have come to Athens before 460. Lastly, it makes it difficult to accept the well-accredited account of Lysias having reached, or passed, the age of eighty; since all traces of his industry, hitherto constant, cease when, at this rate, he would have been no more than sixty-six[1]. The question must be left uncertain. But the modern hypothesis that Lysias was born between 444 and 436 B.C. does not seem, at least, more probable than the ancient hypothesis that he was born about 459[2].

Besides Lysias, Kephalos had two other sons, Polemarchos and Euthydêmos[3]—Polemarchos being the eldest of the three; and a daughter; afterwards married to Brachyllos. The hospitable disposition

---

[1] Blass distinctly admits this :— 'Starb also Lysias bald nach diesem Jahre, so sind freilich jene Angaben über das Alter, welches er erreichte, völlig aufzugeben.' *Att. Bereds.* p. 336.

[2] Stallbaum, in his *Lysiaca ad illustrandas Phaedri Platonici origines* (Leipzig, 1851) pp. 6 f., takes the following dates : Birth of Lysias, 459: Foundation of Thurii, 446: Kephalos comes to Athens, 444: Lysias goes to Thurii, 443: Death of Lysias, 378.

[3] Plato (*Rep.* p. 328 B) mentions Lysias and Euthydêmos as the brothers of Polemarchos. Dionysios (*Lys.* 1) speaks of *two* brothers of Lysias. But the pseudo-Plutarch gives him three — Polemarchos, Eudidos (Euthydêmos), and Brachyllos. Blass seems right in concluding from Demosth. *Neaer.* § 22 that Brachyllos was not brother, but brother-in-law, of Lysias. It is there said that Lysias married the daughter of Brachyllos, his own niece (ἀδελφιδῇ.) Hence, probably, the mistake of the so-called Plutarch.

of Kephalos is marked in the opening of the
Republic, of which the scene is laid at the house
of his eldest son. He complains that Sokrates does
not come often now to see them at the Peiraeus,
and begs that in future he will come to them without
ceremony, as to intimate friends[1]. It is easy to
believe that, in the lifetime of Perikles, the house
of the wealthy Sicilian whom his friendship had
brought to Athens was an intellectual centre, the
scene of many such gatherings as Plato imagined
at the house of Polemarchos; and that Lysias really
grew up, as Dionysios says, in the society of the
most distinguished Athenians[2].

Lysias at Thurii.

At the age of fifteen[3]—his father, according to
one account, being dead[4]—Lysias went to Thurii,
accompanied certainly by his eldest brother Polemarchos; perhaps also by Euthydêmos[5]. At Thurii,
where he passed his youth and early manhood, he
is said to have studied rhetoric under Tisias[6] of
Syracuse, himself the pupil of Korax, reputed
founder of the art. If, as is likely, Tisias was
born about 485 B.C. and did not go to Athens till
about 418, there is nothing impossible in this account. At any rate it is probable that Lysias had
lessons from some teacher of the Sicilian school, a

---

[1] Plat. *Rep.* p. 328 D.

[2] Dionys. *Lys.* 1: συνεπαιδεύθη
τοῖς ἐπιφανεστάτοις Ἀθηναίων. The
pseudo-Plut. repeats the words:
τὸ μὲν πρῶτον συνεπαιδεύετο τοῖς
ἐπιφ. Ἀθην.

[3] Dionys. *Lys.* 1.

[4] [Plut.] *Vit. Lys.*

[5] Dionysios (l. c.) says σὺν ἀδελ-
φοῖς δυσί: the pseudo-Plut. mentions Polemarchos only.

[6] The pseudo-Plut. says παιδευ-
όμενος παρὰ Τισίᾳ καὶ Νικίᾳ τοῖς
Συρακουσίοις. Blass thinks that
the name of the unknown Nikias
arose out of Τισίᾳ by a dittography.

school the trammels of which his maturer genius
so thoroughly shook off. The overthrow of the
Athenian arms in Sicily brought into power an
anti-Athenian faction at Thurii. Lysias and his
brother, with three hundred persons accused of
' Atticising[1],' were driven out, and fled to Athens
in 412 B.C.[2]. A tradition, idle, indeed, but picturesque, connected the Athenian disaster in Sicily
with the last days of Lysias in southern Italy. To
him was ascribed a speech, possessed by the ancients,
in which the captive general Nikias implored the
mercy of his Sicilian conquerors[3].

The next seven years at Athens—from 412 to *His life at Athens*
405—seem to have been years of peace and pros- *from 412 to 405 B.C.*
perity for the brothers. They were the owners of
three houses, one in the town, in which Polemarchos
lived[4]; another in the Peiraeus, occupied by Lysias ;
and, adjoining the latter, a shield-manufactory, employing a hundred and twenty slaves. Informers—
who were especially dangerous to rich foreigners—
did not vex them[5]; they had many friends ; and, in
the liberal discharge of public services, were patterns
to all resident-aliens[6]. The possession of house-

---

[1] Ἀττικισμὸν ἐγκληθεῖσι, Dionys.
Lys. 1.

[2] Dionysios and the pseudo-
Plut. both mark the date by the
archonship of Kallias.

[3] See the short fragment of this
speech ὑπὲρ Νικίου in Sauppe *O. A.*
II. p. 199. Dionysios unhesitatingly
rejected it, and the few remaining
words suffice in themselves to betray a vulgar rhetorician :—κλαίω
τὸν ἀμάχητον καὶ ἀναυμάχητον

ὄλεθρον, κ.τ.λ. But it must have
been at least as old as the latter
part of the fourth century B.C.,
since Theophrastos quoted it
(Dionys. *Lys.* 14).

[4] This follows from Lys. *In Eratosth.* § 16.

[5] *In Eratosth.* § 4.

[6] Cf. *In Eratosth.* § 20, where
Lysias speaks of himself and his
brother as πάσας τὰς χορηγίας χο-
ρηγήσαντας—and, in contrast with

property[1] shows that they belonged—as their father
Kephalos had doubtless belonged—to that privileged
class of resident-aliens who paid no special tax as
such, and who, as being on a par in respect of
taxes with citizens, were called isoteleis. If Lysias
continued his rhetorical studies during this quiet
time, he probably had not yet begun to write
speeches for the law-courts. A rich man, as he
then was, had no motive for taking to a despised
drudgery; and the only extant speech ascribed to
him which refers to a date earlier than 403—that for
Polystratos—is probably spurious. Cicero[2], quoting
Aristotle, says that Lysias once kept a rhetorical
school, but gave it up because Theodôros surpassed
him in technical subtlety. If this story is worth
anything, there is perhaps one reason for referring
it to the years 412—405; it certainly imputes to
Lysias the impatience of a wealthy amateur. At
any rate the ornamental pieces enumerated in the
lists of his works—the encomia, the letters, the
show-speeches—may have belonged in part to this
period of his life. After 403 he wrote for the law-
courts as a profession, and wrote with an industry
which can have left little time for the rhetoric of
display.

*The
Anarchy.*

Soon after the Thirty had taken power in the

the Thirty, οὐχ ὁμοίως μετοικοῦν-
τας ὥσπερ αὐτοὶ ἐπολιτεύοντο.
[1] Boeckh, *Publ. Econ.* Bk. I. c.
24. A resident-alien could under
no circumstances be an owner of
land; and only an isoteles could be
owner of a house.

[2] Cic. *Brut.* c. 48: *nam Lysiam
primo profiteri solitum artem dicendi, deinde, quod Theodorus
esset in arte subtilior, in orationibus ieiunior, orationes eum
scribere aliis coepisse, artem re-
movisse.*

spring of 404, two of them, Theognis and Peison, proposed that measures should be adopted against the resident-aliens; nominally, because that class was disaffected—really, because it was rich. Ten resident-aliens were chosen out for attack, two poor men being included for the sake of appearances. Lysias and Polemarchos were on the list. When Theognis and Peison, with their attendants, came to the house of Lysias in the Peiraeus, they found him entertaining a party of friends. The guests were driven off, and their host was left in the charge of Peison, while Theognis and his companions went to the shield-manufactory close by to take an inventory of the slaves. Lysias, left alone with Peison, asked if he would take a sum of money to save him. 'Yes,' said Peison, 'if it is a large sum.' They agreed on a talent; and Lysias went to bring it from the room where he kept his money-box. Peison, catching sight of the box, called up two servants, and told them to take its whole contents. Thus robbed of more than thrice the amount bargained for, Lysias begged to be left at least enough to take him out of the country. Peison replied that he might consider himself lucky if he got off with his life. They were then going to leave the house, when they met at the door two other emissaries of the Thirty. Finding that Peison was now going to the house of Polemarchos in the town, these men relieved him of Lysias, whom they took to the house of one Damnippos. Theognis was there already with some other prisoners. As Lysias knew Damnippos, he took him aside, and asked him to assist his

escape. Damnippos thought that it would be best
to speak directly to Theognis, who, he was sure,
would do anything for money. While Theognis and
Damnippos were talking in the front-hall, Lysias
slipped through the door, which chanced to be open,
leading from the first court of the house to the
second[1]. He had still two doors to pass through—
luckily they were both unlocked. He escaped to
the house of Archeneôs, the master of a merchant-
ship, close by, and sent him up to Athens to learn
what had become of Polemarchos. Archeneôs came
back with the news that Polemarchos had been met
in the street by Eratosthenes, one of the Thirty,
and taken straight to prison. The same night Lysias took boat to Megara.

Polemarchos received the usual message of the
Thirty[2]—to drink the hemlock. Although the property of which the brothers had been despoiled was
so valuable—including almost the whole stock of
the shield-manufactory, gold and silver plate, furni-
ture, and a large sum of money—the decencies of
burial were refused to Polemarchos. He was laid
out in the prison on a common stretcher,—one
friend gave a cloth to throw over the body, another
a cushion for the head, and so forth. A pair of
gold earrings were taken from the ears of his
widow[3].

---

[1] *In Eratosth.* § 16, τριῶν δὲ
θυρῶν οὐσῶν ἃς ἔδει με διελθεῖν
ἅπασαι ἀνεῳγμέναι ἔτυχον. The first
of these must have been the μέταυ-
λος θύρα, leading from the outer to
the inner αὐλή.

[2] τὸ ὑπ᾽ ἐκείνων εἰθισμένον παράγ-
γελμα, πίνειν κώνειον: *In Eratosth.*
§ 17.

[3] *In Eratosth.* § 19. For the
whole account of the arrest, see
that speech, §§ 6—20.

During the ten or twelve months of the exile— Lysias aids the Exiles. from the spring of 404 to the spring of 403—Lysias seems to have been active in the democratic cause. According to his biographer[1]—whose facts were probably taken from Lysias himself—he presented the army of the patriots with two hundred shields, and with a sum of two thousand drachmas; gained for it, with the help of one Hermon[2], upwards of three hundred recruits; and induced his friend Thrasydaeos of Elis[3] to contribute no less than two talents. Immediately upon the return from the Peiraeus to the city in the spring of 403, Thrasybulos proposed that the citizenship should be conferred upon Lysias; and the proposal was carried in the ekklesia. In one respect, however, it was informal. No measure could, in strictness, come before the popular assembly which was not introduced by a preliminary resolution (probouleuma) of the Senate. But at the moment when this decree was passed, the Senate had not yet been reconstituted after the anarchy[4]; and the probouleuma had therefore been wanting. On this ground Archînos, a

---

[1] [Plut.] *Vit. Lys.* The facts mentioned there may have been taken from the speech of Lysias on the motion of Archînos (*ib.* § 11), and also from that περὶ τῶν ἰδίων εὐεργεσιῶν, (quoted by Harpokration s. vv. Κεῖοι, Φηγαιεῦσι, μεταπύργιον,) if indeed this was distinct from the former.

[2] Ἑρμᾶνι in the *Vit. Lys.* § 7 ought probably to be Ἕρμωνι, as Blass assumes, *Att. Bereds.* p. 340.

[3] [Plut.]*Vit.Lys.* Cf. Xen. *Hellen.*

III. 2. 27.

[4] This appears from the statement of the pseudo-Plut. *Vit. Lys.* § 8, that the proposal was made μετὰ τὴν κάθοδον ἐπ' ἀναρχίας τῆς πρὸ Εὐκλείδου, that is, immediately after the return in the spring of the year 403. Later in the same year Eukleides became archon; and with the revival of the constitutional forms which commenced in his archonship the ἀναρχία was held to have ended.

colleague of Thrasybulos, arraigned the decree (under the Graphê Paranomôn) as unconstitutional, and it was annulled[1]. The whole story has been doubted[2]; but it is difficult to reject it when the Plutarchic biographer expressly refers to the speech made by Lysias in connection with the protest of Archînos[3]. Whether this speech was or was not identical with that of Lysias On his own Services[4] cannot be decided; but the latter must at least have been made upon this occasion.

The pro-
fessional
life of
Lysias.
Stripped of a great part of his fortune by the Thirty Tyrants, and further straitened, probably, by his generosity to the exiles, Lysias seems now to have settled down to hard work at Athens. His activity as a writer of speeches for the law-courts falls—as far as we know—between the years 403 and 380 B.C. That it must have been great and constant is shown by the fact that Dionysios speaks of him as having written 'not fewer than two hundred forensic speeches[5].' No other of the Attic orators was credited with so many as a hundred compositions of all kinds[6]. First in time and first, too, in importance among the extant orations of

---

[1] [Plut.] *Vit. Lys.* ὁ μὲν δῆμος ἐκύρωσε τὴν δωρεάν, ἀπενεγκαμένου δὲ Ἀρχίνου γραφὴν παρανόμων διὰ τὸ ἀπροβούλευτον εἰσαχθῆναι ἑάλω τὸ ψήφισμα.

[2] As by Scheibe (Blass, p. 340), who thinks that the biographer assumed it from the vague allusion in Aeschin. *in Ctes.* § 195: Ἀρχῖνος γὰρ ὁ ἐκ Κοίλης ἐγράψατο παρανόμων Θρασύβουλον τὸν Στειριέα γράψαντά τι παρὰ τοὺς νόμους, ἕνα τῶν

συγκατελθόντων αὐτῷ ἀπὸ Φυλῆς, καὶ εἷλε. This says only, τι.

[3] ἔστι δ' αὐτοῦ καὶ ὁ ὑπὲρ τοῦ ψηφίσματος (λόγος) ὃ ἐγράψατο Ἀρχῖνος, τὴν πολιτείαν αὐτοῦ περιελών: *Vit. Lys.* § 11.

[4] See p. 151, *note* 1.

[5] *De Lys.* c. 17.

[6] Even including doubtful speeches, as Blass observes, *Att. Bereds.* p. 344.

Lysias is that Against Eratosthenes, in whom he *The impeachment of Eratosthenes.* saw not only one of the Thirty Tyrants but the murderer of his brother Polemarchos. It was probably in 403 that Eratosthenes was impeached. The speech of Lysias, memorable as a display of eloquence, valuable, too, as a sufferer's picture of a dreadful time, has this further interest, that it is the only forensic speech known to have been spoken by Lysias himself, and that it marks his only personal contact with the politics of Athens.

Lysias had probably been a professional speech- *Lysias and Sokrates.* writer for about four years when Sokrates was brought to trial in 399. According to the popular account, Lysias wrote a defence for Sokrates to speak in court, but Sokrates declined to use it [1]. In the story itself there is nothing improbable; Kephalos and his son Lysias had been the intimate friends of Sokrates. But it may be suspected that the story arose from a confusion. At some time later than 392 B.C. the sophist Polykrates published an epideictic Accusation of Sokrates [2], and, in reply to it, Lysias wrote a speech In Defence of Sokrates [3]. This was extant in antiquity; and some one who

[1] Diog. Laert. II. 40: [Plut.] *Vit. Lys.*: Cic. *de Orat.* I. 54 § 231: Quint. II. 15 § 30, XI. 1 § 9: Valer. Max. VI. 4. 2: Stob. *Flor.* VII. 56.

[2] The κατηγορία Σωκράτους of Polykrates is mentioned by Suidas s. v. Πολυκράτης: Isokr. *Bus.* §§ 3, 5, and auctor Argum.: Aelian *V. H.* XI. 10: Quint. II. 17, cf. III. 1: Diog. Laert. II. 38. Diogenes notices, from Favorinus, that Poly-

krates had referred to the rebuilding of the walls by Konon: therefore, as Bentley first pointed out (*de Epist. Socr.* § 6, p. 51), the speech cannot have been written before 392 B.C.

[3] Schol. ad Aristid. p. 113. 16 (vol. III. p. 480 Dind.), οἶδε τὸν Σωκράτην πρὸς τοὺς νέους ἀεὶ τὸν Ὀδυσσέα θαυμάζοντα...ὡς Πολυκράτης ἐν τῷ κατ' αὐτοῦ λόγῳ φησὶ καὶ Λυσίας ἐν τῷ πρὸς Πολυκράτην ὑπὲρ αὐτοῦ.

had heard of it, but who knew nothing of the circumstances under which it was written, probably invented the story that it had been offered to, and declined by, the philosopher. The self-denial of Sokrates would be complete when, after rejecting the aid of money, he had rejected the aid of the best contemporary rhetoric[1].

Lysias at Olympia.

Lysias is named in the ordinary text of his own speech On the Property of Aristophanes as taking part in an embassy to Dionysios the elder of Syracuse, an embassy of which the date cannot be put below 389 B.C. But there can be little doubt as to the correctness of the emendation which removes his name from that passage[2]. There is better reason for believing another story in which the name of Lysias is associated with that of the elder Diony-

---

The title of the speech probably was Ὑπὲρ Σωκράτους πρὸς Πολυκρά-την.

[1] Dr L. Hölscher (*Quaestiunculae Lysiacae*, Herford, 1857, pp. 4 ff.) defends the ordinary account, believing that Lysias really composed a defence which Sokrates declined to use. He thinks that the ἀπολογία Σωκράτους mentioned among the works of Lysias by Phot. *Cod.* 262, Antiatt. in Bekker *Anecd.* p. 115. 8, Schol. ad Plat. *Gorg.* p. 331 B, and [Plut.] *Vit. Lys.*, was distinct from the speech ὑπὲρ Σωκράτους written in reply to Polykrates, and cited by the scholiast on Aristides. He remarks that in the Plutarchic life the Apologia is described as ἐστοχασμένη τῶν δικαστῶν—which is meant, he thinks, to mark that it was more practical, more forensic,

than Plato's Apologia Socratis. He observes also that the scholiast on the *Gorgias* (l. c.) notices the speech of Lysias as having contained matter about Anytos and Melêtos. But neither of these references affords any good ground for assuming that there was an Ἀπολογία Σωκράτους by Lysias distinct from his reply to Polykrates. The latter had been read by the scholiast on Aristides. Sauppe shows that the supposed Apologia was at all events not extant in antiquity (*O. A.* II. p. 203).

[2] Lys. *de bonis Aristoph.* § 19, βουλομένου Κόνωνος πέμπειν τινὰ εἰς Σικελίαν [Ἀριστοφάνης] ᾤχετο ὑποστὰς μετὰ Εὐνόμου καὶ Λυσίου, φίλου ὄντος καὶ ξένου, τὸ πλῆθος τὸ ὑμέτερον πλεῖστα ἀγαθὰ πεποιηκότος, κ.τ.λ. Sauppe substitutes Διο-

sios. We have good authority[1] for the statement
that the *Olympiakos*, of which a large fragment
remains, was spoken by Lysias in person at the
Olympic festival of 388 B.C., to which Dionysios
had sent a splendid embassy. In that speech Lysias
pointed out that two great enemies—the despot of
Syracuse in the west, the king of Persia in the east—
threatened Greece; and urged union among Greeks
with all the eagerness and with more than the
sagacity of Isokrates.

As has already been noticed, the indisputably
genuine works of Lysias, so far as they are known,
cease about 380 B.C. The latest, the speech for
Pherenikos of which a fragment remains, belongs to
381 or 380. Of the two speeches for Iphikrates,
also represented by fragments only, one belonged to
371, the other to 354[2]; but Dionysios pronounced
both spurious, partly on the external ground that
Lysias could not then have been living; partly—
which, for us, is the important point—on the internal evidence of style[3]. It seems probable that
Lysias died in, or soon after, 380 B.C., at the age of
about eighty[4].

*Chrono-
logical limit
of his
known
work.*

νυσίου for the words καὶ Λυσίου.
Obviously the words φίλου ὄντος
καὶ ξένου require to be defined
by the mention of the person
whose friend he was. Kayser proposed to insert Διονυσίῳ between
Λυσίου and φίλου. Sauppe's remedy is, as Blass says, simpler and
better.

[1] Dionys. *Lys.* c. 29: Diod. XIV.
109.

[2] See Sauppe, *O. A.* II. p. 178,
190.

[3] Dionys. *Lys.* c. 12.

[4] [Plut.] *Vit. Lys.* ἐτελεύτησεν
ὀγδοήκοντα ἔτη βιούς, ἢ ὥς τινες ἐξ
καὶ ἑβδομήκοντα, ἢ ὥς τινες ὑπὲρ
ὀγδοήκοντα, ἰδὼν Δημοσθένην μειρά-
κιον ὄντα [Schäfer places the birth of
Demosthenes in 384]. Dionys.*Lys.*
c. 12 εἰ γὰρ ὀγδοήκοντα ἔτη γενόμενον θήσει τις τελευτῆσαι Λυσίαν,κ.τ.λ.

The character, as well as the capacity, of Lysias must be judged from the indirect evidence of his own writings. Circumstances kept him out of political life, in which his versatility and shrewdness would probably have held and improved the position which great powers of speech must soon have won. The part which he took during the troubles under the Thirty proved him a generous friend to Athens, as the *Olympiakos* shows him to have been a wise citizen[1] of Greece; but his destiny was not that of a man of action. It is not likely that he regretted this much, though he must have felt his exclusion from the Athenian franchise as the refusal of a reward to which he had claims. His real strength—as far as can be judged now—lay in his singular literary tact. A fine perception of character in all sorts of men, and a faculty for dramatising it, aided by a sense of humour always under control; a certain pervading gracefulness and flexibility of mind; rhetorical skill, masterly in a sense hardly dreamed of at that day, since it could conceal itself—these were his most distinctive qualities and powers. His liberal discharge of public services, and his generosity to the exiles in 404, accord with the disposition which is suggested by the fragments of his letters. He was a man of warm nature, impulsive, hospitable, attached to his friends; fond of pleasure, and freely indulging in it; but, like So-

---

[1] The expression is his own: he claims to give counsel as a good citizen (*Olymp.* § 3)—with the thought in his mind, perhaps, that if he was still but a μέτοικος of Athens he was at least a πολίτης of Hellas.

phokles at the Chian supper-party described by
Ion[1], carrying into social life the same intellectual
quality which marks his best work—the grace and
the temperate brightness of a thoroughly Athenian
mind.

[1] Athenaeos XIII. pp. 603 E—604 D.

CHAPTER VIII.

LYSIAS.

STYLE.

A N appreciation of Lysias is, in one sense, easy for modern criticism. He was a literary artist, and his work bears the stamp of consummate literary skill. The reader may fail to realise the circumstances under which a particular speech was delivered, the force with which it appeals to emotion or to reason, the degree in which it was likely to prove persuasive or convincing. But he cannot fail to be aware that he is reading admirable prose. The merit of Lysias as a writer is secure of recognition. It is his oratorical power which runs some danger of being too lightly valued, unless attention is paid to the conditions under which it was exerted. The speech Against Eratosthenes, indeed, in which he expresses the passionate feeling of his own mind, would alone suffice to prove him in the modern sense eloquent. But a large majority of his other speeches are so comparatively tame, so poor in the qualities of the higher eloquence, that his oratorical reputation, to be understood, needs to be closely interpreted by the scope of his oratory.

Although on a few occasions he himself came forward as a speaker, the business of his life was to write for others. All sorts of men were among his clients; all kinds of causes in turn occupied him. Now he lent his services to the impeachment of an official charged with defrauding the Athenian treasury, or to the prosecution of some adherent of the Thirty, accused of having slandered away the lives of Athenian citizens; now he supplied the words in which a pauper begged that his obol a day from the State might not be stopped, or helped one of the parties to a drunken brawl to demand satisfaction for a black eye. The elderly citizen who appeals against the calumny of an informer to his past services as trierarch or choregus; the young man checked on the threshold of public life by some enemy's protest at his dokimasia for his first office,—in turn borrow their eloquence from Lysias. If he had been content to adopt the standard which he found existing in his profession, he would have written in nearly the same style for all these various ages and conditions. He would have treated all these different cases upon a uniform technical system, merely seeking, in every case alike, to obtain the most powerful effect and the highest degree of ornament by applying certain fixed rules. Lysias was a discoverer when he perceived that a purveyor of words for others, if he would serve his customers in the best way, must give the words the air of being their own. He saw that the monotonous intensity of the fashionable rhetoric—often ludicrously unsuited to the mouth into which it was put—was fatal to real impressiveness; and, instead of lending to all speakers the same false brilliancy, he determined to give to each the vigour of nature. It was the desire of treating appropriately every case entrusted to him, and of making each client speak as an intelligent person, without professional aid, might be expected to speak in certain circumstances, which chiefly determined the style of Lysias.

Lysias the representative of the Plain Style.

This style, imitated by many, but marked in Lysias by an original excellence, made him for antiquity the representative of a class of orators. It was in the latter part of the fourth century B. C. that Greek critics began regularly to distinguish three styles of rhetorical composition, the grand, the plain and the middle. The grand style aims constantly at rising above the common idiom; it seeks ornament of every kind, and rejects nothing as too artificial if it is striking. The plain style may, like the first, employ the utmost efforts of art, but the art is concealed; and, instead of avoiding, it imitates the language of ordinary life. The 'middle' style explains itself by its name. Theophrastos appears to have been the first writer on Rhetoric who attempted such a classification; there is, at least, no hint of it in Aristotle or in the Rhetorica ad Alexandrum[1]. Vague as the

[1] Dionysios, speaking of the third or middle style, declares himself unable to decide whether it was first used by Thrasymachos of Chalkêdon, '*as Theophrastos* *thinks,*' or by some one else: *De Demosth.* c. 3. From this, Francken infers with great probability that the distinction between the three styles was first made by

classification necessarily is, it was frequently modified
according to the taste of individual teachers. The
two extremes—the grand and the plain styles—were
recognised by all; but some discerned two[1], some
three[2] shades between them; while others thought
it needless to distinguish anything intermediate[3].
On the whole, however, the tripartite division kept
its ground down to Roman times. It was adopted,
with variations of detail, by Cicero[4], Dionysios[5] and
Quintilian[6]. The characteristics of the 'plain' style *General characteristics of the Plain Style.*
—with which we are most concerned at present—are
only sketched by Dionysios[7]; but they are more

Theophrastos in his lost work περὶ
λέξεως (*Commentationes Lysiacae*,
p. 9).

[1] Thus Demetrios (περὶ ἑρμην.
c. 36, Walz, *Rh. Graec.* vol. IX. p.
21) distinguishes four types or
χαρακτῆρες—the plain (ἰσχνός), the
grand (μεγαλοπρεπής), the polished
(γλαφυρός), and the forcible (δει-
νός)—meaning by the last a terse,
vigorous style, suited to controversy in court or council.

[2] Syrianos, in his commentary
on the περὶ ἰδεῶν of Hermogenes
(Walz, *Rh. Graec.* vol. VII. p. 93),
says that Hipparchos (a rhetorician who wrote a treatise περὶ
τρόπων, *ib.* VI. p. 337) recognised
five styles—the plain (ἰσχνός), the
copious (ἁδρός—another name for
the μεγαλοπρεπής), the middle (μέ-
σος), the graphic (γραφικός), and
the florid (ἀνθηρός).

[3] Demetrios says that his γλα-
φυρὸς χαρακτήρ was considered by
some as a branch of the ἰσχνός,
and his δεινὸς χαρακτήρ as the

branch of the μεγαλοπρεπής: περὶ
ἑρμ. c. 36, Walz, IX. 21.

[4] Cic. *Orator* c. 6 § 20, *gran-
diloqui—tenues, acuti—medius et
quasi temperatus.*

[5] Dionysios describes the grand
style as ἐξηλλαγμένη, περιττή, ἐγ-
κατάσκευος (*De Demosth.* 1), or
ὑψηλὴ λέξις (*ib.* 34): the plain, as
λιτή, ἀφελής (*ib.* 2), or ἰσχνή, ἀπέ-
ριττος (*ib.* 34): the middle as μέση
(*ib.* 34) or μικτή (*ib.* 3).

[6] Quint. XII. c. 10 § 58. *Unum
subtile* (*genus*), *quod ἰσχνόν vocant,
alterum* grande *atque* robustum,
*quod ἁδρόν dicunt, constituunt;
tertium alii* medium *ex duobus,
alii* floridum (*namque id ἀνθηρόν
appellant*) *addiderunt.*

[7] Dionys. *De Demosth.* c. 2, ἡ
ἑτέρα λέξις, ἡ λιτὴ καὶ ἀφελής, καὶ
δοκοῦσα κατασκευήν τε καὶ ἰσχὺν τὴν
πρὸς ἰδιώτην ἔχειν λόγον καὶ ὁμοιό-
τητα—a vague description, which
tells us only that this style is based
upon ἰδιώτης λόγος—the language
of ordinary life.

precisely given by Cicero. There is a difference, indeed, between the points of view of the two critics. Dionysios treats the three styles historically; Cicero treats them theoretically. The 'middle' style of Cicero differs, therefore, from the 'middle' style of Dionysios in being an ideal. But Cicero's description of the 'plain' style, at least, would probably have been accepted in the main by Dionysios; and it is clear that for Cicero, as for Dionysios, Lysias was the canon of that style. According to Cicero, the chief marks of the 'genus tenue' are these:—1. In regard to composition—a free structure of clauses and sentences, not straining after a rhythmical period[1]. 2. In regard to diction—(*a*) purity[2], (*b*) clearness[3], (*c*) propriety[4]. 3. Abstemious use of rhetorical figures[5].

Originality of Lysias.

With certain exceptions, which will be noticed in their place, Lysias has these characteristics, and is the best representative of the plain style, whether viewed historically or in the abstract. That style gradually came to be used by almost all writers for the ekklesia or the law-courts; but it was Lysias, says Dionysios, who 'perfected' it, and 'brought it to the summit of the excellence proper to it[6].' In order that the originality of Lysias may not be

---

[1] Cic. *Orator* § 77, *Primum igitur eum tanquam e vinculis numerorum eximamus......Solutum quiddam sit, nec vagum tamen.*

[2] *ib.* § 79 *sermo erit purus et Latinus.*

[3] *ib. dilucide planeque dicetur.*

[4] *ib. quid deceat circumspicia-*tur.

[5] *ib.* § 80 *verecundus erit usus oratoriae quasi supellectilis. supellex est enim quodammodo nostra quae est in ornamentis, alia rerum, alia verborum.*

[6] Dionys. *De Demosth.* c. 2, ἐτελείωσε δ' αὐτὴν καὶ εἰς ἀκρὸν ἤγαγε τῆς ἰδίας ἀρετῆς Λυσίας ὁ Κεφάλου.

underrated, attention must be given to the precise
meaning of this statement. It appears to speak of
him merely as having succeeded better than others
in a style used by nearly all writers of speeches for
the law-courts. But what was, in fact, common to
him and them was this only—the avoidance of
decidedly poetical ornament and the employment of
sober prose. This is all that the 'plain' style, as
opposed to the 'elaborate,' necessarily means. That
which he had, and which no other had in the same
degree, was the art of so writing this prose that it
should be in character with the person who spoke it.
Their style was monotonously plain; his was plain too,
but it was more, it was variously natural. Dionysios
shows elsewhere that he appreciated to the full the
originality of Lysias; but he has hardly brought it
out with sufficient clearness in the passage which
has just been noticed. Lysias may, in a general
sense, be regarded as the perfecter of a style already
practised by many others; but it is closer to the
truth to call him the founder of a new one, and of
one in which he was never rivalled[1].

It does not, perhaps, strike the modern mind as
very remarkable that a man whose business was to
write speeches for other people should have conceived

---

[1] The question, 'How far is Lysias the true representative of the
genus tenue?' has been exhaust-
ively discussed by Dr F. Berbig,
in an essay 'Ueber das genus
dicendi tenue des Redners Lysias'
(Gymnasium-program, Cüstrin,
1871: reviewed in the Philologis-
cher Anzeiger III. 5. p. 252). The
essay will be referred to below.
Its general conclusion is that 'In
all his writings Lysias must be
pronounced, by any judgment not
absolutely rigorous, an excellent
model of the plain style;' though
both his composition and his language depart from it in certain
points.

the idea of making the speech appropriate to the person. In order to understand why this conception was, at the time, a proof of genius, it is necessary to remember how rhetoric was then viewed. Prose composition in its infancy was a craft, a close profession, just as much as poetry. Beside the sacred band of 'wise' poets stood the small group of experts skilled to fashion artistic prose. When a man wished for help in a law-suit he applied, as a matter of course, if he could afford it, to one of these; and it was equally a matter of course that the speech supplied to him should bear the same stamp as others turned out by the same machine. There was no pretence of its being the work of the speaker, and no expectation, therefore, that it should reflect his nature; a certain rhetorical colour, certain recognized forms of argument and appeal, were alone looked for. The idea of writing for a client so that he should have in court the whole advantage of professional aid, and, in addition to this, the advantage of appearing to have dispensed with it, was not only novel but daring. This is what Lysias first undertook to do, and did admirably.

Had his style been florid before it became plain? His dramatic purpose—if it may be so called—decided the special characteristics of his style. But, even without this purpose, an instinctive dislike of exaggeration would of itself have given his style some general characteristics, sufficient to distinguish it from that of any of his contemporaries. On this account we must dissent from a view advanced by K. O. Müller in his History of Greek Literature [1].

---

[1] Vol. II. p. 143 (transl. Donaldson).

Lysias had, he thinks, two distinct styles at two
different periods of his life; the earlier, 'forced and
artificial;' the later, plain. Müller recognises the
former in the speech in the Phaedros, and in the
Epitaphios. The turning-point was, he conceives,
the impeachment of Eratosthenes, when 'a real feeling of pain and anger' in the mind of Lysias gave
'a more lively and natural flow both to his spirits
and to his speech.' 'This occasion'—Müller adds—
'convinced Lysias what style of oratory was both the
most suited to his own character and also least
likely to fail in producing an effect upon the judges.'
Ingenious as the theory is, we have no belief in the
fact of any such abrupt transition as it supposes.
That temperate mastery with which Lysias cultivated
the 'plain' style is doubly a marvel if it was only a
sudden practical experience which weaned him from
his first love for a forced and artificial rhetoric.
Converts are not proverbial for discretion; and the
exquisite judgment shown by Lysias after his supposed reformation ought to have prevented its necessity. Like all his contemporaries he must, unquestionably, have had his earliest training in the florid
Sicilian school; but there is nothing to show that its
precepts ever took a strong hold upon him; and there
is overwhelming reason to believe that a genius of
the bent of his must very early have thrown off such
pedantic trammels. It is true that the speech in
the Phaedros —assuming its genuineness—is more
stiffly composed than any of his presumably later
writings: but, on the other hand, it is, as Müller
allows, entirely free from the ornaments of Gorgias.

As for the Epitaphios, its spuriousness is now a generally recognised fact [1].

Plainness and an easy versatility are, then, the general characteristics of Lysias. We propose now to consider in detail his special characteristics; speaking first of his style in the narrower sense, his composition and diction; next of his method of handling subject-matter.

Special characteristics of his style.

His Composition.

Cicero, as we have seen, counts among the marks of the 'plain' style a free structure of sentences and clauses, not straining after a rhythmical period [2]. Dionysios, speaking of êthopoïïa in Lysias, says that he composes 'quite simply and plainly, aware that êthos is best expressed, not in rhythmical periods, but in the lax (or easy) style' (ἐν τῇ διαλελυμένῃ λέξει) [3]. In another place, however, he praises Lysias for a vigour, essential in contests, 'which packs thoughts closely and brings them out roundly' (στρογγύλως) [4]—that is, in terse periods. Both remarks are just. Nothing more strikingly distinguishes Lysias from his predecessors and from nearly all his successors than the degree in which the structure of his sentences varies according to his subject. His speeches may in this respect be classified under three heads. First, those which are of a distinctly public character; in which the composition is thoroughly rhythmical, and which abound with artistic periods, single or combined [5].

---

[1] See below.
[2] Cic. *Orator* § 77, quoted above.
[3] Dionys. *De Lys.* c. 8.
[4] *ib.* c. 6.

[5] In this class, Berbig (in the essay mentioned above ' Ueber das genus dicendi tenue des Redners Lysias,' p. 8) places these speeches:

Secondly, those speeches which, from the nature of
their subjects, blend the private with the public
character; which show not only fewer combinations or groups of periods, but a less careful formation of single periods[1]. Thirdly, the essentially
private speeches; which differ from the second class,
not in the mould of such periods as occur, but
in the larger mixture with these of sentences or clauses
not periodic[2]. Further, in each of these three
classes, a greater freedom of composition distinguishes the narrative from the argument. The narrative parts of the properly public speeches are
usually thrown into what may be called the historical as opposed to the oratorical period; that is,
the sentences are more loosely knit and are drawn
out to a greater length. According as the speech
has more of a private character, these freer periods are more and more relaxed into a simple
series (λέξις εἰρομένη) of longer or shorter clauses.
Yet, while there are so many shades in the composition of Lysias, the colour of the whole is individual.
Isokrates develops period out of period in long, lux-

---

1. Or. XXVII. (κατὰ 'Επικράτους):
2. Or. XXVIII. (κατὰ 'Εργοκλέους):
3. Or. XXIX. (κατὰ Φιλοκράτους):
4. Or. XXXIII. ('Ολυμπιακός): 5.
Or. XXXIV. (περὶ τοῦ μὴ καταλῦσαι
τὴν πολιτείαν.)

[1] *e.g.* 1. Or. XII. (κατὰ 'Ερατοσθένους): 2. Or. XIII. (κατὰ 'Αγο-
ράτου): 3. Or. XVI. (κατὰ Φίλωνος):
4. Or. XIX. (περὶ τῶν 'Αριστοφάνους
χρημάτων.)

[2] In this third class two grades

may be distinguished, according to
the importance of the subject and
the use, greater or less accordingly,
of a periodic style. I. 1. Or. I.
(περὶ τοῦ 'Ερατοσθένους φόνου): 2.
Or. III. (κατὰ Σίμωνος): 3. Or. IV.
(περὶ τραύματος ἐκ προνοίας): 4. Or.
VII. (περὶ τοῦ σηκοῦ). II. 1. Or.
XVII. (περὶ δημοσίων χρημάτων): 2.
Or. XXIII. (κατὰ Παγκλέωνος): 3.
Or. XXXII. (κατὰ Διογείτονος).

uriant sequence; Demosthenes intersperses the most
finished and most vigorous periods with less formally
built sentences which relieve them; Lysias binds his
periods, by twos or threes at the most, into groups
always moderate in size but often monotonous in
form; excelling Isokrates in compactness, but yield-
ing to Demosthenes in life[1].

His Dic-
tion—its
purity.

The diction of Lysias is distinguished in the first
place by its purity.   This is a quality upon which no
modern could have pronounced authoritatively, but
for which the ancient Greek critic vouches.   In the
Augustan age the reaction from florid Asianism to
Atticism had set in strongly, and especial attention
was paid by Greek grammarians to the marks of a
pure Attic style.   Dionysios may be taken as a competent judge.   He pronounces Lysias to be 'perfectly
pure in expression, the best canon of Attic speech,—
not of the old used by Plato and Thucydides,' but of
that which was in vogue in his own time[2].   This
may be seen, he adds, by a comparison with the
writings of Andokides, Kritias and many others.
Two ideas are included under the 'purity' praised
here; abstinence from words either obsolete (γλῶσσαι)
or novel, or too decidedly poetical; and abstinence
from constructions foreign to the idiom of the day—
an excellence defined elsewhere as 'accuracy of
dialect[3].'   Lysias is not rigidly pure in these respects.

---

[1] Cf. Dionys. *De Lys.* c. 6 (speaking of the *terse* periodic style)—ἡ
συστρέφουσα τὰ νοήματα καὶ στρογγύλως ἐκφέρουσα λέξις, Dionysios
says, ταύτην ὀλίγοι μὲν ἐμιμήσαντο,
Δημοσθένης δὲ καὶ ὑπερεβάλετο·
πλὴν οὐχ οὕτως εὐτελῶς οὐδὲ

ἀφελῶς ὥσπερ Λυσίας, χρησά-
μενος αὐτῇ, ἀλλὰ περιέργως καὶ
πικρῶς.

[2] Dionys. *De Lys.* c. 2.

[3] *ib.* c. 13, where the 'purity'
spoken of in c. 2 is defined as consisting of two elements—τὸ καθα-

The only instance of an old-fashioned syntax, indeed,
which has been noticed in him, is the occasional use
of τε as a copula[1]; nor does he use such pedantic
words as were meant by 'glossae;' but rare or poetical words and phrases occur in many places[2]. The
praise of purity must be taken in a general and
relative sense. Of those who came after Lysias,
Isokrates most nearly approached him in this quality[3];
but Isaeos is also commended for it[4].

Next, in contrast with the Sicilian school of rhe- *Simplicity.*
toric, Lysias is characterised by a general avoidance
of ornamental figures. Such figures as occur are
mostly of the kind which men use in daily life without rhetorical consciousness,—hyperbole, metaphor,
prosopopoiïa and the like[5]. As a rule, he expresses
his meaning by ordinary words employed in their
normal sense[6]. His panegyrical speeches and his

ρὸν τῶν ὀνομάτων and ἡ ἀκρίβεια τῆς
διαλέκτου.

[1] This use occurs seven times in
all: Or. I. § 17: XIII. §§ 1, 82 :
XXXI. §§ 1, 5: XXXII. §§ 1, 22. Berbig, p. 13.

[2] *e.g.* Or. XXXIII. § 3 μικρολογη-
σόμενος : § 7 οἰκοῦντες ἀπόρθητοι καὶ
ἀτείχιστοι καὶ ἀστασίαστοι καὶ ἀήτ-
τητοι : Or. IV. § 8 παρωξυμμένος
ὀξύχειρ λίαν καὶ πάροινός ἐστιν : § 9
ἐς τοῦτο βαρυδαιμονίας ἥκει : § 20
ἀνήκεστος συμφορά : Or. XVIII. § 49,
ἀρχαιόπλουτος: Or.XIII.§45 ἀκλεής—
γηροτροφεῖν: Or. XXVI. § 4 ἀείμνη-
στος: Or. XXX. § 35 μισοπονηρεῖν :
Or. XXIV. § 3 δυστυχήματα ἰᾶ-
σθαι : Or. XXXIII. § 7 ἀθάνατος ἐλευ-
θερία.

[3] Dionys. *De Lys.* c. 2 'Ισοκρά-

της—καθαρώτατος δὴ τῶν ἄλλων με-
τά γε Λυσίαν.

[4] Dionys. *De Isaeo.* c. 3.

[5] As an instance of a common
prosopopoiïa see *e.g.* Or. XXI. § 8 οὕτω
παρεσκευασμένην τριήρη πόσα οἴε-
σθε...τοὺς πολεμίους εἰργάσθαι κακά;
Other common figures which occur
in Lysias are synekdoche, *e.g.* Or.
XXXIII. § 9 τὰς ἐλπίδας τῆς σωτη-
ρίας: antonomasia, Or. § 15 ὁ σεμ-
νὸς Στειριεύς : metonymia, Or. XII.
§ 60 τὰς πόλεις ἐπάγοντες : epana-
phora, Or. XXX. § 3 πολλὰ μέν...
πολλὰ δέ : synathroismos, Or.
XXXIII. § 3 καί...καί...καί...καί : pe-
riphrasis, Or. XVIII. § 3 τρόπαιον
ἱστάναι, &c.

[6] Dionys. *De Lys.* c. 3 (ἀρετὴ) ἡ
διὰ τῶν κυρίων τε καὶ κοινῶν καὶ ἐν

letters are said to have presented a few exceptions
to this rule; but all his business-works, as Dionysios
calls them—his speeches for the ekklesia and for the
law-courts—are stamped with this simplicity. He
seems, as his critic says, to speak like the ordinary
man, while he is in fact the most consummate of
artists[1],—a prose poet who knows how to give
an unobtrusive distinction to common language,
and to bring out of it a quiet and peculiar music[2].
Isokrates had the same command of familiar words,
but he was not content to seek effect by artistic
harmonies of these. His ambition was to be ornate;
and hence one of the differences remarked by Dionysios: Isokrates is sometimes vulgar[3]; Lysias never
is. There is one kind of ornament, however, which
Lysias uses largely, and in respect to which he deserts
the character of the plain style. He delights in the
artistic parallelism (or opposition) of clauses. This
may be effected: (1) by simple correspondence of
clauses in length (isokôlon); (2) by correspondence of
word with word in meaning (antitheton proper);
(3) by correspondence of word with word in sound
(paromoion)[4]. Examples are very numerous both in

μέσῳ κειμένων ὀνομάτων ἐκφέρουσα
τὰ νοούμενα.

[1] *ib.* ὁμοίως δὲ τοῖς ἰδιώταις δια-
λέγεσθαι δοκῶν πλεῖστον ὅσον ἰδιώ-
του διαφέρει.

[2] *ib.* κράτιστος ποιητὴς λόγων λε-
λυμένης ἐκ μέτρου λέξεως, ἰδίαν τινὰ
λόγων εὑρηκὼς ἁρμονίαν, ᾗ τὰ ὀνόματα κοσμεῖ τε καὶ ἡδύνει, μηδὲν
ἔχοντα ὀγκῶδες μηδὲ φορτικόν.

[3] Dionys. *De Isocr.* c. 3 σχημα-

τίζει φορτικῶς.

[4] Isokôla and homoioteleuta
constantly occur together: see esp.
Or. XII. (§§ 1, 4, 6, 19, 26, 32, 39,
&c.) and Or. XXXIII. passim. A
special form of the paromoion, viz.
paronomasia, is frequent in Lysias:
e.g. Or. XXXI. § 11 γνώμη—συγγνώ-
μης: § 24 τιμωρηθήσεται—τετιμή-
σεται: Or. XXX. § 29 τὰ πάτρια—
κατὰ πατέρα.

the public and in the private speeches. This love of
antithesis—shown on a larger scale in the terse
periodic composition—is the one thing which sometimes blemishes the êthos in Lysias.

Closely connected with this simplicity is his clear-   *Clearness.*
ness. Lysias is clear in a twofold sense; in thought,
and in expression. Figurative language is often a
source of confusion of thought; and the habitual
avoidance of figures by Lysias is one reason why he
not only speaks but thinks clearly. In regard to
this clearness of expression Dionysios has an excellent remark. This quality might, he observes,
result merely from 'deficiency of power,' i.e. poverty
of language and of fancy which constrained the
speaker to be simple. In the case of Lysias it does,
in fact, result from *wealth of the right words*[1]. He
uses only plain words; but he has enough of these
to express with propriety the most complex idea.
The combination of clearness with conciseness is   *Conciseness.*
achieved by Lysias because he has his language
thoroughly under command; his words are the disciplined servants of his thoughts[2]. Isokrates is clear;
but he is not also concise. In the union of these
two excellences, Isaeos[3] perhaps stands next to
Lysias. There are, indeed, exceptions to the con-

---

[1] *De Lys.* c. 4 καὶ εἰ μὲν δι'
ἀσθένειαν δυνάμεως ἐγίγνετο τὸ
σαφὲς οὐκ ἄξιον ἦν αὐτὸ ἀγαπᾶν·
νῦν δὲ ὁ πλοῦτος τῶν κυρίων
ὀνομάτων ἐκ πολλῆς αὐτῷ περιου-
σίας ἀποδείκνυται ταύτην τὴν ἀρετήν.

[2] *ib.* c. 4 οὐ τοῖς ὀνόμασι δουλεύει
τὰ πράγματα παρ' αὐτῷ, τοῖς δὲ πράγ-
μασιν ἀκολουθεῖ τὰ ὀνόματα.

[3] It is remarkable that Dionysios expressly denies to Demosthenes the *invariable* clearness of Lysias, *De Lys.* c. 4 τῆς μὲν Θουκυδίδου λέξεως καὶ Δημοσθένους, οἳ δει-
νότατοι τὰ πράγματα ἐξειπεῖν ἐγένον-
το, πολλὰ δυσείκαστά ἐστιν ἡμῖν
καὶ ἀσαφῆ.

ciseness of Lysias, as there are exceptions to the purity and the plainness of his diction. Instances occur in which terms nearly synonymous are accumulated, either for the sake of emphasis or merely for the sake of symmetry [1]; but such instances are not frequent.

Vividness. Vividness, ἐνάργεια—'the power of bringing under the senses what is narrated [2]'—is an attribute of the style of Lysias. The dullest hearer cannot fail to have before his eyes the scene described, and to fancy himself actually in presence of the persons introduced as speaking. Lysias derives this graphic force from two things;—judicious use of detail, and perception of character. A good example of it is his description, in the speech Against Eratosthenes, of

---

[1] For *emphasis* (e.g.) in Or. XIII. § 63 οἱ δ' αὐτῶν περιγενόμενοι καὶ σωθέντες, οὓς οὗτος μὲν ἀπέκτεινεν ὠμῶς καὶ θάνατος αὐτῶν κατεγνώσθη, ἡ δὲ τύχη καὶ ὁ δαίμων περιεποίησε ... τιμῶνται ὑφ' ὑμῶν. For *symmetry* (e.g.) in Or. XXVIII. § 3 καὶ γὰρ δὴ δεινὸν ἂν εἴη εἰ νῦν μὲν οὕτως αὐτοὶ πιεζόμενοι ταῖς εἰσφοραῖς συγγνώμην τοῖς κλέπτουσι καὶ τοῖς δωροδοκοῦσιν ἔχοιτε, ἐν δὲ τῷ τέως χρόνῳ καὶ τῶν οἴκων τῶν ὑμετέρων μεγάλων ὄντων καὶ τῶν δημοσίων προσόδων μεγάλων οὐσῶν, θανάτῳ ἐκολάζετε τοὺς τῶν ὑμετέρων ἐπιθυμοῦντας: where, as Blass observes, the words μεγάλων οὐσῶν are superfluous, and the phrase τοὺς τῶν ὑμετέρων ἐπιθυμοῦντας where τοὺς τοιούτους would have sufficed, is meant to balance τοῖς κλέπτουσι καὶ τοῖς δωροδοκοῦσιν.

Another strong instance of redundancy of the former kind—the emphatic—is Or. XXI. § 24 οὐδεπώποτ' ἠλέησα οὐδ' ἐδάκρυσα οὐδ' ἐμνήσθην γυναικὸς οὐδὲ παίδων τῶν ἐμαυτοῦ, οὐδ' ἡγούμην δεινὸν εἶναι εἰ τελευτήσας ὑπὲρ τῆς πατρίδος ὀρφανοὺς καὶ τοῦ πατρὸς ἀπεστερημένους αὐτοὺς καταλείψω. Favorinus, according to Gellius (II. v.), used to say:—'If you remove a single word from a passage of Plato, or alter it, however suitably to the sense, you will still have taken away something from the elegance; if you do so in Lysias, you will have taken away something from the sense.' This praise, as we have seen, needs modification.

[2] Dionys. *De Lys.* c. 7 δύναμίς τις ὑπὸ τὰς αἰσθήσεις ἄγουσα τὰ λεγόμενα.

his own arrest by Theognis and Peison[1]. Dionysios
ascribes vividness, as well as clearness, to Isokrates
also[2]; but there is perhaps only one passage in
the extant work of Isokrates which strictly jus-
tifies this praise[3]. A description may be brilliant
without being in the least degree graphic. The
former quality depends chiefly on the glow of the
describer's imagination; the latter depends on his
truthfulness and skill in grouping around the
main incident its lesser circumstances. A lifelike
picture demands the union of fine colouring and
correct drawing. Isokrates was a brilliant colour-
ist; but he was seldom, like Lysias, an accurate
draughtsman.

From this trait we pass naturally to another *Ēthopoiïa.*
which has just been mentioned as one of its sources—
the faculty of seizing and portraying character. Of
all the gifts of Lysias this is the most distinctive,
and is the one which had greatest influence upon
his style. It is a talent which does not admit of
definition or analysis; it can be understood only by
studying its results. It is shown, as Dionysios says,
in three things—thought, diction, and composition[4];
that is, the ideas, the words, and the style in which
the words are put together, always suit the person
to whom they are ascribed[5]. There is hardly one of

---

[1] *In Eratosth.* §§ 8—17.

[2] *De Isocr.* c. 2.

[3] The passage in the Aeginêtikos
in which the speaker describes his
care of Thrasylochos: §§ 24—27.

[4] *De Lys.* c. 8 τριῶν τε ὄντων
ἐν οἷς καὶ περὶ ἃ τὴν ἀρετὴν ταύτην
συμβέβηκεν εἶναι, διανοίας τε καὶ

λέξεως καὶ τρίτης τῆς συνθέσεως, ἐν ἅπασι τούτοις αὐτὸν ἀποφαίνομαι κατορθοῦν.

[5] Francken (*Commentationes
Lysiacae*, pp. 5—7) thinks it doubtful whether by the ἠθοποιία of Lysias Dionysios meant the appropriate delineation of each several

the extant speeches of Lysias upon which this peculiar power has not left its mark. Many of them, otherwise poor in interest, have a permanent artistic value as describing, with a few quiet touches, this or that type of man. For instance, the Defence which is the subject of the Twenty-first Oration is interesting solely because it embodies to the life that proud consciousness of merit with which a citizen who had deserved well of the State might confront a calumny. In the speech on the Sacred Olive, if the nameless accused is not a person for us, he is at least a character—the man who shrinks from public prominence of any kind, but who at the same time has a shy pride in discharging splendidly all his public duties[1]. The injured husband, again, who has taken upon Eratosthenes the extreme vengeance sanctioned by the law, is the subject of an indirect portrait, in which homeliness is combined with the moral dig-

---

character, or the attribution to all characters alike of a certain attractive simplicity. Francken inclines to the latter view. He refers to cases in which, as he thinks, Lysias has failed, or has not tried, to mark individual character, or in which the general stamp of simplicity is exaggerated. The appreciation of êthos depends much upon taste; it scarcely admits of argument. But it is clear to me what Dionysios, at least, meant by the ἠθοποιΐα of Lysias. He meant the appropriate delineation of each several character. Surely he says so very plainly: *De Lys.* c. 8 οὐ γὰρ διανοουμένους μόνον ὑποτίθεται χρηστὰ καὶ ἐπιεικῆ καὶ μέτρια τοὺς

λέγοντας, ὥστε εἰκόνας εἶναι δοκεῖν τῶν ἠθῶν τοὺς λόγους ἀλλὰ καὶ τὴν λέξιν ἀποδίδωσι τοῖς ἤθεσιν οἰκείαν. Cf. K. O. Müller, *Hist. Gr. Lit.* II. p. 143 (tr. Donaldson):—'Lysias distinguished, with the accuracy of a dramatist, between the different characters into whose mouths he put his speeches, and made everyone, the young and the old, the rich and the poor, the educated and the uneducated, speak according to his quality and condition: this is what the ancient critics praise under the name of his *Êthopoiïa.* The prevalent tone, however, was that of the average man.'

[1] *De sacra Olea* §§ 1—3, 30.

nity of a citizen standing upon his rights[1]. The
steady Athenian householder of the old type, and the
adventurous patriot of the new, are sketched in the
speech On the Property of Aristophanes[2]. The accuser
of Diogeiton, unwilling to prosecute a relative, but
resolved to have a shameful wrong redressed;—Diogeiton's mother, pleading with him for her sons;—are
pictures all the more effective because they have been
produced without apparent effort[3]. But of all such
delineations—and, as Dionysios says, *no* character in
Lysias is inartistically drawn or lifeless[4]—perhaps
the cleverest and certainly the most attractive is
that of Mantitheos, the brilliant young Athenian
who is vindicating his past life before the Senate.
Nowhere is the ethical art of Lysias more ably shown
than in the ingenuous words of apology with which,
as by an afterthought, Mantitheos concludes his
frank and highspirited defence :—

'I have understood, Senators, that some people
are annoyed with me for this too—that I presumed,
though rather young, to speak in the Assembly. It
was about my own affairs that I was first compelled
to speak in public; after that, however, I *do* suspect
myself of having been more ambitiously inclined than
I need have been,—partly through thinking of my
family, who have never ceased to be statesmen,—
partly because I saw that you (to tell the truth)

---

[1] *De caed. Eratosth.* (Or. i.)
§§ 5 ff., 47—50.

[2] *De Aristoph. bonis* §§ 18—
23, 55—64.

[3] *In Diogeit.* §§ 1—3, 12—17.

[4] *De Lys. c.* 8 ἁπλῶς γὰρ οὐδὲ
εὑρεῖν δύναμαι παρὰ τῷ ῥήτορι τούτῳ
πρόσωπον οὔτε ἀνηθοποίητον οὔτε
ἄψυχον.

respect none but such men; so that, seeing this to be your opinion, who would not be invited to act and speak in behalf of the State? And besides— why should you be vexed with such men? The judgment upon them rests with none but your- selves[1].'

The 'propriety' of Lysias.

The 'propriety' which has always been praised in Lysias depends mainly on this discernment of what suits the character of each speaker; but it includes more—it has respect also to the hearers and to the subject, and generally to all the circumstances of the case. The judge, the ekklesiast, the listener in the crowd at a festival are not addressed in the same vein; different excellences of style characterise the opening, the narrative, the argument, the final appeal[2].

His 'charm.'

It remains to say a few words on the peculiar and crowning excellence of Lysias in the province of expression,—his famous but inexplicable 'charm.' It is noticeable that while his Roman critics merely praise his elegance and polish, regarding it as a simple result of his art[3], the finer sense of his Greek

[1] *Pro Mantith.* §§ 20, 21.

[2] The distinction between *Êtho- poiia* and the *Propriety* praised in Lysias will appear from a care- ful reading of Dionys. *De Lys.* cc. 8, 9. Êthopoiïa is the adaptation of the speech to the intrinsic cha- racter of the speaker. Propriety is the adaptation of the speech to the circumstances;—on the one hand, to the age, quality, occupa- tion, &c. of the speaker; on the other hand, to the cause and to the audience.

[3] Cic. *Brut.* § 35 *egregie sub- tilis scriptor atque elegans:* ib. § 285, *ieiunitas polita, urbana, ele- gans.* Quint. x. 1. 78 *subtilis atque elegans:* IX. 4. 17 *gratia quae in eo maxima est simplicis atque inaffectati coloris.* It must be allowed to Cicero that he felt the plainness of Lysias to have a charm of its own. But he did not, like Dionysios, feel this charm to be something independent of the plainness, which could be used as a distinct test of genuine work.

critic apprehends a certain nameless grace or charm,
which cannot be directly traced to art,—which cannot be analysed or accounted for: it is something
peculiar to him, of which all that can be said is that
it is there.   What, asks Dionysios, is the freshness
of a beautiful face?   What is fine harmony in the
movements and windings of music?   What is rhythm
in the measurement of times?   As these things baffle
definition, so does the charm of Lysias.   It cannot
be taken to pieces by reasoning; it must be seized
by a cultivated instinct[1].   It is the final criterion of
his genuine work.   'When I am puzzled about one of
the speeches ascribed to him, and when it is hard for
me to find the truth by other marks, I have recourse
to this excellence, as to the last piece on the board.
Then, if the Graces of Speech seem to me to make
the writing fair, I count it to be of the soul of Lysias;
and I care not to look further into it.   But if the
stamp of the language has no winningness, no loveliness, I am chagrined, and suspect that after all
the speech is not by Lysias; and I do no more violence to my instinct, even though in all else the
speech seems to me clever and well-finished; believing
that to write well, in special styles other than this,
is given to many men; but that to write winningly,
gracefully, with loveliness, is the gift of Lysias.'[2]

See *Orator* § 78, *nam ut mulieres
esse dicuntur nonnullae inorna-
tae, quas id ipsum deceat, sic* haec
*subtilis oratio atque incompta de-
lectat. fit enim quiddam in utro-
que, quo sit venustius, sed non ut
appareat.*

[1] Dionys. *De Lys.* c. 11.   Note

the words—τίς ἡ παρ' αὐτῷ χάρις
ἐστι, βουλομένοις μαθεῖν ὑποθείμην
ἂν ἐπιτηδεύειν χρόνῳ μακρῷ καὶ μακρᾷ
τριβῇ, καὶ ἀλόγῳ πάθει τὴν ἄλο-
γον συνασκεῖν αἴσθησιν—'and
to train their critical sense by a
feeling as instinctive as itself.'

[2] *1b.*

A modern reader would be sanguine if he hoped
to analyse the distinctive charm of Lysias more
closely than Dionysios found himself able to do.
He may be content if study by degrees gives him a
dim apprehension of something which he believes
that he could use, as Dionysios used the qualities
detected by his 'instinct,' in deciding between the
genuine and the false. Evidently the same cause
which in great measure disqualifies a modern for
estimating the 'purity' of the language of Lysias
also disqualifies him for estimating its charm. This
charm may be supposed to have consisted partly in
a certain felicity of expression,—Lysias having a
knack of using the word which, for some undefinable
reason, was felt to be curiously right; partly in a
certain essential urbanity, the reflection of a nature
at once genial and refined. The first quality is evidently beyond the sure appreciation of a modern
ear: the second less so, yet scarcely to be estimated
with nicety, since here too shades of expression are
concerned. At best a student of Lysias may hope
to attain a tolerably true perception of what he
could *not* have written: but hardly the faculty of
rejoicing that he wrote just as he did.

*His treat-
ment of
subject-
matter.*

Having now noticed the leading characteristics
of Lysias in regard to form of language, we will
consider some of his characteristics in the other
great department of his art—the treatment of the
subject-matter. In this the ancient critics distinguished two chief elements, Invention and Arrangement[1].

---

[1] εὕρεσις—τάξις: Dionys. *De Lys.* c. 15.

By 'invention' was meant the faculty of dis- <small>*Invention.*</small>
covering the arguments available in any given circumstances; the art, in short, of making the most
of a case. Sokrates, criticising the speech in the
Phaedros, is made to express contempt for the in-
ventive power of Lysias[1]. Arguments, however,
which would not pass with a dialectician, might do
very well for a jury. If Plato found Lysias barren
of logical resource, Dionysios emphatically praises
his fertile cleverness in discovering every weapon
of controversy which the facts of a case could yield
to the most penetrating search[2]. The latter part
of the speech against Agoratos may be taken as a
good example of this exhaustive ingenuity[3]. It is
a fault, indeed, that there the speaker attempts to
make too many small points in succession; and one,
at least, of these is a curious instance of overdone
subtlety[4].

In regard to arrangement, Lysias is distinguished <small>*Arrange-ment.*</small>
from all other Greek orators by a uniform simplicity.
His speeches consist usually of four parts, which
follow each other in a regular order : proem, narrative, proof, epilogue[5]. In some cases, the nature of
the subject renders a narrative, in the proper sense,
unnecessary; in others, the narrative is at the same
time the proof; in a few, the proem is almost or

---

[1] Plat. *Phaedr*. pp. 234 E—236 A.
[2] Dionys. *Lys.* c. 13.
[3] *In Agorat.* §§ 49—90.
[4] *ib.* §§ 70—90, in which it is
argued that the amnesty of 403
does not hold good as between two
members of the same political

party.
[5] ἔστι δὲ τὰ τῆς ὑποθέσεως στοι-
χεῖα τέσσαρα, προοίμιον, διήγησις, πίστεις, ἐπίλογος: Dionys.
Art. Rhet. x. c. 12. Aristotle's
enumeration is προοίμιον, πρόθεσις,
πίστις, ἐπίλογος : *Rhet.* III. 13.

entirely dispensed with. But in no case is there
anything more elaborate than this fourfold partition,
—and in no case is the sequence of the parts altered.
This simple arrangement, contrasting with the manifold subdivisions which Plato notices as used by the
rhetoricians of his day[1], is usually said to have been
first made by Isokrates[2]. This may be true in the
sense that it was he who first stated it theoretically.
In practice, however, it had already been employed
by Lysias; and more strictly than by Isokrates
himself[3]. The difference between their systems,
according to Dionysios, is precisely this;—Lysias
uses always the same simple framework, never interpolating, subdividing or defining[4]; Isokrates knows
how to break the uniformity by transpositions of his
own devising, or by novel episodes[5]. The same difference, in a stronger form, separates Lysias here
from his imitator in much else, Isaeos. Every kind
of artifice is used by Isaeos in shifting, subdividing,
recombining the four rudimentary elements of the
speech according to the special conditions of the
case[6]. It was this versatile tact in disposing his
forces—this generalship[7], as Dionysios in one place
calls it—which chiefly procured for Isaeos the reputation of unequalled adroitness in fighting a bad

---

[1] *Phaedr.* pp. 266 E, 267 E. Cf.
Arist. *Rhet.* IV. 13.

[2] Dionys. *Lys.* 16: Sauppe, *O.A.*
II. 224: Cope, *Introd. to Arist.
Rhetoric*, p. 332.

[3] Westermann (*Griesch. Bereds.*
p. 75) seems to recognise Lysias as
the inventor of the fourfold partition.

[4] Dionys. *De Lys.* c. 15.

[5] Id. *De Isocr.* c. 4, τὸ διαλαμ-
βάνεσθαι τὴν ὁμοειδίαν ἰδίαις μετα-
βολαῖς καὶ ξένοις ἐπεισοδίοις.

[6] Id. *De Isae.* c. 14.

[7] τοὺς δὲ δικαστὰς καταστρατη-
γεῖ, *De Isae* 3.

cause[1]. Lysias had consummate literary skill and
much acuteness; but his weapons were better than
his plan of campaign; he was not a subtle tactician.
'In arranging what he has invented he is commonplace, frank, guileless;'[2] while Isaeos 'plays all manner of ruses upon his adversary,'[3] Lysias 'uses no
sort of knavery.'[4] Invention and selection are admirable in him: arrangement is best studied in his
successors[5].

If we turn from his general plan to his execution
of its several parts, Lysias will be found to shew
very different degrees of merit in proem, narrative,
proof and epilogue.

His proem, or opening, is always excellent, always *Proem.*
gracefully and accurately appropriate to the matter
in hand. This inexhaustible fertility of resource
calls forth the special commendation of Dionysios.
'The power shown in his proems will appear especially marvellous if it is considered that, though he
wrote not fewer than 200 forensic speeches, there is
not one in which he is found to have used a preface
which is not plausible, or which is not closely connected with the case. Indeed, he has not twice hit
upon the same syllogisms, or twice drifted into the
same thoughts. Yet even those who have written

---

[1] His reputation in this respect
was of a somewhat sinister kind:—
ἦν δὲ περὶ αὐτοῦ δόξα παρὰ τοῖς
τότε γοητείας καὶ ἀπάτης, ὡς δεινὸς
ἀνὴρ τεχνιτεῦσαι λόγους ἐπὶ τὰ πο-
νηρότερα. Dionys. *De Isae.* 4.

[2] ἔστιν ἀπέριττός τις καὶ ἐλεύθε-
ρος καὶ ἀπόνηρος οἰκονομῆσαι τὰ

εὑρεθέντα: Dionys. *De Lys.* c. 15.

[3] πρὸς τὸν ἀντίδικον διαπονη-
ρεύεται, *De Isae.* c. 3.

[4] οὔτε γὰρ προκατασκευαῖς [κ.τ.λ.],
...οὔτε ταῖς ἄλλαις τοιαύταις παν-
ουργίαις εὑρίσκεται χρώμενος:
De Lys. c. 15.

[5] *Ib.*

little are found to have had this mischance,—that, I mean, of repeating commonplaces ; to say nothing of the fact that nearly all of them borrow the prefatory remarks of others, and think no shame of doing so.'[1] The opening of the speech against Diogeiton may be cited as an example of a difficult case introduced with singular delicacy and tact.

Narrative.   The same kind of cleverness which never fails to make a good beginning finds a more important scope in the next stage of the speech.   In narrative Lysias is masterly.   His statements of facts are distinguished by conciseness, clearness and charm, and by a power of producing conviction without apparent effort to convince[2].   If these qualities mark almost equally some of the narratives in the private orations of Demosthenes[3], it is yet Lysias and not Demosthenes to whom Dionysios points as the canon of excellence in this kind[4].   He goes so far as to say that he believes the rules for narrative given in the current rhetorical treatises to have been derived from study of models supplied by Lysias.

Proof.   In the third province—that of proof—this supremacy is not maintained.   Rhetorical proofs are of three kinds: (1) direct logical proofs which appeal to the

---

[1] Dionys. *De Lys.* c. 17.

[2] His narratives τὴν πίστιν ἅμα λεληθότως συνεπιφέρουσιν, *id. De Lys.* c. 18.

[3] After comparing an extract from the lost speech of Lysias Against Tisis with an extract from the speech of Demosthenes Against Konon, Dionysios asks—ταῦτα οὐ

καθαρὰ καὶ ἀκριβῆ καὶ σαφῆ καὶ διὰ τῶν κυρίων καὶ κοινῶν ὀνομάτων κατεσκευασμένα, ὥσπερ τὰ Λυσίου; and goes on to notice other excellences which both have alike. *De Demosth.* c. 13.

[4] ὅρον τε καὶ κανόνα τῆς ἰδέας ταύτης αὐτὸν ἀποφαίνομαι : *De Lys.* c. 18.

reason; and indirect moral proofs which appeal (2) to the moral sense, and (3) to the feelings.

In the first sort Lysias is strong both by acuteness in discovering, and by judgment in selecting, arguments. In the second he is effective also; and succeeds, even when he has few facts to go upon, in making characters seem attractive or the reverse by incidental touches. In the third he is comparatively weak; he cannot heighten the force of a plea, represent a wrong, or invoke compassion[1], with sufficient spirit and intensity. Hence in the fourth and last *Epilogue.* department, the epilogue, he shows, indeed, the neatness which suits recapitulation, but not the power which ought to elevate an appeal. The nature of his progress through a speech is well described by an image which his Greek critic employs[2]. Like a soft southern breeze, his facile inspiration wafts him smoothly through the first and second stages of his voyage; at the third it droops; in the last it dies.

The manner in which Lysias handles his subject-matter has now been spoken of so far as concerns its technical aspect. But, besides these characteristics of the artist which may be discovered in particular parts, there are certain general qualities, resulting from the character of the man, which colour the whole; and a word must now be said of these.

---

[1] In the technical language of Dionysios, Lysias understands οὔτε αὐξήσεις οὔτε δεινώσεις οὔτε οἴκτους: *De Lys.* c. 19.

[2] αὕτη μέντοι (ἡ χάρις), καθάπερ νότιός τις αὖρα, μέχρι προοιμίου καὶ διηγήσεως αὐτὸν ἄγει· ὅταν δὲ εἰς τοὺς ἀποδεικτικοὺς ἔλθῃ λόγους, ἀμυδρά τις γίγνεται καὶ ἀσθενής· ἐν δὲ δὴ τοῖς παθητικοῖς εἰς τέλος ἀποσβέννυται: Dionys. *De Demosth.* c. 13.

The tact of Lysias.

Foremost among such qualities is tact. One of its special manifestations is quick sympathy with the character of the speaker; another is perception of the style in which a certain subject should be treated or a certain class of hearers addressed. Both these have already been noticed. But, above and beyond these, there is a certain sureness in the whole conduct of a case, a certain remoteness from liability to blunder, which is the most general indication of the tact of Lysias. Among his genuine extant speeches there is only one which perhaps in some degree offers an exception to the rule;—the speech against Evandros[1]. In the case of the speech against Andokides, the conspicuous absence of a fine discretion is one of the most conclusive proofs that Lysias was not the author[2]. In relation to treatment, this tact is precisely what the 'charm' praised by Dionysios is in relation to language; it is that quality, the presence or absence of which is the best general criterion of what Lysias did or did not write.

His humour.

A quality which the last almost implies is humour; and this Lysias certainly had. The description of an incorrigible borrower, in the fragment of the lost speech against the Sokratic Aeschines, shows this humour tending to broad farce[3], and illustrates

[1] See the remarks below upon this speech.

[2] The internal evidence against the authenticity of the speech Against Andokides is discussed below.

[3] Fragment 1 in Sauppe, *O. A.* II. p. 172. The passage especially meant here begins at ἀλλὰ γάρ,

ὦ ἄνδρες δικασταί, οὐκ εἰς ἐμὲ μόνον τοιοῦτός ἐστιν, and goes down to ἢ τούτῳ συμβάλλειν :—

'But indeed, judges, I am not the only person to whom he behaves in this way; he is the same to every one else who has had to do with him. Have not the neighbouring shopkeepers, from whom

what Demetrius means by the 'somewhat comic
graces'[1] of Lysias.　But, as a rule, it is seen only
in sudden touches, which amuse chiefly because they
surprise; as in the speech for Mantitheos, and most
of all in that for the Invalid[2].　Really powerful *Sarcasm.*
sarcasm must come from earnest feeling; and Lysias,
though intellectual acuteness gave him command of
irony, was weak in sarcasm for the same reason that
he was not great in pathos.　There is, properly
speaking, only one extant speech—that against Nikomachos—in which sarcasm is a principal weapon[3].
Here he is moderately successful, but not in the
best way; for, just as in his attack upon Aeschines,
vehemence, tending to coarseness, takes the place of
moral indignation.

　The language, the method, the genius of Lysias *Defects of*
have now been considered in reference to their chief *Lysias as an orator.*
positive characteristics.　But no attempt to estimate
what Lysias was would be true or complete if it failed

he gets on credit goods for which
he never pays, shut up their shops
and gone to law with him? Are
not his neighbours so cruelly used
by him that they have left their
houses and are trying to take
others at a distance? Whenever
he has collected club-subscriptions,
he fails to hand over the payments
of the other members, and they are
wrecked on this little tradesman
like chariots at the turning-post
of the course. Such a crowd goes
at daybreak to his house to demand the sums due to them, that
passers-by fancy the people have
come to attend a funeral. As for

the inhabitants of the Peiraeus
they are in such a mind that they
think it much safer to sail to the
Adriatic than to encounter this
man.'

[1] Demetr. περὶ ἑρμηνείας § 128
(Walz, *Rhet. Gr.* IX. 58): τῶν δὲ
χαρίτων αἱ μέν εἰσι μείζονες καὶ σεμ-
νότεραι, αἱ δὲ εὐτελεῖς μᾶλλον καὶ
κωμικώτεραι, οἷον αἱ Ἀριστοτέ-
λους χάριτες καὶ Σώφρονος καὶ Λυσίου.

[2] e.g. *In Mantith.* (Or. XVI.)
§ 15: *Pro Inval.* (Or. XXIV.) § 9.
Cf. *De sacra Olea* (Or. VII.) § 1, 14.

[3] See esp. *In Nikom.* (Or. XXX.)
§§ 11, 27.

to point out what he was not. However high the
rank which he may claim as a literary artist, he cannot, as an orator, take the highest. The defects
which exclude him from it are chiefly two ; and these
are to a certain extent the defects of his qualities.
As he excelled in analysis of character and in elegance,
so he was, as a rule, deficient in pathos and in fire.

The limits
of pathos
in Lysias.
It would be untrue to say that Lysias never
appeals to the feelings with effect, and unfair to
assume that he lacked the power of appealing to
them with force. But the bent of his mind was
critical; his artistic instinct shrank from exaggeration
of every sort ; and, instead of giving fervent expression to his own sense of what was pitiable or terrible
in any set of circumstances, it was his manner merely
to draw a suggestive picture of the circumstances
themselves. This self-restraint will be best understood by comparing a passage of Lysias with a similar
passage of Andokides. The speech On the Mysteries
describes the scene in the prison when mothers, sisters, wives came to visit the victims of the informer
Diokleides[1]. A like scene is described in the speech
Against Agoratos, when the persons whom he had
denounced took farewell in prison of their kins-
women[2]. But the two orators take different means
of producing a tragic effect. 'There were cries and
lamentations,' says Andokides, 'weeping and wailing
for the miseries of the hour.'[3] Lysias simply remarks
that the wife who came to see her husband had
already put on mourning[4]. For hearers of a certain

[1] Andok. *De Myst.* §§ 48—51.
[2] Lys. *In Agorat.* §§ 39—42.
[3] *De Myst.* § 48.
[4] *In Agorat.* § 40.

class the pathos of facts is more eloquent than an express appeal; but the speaker who is content to rely upon it renounces the hope of being found pathetic by the multitude. It was only now and then that, without going beyond the limits which his own taste imposed, Lysias could expect to stir general sympathy. In the defence which he wrote for the nephews of Nikias, the last survivors of a house made desolate by violent deaths and now threatened with spoliation, he found such an opportunity. He used it well, because, though declamation would have been easy, he abstained from everything rhetorical and hollow. The few words in which the defendant speaks of his claim to the protection of the court are plain and dignified :—

'Judges, I have no one to put up to plead for us; for of our kinsmen some have died in war, after showing themselves brave men, in the effort to make Athens great; some, in the cause of the democracy and of your freedom, have died by the hemlock of the Thirty; and so the merits of our kinsmen, and the misfortunes of the State, have become the causes of our friendlessness. It befits you to think of these things and to help us with good will, considering that under a democracy those deserve to be well-treated at your hands who, under an oligarchy, had their share of the troubles.'[1]

After inquiring how far Lysias fails in pathos, it remains to speak of the other principal defect noticed above. How far, and in what sense, does he want fire? By 'fire' is meant here the passion of a speaker

The eloquence of Lysias rarely passionate.

---

[1] *De bonis Niciae fratris* (Or. XVIII.) §§ 24, 25.

stirred with great ideas. Dionysios says (in effect)
that, besides pathos, Lysias wants two other things,
grandeur and spirit[1].   He has not—we are told—
the intensity or the force[2] of Demosthenes ; he
touches, but does not pierce, the heart[3]; he charms,
but fails to astonish or to appal[4].   This is true ;
but it should be remembered that in a great
majority of the causes with which he had to deal
the attempt at sublimity would have been ridi-
culous.   It may be granted that, had Lysias been
called upon to plead for Olynthos or to denounce
Philip, he would not have approached even distantly
the lofty vehemence of Demosthenes.   The absence
of passion cannot properly be regarded as a defect in
his extant speeches ; but they at least suggest that
under no circumstances could he have excelled in
passionate eloquence.   They indicate a power which
sufficed to elaborate them, rather than a power which
gave them their special qualities out of an affluence
of resource.   Two speeches, however, must be named,
one of which shows (in what remains of it) the inspiration of a great idea, the other, the inspiration
of an ardent feeling.   These are the *Olympiakos*
and the speech Against Eratosthenes.   If in each
of these Lysias has shown himself worthy of his subject, the inference in his favour should be strengthened by the fact that, so far as we know, these are
the noblest subjects which he treated.

---

[1] Dionysios says that the style
of Lysias is not ὑψηλή and μεγαλοπρεπής: nor θυμοῦ καὶ πνεύματος
μεστή: *De Lys.* c. 13.

[2] τόνος—ἰσχύς: Dionys. *Demosth.*
13.

[3] He wants τὸ πικρόν: id. *Lys.*
13.

[4] His style being neither θαυ-
μαστή nor καταπληκτική: *ib.*

In the *Olympiakos* he is enforcing the necessity
of union among Greeks and calling upon Sparta to
take the lead :—

'It befits us, then, to desist from war among
ourselves and to cleave, with a single purpose, to
the public weal, ashamed for the past and appre-
hensive for the future ; it befits us to imitate our
forefathers, who, when the barbarians coveted the
land of others, inflicted upon them the loss of their
own ; and who, after driving out the tyrants, established liberty for all men alike.   But I wonder most
of all at the Lacedaemonians, and at the policy which
can induce them to view passively the conflagration
of Greece.   They are the leaders of the Greeks, as
they deserve to be, both for their inborn gallantry
and for their warlike science ; they alone dwell
exempt from ravage, though unsheltered by walls ;
unvexed by faction ; strangers to defeat ; with
usages which never vary ; thus warranting the hope
that the freedom which they have achieved is immortal, and that, having proved themselves in past
perils the deliverers of Greece, they are now thought-
ful for her future.'[1]

In the speech Against Eratosthenes, he concludes
the impeachment with an appeal to the two parties
who had alike suffered from the Thirty Tyrants ;—
the Townsmen, or those who had remained at Athens
under the oligarchy ; and the democratic exiles who
had held the Peiraeus :—

'I wish, before I go down, to recall a few things

---

[1] *Olympiakos* (Or. XXXIII.) §§ 6, 7.

to the recollection of both parties, the party of the Town and the party of the Peiraeus; in order that, in passing sentence, you may have before you as warnings the calamities which have come upon you through these men.

'And you, first, of the Town—reflect that under their iron rule you were forced to wage with brothers, with sons, with citizens a war of such a sort that, having been vanquished, you are the equals of the conquerors, whereas, had you conquered, you would have been the slaves of the Tyrants. They would have gained wealth for their own houses from the administration; you have impoverished yours in the war with one another; for they did not deign that you should thrive along with them, though they forced you to become odious in their company; such being their consummate arrogance that, instead of seeking to win your loyalty by giving you partnership in their prizes, they fancied themselves friendly if they allowed you a share of their dishonours. Now, therefore, that you are in security, take vengeance to the utmost of your power both for yourselves and for the men of the Peiraeus; reflecting that these men, villains that they are, were your masters, but that now good men are your fellow-citizens,—your fellow-soldiers against the enemy, your fellow-counsellors in the interest of the State; remembering, too, those allies whom these men posted on the acropolis as sentinels over their despotism and your servitude. To you—though much more might be said—I say thus much only.

'But you of the Peiraeus—think, in the first

place, of your arms—think how, after fighting many
a battle on foreign soil, you were stripped of those
arms, not by the enemy, but by these men in time
of peace; think, next, how you were warned by
public criers from the city bequeathed to you by
your fathers, and how your surrender was demanded
of the cities in which you were exiles. Resent these
things as you resented them in banishment; and
recollect, at the same time, the other evils that
you have suffered at their hands;—how some were
snatched out of the marketplace or from temples and
put to a violent death; how others were torn from
children, parents, or wife, and forced to become their
own murderers, nor allowed the common decencies of
burial, by men who believed their own empire to be
surer than the vengeance from on high.

'And you, the remnant who escaped death, after
perils in many places, after wanderings to many
cities and expulsion from all, beggared of the ne-
cessaries of life, parted from children, left in a
fatherland which was hostile or in the land of
strangers, came through many obstacles to the Peiraeus. Dangers many and great confronted you;
but you proved yourselves brave men; you freed
some, you restored others to their country.

'Had you been unfortunate and missed those
aims, you yourselves would now be exiles, in fear of
suffering what you suffered before. Owing to the
character of these men, neither temples nor altars,
which even in the sight of evil-doers have a protecting virtue, would have availed you against wrong;—
while those of your children who are here would

have been enduring the outrages of these men, and
those who are in a foreign land, in the absence of
all succour, would, for the smallest debt, have been
enslaved.

'I do not wish, however, to speak of what might
have been, seeing that what these men have done is
beyond my power to tell; and indeed it is a task
not for one accuser, or for two, but for a host.

'Yet is my indignation perfect for the temples
which these men bartered away or defiled by entering
them; for the city which they humbled; for the
arsenals which they dismantled; for the dead, whom
you, since you could not rescue them alive, must
vindicate in their death. And I think that they
are listening to us, and will be aware of you when
you give your verdict, deeming that such as absolve
these men have passed sentence upon *them*, and that
such as exact retribution from these have taken vengeance in *their* names.

'I will cease accusing. You have heard—seen—
suffered: you have them: judge.'[1]

*Place of
Lysias in
the history
of Rhetoric.*
On reviewing the general position of Lysias
among the Attic orators, it will be seen to result
mainly from his discovery, made at a time when
Rhetoric had not yet outlived the crudest taste for
finery, that the most complete art is that which
hides itself. Aided not only by a delicate mastery of
language but by a peculiar gift for reading and expressing character, he created a style of which the
chief mark was various naturalness. It was long
before the art of speaking reached, in general prac-

----

[1] *In Eratosth.* §§ 92—100.

tice, that sober maturity which his precocious tact
had given to it in a limited field; it was long before
his successors freed themselves to any great extent—
few wholly freed themselves—from the well-worn
allurements which he had decisively rejected when
they were freshest. But at least no one of those who
came after dared to neglect the lesson taught by
Lysias; the attempt to be natural, however artifici-
ally or rarely, was henceforward a new element in
the task which professors of eloquence conceived to
be set before them. Lysias remains, for all after-
times, the master of the plain style.

This supremacy in a definite province is allowed
to him by the general voice of antiquity through
the centuries in which its culture was finest; the
praise becoming, however, less discriminating as the
instinct which directed it became less sure.

The ancient critics upon Lysias.

Plato's satire[1] upon Lysias—for not having seen
that the writing of love-letters is a branch of
Dialectic—is joined to a notice of the clearness,
compactness, finished polish of his language[2]; and
it would perhaps be unfair to Plato to assume that
in the one place where he seems at all just to

---

[1] Plat. *Phaedr*. p. 264 B : οὐ
χύδην δοκεῖ βεβλῆσθαι τὰ τοῦ λόγου;
ἢ φαίνεται τὸ δεύτερον εἰρημένον ἔκ
τινος ἀνάγκης δεῖν δεύτερον τεθῆναι;
It is on this ground—the *unphilo-
sophic* character of Lysias—that
Plato gives such a decided preference to Isokrates. Compare the
remark of Dionysios that Isaeos
differs from Lysias in this among
other things—τῷ μὴ κατ᾽ ἐνθύμημά
τι λέγειν ἀλλὰ καὶ κατ᾽ ἐπιχείρημα

(*De Is.* 16). That is, Isaeos frequently makes an attempt (ἐπιχείρημα) at strict logical proof; whereas Lysias rarely goes beyond the
rhetorical syllogism (ἐνθύμημα).

[2] *Phaedr.* p. 234 E: τί δέ; καὶ
ταύτῃ δεῖ τὸν λόγον ἐπαινεθῆναι, ὡς
τὰ δέοντα εἰρηκότος τοῦ ποιητοῦ, ἀλλ᾽
οὐκ ἐκείνῃ μόνον, ὅτι σαφῆ καὶ
στρογγύλα, καὶ ἀκριβῶς ἕκαστα
τῶν ὀνομάτων ἀποτετόρνευται;

Lysias he meant to be altogether ironical. Isaeos
was a careful student of Lysias [1]. If Aristotle [2]
seldom quoted him, if Theophrastos [3] appears to have
missed and Demetrios [4] to have underrated his peculiar merits, one of the first orators of their generation,
Deinarchos [5], often took him for a model. When

---

[1] Dionys. *De Is.* 2: [Plut.] *vit.*
Isae.

[2] In the extant works of Aristotle there occur but two quota-
tions from authentic speeches of
Lysias: (1) In *Rhet.* iii. ad fin.
εἴρηκα, ἀκηκόατε, ἔχετε, κρίνατε :
cited as an example of effective
asyndeton. This is probably an
inaccurate citation of the ἀκηκόατε,
ἑωράκατε, πεπόνθατε, ἔχετε, δικάζετε
with which the speech Against Eratosthenes closes. (2) In *Rhet.* ii.
c. 23 § 18 there is a quotation
from § 11 of the speech of Lysias
περὶ τῆς πολιτείας (Or. xxxiv.): εἰ
φεύγοντες μὲν ἐμαχόμεθα ὅπως κατ-
έλθωμεν, κατελθόντες δὲ φευξόμεθα
ὅπως μὴ μαχώμεθα.
The citation in *Rhet.* iii. c. 10
§ 7 (διότι ἄξιον ἦν ἐπὶ τῷ τάφῳ—
συγκαταθαπτομένης τῇ ἀρετῇ αὐτῶν
τῆς ἐλευθερίας) from § 60 of the
ἐπιτάφιος ascribed to Lysias (Or.
ii.) cannot be reckoned, since that
speech is unquestionably spurious.
Blass remarks that the words quoted by Demetrios (περὶ ἑρμ. § 28)
from a lost work of Aristotle περὶ
δικαιοσύνης resemble what we read
in § 39 of the speech Against Eratosthenes. (*Att. Bereds.* p. 377,
note 3.)

[3] Dionysios expresses indignant
astonishment at the assertion of
Theophrastos (ἐν τοῖς περὶ λέξεως)
that Lysias had a taste for vulgar

redundancy of ornament (φορτι-
κῶν καὶ περιέργων αὐτὸν οἴεται
ζηλωτὴν γενέσθαι λόγων). Moderns
may share this surprise, when they
find that Theophrastos referred
in support of his opinion to a
speech said to have been composed
by Lysias for the captive general
Nikias. The few words quoted by
Theophrastos suffice to indicate
the work of a third-rate rhetorician : see above, p. 147. Cf. Sauppe's
remarks on the fragment, *O.A.* ii.
p. 199.

[4] In a passage of the περὶ ἑρμηνείας (§ 128) already noticed, the
epithets which Demetrios gives to
the 'graces' of Lysias are εὐτελεῖς
—κωμικώτεραι. It is significant
that Demetrios should have mistaken ἀφέλεια for εὐτέλεια, plainness for paltriness. He lived at
the time when Greek eloquence,
in the first stage of its decline,
was beginning to affect the tawdry
ornament of the Rhodian school.
(See Westerm. *Griesch. Bereds.*
p. 165.)

[5] Dionysios names certain
speeches of Deinarchos as bearing
especially the Λυσιακὸς χαρακτήρ.
Hypereides and (of course) Demosthenes were the two other masters by whom Deinarchos was
chiefly influenced. (Dionys. *De
Dein.* c. 5.)

Among the less eminent imita-

the taste for Attic simplicity, lost during two centuries in the schools of Asia, revived at Rome, Lysias
was recognised as its truest representative. Though
most of his Roman imitators appear to have become
feeble in seeking to be plain, one of them, Licinius
Calvus, is allowed at least the praise of elegance[1].
Cicero's criticism of Lysias is not close; it does not
analyse with any exactness the special qualities of
his style; but the general appreciation which it
shows is just. For Cicero, Lysias is the model, not
of a plain style merely, but of Attic refinement[2];
he has also the highest degree of vigour[3]; and
though grandeur was seldom possible in the treatment of such subjects as he chose, some passages
of his speeches have elevation[4]. Yet, while Demosthenes could use the simplicity of Lysias, it
is doubtful (Cicero thinks) whether Lysias could
ever have risen to the height of Demosthenes[5];

tors of Lysias who belonged nearly
to the age of Deinarchos, Cicero
names Charisios and Hegesias of
Magnesia (*Brut.* § 286 : *Orator*
§ 226).

[1] Cic. *Brutus* § 283 *Accuratius
quoddam dicendi et exquisitius
afferebat genus.* He treated this
style *scienter eleganterque*, though
with a certain self-conscious and
overwrought care which deprived
it of freshness and force.

[2] *De Oratore* III. 7 § 28 *Sua-
vitatem Isocrates,* subtilitatem
*Lysias, acumen Hyperides, soni-
tum Aeschines, vim Demosthenes
habuit.* Compare *Orator* § 29
intelligamus hoc esse Atticum in

*Lysia, non quod tenuis sit atque
inornatus, sed quod nihil habeat
insolens aut ineptum.*

[3] *Brutus* § 64 *Quanquam in
Lysia saepe sunt etiam lacerti,
ita sic ut fieri nihil possit valen-
tius.*

[4] *De opt. gen. Oratorum* § 9 *Est
enim (Lysias) multis locis gran-
dior; sed quia et privatas ille
plerasque et eas ipsas aliis et par-
varum rerum caussulas scripsit,
videtur esse ieiunior, quom se ipse
consulto ad minutarum genera
caussarum limaverit.*

[5] *ib.* § 10 *Ita fit ut Demosthenes
certe possit summisse dicere, elate
Lysias fortasse non possit.*

Lysias is 'almost' a second Demosthenes[1], or, what is the same thing, 'almost' a perfect orator[2]; but his mastery is limited to a province. The Augustan age produced by far the best and fullest of known ancient criticisms upon Lysias, that of Dionysios[3]. The verdict of Caecilius has perished with his work on the Ten Orators; but the remark preserved from it, that Lysias was abler in the invention than in the arrangement of arguments[4], shows discernment. This quality marks in a less degree the judgments of subsequent writers. Quintilian[5] only commends Lysias in general terms for plain elegance of language and mastery of clear exposition; Hermogenes[6] especially praises, not his winningness, but his hidden force, classing him, with Isaeos and Hypereides, next to Demosthenes in political eloquence. Photios[7] goes wide of the

---

[1] *Orator* § 226, *Lysiam—alterum paene Demosthenem.*

[2] *Brutus* § 35 *Quem iam prope audeas oratorem perfectum dicere; nam plane quidem perfectum, et cui nihil admodum desit, Demosthenem facile dixeris.*

[3] Besides the special essay on Lysias, and the short notice in the κρίσις ἀρχαίων v. 1, there is much criticism upon him in the essays upon Isokrates, Isaeos, Demosthenes and Deinarchos. It is necessary to study these in connexion with the essay on Lysias; they explain, or limit, many statements found there.

[4] The criticism is cited, and contested, by Photios, p. 489 B, quoted below.

[5] Quint. IX. 4. 16: X. 1. 78 (Lysias)...*quo nihil, si oratori satis est docere, quaeras perfectius.*

[6] In the περὶ ἰδεῶν II. c. 41 Hermogenes ranks Lysias, with Isaeos and Hypereides, next to Demosthenes in mastery of the πολιτικὸς λόγος. In his chapter περὶ δεινότητος (περὶ ἰδ. II. 9) he says that there are three kinds of δεινότης, —that which is and seems, that which seems and is not, and that which is but does not seem. The last, or hidden, δεινότης is, he thinks, most perfectly exemplified in Lysias.

[7] Photios *cod.* 262: ἔστι δὲ ὁ Λυσίας δεινὸς μὲν παθήνασθαι, ἐπιτήδειος δὲ τοὺς πρὸς αὔξησιν διαθεῖναι λόγους.—Id. p. 489 B. 13: Και-

mark; he praises Lysias for those things in which he was relatively weak, pathos and sublime intensity; and disputes the just observation of Caecilius that Lysias excelled in invention rather than in arrangement.

A few words will be enough to mark the broad differences between Lysias and those three of his successors who may best be compared with him,— Isaeos, Isokrates and Demosthenes. Isokrates, like Lysias, has purity of diction and accuracy of idiom; command of plain language (though he is seldom content with it); power of describing, though not of dramatizing, character; propriety and persuasiveness. But while Lysias hides his art in order to be more winning, Isokrates aims openly at the highest artificial ornament, and escapes being frivolous or frigid only by the greatness of most of his subjects and the earnestness with which he treats them. Isaeos, a direct student of Lysias, resembles him most in his diction, which is not only, like that of Isokrates, clear and pure, but concise also; further, he strives, like his master, to conceal his art, but never quite succeeds in this. The excellence of Demosthenes comprises that of Lysias, since, while the latter is natural by art, the former is so by the necessary sincerity of genius; but Demosthenes is not, like Lysias, plain; nor has he the same delicate charm; grandeur and irresistible power take its place.

Lysias and his Successors.

κίλιος δὲ ἁμαρτάνει εὑρετικὸν μὲν τὸν ἄνδρα εἴπερ ἄλλόν τινὰ συνομολογῶν, οἰκονομῆσαι δὲ τὰ εὑρεθέντα οὐχ οὕτως ἱκανόν· καὶ γὰρ κἂν τούτῳ τῷ μέρει τῆς.ἀρετῆς τοῦ λόγου οὐδενὸς ὁρᾶται καταδεέστερος—injudicious praise indeed.

*Services of
Lysias to
the prose
idiom.*

Lastly—it should be remembered that it is not only as an orator but also, and even more, as a writer that Lysias is important; that, great as were his services to the theory and practice of eloquence, he did greater service still to the Greek language. He brought the everyday idiom into a closer relation than it had ever before had with the literary idiom, and set the first example of perfect elegance joined to plainness; deserving the praise that, as in fineness of ethical portraiture he is the Sophokles, in delicate control of thoroughly idiomatic speech he is the Euripides of Attic prose.

CHAPTER IX.

LYSIAS.

WORKS.

The Extant Collection.—Epideictic and Deliberative Speeches.

THE Plutarchic biographer of Lysias says :—' 425 compositions pass under his name ; of which 233 are pronounced genuine by Dionysios and Caecilius'.[1] The precise number 233 was probably given by Dionysios *or* Caecilius, not by both; but it may be taken as representing roughly the proportion of genuine to spurious allowed by the Augustan Atticists. It is not difficult to understand how the list of works attributed to Lysias had become so large and so inaccurate. His fertility was known to have been great ; his style was distinguished less by any salient features than by marks needing for their recognition a finer sense, especially an instinct for the niceties of Attic idiom ; and it was not until the Attic revival under Augustus that such an

---

[1] [Plut.] *Vit. Lys.* φέρονται δ' αὐτοῦ λόγοι τετρακόσιοι εἴκοσι πέντε· τούτων γνησίους φασὶν οἱ περὶ Διονύσιον καὶ Καικίλιον εἶναι διακοσίους τριάκοντα. Photios, in his transcript of the passage (*cod.* 262), has διακοσίους τριάκοντα τρεῖς : and probably τρεῖς is to be replaced in [Plut.].

The general term λόγοι is to be understood as including Letters : Cf. Dionys. *de Lys.* 1, γράψας λόγους ᾿εἰς δικαστήρια...πρὸς δὲ τούτοις...ἐπιστολικούς. — Suidas (s. v. Λυσίας) says λόγοι δ' αὐτοῦ λέγονται εἶναι γνήσιοι ὑπὲρ τοὺς τ′ (300)— perhaps a mere slip for σ′ (200).

instinct, dead during two centuries, was brought
back to an artificial life.   Meanwhile the grammarians of Pergamos and Alexandria, presuming on
the reputation of Lysias for industry, had probably
been lavish in ascribing to him such anonymous
forensic speeches as bore the general stamp of the
'plain' style.

*Proportion
of Extant
to Lost
Works.*

Thirty-four speeches, entire, or represented by
large fragments, are extant under the name of
Lysias.   A hundred and twenty-seven lost speeches
are known from smaller fragments or by their titles.
Three letters, cited by grammarians, are identified
by the names of the persons to whom they were
addressed.   If to this list is added the disputed
Erôtikos in Plato's Phaedros, 165 of the 425 compositions mentioned in the Plutarchic Life have been
accounted for ; 260 remain unknown[1].

*Condition
of the
Extant
Speeches.*

Of the 34 speeches now usually reckoned as
extant, three are mere fragments, though large fragments, preserved by Dionysios alone, and printed
with the rest only in the more recent editions of
Lysias.   These are nos. XXXII. (Against Diogeiton);
XXXIII. (Olympiakos) ; XXXIV. (Defence of the Constitution).   Of the other 31 speeches eight are
more or less mutilated.   In the first place an entire
quaternion (eight pages), and three pages of another,
are wanting in the Palatine MS.   The lost quaternion
contained the end of Or. XXV. (Defence on a
Charge of abolishing the Commonwealth), the speech

---

[1] For the titles and fragments
of the 127 lost speeches, and of the
letters, see Sauppe *Or. Att.* II. pp.
170—210.   Blass reckons 170 (instead of 165) compositions known by
name: *Att. Bereds.* pp. 348—365.

Against Nikides, and the beginning of Or. XXVI.
(Against Evandros). The imperfect quaternion contained on its first two pages the end of Or. V. (For
Kallias), and the beginning of Or. VI. (For Andokides); on its last page, a passage in Or. VI. corresponding to the lacuna in § 49 after ἀνταποδούς. In
the next place the archetype of the Palatine MS.
itself was defective. The gaps are at the beginning
of Or. IV. (On Wounding with Intent); at the end
of Or. XVII. (On the Property of Eraton); at the
beginning of Or. XVIII. (On the Property of Eukrates); and at the beginning of Or. XXI. (On a Charge
of taking Bribes.) Thus of the 34 speeches only 23
are entire[1].

Leaving aside the three speeches known only *Arrange-*
from Dionysios, the other 31, as arranged in the *MSS.*
MSS., form three divisions. The first division consists of the solitary epideictic speech, No. II. (the
Epitaphios)—interpolated, as it were, by accident,
and (considering its almost certain spuriousness)
possibly at a late time. The second division consists
of Orations I. and III. to XI. inclusive,—all forensic,
except VIII., and arranged with an attempt at classification of subjects. Oration I. refers to a case of
murder; III. and IV. to cases of wounding with
murderous intent; V. VI. VII. deal with cases of
impiety; VIII.—XI. (inclusive) concern, directly or
indirectly, cases of libel (κακηγορία);—No. VIII.,
though not forensic, being numbered with these

---

[1] These facts are taken partly
from Baiter and Sauppe's edition
of the text of Lysias, and the critical notes thereto; partly from
the references of Blass to Sauppe's
Epistola Critica (*Att. Bereds.* pp.
368—371).

for convenience. In the third division, consisting
of Orations XII.—XXXI. inclusive, no such system of
arrangement can be discovered; but the twenty
speeches have this in common, that all relate to
causes either formally or virtually public. Oration
XVII. (On Eraton's Property—in the MSS. περὶ
δημοσίων ἀδικημάτων), though not formally public,
is so virtually, as concerning a confiscation to the
treasury; the case dealt with by Or. XXIII. (Against
Pankleon), though private in form, is so far akin
to a public cause that it turns upon a disputed claim
to Athenian citizenship.

It seems probable that each of these two divisions—Or. I. with III. to XI., and Or. XII. to XXXI.—
is a fragment of a manuscript edition which originally comprised all the speeches of Lysias; but
whether both fragments belong to the same edition can hardly be decided[1].

The extant speeches of Lysias may be considered
under the heads of Epideictic, Deliberative and
Forensic. After these, it will remain to speak of
the Miscellaneous Writings ascribed to him, represented by the Address to his Companions (Or. VIII.)
and the Platonic Erôtikos. Lastly the Fragments
of speeches and letters will claim notice.

---

[1] If both fragments belong to
the same edition, then this edition
would seem to have contained
(1) the public speeches, classed together as such, but not arranged
according to subjects, with the
great speeches Against Eratosthenes and Against Agoratos (XII.
XIII.) at their head: (2) the private
speeches—whether technically private, or only virtually so, as concerning the individual more than
the State—arranged according to
subjects. But then it is difficult to
explain why Orat. VI., Against
Andokides—essentially a δημόσιος
λόγος—should appear among the
latter.

Epideictic Speeches.

Of the Epideictic speeches of Lysias at least
one genuine specimen remains—the fragment of an
oration delivered at the Olympic festival. The *Oratory*
at the Pan-
fashion of addressing a set harangue to the Pan- *hellenic*
festivals.
hellenic concourse at the great national meetings had
been set by the earliest sophists. Hippias 'used
to charm Greece at Olympia with ornate and elaborate speeches.'[1] The Olympic oration of Gorgias
was renowned; and at Delphi his golden statue stood
in the temple where, during the panegyris, he had
'thundered his Pythian speech from the altar.'[2] If
only as displays of rhetorical art, such harangues
were in harmony with the character of the great
Panhellenic meetings, the central idea of which was
open competition in every sort of excellence, physical
and mental. But the speaker at such a time would
have certain practical themes suggested to him by
the occasion itself, and would enjoy a rare opportunity of treating them with practical effect. He could
interpret and apply to passing events the thought,
necessarily present to every mind in such an assem-
blage, of a common Hellenic brotherhood. Gorgias
had not failed to strike this chord. 'His speech
at Olympia dealt with the largest of political questions. Seeing Greece torn by faction, he became a
counsellor of concord, seeking to turn the Greeks
against the barbarians, and advising them to take

---

[1] ἔθελγε τὴν Ἑλλάδα ἐν Ὀλυμ-   I. 11.
πίᾳ λόγοις ποικίλοις καὶ πεφροντι-   [2] τὸν λόγον τὸν Πυθικὸν ἀπὸ τοῦ
σμένοις εὖ, Philostr. *Vit. Sophist.*   βωμοῦ ἤχησεν, *ib.* I. 9.

for the prizes of their arms not each others' cities but the land of the barbarians.'[1] Hellenic nationality as a tie no less real than local citizenship, the Hellenic cause as paramount to all individual interests, must, in one form or another, have always been the foremost topic of speakers at the Panhellenic festivals.

The Olympiakos. This topic had a special significance at the moment when the Olympiakos of Lysias was spoken[2]. It was spoken, according to Diodôros, in the first year of the 98th Olympiad, 388 B.C.—the year before the Peace of Antalkidas, by which the Corinthian War was brought to a close. Athens, Thebes, Argos and Corinth had in 388 been seven years at war with Sparta. During this time two powers, both dangerous to the freedom of Greece, had been rapidly growing. In the east the naval strength of Persia had become greater than it had been for a century. In the west Dionysios, tyrant, since 405, of Syracuse, had reduced Naxos, Katana and Leontini; had twice defeated Carthage; and was threatening the Greek towns of Italy.

The Embassy from Dionysios. A magnificent embassy from the court of Dionysios, with his brother Thearides at its head, appeared at the Olympic festival of 388. Tents embroidered with gold were pitched in the sacred enclosure; a number of splendid chariots were entered in the name of Dionysios for the four-horse chariot-race;

[1] Philostr. *l. c.*
[2] XIV. 107, 109. Grote (x. 103, *note*) rejects the statement of Diodôros, and assumes 384 B.C.—the next festival—as the date; but on grounds which do not appear conclusive. The oration distinctly speaks of as war a going on at the time: ὥστε ἄξιον τὸν μὲν πρὸς ἀλλήλους πόλεμον καταθέσθαι, § 6: and in 384 the Corinthian war had been over for three years.

while rhapsodists, whose skill in recitation attracted
crowds, repeated poems composed by their royal
master[1]. While eye and ear were thus allured by
the glories of the Syracusan tyrant, Lysias lifted
up his voice to remind the assembled Greeks that in
Dionysios they must recognise one of the two great
enemies of Greece. Let them not admit to their
sacred festival the representatives of an impious
despotism. Let them remember that their duty is
to overthrow that tyranny and to set Sicily free ;
and let the war be begun forthwith by an attack
upon those glittering tents[2].

Only the first part of the speech has been preserved ; but, to judge from the scale on which the
topics are treated and from the point in the argument which the extract reaches, the whole cannot
have been much longer.

After praising Herakles for having founded the Olympic *Analysis.*
festival in order to promote goodwill among all Hellenes
(§§ 1, 2), the speaker says that he is not going to trifle with
words like a mere sophist, but to offer serious counsel upon
the dangers of Greece. Part of the Greek world is already
subject to barbarians, part to tyrants. Artaxerxes is rich
in ships and money; so is Dionysios. Greeks must lay aside
civil strife, and unite like their fathers against their common
foes. (§§ 3—6.) The Lacedaemonians are the acknowledged
leaders of Greece, unconquered abroad, untroubled by faction
at home. Why do they not bestir themselves ? (§ 7)
Instant action is needful. Greece must not wait until the
enemy in the east and the enemy in the west close in upon
her together. (§§ 8, 9.)

Here the extract ends—probably at the point *Remarks.*
where Lysias addressed himself more particularly

---

[1] Diod. xiv. 109.   [2] Dionys. *Lys.* c. 29.

The Olympiakos compared with the Panegyrikos.

to the state of Sicily, before concluding with an invective against the envoys of Dionysios. It is natural to compare with this fragment the great speech in which eight years later the same subject was treated,—the Panegyrikos of Isokrates. In each case a Panhellenic audience is reminded of the political unity of Hellas and is urged to common action against the barbarian; in each case there is an appeal to the most powerful of the Greeks to become organisers and leaders of the rest; in each case the speaker claims to be a more practical adviser than his predecessors. This last claim would not be easy to decide. It would be hard to say which was the more hopeful scheme; in 388, that Sparta should persuade the other Greek cities to lay aside all jealousies and unite for the common defence under her leadership; or in 380, that Sparta and Athens should jointly achieve that task, and act as harmonious colleagues in such a leadership. As regards form, the vigorous plainness which stamps the fragment of the Olympiakos is perhaps in better keeping with counsel given at a grave national crisis than is the artistic finish of the Panegyrikos. Dionysios says that in the epideictic style Lysias is 'somewhat languid,' and wants that power of 'rousing the hearer' which Isokrates, like Demosthenes, possessed[1]. It is not certainly in this fragment that we find the justification of the criticism.

The Epitaphios.

The Funeral Oration ascribed to Lysias purports to have been spoken, in the course of the Corinthian

[1] Dionys. *de Lys.* c. 28, ἐν μέν δη τοῖς ἐπιδεικτικοῖς λόγοις μαλακώτε- ρος...οὐ διεγείρει δὲ τὸν ἀκροατὴν ὥσπερ Ἰσοκράτης ἢ Δημοσθένης.

War, over Athenians who had been sent to the
support of Corinth. The precise date cannot be
determined. In § 59 there is an allusion to the battle
of Knidos in 394, and to the visit of the Persian
fleet to Greece in 393; and in § 63 there is an
allusion to the rebuilding of the walls of Athens in
the latter year. If it were supposed that the speech
was retouched after delivery, it might have been
spoken over those who fell in the battle of Corinth
in 394. Otherwise the fight in the Long Walls of
Corinth in 392, or that in 391 when Agesilaos took
Lechaeum, might be assumed as the occasion. To
any one of these three hypotheses there is, indeed,
the objection that the speaker seems to refer to the
battle in question as one in which the deceased
were on the winning side (§ 70).

The oration opens by contrasting the greatness of the *Analysis.*
theme with the shortness of the time allowed to the speaker
for preparation (§§ 1—3). It goes on, in the usual fashion
of such discourses, to commemorate the exploits of Athens
from the earliest times. It relates the war in which Theseus
repelled the Amazons; the part taken by Athenians in
obtaining burial for the Argives who fell before Thebes in
the war of the Seven; the brave refusal of Athens to give
up the children of Herakles to Eurystheus (§§ 4—16). Then
a brief digression on the character of the Athenians as au-
tochthones, and on the early growth of democracy (§§ 17—19).
The Persian wars—the siege of Aegina in 458—and the
expulsion of the Thirty Tyrants are successively noticed,
with remarks on the contrast between the Athenian and
the Spartan empire. (§§ 20—66.) Then comes a curiously
short tribute to the departed (§§ 67—70), and a most gloomy
address to their surviving relatives (§§ 71—76); followed
by the usual commonplace about the immortal honours of
the dead (§§ 77—81).

Character and authorship of the Epitaphios.

Two questions have to be considered in regard to the Epitaphios; whether it was written for a real occasion or merely as an exercise; and whether it is or is not the work of Lysias[1].

If it was written for a real occasion, then it can hardly be his work; for Lysias, not being an Athenian citizen, could not have spoken it himself; and it is unlikely that he should have composed it for another, since the citizen chosen by the Senate to pronounce a funeral harangue was usually an orator of repute[2]. But two things are in favour of the view that the Epitaphios was a mere rhetorical exercise; first, the character of the references to supposed contemporary events,—references particular enough to have been inserted by a composer anxious for the appearance of reality, yet not exactly corresponding with any known situation; secondly, the neglect of topics which a mere exercise could afford to ignore, but which in a real oration would, according to all fitness and all usage, be prominent—the topics of practical advice and of consolation. This Epitaphios says little enough

---

[1] The case for, and the case against, the authenticity of the Epitaphios are well argued in two essays—(1) *Lysias Epitaphios als echt erwiesen*, by Dr Le Beau, Stuttgart, 1863: (2) *De Epitaphio Lysiae Oratori falso tributo*, by H. Eckert, Berlin [1865 ?]. Le Beau's able essay is clear and admirably thorough, but defends a hopeless cause: Eckert's is a full re-statement, in reply to Le Beau, of the arguments against the genuineness.

[2] Cf. Thuc. II. 34, ἀνὴρ ᾑρημένος ὑπὸ τῆς πόλεως ὃς ἂν γνώμῃ τε δοκῇ μὴ ἀξύνετος εἶναι καὶ ἀξιώσει προήκῃ. A third hypothesis has been advanced by Le Beau (pp. 37 ff.)—that the oration was written by Lysias to be spoken by the Archon Polemarch at one of the annual commemorations of citizens who had died during the past year; but Eckert maintains that such annual commemorations were not instituted before the time of Alexander (pp. 6 ff.).

about the dead; it scarcely attempts to exhort or to
comfort the living. If, then, we may assume what
the general character of the speech indicates—that
it was composed merely as a rhetorical essay—the
next question is—Was Lysias the author? The external evidence is inconclusive. Harpokration and
Theon[1] ascribe it without suspicion to Lysias. Aristotle quotes from '*the* Epitaphios' a passage which
is found in our speech, but does not name Lysias,
though in the same chapter he cites Perikles, Isokrates and others by name. Nothing, however, can
fairly be inferred from this except that in Aristotle's
time the speech was celebrated[2]. Dionysios nowhere mentions an Epitaphios by Lysias; and his
silence is suspicious. Turning from the external
to the internal evidence, we find that this is
overwhelmingly against the authorship of Lysias.
All his leading characteristics—simplicity, grace,
clearness, the sense of symmetry—are conspicuous
by their absence. The structure of the whole is
clumsy; the special topics are ill-arranged, and
receive a treatment sometimes meagre, sometimes
extravagantly diffuse; the language is affected,
turgid and in many places obscure to a degree which
makes it inconceivable that this oration and the
fragment of the Olympiakos can be the work of the

---

[1] Theon, προγυμνάσματα p. 164
(Spengel, *Rhet. Gr.* II. p. 68) ἔχο-
μεν δὲ καὶ Ἰσοκράτους μὲν τὰ ἐγκώ-
μια, Πλάτωνος δὲ καὶ Θουκυδίδου
καὶ Ὑπερείδου καὶ Λυσίου τοὺς ἐπι-
ταφίους.

[2] Arist. *Rhet.* III. 10 καὶ οἷον ἐν

τῷ ἐπιταφίῳ, διότι ἄξιον ἦν ἐπὶ
τῷ τάφῳ τῷ τῶν ἐν Σαλαμῖνι
τελευτησάντων κείρασθαι τὴν
Ἑλλάδα, κ.τ.λ. The passage occurs in nearly the same words in
§ 60 of our Epitaphios.

same man[1]. There are several resemblances of expression between this Epitaphios and the Panegyrikos of Isokrates, and these have often been
explained by supposing Isokrates to have borrowed
from Lysias. But let any careful reader note how
thoroughly the more rhetorical parts of the Epitaphios bear the stamp of a cento, and he will
prefer to suppose that some very inferior writer has
borrowed from Isokrates[2]. No weight can be allowed
to the argument that Plato in the Menexenos (386
B.C. ?) had this particular Epitaphios in view. The
Menexenos goes, indeed, over very nearly the same
range of subjects; but these subjects were the commonplaces of commemorative oratory, and the coincidence
is no warrant for assuming a direct imitation. If
it may be taken for granted that Aristotle's citation
in the Rhetoric is from our Epitaphios, the composition of the speech, whoever was the author, may
be placed between 380 and 340 B.C.[3]. In any case,
considering the general character of the Greek[4], it
can scarcely be put much below the first half of the
second century B.C.

[1] Eckert, in the essay referred
to above, examines at length (pp.
19—48) the arrangement (τάξις),
'invention' (εὕρεσις), and diction
(λέξις) of the speech, and shows
how thoroughly each is foreign
to the manner of Lysias. It has
not been judged necessary here to
follow his analysis into details.
The broad impression left upon the
mind by the speech as a whole will
be enough for most readers. As
Dobree said—'Lysias in genere epi-
deictico quantumvis plenus et dif-

fluens ; nugax, salebrosus, indiges-
tus nunquam esse potuit.' (*Advers.*
I. p. 15.)

[2] Cf. Panegyr. § 72, with Epitaph. § 9 : Pan. § 88 with E. § 29 :
Pan. § 115 with E. § 59 ; &c. 'Illic'
(i.e. in the Panegyrikos), says Dobree, ' summum oratorem videas,
hic nugacem compilatorem.'

[3] Aristotle's *Rhetoric* having
been written probably during his
second residence at Athens, 335—
323 B.C.: see Grote's Aristotle, I. 34.

[4] ' Sermone utitur sat bene Grae-

DELIBERATIVE SPEECH.

The speeches of Lysias for the ekklesia have had the same fate as his epideictic speeches. These, too, are represented by one fragment alone—that which now stands last in the collection as Oration XXXIV. Like the fragment of the Olympiakos, it is given by Dionysios as a specimen of a class. The title which it usually bears describes it as a Plea against abolishing the ancient Constitution of Athens. When, after the fall of the Thirty, the democracy was restored in 403, it was the aim of Sparta to restrict it. One Phormisios proposed in the ekklesia that only landowners should have the franchise, a measure which, according to Dionysios, would have excluded about five thousand citizens. The speech from which he gives an extract was made against this motion during a debate in the ekklesia. It appears to have been written by Lysias for some wealthy citizen who was not personally affected by the proposal, and may probably be regarded as the earliest of the orator's works now known.

Or. xxxiv., *a Plea for the Constitution.*

A censure on the proposers and supporters of the motion is followed by a statement of the speaker's political faith. Nothing but a full democracy, he says, can save the country. When Athens was imperial, did she limit the franchise? On the contrary, she gave one of the special privileges of citizenship to the Euboeans. Then, to take

Analysis.

co atque Attico, et in universum spectanti non videtur in sermonis puritatem et verborum delectum   admodum peccasse' (Dobree *Adv.* p. 14). Cf. Eckert, p. 52.

the landowners' point of view, it is not they who have ever
profited by oligarchies. In fact it is just on their property
that the advocates of this, as of former oligarchies, have
designs. (§§ 1—5.)

If it is said that Athens can be safe only by obeying
Sparta, it should be remembered how desperate are the
terms which Sparta would like to impose. Surely it
is better to die fighting for one's rights than to pass sentence of death upon oneself. But there is a danger for
Sparta also, which will to a certain extent restrain her. She
leaves Argos and Mantineia at peace, because she knows
that nothing can be gained, and that much would be risked,
by driving them to extremities: she will feel the same in
regard to Athens. This was the policy of Athens herself
when she was greatest. (§§ 6—9.) It would be strange if
the democrats who fought bravely in exile should lose
heart now that they are restored; if the sons of men who
saved Hellas should shrink from delivering Athens. (§§ 10,
11.)

Dionysios remarks on this speech that there is
nothing to prove that it was actually delivered on the
occasion supposed, but that 'at all events it is in a
style suitable for debate.'[1] For that very reason, the
smooth finish of the extract from the Olympiakos is
not to be looked for here ; a rougher vigour takes its
place. Regarded historically, it has one point of interest—the analogy suggested between Sparta's con-
temptuous forbearance towards Argos and Mantineia
and her probable attitude towards Athens. Nothing
could show more strikingly the prostrate condition
in which Athens was left by the Thirty Tyrants
than that a speaker in the ekklesia should have ven-
tured to use such an illustration.

---

[1] *De Lys.* c. 32 εἰ μὲν οὖν ἐρρήθη τότε, ἄδηλον· σύγκειται· γοῦν ὡς πρὸς
ἀγῶνα ἐπιτηδείως.

CHAPTER X.

LYSIAS.

WORKS.

FORENSIC SPEECHES IN PUBLIC CAUSES.

IN classifying forensic speeches the first thing to be done is to fix the principle of distinction between the public and the private. One method is to con- *Principle of distinction between 'public' and 'private' law-speeches.* sider solely the form of procedure, and to distinguish 'public' and 'private' as they were technically distinguished by Greek law. Another method is to consider rather the substance than the form of each cause, and to arrange the causes according as their practical interest was more directly for the State or for the individual. Blass adopts the latter plan[1].

---

[1] Blass's classification is as follows :—

I. *Public Causes:* Against Epikrates [Or. xxvii]: Against Ergokles [xxviii] : Against Philokrates [xxix]: Against Nikomachos [xxx]: Against the Corndealers [xxii]: Against Evandros [xxvi]: Against Philon [xxxi] : Against Alkibiades [xiv, xv] : Defence on Charge of Taking Bribes [xxi]: For Polystratos [xx]: Defence on a Charge of seeking to abolish the Democracy [xxv]: For Mantitheos [xvi] :

On the Property of the Brother of Nikias [xviii]: On the Property of Aristophanes [xix].

II. *Private Causes in which the person of the accused, or the consequences of the offence in question, had a specially high importance for the Commonweal* (*Att. Bereds.* p. 539). Against Eratosthenes [xii]: Against Agoratos [xiii] : Against Andokides [vi].

III. *Properly Private Causes.* On the Murder of Eratosthenes [i]: Against Simon [iii]: On Wound-

The speech On the Murder of Eratosthenes [Or. I.],
for instance, is referred by Blass to the private class,
since the cause, though formally public (as being a
γραφὴ φόνου), was of no properly political interest.
The obvious objection to such a mode of classification
is its uncertainty.   The definite technical distinction
once abandoned, it becomes hard to say what is or is
not a 'public' cause.   Thus the speeches Against
Eratosthenes [Or. XII.] and Against Agoratos [Or.
XIII.] are placed by Blass in a rank by themselves,
intermediate between the properly public and the
properly private, because in each case, though an
individual is mainly concerned, the issue is of
high moment to the State.   Such differences have
a real *literary* importance, and have already been
recognised (p. 166) as corresponding to different
shades of style.   But they appear too indefinite to
form a good basis for scientific classification.   The
necessity of drawing a doubtful or arbitrary line is
avoided by taking the classification supplied by
Greek law itself.   Classified as public and private
(δημόσιοι and ἰδιωτικοί) in the Greek sense, the
speeches of Lysias will stand thus:—

A.—Speeches in Public Causes.

I.   *Causes relating to Offences directly against
the State (γραφαὶ δημοσίων ἀδικημάτων); such as trea-*

ing with Intent [IV]: For Kallias
[V]: On the Sacred Olive [VII]:
For the Soldier [IX]: Against
Theomnêstos [X, XI]: Against Dio-
geiton [XXXII]: On the Property
of Eraton [XVII]: Against Pankleon
[XXIII].

IV. *Bagatelle Speeches.* For the
Invalid [XXIV]: To his Companions
[VIII].—*Att. Bereds.* pp. 445—660.

son, malversation in office, embezzlement of public moneys.

1. For Polystratos [Or. xx.].
2. Defence on a Charge of Taking Bribes [Or. xxi.].
3. Against Ergokles [Or. xxviii.].
4. Against Epikrates [Or. xxvii.].
5. Against Nikomachos [Or. xxx.].
6. Against the Corndealers [Or. xxii.].

II. *Cause relating to Unconstitutional Procedure* (γραφὴ πορανόμων).

On the Property of the Brother of Nikias [Or. xviii.].

III. *Causes relating to Claims for Money withheld from the State* (ἀπογραφαί.)

1. For the Soldier [Or. ix.].
2. On the Property of Aristophanes [Or. xix.].
3. Against Philokrates [Or. xxix.].

IV. *Causes relating to a Scrutiny* (δοκιμασία), *especially the Scrutiny by the Senate of Officials designate.*

1. Against Evandros [Or. xxvi.].
2. For Mantitheos [Or. xvi.].
3. Against Philon [Or. xxxi.].
4. Defence on a Charge of seeking to abolish the Democracy [Or. xxv.].
5. For the Invalid [Or. xxiv.].

V. *Causes relating to Military Offences* (γραφαί λειποταξίου, ἀστρατείας, κ. τ. λ.).

1. Against Alkibiades, I. [Or. xiv.].
2. Against Alkibiades, II. [Or. xv.].

VI. *Causes relating to Murder or Intent to murder* (γραφαὶ φόνου, τραύματος ἐκ προνοίας).

    1.   Against Eratosthenes [Or. xii.].

    2.   Against Agoratos [Or. xiii.].

    3.   On the Murder of Eratosthenes [Or. i.].

    4.   Against Simon [Or. iii.].

    5.   On Wounding with Intent [Or. iv.].

VII. *Causes relating to Impiety* (γραφαὶ ἀσεβείας).

    1.   Against Andokides [Or. vi.].

    2.   For Kallias [Or. v.].

    3.   On the Sacred Olive [vii.].

B.—Speeches in Private Causes.

I. *Action for libel* (δίκη κακηγορίας).

    Against Theomnêstos[1] [Or. x.].

II. *Action by a Ward against a Guardian* (δίκη ἐπιτροπῆς).

    Against Diogeiton [Or. xxxii.].

III. *Trial of a Claim to Property* (διαδικασία).

    On the Property of Eraton[2] [Or. xvii.].

IV. *Answer to a Special Plea* (πρὸς παραγραφήν).

    Against Pankleon [Or. xxiii.].

---

[1] The MSS. give κατὰ Θεομνήστου A. as Or. x. and κατὰ Θεομνήστου B. as Or. xi. But the so-called Second Speech is a mere epitome of the first: see below.

[2] Entitled in the MSS. περὶ δημοσίων ἀδικημάτων.

Speeches in Public Causes.

I. Causes relating to Offences directly against the State (γραφαὶ δημοσίων ἀδικημάτων).

1. *For Polystratos.* [Or. xx.]—Harpokration describes this as a 'Defence for Polystratos on a charge of seeking to abolish the Democracy.'[1] But from the speech itself the precise nature of the charge cannot be gathered. All that can be safely inferred is that the offence alleged was of a political nature, and was connected with the oligarchical revolution of 411 B.C. Polystratos had held several offices under the oligarchy (§ 5), and had been elected to a vacancy in the Council of the Four Hundred just eight days before the defeat of the Athenian fleet by the Spartans at Eretria, immediately after which the government fell (§ 14). His most important employment had been that of enrolling the 5000 persons to whom the Council conceded the franchise; and he takes credit for having placed, in his capacity of registrar, 9000 instead of 5000 on the roll. It was only in their last peril that the Oligarchy took steps for giving a real existence to the nominal body of 5000; and this agrees with the account of Polystratos, who dates his registrarship from his entry into the Council only eight days before its overthrow (§ 14). When the democracy was re-established, Polystratos was prosecuted and heavily fined; probably on the ground of malversation in some office which he had held under the Oligarchy.

In the present case malversation in his registrar-

I. 1. For Polystratos.

Probable nature of the charge.

[1] s.v. Πολύστρατος—ὑπὲρ Π. δήμου καταλύσεως ἀπολογία.

ship may have been the special charge against him.
The penalty threatened was pecuniary; but he says
that, as he has no money with which to meet it, the
result for him, if condemned, will be disfranchisement
as a state-debtor.

Date. The date must lie between 411 and 405. The
war in the Hellespont is noticed (§ 29); but there
is no reference to Arginusae or subsequent events;
and the early part of 407 is therefore the latest date
which appears probable.

Polystratos, who was a man past sixty (§ 10), is
represented by the eldest of his three sons (§ 24).

Analysis. The first part of the speech sets forth that Polystratos
was one of the least prominent and least culpable of the
oligarchs; that he had already suffered severely, and is now
accused maliciously; and that the general tenor of his past
life proves his patriotism (§§ 1—23). The speaker then
relates his own services in Sicily after the disaster of 413,
and reads a patriotic letter written to him by his father at
that time. He recounts also the services of his brothers,
the second and third sons of Polystratos; of whom the former
had been active at the Hellespont, and the latter at home
(§§ 24—29). In return for all that the father and his three
sons have done for the city, they ask only to be spared a
verdict which would rob them of citizenship (§§ 30—36).

The speech probably spurious. The only ancient notice of this speech is by Harpokration, who once refers to it; then, indeed, with-
out suspicion[1]. But the general opinion of recent
critics[2] pronounces it spurious. In one respect alone

[1] s. v. Πολύστρατος.
[2] As of Baiter, Sauppe and Blass.
It is curious to find—in an essay
published at Munich in 1830, *Dis-
sertatio de locis quibusdam Lysiae*
arte critica persanandis, by J.
Franz—numerous minute emen-
dations proposed in the text of this
speech (pp. 7—10), all depending on
close observation of the language of

it has at first sight a resemblance to the style of
Lysias. It is thoroughly natural. Yet the naturalness is not that of Lysias. It is the absence, not
the concealment, of art; the simplicity, not of a
master, but of a composer wholly untrained. A want
of logical method renders the statements in the first
part (§§ 1—23) confused, and the language throughout clumsy, sometimes obscure. Instead of the compact sentences of Lysias there are long strings of
clauses loosely joined;—see especially § 14. Were
the speech genuine, it would be the only known
forensic speech of Lysias earlier than the fall of the
Thirty Tyrants. But it seems hardly doubtful that
it must be rejected.

2. *Defence on a Charge of Taking Bribes.*
[Or. XXI.]—The first part of this speech, in which the
accused met the specific charges against him, has
been lost; the part which remains contains only his
appeal to his previous character generally. The precise nature of the charge is therefore doubtful. In
§ 21 the speaker asks that he may not be adjudged
guilty of taking bribes; hence the title given to the
fragment. The accused had probably held some
office, and was charged, when he gave account of it,
with corrupt practices.

*I. 2. De-
fence on a
Charge of
Taking
Bribes.*

A clue to the date is given by the fact that the
speaker became of full age (i. e. eighteen) in the
archonship of Theopompos (§ 1), 411 B.C.; and had
performed leiturgies yearly to the archonship of
Eukleides (§ 4), 403 B.C. No reason appears why his

Date.

Lysias; while the general character
of the whole composition—so unlike that of its reputed author's
work—entirely escapes criticism.

public services should have ceased abruptly in that year. On the other hand, if he had performed leiturgies later than 403 B.C., he would probably have mentioned them. The year of the speech may therefore be conjectured to be 402, and the age of the speaker 26 [1].

Analysis.

Having already answered the accusers in detail, he goes on, in the extant fragment, to enumerate his public services. As choregus and trierarch he has spent upwards of ten talents in eight years—more than four times the amount which would have satisfied legal requirements (§§ 1—5). His trireme, when he was trierarch, was so good that Alkibiades, as admiral, had done him the unwelcome honour of sailing in it (§ 7); and it was one of the twelve which made good their escape from Aegospotami (§ 10).

He might fairly claim some substantial recognition of these costly services; but he asks only not to be deprived of his own property (§§ 11—19). In conclusion he reminds the judges that one who had risked his life and whole fortune for the State was not likely to have taken bribes to defraud it (§§ 21, 22). Beggary had often enough hung over his wife and children when he was fighting for Athens; it would be hard if it should at last actually befall them by the sentence of an Athenian court (§§ 24—52).

The êthos.

Lysias shows here strikingly his power of adapting language to character; the êthos is the merit of the speech. It expresses the strong, honest feeling of a man who has made sacrifices for his country, who is conscious of his desert, and who claims, rather than begs, acquittal. 'I think, judges, that it would be much fairer for you to be indicted by the revenue-officers for keeping my property, than for me to be

---

[1] Blass, *Att. Ber.* p. 496.

now in peril on a charge of keeping the property
of the Treasury…I am not proud of what is left
to me, but of what I have spent upon you. My
fortune came to me from others—the credit for its
use is my own.' (§§ 16, 17.)

3. *Against Ergokles.* [Or. XXVIII.]—In 390 I. 3.
B.C. a fleet of forty triremes was sent to the coast *Against Ergokles.*
of Asia Minor under the command of Thrasybulos.
After many successes in the Hellespont and
a victory over the Lacedaemonians at Lesbos,
Thrasybulos was slain at Aspendos in Pamphylia
by a party of natives who surprised his camp
by night[1]. Meanwhile anger had been excited at
Athens by reports that the commanders of the expedition had embezzled moneys levied on the towns
in Asia, and had been treacherous to the cause of
the city. A decree was passed demanding an account
of all funds so raised, and recalling the commanders.
Thrasybulos died before he could obey the summons;
his colleagues, of whom Ergokles was one, were *Date.*
brought to trial in 389 B.C. The procedure was
apparently by impeachment. Ergokles was condemned to death and his property was confiscated[2].

The short speech of Lysias was spoken by one of
the Public Prosecutors; who, as others had already
gone fully into the charges, does little more than
recapitulate them.

Ergokles is charged with having betrayed Greek towns *Analysis.*

---

[1] Xen. *Hellen.* IV. viii. 25—30.
[2] See § 2 of the speech Against
Philokrates, who was accused of
having in his hands part of the
confiscated property of Ergokles.

in Asia, with having injured citizens and friends of Athens, and with having enriched himself at the public cost. All this time the fleet was allowed to go to ruin, with the connivance of Thrasybulos—who would never have been given the command, had it been foreseen that only his 'flatterers' (§ 4) were to benefit by it (§§ 1—7). Thrasybulos had done well to die; the partners of his guilt are now seeking to buy their lives by wholesale bribery; but this must not be suffered (§§ 8—11). Ergokles pleads his patriotism at the restoration of the democracy; but he has since shown himself worse than the Tyrants (§§ 12—14). His condemnation and that of his associates is necessary as an example to Greece, and is due to the cities, such as Halikarnassos[1], which they betrayed (§§ 15—17).

Decision and vigorous brevity are the chief characteristics of this speech, as of that Against Epikrates (xxvii.) and that Against Philokrates (xxix.); both of which, like this, were spoken by Public Prosecutors. An address by an official afforded less scope for artistic individual colouring than a speech which had to be fitted to the character and circumstances of a private speaker.

I. 4.
*Against
Epikrates.*

4. *Against Epikrates.* [Or. xxvii.]—The title, 'Against Epikrates and his Fellow-Envoys,' which one Theodôros[2] affixed to this speech, is clearly wrong. In the first place each of the 'Fellow-Envoys' would have been the subject of a separate

---

[1] Xenophon does not name Halikarnassos: but he describes Thrasybulos, after his victory at Lesbos, as levying money for his troops from some towns on the Greek coast:—ἐκ δὲ τούτου τὰς μὲν προσηγάγετο τῶν πόλεων, ἐκ δὲ τῶν οὐ προσχωρουσῶνλεηλατῶν χρήματα τοῖς στρατιώταις ἔσπευσεν εἰς τὴν Ῥόδον ἀφικέσθαι. ὅπως δ' ἂν καὶ ἐκεῖ ὡς ἐρρωμενέστατον τὸ στράτευμα ποιήσαιτο, ἐξ ἄλλων τε πόλεων ἠργυρολόγει, κ.τ.λ. (*H.* iv. viii. 30).

[2] The MSS. having ΚΑΤΑ ΕΠΙ-

accusation; in the next place, there is absolutely
no reference to an embassy except in the opening
words[1], which have probably been interpolated to
match the title. The grammarian, it can hardly
be doubted, was thinking of the Epikrates mentioned by Demosthenes as having been condemned,
with his colleagues in an embassy, by a decree of
the people[2]. Whether this Epikrates is the same
person or not, cannot be decided. But, in the present case, the charge against him is of having embezzled public moneys while he held the office of
comptroller of the treasury (§ 3). The charge must
have been made either at his audit (εὐθῦναι) or
by a special impeachment (εἰσαγγελία.) The only
clue to the date is the fact that a war had now
lasted some time (§ 10). The latter part of the *Date.*
Corinthian War—about the year 389—is probably
indicated.

Like the speech against Ergokles, this was preceded by others for the prosecution, and gives therefore only a general view of the case.

Corrupt officers of the treasury, like Ergokles, often tell *Analysis.*
the judges, in asking for a verdict against some one whom
they have wrongfully accused, that if it is not given, the city
will soon lack funds to pay its public servants. And now this
lack of funds is caused by the corrupt officials themselves.
The State must punish heavily those guardians of the revenue

KΡΑΤΟΥΣ ΚΑΙ ΤΩΝ ΣΥΜΠΡΕΣ-
ΒΕΥΤΩΝ ΕΠΙΛΟΓΟΣ ΩΣ ΘΕΟΔΩ-
ΡΟΣ.
[1] κατηγόρηται μέν, ὦ ἄνδρες Ἀθη-
ναῖοι, Ἐπικράτους ἱκανὰ καὶ τῶν συμ-

πρεσβευτῶν· ἐνθυμεῖσθαι δὲ χρή,
κ.τ.λ. The words καὶ τῶν συμπρεσ-
βευτῶν are probably spurious.
[2] *De Falsa Legat.* § 277: Blass,
p. 445.

who so often procure the confiscation of private property while
they enrich themselves out of the property of the public
(§§ 1—7). If such men were condemned without the forms
of a trial, it would be no breach of justice; their guilt is notorious. This is war-time; yet these men can not only pay
heavy taxes, but at the same time live in the best houses—men
who, in quieter times, had not bread to eat (§§ 8—10). No
appeal to mercy should be admitted from such a quarter.
The courts have lately been too lenient. Epikrates and his
like must be made to suffer loss, since they are insensible to
shame (§§ 11—16).

5. *Against Nikomachos.* [Or. xxx.].—Soon after
the fall of the First Oligarchy in 411 B.C., a decree
of the ekklesia (probably in 410) appointed a board
of special Commissioners (Nomothetae[1]) for the revision of the laws; especially for the recension of
those old laws of Solon, written on the sides of the
wooden prisms called Kurbeis or Axones, which now
needed to be freed from corruptions and interpola-
tions. Nikomachos[2] was a member of the Commis-

---

[1] Nikomachos is called in §§ 2
and 27 νομοθέτης. This was probably the ordinary official designation of the special Commissioners
both in 411 and 403: the title ἀναγραφεὺς τῶν νόμων, 'Recorder' of
the laws, also applied to Nikomachos in § 2, being sometimes used,
perhaps, to distinguish the special
from the ordinary Nomothetae.—
Rauchenstein notices in Demosth.
Olynth. iii. § 10 another trace of
the occasional appointment of special Nomothetae: see his Introduction to this speech, *A usgewählte
Reden des Lysias*, p. 130, n.

[2] In § 11, as once in a quotation
by Harpokration (s. v. ἐπιβολή),
Nikomachos is called Nikomachi-
des:—πείθουσι Νικομαχίδην νόμον
ἀποδεῖξαι ὡς χρὴ καὶ τὴν βουλὴν συν-
δικάζειν. Rauchenstein (ad loc.)
thinks that is merely an instance
of the patronymic used convertibly
with the simple name, as Eubulides
for Eubulos in Or. xix. § 29;
cf. Androkleides for Androkles
in Isae. Or. vi. 46. Blass, with
more likelihood, suspects a mere
blunder. Is it possible that in § 11
we ought to insert τοῦτον after
πείθουσι, and understand:—'they
persuade the defendant to enun-
tiate a law of which he was him-

sion. Four months were assigned for the work[1]; but Nikomachos contrived to extend his share of it over six years—*i.e.* until the overthrow of the democracy in 404—without rendering an account.

After the fall of the Second Oligarchy in 403, a second Revising Commission was appointed by the Senate. These special Nomothetae were to report *within one month* to the Senate and the 500 ordinary Nomothetae selected by the demes[2]. Nikomachos was again employed; his special duty on this occasion being to revise the laws which concerned the public sacrifices[3]. Again he failed to discharge his task within the prescribed term. At the date of this speech he had held office for four years. The speech probably belongs, therefore, to 399 B.C. Nikomachos is accused before the Board of Auditors (the ten Logistae) of having failed to render an account of his office (ἀλογίου δίκη)[4].

self the parent' (Νικομαχίδην νόμον) —a law invented by Nikomachos for the occasion? This would be quite in keeping with the sarcastic tone of the speech.

[1] § 2 προσταχθὲν γὰρ αὐτῷ τεσσάρων μηνῶν ἀναγράψαι...ἑξέτη τὴν ἀρχὴν ἐποιήσατο.

[2] The psephisma of 403 for the revision of the laws is given in full by Andokides in the speech On the Mysteries, § 83.

[3] See § 25, καὶ τῶν ὁσίων καὶ τῶν ἱερῶν ἀναγραφεὺς γενόμενος εἰς ἀμφότερα ταῦτα ἡμάρτηκεν. Here τῶν ὁσίων refers to the first Commission of 410 B.C., when the laws entrusted to the revision of Nikomachos were only secular; τῶν ἱερῶν to the second Commission of 403 B.C., when the laws which came under his revision were those relating to public worship.

[4] The description in the MSS. heading of the speech—εὐθυνῶν κατηγορία—is inaccurate, as Rauchenstein points out (*Introd.* p. 131). This would mean that Nikomachos had rendered an account, and that, when he rendered it, an accusation was brought against him by some citizen; which would then have been heard by the εὔθυνοι. The charge against Nikomachos was that he had never rendered any account to the Logistae. The points of law connected with this speech are discussed in an essay

The speaker is one of several accusers (§ 34), probably not the principal; the penalty demanded is death (§§ 23, 27.)

Analysis.   The first part of the speech sets forth the antecedents of Nikomachos. His father was a public slave; he himself, after late enrolment in a phratria, became an under-scribe to a magistrate. His present offence was not the first of the kind which he had committed. After the First Oligarchy, as after the Second, commissioners for the revision of the laws were appointed. Nikomachos had been one of these also; and had retained the appointment for six years (§ 2)— (that is, till 404 B.C.)—(§§ 1—6).

He will perhaps try to cast upon his accuser the suspicion of oligarchical sympathies. It ought not to be forgotten that it was he himself who, by a forged law, enabled the oligarchs to destroy Kleophon[1] in 405. His sufferings under the Thirty were involuntary, and cannot be set against an action which was deliberate (§§ 7—16). The speaker will be taunted by Nikomachos with impiety because he complained in the ekklesia of the number of public sacrifices which this self-authorised legislator had ordered. But the truth is that, by ordering a number of new sacrifices, Nikomachos has caused those prescribed by the laws of Solon (τὰ ἐκ τῶν κύρβεων, § 17) to be neglected; and has in two years spent twelve talents more than was necessary (§ 21). Hence the city, from want of funds, has been driven to confiscations (§ 22). Nikomachos ought to suffer the extreme penalty, as a warning to the corrupt officials who, confident in their powers of speech, are reckless of public or private misery (§§ 17—25).

Neither service in war, nor liberality at home, nor the merit of ancestors, nor the hope of his own gratitude, can

---

entitled *Diatribe in Lysae orationem in Nikomachum*, by F. V. Weijers, Leyden, 1839.

[1] Kleophon, ὁ λυροποιός, the demagogue: Ar. *Ran.* 677: Arist.

Rhet. I. 15, etc. Cf. Lys. *de bonis Aristoph.* (Or. XIX) § 48: Κλεοφῶντα πάντες ἴστε ὅτι πολλὰ ἔτη διεχείρισε τὰ τῆς πόλεως πάντα.

be pleaded as a reason for acquitting him. The people themselves might well be denounced for entrusting to such as he the powers once held by a Solon, a Themistokles, a Perikles (§ 28). Nikomachos has sought in vain to bribe his accusers; let his judges do their duty as firmly (§§ 26—35).

Unsparing and rather coarse sarcasm is the strength of this attack. Throughout, Nikomachos is treated, not as the recorder of laws, but as the son of the public slave, as the ex-under-scribe. 'Are we to acquit him for his ancestors?' asks the accuser. 'Nay, for his own sake he deserves death; and for theirs—the slave-market' (§ 27).

6. *Against the Corndealers.* [Or. XXII.].—The Guild of Corndealers (σιτοπῶλαι) was composed of aliens (§ 5) resident in the Peiraeus, who bought corn as it came into port and sold it in small quantities to the citizens. The trade was a good one, and was watched with jealousy both by citizens and by wholesale importers (ἔμποροι, § 27). Stringent laws, administered by a board of Corn-Inspectors (σιτοφύλακες, § 8), were framed to limit the gains of the retaildealers. One of these laws forbade them to charge more than one obol a bushel over cost-price (§ 8); another, in order to check monopoly, provided that no one should buy more than 50 phormoi (about 50 bushels) of corn at one time (§ 6).

It is this second law which is here alleged to have been broken by the guild or by some of its members. The case is tried before an ordinary court under the presidency of the Thesmothetae: the penalty is death.

The date of the speech cannot be fixed. All that

can be said is that it was certainly later than the beginning of the Corinthian War in 394 B.C.; possibly later than the Peace of Antalkidas in 387 B.C.[1]

Analysis.   The speaker begins by deprecating the notion that the charge preferred by him is vexatious or spiteful. On the contrary, he says, he was at the beginning of the business suspected of unduly favouring the Guild. An impeachment was first laid before the Senate, who were inclined to deliver the Corndealers then and there to the Eleven. It was he who then counselled moderation and the observance of the usual legal course. Accordingly the case was heard before the Senate (which was itself the preliminary court in cases of impeachment). No one came forward as accuser; and the speaker then made the accusation himself. The case was sent by the Senate for trial by an ordinary court (§§ 1—4).

One of the Corndealers is then questioned, and admits having bought more than fifty bushels at once, but says that he did so by the recommendation of the Corn-Inspectors. The speaker shows, first, that this is no defence; next, that the statement is false (§§ 5—10). The dealers plead that their object in buying large quantities was to be able to sell cheap; but their claim to public spirit can be refuted (§§ 11—16). They have acknowledged their combination against the wholesale importers. Their death is the satisfaction due to these and to the officials who have so often been punished for inability to check such frauds (§§ 17—22).

Compact and clear, without any attempt at ornament, this short speech is at least good of its kind,—a specimen of the strictly business-like style of Lysias.

---

[1] See § 14, which speaks of the rumours spread by the Corndealers in order to raise the price of corn :—ἢ τὰς ναῦς διεφθάρθαι τὰς ἐν τῷ Πόντῳ ἢ ὑπὸ Λακεδαιμονίων ἐκπλεούσας συνειλῆφθαι ἢ τὰ ἐμπόρια κεκλεῖσθαι ἢ τὰς σπονδὰς μέλλειν ἀπορρηθήσεσθαι. 'The ships in the Euxine' are the ships which brought corn to Athens from those regions : cf. Xen. *H.* I. 35. The σπονδαί possibly refer to the Peace of Antalkidas or to negociations which preceded it.

II. Indictment for proposing an Unconstitu-
tional Measure (γραφὴ παρανόμων).

On the Confiscation of the Property of the Brother II. 1. *On the*
of Nikias. [Or. XVIII.]—Eukrates, brother of the *Confisca-*
tion of the
Property of
General Nikias, was put to death by the Thirty *the Brother*
of Nikias.
Tyrants in 404 B. C. Several years afterwards a
certain Poliochos[1] proposed and carried in the ekklesia a decree for confiscating the estate left by
Eukrates. In this speech the elder of the two sons
of Eukrates pleads against the execution of the
decree.

The legal form of the cause is doubtful. Two *Form of the*
cause.
views are possible. (1) The sons of Eukrates may
have indicted Poliochos under the Graphê Paranomôn for proposing an unconstitutional measure. In
this case the speech is an Accusation. (2) Poliochos may have indicted the sons of Eukrates for
withholding property due to the State under the
decree; the action being in form an apographê, or
claim for moneys withheld from the Treasury. In
this case the speech is a Defence[2].

One point is in favour of the latter view. The
speaker appeals in his peroration, first, to the judges

---

[1] There is some doubt about the
name. The MSS. have Πολίαχος
or Πόλισχος : Galen, in his citation
(XVIII. 2, 657 Kühn), Πολιοῦχος.
Taylor has been followed by Sauppe
and other recent editors in reading
Πολίοχος, a proper name recognised by Harpokration.

[2] Francken (*Commentationes Ly-*

siacae, pp. 124 ff.) thinks that Ha-
maker has proved beyond all
doubt that the cause is an ἀπογραφή, not a γραφὴ παρανόμων.
But the arguments brought are
unavailing without a satisfactory
emendation of the words in § 14—to
be noticed presently.

generally, then to the Syndici (§ 26). Now these
fiscal officers would have had the presidency of the
court in a cause affecting the treasury. But it is
not clear why they should have had jurisdiction in a
trial under the Graphê Paranomôn.

On the other hand, a passage in § 14 supports
the first view. 'All men will know' [i. e. if Poliochos gains the cause] 'that on the former occasion
you fined[1] in 1000 drachmas the man who wished to
confiscate our land, whereas on this occasion he has
carried his proposal; and that, therefore, in these
two cases Athenian judges gave two opposite ver-
dicts, *the same man being on his trial for a breach of
the Constitution.*'

The last words—παρανόμων φεύγοντος τοῦ αὐτοῦ
ἀνδρός—may possibly be corrupt[2]. But if they are
right, then they prove that this trial, like the former,
was a Graphê Paranomôn against Poliochos. And
this is confirmed by the fact that 'Against Poliochos' is the title under which the speech is cited by
Galen[3]. On the whole, the probabilities appear to
lean to this side. But the evidence does not suffice
to decide the question.

Date. The date may be inferred from two circumstances.
(1) The speaker and his brothers were children in

---

[1] Scheibe's emendation of ἐζημι-
ώσατε for ἐζημίωσε seems certain.

[2] Francken (*Comm. Lys.* p. 126)
suggests that Lysias may have
written something like παρανόμων
φυγόντος τότε τοῦ ἀνδρός [not τοῦ
αὐτοῦ ἀνδρός, as Blass quotes it,
Att. Bereds. p. 524], νῦν δὲ νικήσαντος. But this is too violent a
change: and besides, as Blass says,
one would require τότε μὲν παρανόμων φυγόντος, νῦν δὲ νικήσαντος.

[3] Vol. XVIII. 2. 657 (Kühn), ap.
Sauppe *Or. Att.* p. 112 and Blass
Att. Bereds. p. 522. It seems very
probable that κατὰ Πολιόχου is the
right title.

404 (§ 10), but are now adults, holding the office of trierarchs (§ 21). (2) On the other hand, Athens and Sparta are at peace (§ 15). The Corinthian War (394—387 B.C.), therefore, either has not begun or is over. And as the son of Nikêratos (§ 10), the first cousin of the speaker, is not mentioned as having yet taken any part in public affairs, the earlier date is more likely—396 or 395 B.C., approximately.

The following stemma shows the relationship of the persons with whom the speech is concerned :— *Stemma of the family of Nikias.*

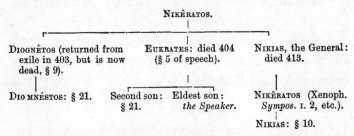

NIKÊRATOS.

DIOGNÊTOS (returned from exile in 403, but is now dead, § 9).

EUKRATES: died 404 (§ 5 of speech).

NIKIAS, the General: died 413.

DIO MNÊSTOS: § 21.   Second son: § 21.   Eldest son: *the Speaker.*   NIKÊRATOS (Xenoph. *Sympos.* I. 2, etc.).

NIKIAS: § 10.

The speaker begins by dwelling on the public services *Analysis.* of his uncles Nikias and Diognêtos and his father Eukrates (§§ 1—12). He next argues that a confiscation is never in any true sense a gain to the State. First, it endangers the most precious of all the city's treasures—concord among citizens. In the next place, property thus confiscated is always sold below its true value, and part even of the sum which it fetches is made away with by the proposer of the measure. Left in the hands of patriotic owners—like the speaker, his brother, and his cousin, who, all three, are trierarchs—it is far more profitable to the State (§§ 13—23).

They can produce no relatives to weep and pray for them; they are the last of their house ; they can only appeal to the judges to protect the kinsmen of those who suffered for the democracy. Let the judges remember the time when, in exile and poverty, they prayed to the gods for a day when they might be able to show their gratitude to the children of their champions. This gratitude is claimed now. The danger which threatens the accused is nothing less than utter ruin (§§ 24—27).

Distinctive quality of the Speech.

This fragment is interesting as giving a sequel, in the history of his family, to the personal fortunes of Nikias; it is interesting, too, as being distinguished by a quality somewhat rare in the works of Lysias. Few of his speeches have so much pathos. The address is emphatically an appeal to pity; and excites it less by direct appeals than by its simplicity and a tone of manly self-restraint. One passage is especially striking—the description of Diognêtos bringing the orphan children of his brothers to Pausanias, and imploring the Spartan king to remember all that their fathers had suffered (§ 10).

III. Claims for Moneys withheld from the State.

III. 1. For the Soldier.

1. *For the Soldier.* [Or. ix.]—The accused, Polyaenos, is prosecuted under a writ (ἀπογραφή, §§ 3, 21) for the recovery of a fine alleged to be due from him to the Treasury. He states that, two years before, he had returned to Athens from a campaign, but had not been two months at home before he was again placed upon the list for active service. Hereupon he appealed to the General of his tribe (τῷ στρατηγῷ, § 4); but obtained no redress. He spoke indignantly on the subject in conversation at one of the banker's tables in the marketplace; and, this having been reported to the authorities, he was fined under the law against reviling magistrates. The Generals did not, however, take any steps to

levy the fine; but at the expiration of their year
of office, left a note of it with the Stewards of
the Treasury (τοῖς ταμίαις, § 6). These, after inquiry, were satisfied that the fine had been inflicted
maliciously (§ 7), and cancelled it. The accusers,
ignoring this decision, now prosecute the soldier,
at an interval of more than a year, as a state-debtor.
In case of conviction the penalty would be the payment of twice the original fine; but not the loss of
civic rights. (§ 21.) From § 4 the speech may be
referred to the time of the Corinthian War,. 394—
387 B.C.

After complaining that his adversaries have wandered *Analysis.*
from the special issue into general attacks upon his character
the speaker sketches the facts of the case (§§ 1—7). He
then argues, first, that the fine was originally illegal, since
the offence contemplated by the law was that of speaking
against a magistrate in court (ἐν συνεδρίῳ, § 6), which he
had not done; secondly, that in any case the reversal of
the sentence by the stewards had absolved him (§§ 8—12).

The malice of his enemies had been provoked, he says,
by the favour which he had formerly enjoyed with Sôs-
tratos, an influential citizen. They are resolved to ruin
him. The matter at issue is nominally a fine, but really
his citizenship; for, if the court also takes part against him,
he will be driven to fly from a city in which justice is not
to be had (§§ 13—22).

Harpokration doubted the authenticity of this *Question of*
speech[1]; some recent critics have decisively rejected *genuine-*
it[2]. There are several traces of mutilation in the *ness.*
extant version. Thus the direct question with which

---

[1] s. v. δικαίωσις:—Λυσίας ἐν τῷ
περὶ στρατιώτου, εἰ γνήσιος.

[2] Especially Francken, *Commen-*

tationes Lysiacae pp. 64 f.: Blass,
Att. Bereds. pp. 606 f.

the speech opens is oddly abrupt ; in § 5 a conversation is referred to (τὰ προειρημένα) as if it had been
given in terms ; and in § 9 the speaker alludes to
witnesses whom he has called, but of whom there
is no other trace. It would be easier to vindicate
the authorship of Lysias if the speech, as it stands,
could be assumed to be a mere extract or epitome,
like the so-called Second Speech Against Theomnêstos. But the epitomic character, distinct there,
is absent here ; there, proem and epilogue have been
compressed ; here their redundancies of expression
are left untouched.

Francken thinks that the language is in some
points doubtful Attic[1]; and that the law is question-
able[2]. He argues further that, if the text is right
in § 6, 'Ktesikles the archon,' there mentioned, must
be the archon of Ol. CXI. 3, 334 B.C.; and notices
that, in that year, an armament was prepared, but
not despatched, by Athens[3]—which agrees with the
fact that Polyaenos, when enrolled the second time,
was not called upon to serve. These arguments
seem to point to different conclusions. If the diction
and the law are not classically Attic, then the speech
is a late work, probably a rhetorical exercise. If

---

[1] *e. g.* ἐντός for ἔνδον in § 10—
already noticed by Dobree; δικαίωσις for δικαίωμα ('plea' or 'argument') in § 8, noticed by Harpokr.;
τὸ πέρας in the sense of 'at last' in
§ 17.

[2] He infers from Dem. *Meid.*
§ 33 that the penalty for reviling
a magistrate *in court*, as for striking τὸν ἄρχοντα ἐστεφανωμένον,
would have been, not a fine, but
atimia; and he thinks it strange
that the ταμίαι, inferior magistrates,
should summon their superiors,
the strategi, before them (§ 7). We
do not know enough to decide such
points : and nothing can be safely
argued from them.

[3] See Schäfer, *Demosthenes und
seine Zeit*, vol. III. p. 162.

Ktesikles is the Ktesikles of 334, then the speech
was probably written for a real cause of about that
date[1].

Far stronger than these special objections is *The general style proves the Speech spurious.*
the general objection arising from the style. This,
indeed, appears conclusive. The passage in §§ 15—
18, where the speaker attacks his adversaries, could
hardly have come from Lysias. It is overwrought in
tone, overloaded with antitheses, and too epideictic
for its place. The whole defence is meagre, yet
not concise—a reversal of the manner of Lysias.
It was probably written by a bad imitator of his
style; but for a real cause rather than as an exercise[2].

2. *On the Property of Aristophanes.* [Or. *III. 2. On the Property of Aristophanes.*
XIX.]—Nikophêmos, father of Aristophanes, was the
friend of Konon, and his comrade in the naval campaigns of 394— 390 B.C. When Konon visited the
Persian Court in 394, he left Nikophêmos and Hierô-
nymos in joint command of the Persian fleet[3]; and
when he took Kythêra in 393 Nikophêmos was appointed harmost[4]. While Konon and Nikophêmos had
their home at Cyprus (§ 36), their sons, Timotheos and
Aristophanes, lived at Athens; the latter poor, until

---

[1] Blass assumes (*Att. Bereds.* p.
607) that Ktesikles was one of the
strategi, and this is certainly easier.
But, in that case, the words τοῦ
ἄρχοντος must be a gloss; added
by a commentator who associated
the name only with the archon of
334. A strategus could not have
been called ἄρχων.

[2] I cannot see that, as Blass
thinks, a sophistic exercise is indicated by the accumulation of

unknown proper names in § 5;—
by the fact of the 'influential' Sô-
stratos (§ 13) being lost to fame;—by
the absence of clearness in the
statement of the case;—or by the
uncertainty of the date. The subject would surely have been a poor
one for a declamation.

[3] Diod. XIV. 81: Νικόδημος, in
that passage, being a mere clerical
error for Νικόφημος.

[4] Xen. *Hellen.* IV. viii. 8.

the battle of Knidos in 394 and the campaigns of the
following years brought some wealth to his father
and himself (§ 28). On two important occasions
Aristophanes was engaged in the service of the
State. He went on an embassy to Sicily (in what
year is doubtful) with proposals from Evagoras, king
of Cyprus, to Dionysios; and succeeded in dissuading
the latter from affording his promised aid to Sparta
(§§ 19, 20). Again in 389 B.C. he sailed with an
Athenian expedition to the aid of Evagoras (§§ 21—
23). From this expedition he never returned. He
and his father Nikophêmos were suddenly put to
death at Cyprus without trial (§ 7); doubtless on a
suspicion of treachery or of embezzlement similar
to that which raised a storm of indignation against
Thrasybulos and his colleagues in 390 B.C.

*Origin of
the Action.*
After the death of Aristophanes, one Aeschines
proposed the confiscation of his property. The proposal, like that of Poliochos in the case of the property
of Eukrates, was resisted on the ground of illegality,
and a speech was written by Lysias against it[1]. It
was, however, carried into effect, and so stringently
that not even the debts left by Aristophanes were
discharged, nor was the dowry of his widow repaid
to her family (§ 32). But the amount of property
which was found disappointed the general belief in
the wealth of Nikophêmos (§§ 11, 53). It was

---

[1] Harpokration s. v. Χύτροι:—
Λυσίας ἐν τῷ κατ᾽ Αἰσχίνου περὶ τῆς
δημεύσεως τῶν Ἀριστοφάνους χρημάτων: Sauppe *O. A.* II. p. 173. In
his *Onomasticum Fragmentorum*
Sauppe seems to identify this Aeschines with the Sokratic, against
whom Lysias wrote on another
occasion. That the proposal of
Aeschines was met with a γραφὴ
παρανόμων is indicated in § 8 of
Or. XIX.

thought that something must have been withheld;
and suspicion fell upon the father-in-law of Aristophanes. A writ was therefore issued against him
for the recovery of moneys due to the treasury (§ 11).
Before the trial came on, he died, at the age of more
than seventy (§ 60); and his only son, a man of
thirty (§ 55), was left to defend the action. The
Fiscal Board of Syndici were the presidents of the
court.

The date is indicated by § 50. It is there *Date.*
said that Diotimos had lately (ἔναγχος) been accused of having forty talents unaccounted for in
his possession; but had, on returning to Athens,
disproved the charge. Diotimos had held a command in the Hellespont in 388 and 387[1] B.C.; 387
is therefore probably the year of the speech.

The defence is approached with timidity, as if under *Analysis.*
the consciousness that a strong prejudice has to be met.
The speaker represents the gravity of the task which has
devolved upon him; his father's good fame, his own, and
all his fortunes are at stake. He sets forth the restless
malice of his accusers, and reminds the court that experience
has proved how little such accusations are to be trusted[2].
The cruel fate of Nikophêmos and Aristophanes;—the desti-
tution of his brother-in-law's children, and the persecutions
to which his own family have been exposed in addition to
the burden thus thrown upon them;—the current delusions,
lastly, about the wealth of Nikophêmos, delusions so dangerous in the present impoverished state of the Treasury—all
these are urged as claims to the sympathetic attention of
the court. (§§ 1—11.)

---

[1] Xen. *H.* v.´ 1. 25.
[2] On the almost verbal coincidence between §§ 2—5 of this proem
and §§ 1, 6, 7 of Andok. *De Mysteriis*, see above, p. 117.

The next division of the speech is devoted to showing that Aristophanes was not originally a rich man, and was at all times lavish. He was not chosen by the speaker's father as a son-in-law on account of his wealth : indeed, his last act before sailing for Cyprus was to come to their house and borrow seven minae ; and it could be proved that shortly afterwards he was in want of a very small sum of ready money. Then follows a formal inventory of the property left by the deceased (§§ 12—27).

But why, it may be asked, was this property so small? Aristophanes had scarcely any fortune until four years before his death ; and within these four years he was twice choregus, besides buying a house and lands. The defendant had taken precautions for the due transference to the Government of every article left in the house of Aristophanes : a watch had even been set to see that the doors were not torn off, as sometimes happened to confiscated houses. He is ready to take the most solemn oath before the Syndici that nothing remains in his hands ; nay, that his sisters' dowry and the debt of seven minae still remain unpaid. Supposing that the property of Timotheos, son of Konon, were confiscated and only four talents realized, would *his* relatives be thought to deserve ruin? Yet the father of Timotheos was at least ten times as rich as the father of Aristophanes (§§ 28—41). There are many instances in which the popular estimate of a man's fortune has been proved, at his death or on inquiry during his lifetime, to have been enormously exaggerated. The recent case of Diotimos (§ 50) and the case of the great Alkibiades (§ 52) are among those in point.   (§§ 42—54.)

The good character borne by himself and by his father ought to be remembered. If their property were confiscated now, the State would not get two talents. At this moment he is a trierarch: his father spent his fortune on the State and for its honour; he kept good horses, had athletes in his pay, and won victories at the Isthmos and at Nemea (§ 63). On all these grounds the defendant claims the protection of the court against a malignant attack (§§ 55—64).

This very clever speech gives a formidable idea of the dangers to which an Athenian of the time was exposed if he or any member of his family was supposed to have made a fortune on foreign service. The city was poor[1]; it was full of informers, ready to prefer any accusation on the chance of sharing the spoil; and by a vague charge of treachery or embezzlement abroad it was easy to inflame the ekklesia[2]. There is nothing to show why Aristophanes or his father were put to death without trial. The point which is most strikingly brought out by this defence is the strength of the popular feeling which it had to combat. It is remarkable in how diffident a tone the speaker begins, how careful he is to put in the front of his case everything that can excite compassion, how he avoids directly praising or even defending Aristophanes. He gradually insinuates that Aristophanes was a worthy man—poor, but generous and patriotic. The speech is nearly half over before it comes directly to the real issue (§ 28), and argues that Aristophanes cannot, in fact, have left more property than appeared. Perhaps the modesty of the speaker is a little overwrought; but there is consummate art in the sketch of his father, the quiet citizen of the

---

[1] See especially § 11, χαλεπὸν μὲν οὖν ἀπολογεῖσθαι πρὸς σπάνιν ἀργυρίου ἣ νῦν ἐστιν ἐν τῇ πόλει. Compare Or. xxx (Against Nikomachos) § 22, and the case of Eraton (Or. xvii): Francken, *Comment. Lysiacae*, p. 130.

[2] Rauchenstein, in his Introduction to this Speech (p. 146), aptly quotes Or. xxvii (Against Epikrates) § 11: οὐκέτι ὧν οὗτοι (the corrupt demagogues) κλέπτουσι ὀργίζεσθε, ἀλλ᾽ ὧν αὐτοὶ λαμβάνετε χάριν ἴστε, ὥσπερ ὑμεῖς τὰ τούτων μισθοφοροῦντες ἀλλ᾽ οὐ τούτων τὰ ὑμέτερα κλεπτόντων.

old school, and of Aristophanes, the adventurous patriot of the new. On the whole, this is one of the masterpieces of Lysias, in which all the resources of his tact were brought into play by a subject difficult enough to be worthy of them.

3. *Against Philokrates.* [Or. xxix.]—This case may be regarded as a sequel to that of Ergokles [Or. xxviii][1]. Philokrates had sailed, as steward or purser (ταμίας § 3), under command of Ergokles as trierarch. Ergokles had now been put to death and his property had been confiscated. But a sum of thirty talents, which he was said to have gained by corrupt practices, had not been found (§ 2). A writ was therefore issued against Philokrates on the supposition that, since he had been in the confidence of Ergokles, he must know what had become of the money.

The speaker is one of several Public Prosecutors (συνήγοροι) and, as in the case of Ergokles, merely follows others with a summary of the leading points. The case Against Philokrates has been stated, and the evidence cited, by former speakers; this is the concluding speech for the prosecution; hence the title of epilogue or peroration[2] given in the

---

[1] See above, p. 221.

[2] Κατὰ Φιλοκράτους ἐπίλογος. The speaker says in § 1 that many persons who had promised to appear against Philokrates have not done so; but obviously this does not justify Francken's inference,—' Altera pars inscriptionis (ἐπίλογος) manifesto falsa est; statim enim ab initio totidem verbis neminem esse praeter se accusatorem orator testatur' (*Comment. Lys.* p. 226). The absence of witnesses and proofs in this speech is conclusive, as Blass says (*Att. Bereds.* p. 454), on the other side.

MSS. to this as well as to the speech Against Ergokles. The date is probably the year of the trial of Ergokles—389 B.C.

Many persons, says the speaker, who had promised to appear against Philokrates have failed; an additional proof that he has the money, and has been able to buy off numerous accusers. The thirty talents have not been discovered: who can have them but the most intimate friend of Ergokles, his subaltern and his steward? It rests with Philokrates to show either that Ergokles was wrongly condemned, or that some one else now has the missing sum (§§ 1—5). Three talents, it is well known, had been promised to public speakers if they could save Ergokles. Philokrates has got this money back, and has possessed himself of the rest of his late chief's property; yet now he has the effrontery to pretend that he was his enemy. Is it likely that in that case he would have volunteered to sail with him as trierarch? (§§ 6, 7.)

The Athenians ought to defend their own interests, and compel Philokrates to give up their property. It is hard if those who cannot pay taxes incur the public anger, while the embezzlers of State-property escape. Indeed, the accomplices of Ergokles deserve not only a pecuniary penalty, but the same punishment which he suffered—death. While his trial was pending, his friends went about boasting that they had bribed upwards of 2000 men (§ 12). Let it be proved to them that no amount of bribery can save evil-doers. If the citizens are wise, they will reclaim what is their own (§§ 8—14).

Like the speeches Against Ergokles and Against Epikrates, this is the address of an official prosecutor, and of one who had but a subordinate part to perform. It has the characteristic excellences of the other two, compactness and vigour; but it is necessarily inferior to the speech Against Ergokles, in which the greater importance of the cause calls forth more oratorical vigour.

IV. CAUSES RELATING TO A SCRUTINY (δοκιμασία)
BEFORE THE SENATE ; ESPECIALLY OF OFFICIALS
DESIGNATE.

IV. 1.
*Against
Evandros.*

1. *Against Evandros.* [Or. XXVI.]—In the second
year of the 99th Olympiad (38½ B.C.) Leôdamas[1] drew
the lot to be First Archon for the following year;
and Evandros was at the same time designated
First Archon in reserve[2]. Leôdamas, before entering
upon the archonship, had to pass a scrutiny (δοκιμασία) before the Senate. On this occasion he was
accused by Thrasybulos of Collytos; the Senate rejected him; and the office thus came to Evandros.
But Evandros also had to pass a scrutiny; and the
present speech is made to the Senate in order to
prove that he is ineligible.

Date.

The case is heard on the last day but one of Ol.
99. 2, *i.e.* at about midsummer of our year 382 B.C.[3].
The last day of the Attic year was a public holiday,
on which no law-court could sit, and on which a
sacrifice to Zeus Sôtêr was celebrated by the First

---

[1] Not the orator of Acharnae,
who was the advocate of Leptines
in 355 B.C., but a man of whom nothing is known except from this
speech and from a notice in Arist.
Rh. II. 23. Thrasybulos had said
in his accusation that the name of
Leôdamas had been inscribed on a
pillar [recording traitors &c.] on
the acropolis (ἦν στηλίτης γεγονὼς
ἐν τῇ ἀκροπόλει), but was erased in
the time of the Thirty. Leôdamas
answered that he was not likely to
have erased it then. The Thirty
would have trusted him the more
for his enmity to the people being

registered (ἐγγεγραμμένης τῆς ἔχθρας
πρὸς τὸν δῆμον).

[2] ἐπέλαχε : Harpokr. s. v. Cf.
Aesch. *in Ktes.* § 62.

[3] The Olympic year, reckoned
from July to July, is counted as
that year B.C. in which its first
half falls. The year 382 B.C. comprised the second half of Ol. 99. 2
and the first half of Ol. 99. 3.
Hence the date of this speech,
which belongs to the end of Ol.
99. 2, is, in strictness, 382 B.C.; and
the following Greek year, Ol. 99. 3,
in which Evandros was Archon, is
also *conventionally* 382 B.C.

Archon.   If, therefore, the Senate rejected Evandros, no time remained for an appeal to an ordinary court; and the State would be left without its chief magistrate at one of its great solemnities (§ 6).

The election of Evandros was, in fact, ratified; for *Evandros actually* he appears in the lists as Archon for the following *Archon in 382 B.C.* year, Ol. 99. 3.   This date is confirmed by allusions in the speech.

Thrasybulos the Collytean is charged in § 23 with having estranged Boeotia from Athens and with having lost Athenian ships.   The first accusation refers to the establishment of oligarchies in the Boeotian cities, through Spartan influence, after the Peace of Antalkidas; and is curiously illustrated by the reference of Aeschines to Thrasybulos of Collytos as a man of great influence at Thebes[1].   The second accusation refers to an incident of the war on the Hellespont five years before.   In 387 B. C. eight triremes under the command of this Thrasybulos were captured by Antalkidas near Abydos[2].

All the first part of the speech has been lost in those eight pages of the Palatine MS. which contained the conclusion of the Twenty-fifth Speech and the whole of that Against Nikides[3].   The special charges made by the accuser, and the depositions to which he alludes (§ 8), were in this part.   What remains is chiefly his answer to certain pleas which he conceives that Evandros may urge.

[1] Aeschin. *in Ktes.* § 138.
[2] Xen. *Hellen.* v. 1. 27.   Xenophon's account, it may be observed, gives no support to the accuser's statement (§ 23) that Thrasybulos *betrayed* his ships.
[3] See p. 200.

It is hard —the speaker says—that, not content with impunity for his offences against the people, Evandros should ask for office. Evandros relies on the recent sobriety (ἡσυχιότης, § 5) of his life—which has been compulsory: and on his father's liberality—who used the influence thus gained to overthrow the democracy (§§ 1—5). He has contrived to delay his scrutiny until the last day but one of the year, when there is no time to appoint another First Archon. But the sacrifices of the morrow will surely be more pleasing to the gods, though offered only by the King Archon and his colleagues, than if the celebrant were a man whose hands are stained with the blood shed in the days of the Thirty Tyrants (§§ 6—8). One of the principal objects of the law of Scrutinies (ὁ περὶ τῶν δοκιμασιῶν νόμος, § 9) is to exclude from office in a democracy those who have abused power under an oligarchy. The mere fact of having been an ordinary knight or senator under the Thirty disqualifies a man for a place in the Council of Five Hundred. Evandros was more than this; he was guilty of special crimes against the people; and shall he be First Archon? He will thus become a member of the Areiopagos for life, and murderers will be tried by a murderer. And this through the influence of Thrasybulos, a traitor to Athens. It must not be supposed that the speaker opposes Evandros for the sake of Leôdamas. Leôdamas would be well pleased that the Senate should prove itself oligarchical by confirming so unpopular an appointment (§§ 10—15).

Evandros appeals to the Amnesty [of 403 B.C.]; but that Amnesty did not mean that the honours, as well as the toleration, of the State should be accorded to its recent enemies (§§ 16—20). Let the Senate compare the accuser with the advocate of Evandros. The accuser is pure of all connection with oligarchies; his ancestors fought against the Peisistratidae; his family have exhausted a large fortune upon the State. Thrasybulos has alienated the Boeotians from Athens; has lost her ships, and brought her to despair. If the Court reflects which of these two men ought rather to prevail, it will decide rightly upon the claims of Evandros (§§ 21—24).

Unwillingness to mar a great annual festival may have influenced the Senate when they confirmed the election; but there is no proof that the grounds upon which it was opposed were good. The accuser must have felt that his case was well-nigh hopeless. This, *Tone of the Speech.* and the feeling of Lysias himself towards all who had been concerned in the violence of the Anarchy, will partly account for the extreme bitterness and unfairness of this speech. In two places the tone is especially marked. First, where the accuser admits that since the restoration of the democracy Evandros has been a thoroughly good citizen, and then argues that he deserves no credit for it (§§ 3—5); again, where he maintains that the dokimasia was instituted for the express purpose of keeping oligarchs out of office (§ 9). The outburst against Thrasybulos at the end is of a piece with this (§ 23). A certain boldness of expression, hardly congenial to Lysias, corresponds with the excited tone of the speech[1], which has the air of having been written in haste, to support a cause already desperate.

2. *For Mantitheos.* [Or. XVI.]—The name oc- *IV. 2. For Mantitheos.* curs only in the title, which, contrary to the general rule, is perhaps of the same age as the speech—'A Defence for Mantitheos on his Scrutiny before the Senate.' What the office was to which this scrutiny related, can only be guessed; perhaps it was that of an ordinary senator, since in § 8 the speaker cites instances of persons who had really done what he is charged with doing, and had yet been admitted to the Senate. The complaint against him was that his

---

[1] See especially §§ 3, 4.

name appeared on the list (σανίς, cf. § 6) of those
who had served as Knights in the time of the Thirty.
As the speech Against Evandros shows (§ 10), the fact
of such service under the Tyrants became, after the
restoration of the democracy, a disqualification for
the office of senator. Mantitheos must, then, have
been at least eighteen years of age in 405 B. C., and
so must have been born before 422. He refers to his
share in campaigns subsequent to that of 394 B.C.
(§§ 15—18). On the other hand, the tone of the joke
in § 15 rather suggests that Thrasybulos, its object,
was still alive ;—that is, that the speech is earlier

Date. than 389 B. C.[1]. The date may have been about
392 B.C. The speaker, who was taunted with youthful presumption (§ 20), cannot have been much more
than thirty.

Analysis. The first disproves the charge against him of having
served as a Knight under the Thirty Tyrants. Before the
disaster on the Hellespont [405 B.C.], his father had sent him
and his brother to the Euxine, to Satyros [king of the Kim-
merian Bosporos]; and they did not return to Athens till
five days before the democratic exiles captured the Peiraeus
[404 B.C.] (§ 4). The appearance of his name upon the list of
Knights at that time proves nothing; the list has many false
entries and many omissions. Here is a better proof on the
other side :—when the democracy was restored, the phylarch
(captain of cavalry) of each tribe was directed to recover
from each Knight who had served under the Tyrants *the sum
paid to him by the State for his equipment* when he was first
enrolled (κατάστασις, § 6). Now Mantitheos was never called
upon to refund, nor brought before the Fiscal Board (σύν-
δικοι, § 7)—(§§ 1—8).

[1] Thrasybulos died in Ol. 97. 3
(Diod. xiv. 94, 99 : Xen. *Hellen.*
iv. 8. 30), i.e. 390—389 B.C.: probably, as Clinton (*F. H.*) says, in
the early part of 389.

Having disproved the charge against him, he goes on to urge his positive merits. His private life has been blameless. After his father's death, he portioned his two sisters and helped his brother. Men who are fond of dice and wine have a marked aversion to him (§ 11). Then his public services have been constant. He volunteered on the expedition for the relief of Haliartos [395 B.C.] (§ 13). In the next year he fought in the disastrous battle of Corinth, and retreated later than 'the majestic Steirian [Thrasybulos], who has taunted all the world with cowardice' (§ 15). In the autumn of the same year [394 B. C.] he and his company volunteered for service against Agesilaos in Boeotia. Since then, he has constantly served in the field or in garrison (§ 18).—(§§ 9—19).

Some have taunted him with forwardness because, though so young, he has spoken in the ekklesia. His own affairs, however, compelled him to do so at first. Perhaps, indeed, he has been too ambitious. But he could not help thinking of his forefathers, who had always been in public life and served the State; and he saw that Athenians, to tell the truth, respected none but those who could act and speak for the city. 'And why should you be annoyed with such men? You yourselves and none else are their judges' (§§ 20, 21).

Perhaps hardly anything in Greek literature has *The character of Mantitheos.* a fresher or brighter charm than this short speech— the natural, wonderfully vivid expression of an attractive character. Mantitheos is the brilliant, ambitious young Athenian, burning to fulfil the Homeric ideal by distinguishing himself in council as in war; an Alkibiades made harmless by the sentiment of chivalry. The general tone of simple self-reliance, and possibly the gibe at Thrasybulos, may have been found refreshing by elderly senators. Mantitheos had really done good service in the field; and his statement of this is followed by an ingenuous apology for over-eagerness to shine in the ekklesia. The last passage is masterly. The virtue of 'minding one's own affairs' (ἀπραγμοσύνη) was often praised at Athens; but Mantitheos goes to the centre of Athenian instincts when he tells the judges that 'to say the truth' they respect no men who do not take part in public life[1].

IV. 3.
Against
Philon.

3. *Against Philon.* [Or. XXXI.]—This speech may be considered as a companion-piece to the last; being an Accusation, as the other is probably a Defence, at a dokimasia for the Senate. Philon—a man otherwise unknown—had been chosen by lot a member of the Senate of Five Hundred; and had appeared before that body, with others designated to places in it, in order to pass the scrutiny. The speaker, himself a senator, comes forward to oppose the admission of Philon. The date cannot be fixed. Philon is accused of having gone about Attica, plundering 'the oldest of the citizens,' who had stayed quietly in their

Probable
Date.

demes (§ 18); and some of these citizens were still alive: some time between 404 and 395 B.C. may therefore be assumed.

Analysis.

The speaker begins by protesting that no private enmity, but only regard to his oath as senator, induces him to appear against Philon. What is the definition of a worthy senator? One who both is, and desires to be, a citizen (§ 5). Now when the troubles came on Athens [405 B.C.], Philon proved how little he valued his citizenship. He neither stayed with the oligarchs in the town, nor joined the exiles at Phylê,

---

[1] The speech is described by Dobree (*Adv.* I. 192) as 'vividis et paene comicis coloribus exprimens στρατικὴν αὐθάδειαν ea simul arte ut hoc ipso placeat'—a description which does no justice to the delicacy of the delineation. 'Ex verbis Dobrei alterum quendam Pyrpolinicen expectes,' as Francken says (*Comment. Lys.* p. 118).

but went to Orôpus—paid the resident-alien's tax, and lived
under the protection of a patron. This shall be proved by
witnesses (§§ 1—14). If he says that he was unfit for fighting, it can be shown that his name does not appear among
those of the citizens who, instead of personal service, paid
money or armed their demesmen (§§ 15, 16). Nor was he
merely passive : he did positive wrong to aged citizens of
Athens whom he met with in the country (§§ 17—19). This
corresponds with his treatment of his own mother, who transferred the keeping of her money from her son to a stranger
(§§ 20—23). Why should such as he be a senator? The
betrayer of a garrison, a fleet, or a camp is punished; but
Philon has betrayed the State itself (§§ 24—26).

'He has broken no law,' he says. No : for an offence so
enormous was never expressly contemplated by any legislator
(§§ 27, 28). If the aliens who helped Athens in her need
were honoured, surely the citizens who abandoned her should
be disgraced. The advocates who claim honour for Philon
now would have done better had they advised him to deserve
it then (§§ 29—33). Let each senator ask himself why *he*
was admitted to that dignity, and he will see why Philon
ought to be shut out from it (§ 34).

The tone of this address is in contrast with that *The attack strong, but temperate.*
of the protest against the election of Evandros : it is
severe and decided, but not bitter or unfair. A character which seems to have been really contemptible
is drawn without passion, each statement being supported by evidence; and the assertion of the speaker,
that only a sense of duty prompted him to accuse, is
at least not contradicted by his method. The style
is rhetorical, and rather more openly artificial than
is usual with Lysias (see esp. §§ 11, 32); but it has
all his compactness and force—of which the short
appeal at the end is a good example. One point of *Allusion to the crime of Neutrality.*
historical interest comes out. Philon is accused of

having taken part, in 405 B.C., neither with oligarchs nor with democrats. He pleads :—' Had it been an offence not to be present at such a time, a law would have been made expressly on that subject.' The answer is, that, owing to the inconceivable enormity of the offence, no law has been enacted on the subject (§ 27). So completely had Solon's enactment against neutrality—to which the speaker could have appealed with so much rhetorical effect—passed out of the remembrance of that generation[1].

IV. 4. *Defence on a Charge of seeking to abolish the Democracy.*

4. *Defence on a Charge of seeking to abolish the Democracy.* [Or. xxv.]—This title, given to the speech in the MSS., is clearly wrong. The speaker is, indeed, chiefly concerned to prove that he is guiltless of any share in the crimes of the Thirty Tyrants; but it is clear that he was not upon his trial for high treason. There is no reference to any penalties which threatened him. The question is whether he shall, or shall not, be admitted to certain privileges. Thus in § 3 he insists on his claim to participation in the advantages of citizenship; in § 4 he speaks of rights which citizens who have done no evil ought to share with positive benefactors of the State; in § 14 he says to the judges :—' If, when I might have had

---

[1] Rauchenstein, in his introduction to the speech (p. 116), brings together the chief passages in which Solon's law is mentioned :—Plut. *Sol.* c. 20 (ἄτιμον εἶναι τὸν ἐν στάσει μηδετέρας μερίδος γενόμενον): Cic. *ad Att.* x. 1: Gellius ii. 12 (translating an extract from Aristotle —perhaps from his πολιτεῖαι) *si ob hanc discordiam dissensionemque seditio atque discessio populi in* *duas partes fieret et ob eam caussam irritatis animis utrinque arma caperentur pugnareturque, tum qui in eo tempore in eoque casu civilis discordiae non alterutri parti se adiunxerit sed solitarius separatusque a communi malo civitatis secesserit, is domo patria fortunisque omnibus careto, exul extorrisque esto.*

office, I declined it, I have a right to receive honour from you *now*.' Clearly this speech was delivered on the occasion of a dokimasia for some office to which the speaker had been designated, but his admission to which was opposed. The cause is heard by an ordinary court—probably under the presidency of the Thesmothetae[1]—and on appeal from a decision for the speaker already given by the Senate. The date must be placed between 402 and 400 B.C.; probably nearer to the lower limit[2]. The accusers were Epigenes, Diophanes and Kleisthenes (§ 25). The defendant is not named.

The Speech really connected with a Dokimasia.

Date.

It would not be strange, he says, if the speeches made against him had excited the indignation of the judges against all, without distinction, who had remained at Athens under the Thirty. Much more might, indeed, have been said about the crimes of the Tyrants. But it is unmeaning to charge those crimes upon men who had no share in them. If he

Analysis.

---

[1] Since the Thesmothetae had jurisdiction in causes connected with δοκιμασίαι: Pollux 8. 44.

[2] Rauchenstein (*Introduct.* p. 91) supposes 402 B.C.; Blass (*Att. Bereds.* p. 509) prefers 401 or 400.

The arguments for the *earlier* date are these :—(1) The general tone of the speech, referring to the troubles of the Anarchy as recent: (2) § 17, where the speaker says προθυμήσομαι χρηστὸς εἶναι—as if he had not yet had time to prove his reformed character : (3) §§ 23 —24, where the exiled adherents of the Thirty are described as still hoping for a reaction at Athens: (4) § 28, from which (Rauchenstein thinks) it appears that the law of Archînos was not yet passed—a law enacted soon after the resto-ration of the democracy, providing that persons against whom, in despite of the Amnesty, accusations were brought in violation of the Amnesty, should be allowed at once to enter a παραγραφή, and to speak *first* at its hearing (Isokr. *Kall.* § 2).

For the *later* date it is argued (1) that in one place at least—§ 21 —the events under the Thirty are spoken of as if some considerable interval had elapsed; (2) that the restored democracy was old enough for abuses to have grown up,—§ 30 [this is, I think, a strong point]: (3) that § 28 does not prove the law of Archînos to be non-existent, since that law would have had no bearing on a δοκιμασία.

can prove that he is innocent, he may surely claim at least
the ordinary privileges of citizenship in common with men
of more distinguished services (§§ 1—6).   No man is born
an oligarch or a democrat.   He becomes one or the other
according to his private interest (τῶν ἰδίᾳ συμφερόντων, § 10).
This is proved by history.   Phrynichos and Peisandros were
demagogues before they became oligarchs.   Men who helped
to overthrow the Four Hundred were afterwards numbered
with the Thirty: many of the Four Hundred themselves
were with the democrats at the Peiraeus ; some of those who
had expelled the Four Hundred were afterwards among the
Thirty ; and some of the men who gave in their names for
the march against Eleusis, after going forth with the people,
were besieged along with the Tyrants[1].

The explanation is simply that their interests varied at
different times.   Now, the interest of the speaker lay wholly
with the democracy.   He had been five times trierarch and
had been in four sea-fights (§ 12).   The establishment of the
Thirty destroyed his chance of reward for these services.
Neither under the First Oligarchy nor under the Second did
he hold office (§§ 7—14).   If he did no wrong in the Anarchy, much more will he be a good citizen under the restored
Democracy.   The victims of the Tyrants must not be con-
founded with their agents.   It was the error of the Thirty
that they visited the sins of a few corrupt demagogues on

---

[1] § 9 εἰσὶ δὲ οἵτινες τῶν Ἐλευ-
σῖνάδε ἀπογραψαμένων, ἐξελθόντες μεθ᾽ ὑμῶν, ἐπολιορκοῦντο μετ᾽ αὐτῶν. The Thirty Tyrants,
when their government fell and
was succeeded by that of the Ten,
withdrew to Eleusis.   After the restoration of the democracy, an expedition was made from Athens
against Eleusis, and they were dis-
lodged : Xen. *Hell.* II. iv. 39, 43.

The question is, whether οἱ Ἐλευ-
σῖνάδε ἀπογραψάμενοι are (1) men
who enrolled themselves at Athens
for this expedition, but afterwards

deserted to the Tyrants—in which
case ἐξελθόντες means 'having
marched out :' or (2) men who,
having been driven from Athens
by the Thirty, remained in Attica,
and, instead of joining the democrats, joined the tyrants at Eleusis
—in which case ἐξελθόντες means
'having left Athens' under stress
of the Tyranny.   I prefer the
former view as giving (*a*) a clearer
meaning to ἀπογραψαμένων, (*b*) a
clearer contrast between ἐξελθόντες
μεθ᾽ ὑμῶν and ἐπολιορκοῦντο μετ᾽
αὐτῶν.

all the citizens: let not the people so err now (§§ 15—20). Dissensions among the Thirty gave the exiles their first hopes of success; let not disunion in the democracy now give occasion to the enemies of Athens, but let the oaths of amnesty be kept towards all (§§ 21—24). After the fall of the Four Hundred, the rigours which bad advisers caused to be adopted against their political opponents brought the city to ruin. And now sycophants, counselling a revengeful policy, oppose themselves to the views of those who were really active in restoring the democracy. Such men show what they would have been had they shared the power of the Thirty. The friends of the city advise differently. Let the Amnesty hold good for all. When those who are really answerable for the past troubles are brought to account, severity is excusable; but innocent men must not be mixed up with them (§§ 25—35).

The speaker had evidently been closely connected with the party of the Tyrants; for though he states his services to the democracy before 405 B.C., of his political character since that time he has nothing better to say than that it has been harmless; indeed, he implies a contrast between himself and those who had been true to the democracy at its need (§ 4). It is hard to understand the high praise which *The Speech over-praised.* has been given to this speech by some critics of Lysias[1]; it is barely conceivable that one of the ablest of them should count it his best work[2]. The speaker's interpretation of the Amnesty is, indeed, larger and truer than the opposite view taken by the accuser of Evandros[3]; and his elaborate exposition of the doctrine that political creed is purely an affair of self-

---

[1] As by Reiske ('egregia, luculenta, Lysiae nomine dignissima,' *Or. Att.* v. p. 759): and by Francken (*Comment. Lys.* p. 184).

[2] 'Lysiam relegenti videtur haec oratio esse omnium optima.' Dobree, *Adv.* I. 247.

[3] *Or.* XXVI. §§ 16—20 : see above, p. 244.

interest may claim the praise of candour. The style
has vigour, but neither brilliancy nor dignity; and
the êthos of the speaker, as a moderately intelligent
and thoroughly practical man, can scarcely be accounted persuasive[1].

IV. 5. For the Invalid.

5. *For the Invalid.* [Or. xxiv.]—This speech
may conveniently be classed with the four preceding, since it was written for a dokimasia, although
the scrutiny in this case was of a different kind. At
Public Charity at Athens. Athens a certain allowance was made by the State to
the ἀδύνατοι[2]: that is, to persons who were unable,
through bodily ailment, to earn a livelihood, and who
had less than three minae of private property. Once
a year, or perhaps oftener, the list of applicants for
such relief was scrutinised by the Senate[3] and then
passed by the ekklesia (§ 22). It is on the occasion
of such a scrutiny that the present speech is made.
The speaker had for years (§ 8) been in receipt of an
obol daily (§ 26) from the State; but lately it had
been attempted to show that he was not entitled to
public relief. This objection is termed in the title to
the speech (not in the speech itself) an eisangelia;
but had, of course, nothing in common with eisan-
geliae technically so called except that it was an

---

[1] It is difficult not to suspect
that Lysias—himself a loyal friend
of the democracy in two disasters—
wrote this defence of easy tergi-
versation with deliberate, though
disguised, irony; irony which perhaps ran no danger from the acuteness of his client.

[2] It is not clear whether the
term ἀδύνατος, in this technical
sense, referred *only* to bodily in-

firmity, or included (as Francken
thinks, p. 171 n.) also the idea
of poverty. The Invalid was said
by his adversary (1) τῷ σώματι
δύνασθαι καὶ οὐκ εἶναι τῶν ἀδυνάτων,
§ 4, and (2) δύνασθαι συνεῖναι δυ-
ναμένοις ἀνθρώποις ἀναλίσκειν § 5,
a phrase evidently as an antithesis
—possibly humorous—to ἀδύνατος.

[3] Aeschin. *in Timarch.* § 104.

accusation laid immediately before the Senate. The *Date.*
date appears from § 25 to have been later than
403 B. C.

Having premised that jealousy is the only conceivable *Analysis.*
motive for this attack upon him, the speaker comes to the
two objections which have been made to his receiving the
public alms:—that he is not really a cripple; and that he
has a trade (§§ 1—4). He answers the second objection
first (§§ 5—9); and then refutes the other with a good deal
of grim humour (§§ 10—14). Lastly, he defends his general
character (§§ 15—20), and concludes with an entreaty not to
be deprived of his obol a day (§§ 21—27).

Harpokration seems[1] to have doubted the genuine- *No ground
for doubt-
ing the
genuine-
ness.*
ness of this speech; possibly on the ground taken by
Boeckh[2]—that Lysias would not have written, nor the
Senate endured, so elaborate an address on such a
subject. This seems a most unsafe argument against
a composition excellent of its kind, and excellent in a
way suggestive of Lysias. The humour, broad, but
stopping short of burlesque, exactly suits the condition of the speaker; and there is true art in the
ironical pathos of the invalid, when, using an Attic
illustration, he remarks that his infirmity is disputed
with him by his adversary as eagerly as if it were an
heiress (§ 14).

---

[1] *seems*, for his words are (s. v.
ἀδύνατος), ἔστι δὲ καὶ λόγος τις ὡς
Λυσίου περὶ τοῦ ἀδυνάτου: some
MSS. having ὡς λέγεται Λυσίου
(Blass, *Att. Bereds.* p. 648).

[2] *Staatsh.* I. p. 260 ff. referred
to by Blass *l. c.* Blass classes
this speech with such 'bagatelle'
speeches as λόγος περὶ τῆς ἐγγυθήκης, λόγος περὶ τοῦ χρυσοῦ τρίποδος, &c., ascribed to Lysias; and

remarks that all such trifles, without distinction, were held spurious
by the old critics, whom Harpokration and Athenaeos follow. But it
should be noticed that Athenaeos,
while he adds εἰ γνήσιος to his
mention of the περὶ τοῦ χρ. τρίποδος
(VI. p. 231 B), only says of the περὶ
τῆς ἐγγυθήκης that it is 'ascribed'
to Lysias—acquiescing, apparently,
in the ascription (v. p. 209 F).

V.   CAUSES RELATING TO MILITARY OFFENCES
(λιποταξίου—ἀστρατείας).

V. 1.
Against Al-
kibiades, I.
2. Against
Alkibiades,
II.

1.   *Against Alkibiades, on a Charge of Desertion* [Or. XIV.].

2.   *Against Alkibiades, on a Charge of Failure to Serve* [Or. XV.].

The two
Speeches
concern the
same fact.

These speeches do not refer to two distinct accusations, but are merely two different ways of stating the same accusation. Alkibiades, son of the famous Alkibiades, had taken part in the expedition sent from Athens to the relief of Haliartos when Boeotia was invaded by Lysander in 395 B.C. But, instead of serving with the heavy-armed infantry, he had chosen to serve with the cavalry, although he had not passed the scrutiny (dokimasia) required before enrolment among the Knights. His accusers might have indicted him under a special law which attached the penalty of disfranchisement to such a fraud (Or. XIV. § 8). They preferred, however, to bring against him a more invidious charge—desertion of military duty.

Law about
Military
Offences.

The principal military offences were dealt with at Athens by one law. Under this law a citizen was liable to indictment and if convicted to disfranchisement for 1. Failure to join the army—ἀστρατείας : 2. Cowardice in battle—δειλίας : 3. Desertion of his post—λιποταξίου. This third term properly denoted an offence distinct from the other two. But it was sometimes so extended as to include either of the other two[1]. Now Alkibiades had served, indeed,

---

[1] It does not appear quite certain whether there was a γραφὴ δειλίας distinct from a γραφὴ λιποταξίου. In § 6 of the First Speech Against

but had not served with the hoplites. His offence, then, might be looked at from two points of view. He might be considered as a man who, on service, had been found out of his place, and who was liable to an indictment for Desertion of his Post—γραφὴ λιποταξίου. Or he might be considered as a man who had never been present in his place, and who was liable to an indictment for Failure to Serve—γραφὴ ἀστρατείας. The First Speech takes the former point of view ; the Second takes the latter.

The date and occasion of the speeches are not *Date.* directly indicated, but can be determined almost certainly. This was the first military trial since 'the peace' (XIV. § 4) ;—a campaign had just taken place, but no battle had been fought (§ 5), though the generals had given satisfaction to the State (XV. § 1). All this corresponds with the campaign of the year 395. It was the first since the peace, or rather truce, with Sparta in the spring of 404. No battle had been fought, because, before the

---

Alkibiades they appear to be identified. But in the following passages (among others) they are distinguished :—Aeschin. *in Ctes.* §175 Σόλων—ἐν τοῖς αὐτοῖς ἐπιτιμίοις ᾤετο δεῖν ἐνέχεσθαι τὸν ἀστράτευτον καὶ τὸν λελοιπότα τὴν τάξιν καὶ τὸν δειλὸν ὁμοίως : Andok. *de Myst.* § 73 ὅποσοι λίποιεν τὴν τάξιν ἢ ἀστρατείας ἢ δειλίας ἢ ἀναυμαχίου ὄφλοιεν ἢ τὴν ἀσπίδα ἀποβάλοιεν : and Plato's distinction (*Legg.* XII. 943 F) of ἀστρατείας —λιποταξίου—ῥιφθέντων (the last equivalent to δειλίας) may be sup-

posed to correspond to a like distinction in the actual Attic law. Obviously a γραφὴ λιποταξίου might be needed for cases in which a γραφὴ δειλίας could not be preferred. On the other hand, the γραφὴ λιποταξίου might probably include the case of ἀστρατεία : just as the δίκη λιπομαρτυρίου (compared by Francken, *Comment. Lys.* p. 111) lay against a man who *refused* to give evidence; not merely against one who, having undertaken to do so, failed to appear.

Athenian force arrived at Haliartos, the Lacedaemonians had already been defeated, and Lysandros
slain. The Athenian Generals had only to assist
at the arrangement of the humiliating truce under
which Pausanias led his army out of Boeotia[1]. In
395 B.C. the younger Alkibiades must have been
about twenty years of age[2].

The Court was composed of soldiers (στρατιώτας
δικάζειν, Or. XIV. § 5), the Generals presiding (τῶν
στρατηγῶν δέομαι, XV. 1). Archestratides, the chief
accuser, had opened the cause and produced the
evidence; these two speakers are his friends and
supporters. (Or. XIV. 3 ; XV. 12.)

*Analysis.—
First
Speech.*   The accuser explains his appearance in that capacity.
An explanation is, indeed, hardly necessary, considering the
character of Alkibiades; but in his own case a feud in-
herited from his father supplies a special motive. (§§ 1—3.)
He then addresses himself to a technical point. The law
against Desertion is so worded (it has been argued) that
it does not apply where there has been no battle. He
answers that one of the two offences which that law con-
templates—namely Failure to Serve—is manifestly proved
against Alkibiades, who did not take his place among the
hoplites. Of the other offence—Desertion of his Post through
cowardice—he is virtually guilty, since his reason for preferring
to serve with the cavalry was that there he would run less
risk. Others, who were really knights, waived their privilege
in this instance[3], and served as hoplites. Alkibiades seized
a privilege to which he had no claim (§ 10). Such audacity

---

[1] Xen. *Hellen.* III. v. 16.

[2] Since from Isokr. *de Bigis* (*Or.*
XVI) § 45 it appears that the
younger Alkibiades was born in,
or just before, 415 B.C.

[3] This statement is exactly illustrated by the Speech For Man-

titheos (Or. XVI) § 12, where Mantitheos, speaking of this very
expedition to Haliartos, says :—ὅτε
...εἰς Ἀλίαρτον ἔδει βοηθεῖν, ὑπὸ
Ὀρθοβούλου κατειλεγμένος ἱππεύειν,
...ἑτέρων ἀναβάντων ἐπὶ τοὺς
ἵππους ἀδοκιμάστων παρὰ τὸν

must be punished for public example. Let the soldiers
who sit in judgment remember how much each of them
sacrificed to his duty, and then decide what punishment is
merited by such contempt of duty (§§ 4—15). The advocates of Alkibiades will plead his youth and his parentage.
Neither his own nor his father's character deserves sympathy.
If relatives plead for him, it is they who ought to have restrained him; if officials, they must show that he is legally
innocent.   (§§ 16—22.)

Then follows a bitter attack upon the defendant and his
father. Alkibiades the younger is described as vicious from
his youth, and as a traitor to his own father[1]; all the treasons
of the elder Alkibiades are recounted at length. He prompted
the Spartan occupation of Dekeleia—he incited Chios to
revolt—he preferred a home even in Thrace to Athens. He
betrayed the Athenian fleet to Lysandros: both his great-
grandfathers, Megakles and Alkibiades, were *ostracised*.
(§§ 23—40.) An attack on the family in their private relations, as stained with every impurity and impiety, leads to
the conclusion. Much, the accuser says, has been omitted:
the judges must imagine it. He then causes to be read the
laws on which he relies; the judicial oath; and the indictment.   (§§ 41—47.)

The Generals, the presidents of the Court, say that they *Second
Speech.*
allowed Alkibiades as a special favour to serve with the
cavalry. Why, in that case, was he rejected by the
phylarch of his own tribe, and not struck off the list of
hoplites by the taxiarch? Why, when he took the field, was
he treated with scorn by all the knights, and driven to
place himself among the mounted bowmen? It is strange
if the Generals can enrol a man among the knights at their

νόμον ἐγὼ προσελθὼν ἔφην τῷ Ὀρ-
θοβούλῳ ἐξαλεῖψαί με ἐκ τοῦ
καταλόγου.

[1] An allusion in § 26 is obscure.
It is said that the younger Alkibiades μετὰ Θεοτίμου ἐπιβουλεύσας
τῷ πατρὶ Ὠρεοὺς προὔδωκεν.

Francken suggests Ὀρνεάς (the
town in the Argeia); and thinks
that the young Alkibiades may
have had something to do with
a betrayal of that place to the Lacedaemonians in 416 B.C.: cf.
Thuc. VI. 7 (*Comment. Lys.* p. 106).

pleasure, when they cannot so enrol him among the hoplites. If, however, the Generals have exceeded their real powers, then the Court cannot recognise their arbitrary act. (§§ 1—8.) The law is, indeed, severe; but the judges must administer it as unflinchingly as if they were marching against the enemy (§§ 9—12).

Feeling towards the elder Alkibiades. The first especially, of these two speeches should be compared with the Defence written shortly before by Isokrates—probably in 397 or 396 B.C.—for the same man. Both bear striking witness to the hatred felt for the memory of the elder Alkibiades in the early years of the restored democracy. Here, denunciations of the father fill about one-half of the speech against the son; there, the son devotes more than three-fourths of his address to a defence of his father. The speech Against Alkibiades ascribed to Andokides, but probably the work of a late sophist, indirectly illustrates the same feeling; being, in fact, an epitome of the scandalous stories about Alkibiades current at the same period.

Doubt of the genuineness—not well founded. Harpokration refers to Oration XIV. with a doubt of its authenticity[1]; Oration XV. is cited by no ancient author. The genuineness of each has been called in question by modern critics[2]; chiefly on grounds of internal evidence. It has been noticed that the composition varies in some points from the usual Lysian character; and that the special marks

---

[1] s. v. Ἀλκιβιάδης.

[2] See Francken (*Comment. Lys.* pp. 110—115), who refers to the doubts of Boeckh and others, but himself expresses positive suspicion only of Or. xv: Blass (*Att. Bereds.* pp. 491—4), who adds Scheibe to the sceptics, and himself inclines to doubt *both* speeches; though allowing, with Francken, that they certainly are not mere sophistic exercises. Taylor thought the *second* spurious (Reiske *Or. Att.* v. 553).

of his power are absent[1]. The two speeches must
stand or fall together. If not the work of Lysias,
they are certainly the work of a contemporary writer
for the law-courts. But the evidence, external or
internal, against their genuineness appears too slight
to warrant even a strong suspicion.

VI. CAUSES RELATING TO MURDER OR INTENT
TO MURDER (γραφαὶ φόνου—τραύματος ἐκ προνοίας).

1. *Against Eratosthenes.* [Or. XII.]—Polemar- VI. 1.
chos, brother of Lysias, had been put to death by *Against Eratosthenes.*
the Thirty Tyrants. Eratosthenes, one of their
number, was the man who had arrested him and
taken him to prison. In this speech Lysias, himself
the speaker, charges Eratosthenes with the murder
of Polemarchos, and, generally, with his share in the
Tyranny.

A question has to be considered in regard to the *Form of procedure.*
form of the accusation. Was Eratosthenes prosecuted
under an ordinary indictment for murder? Or was
he accused on the occasion of his coming forward to
render account of his office as one of the Thirty?

On the former supposition it is hard to say before
what court the trial took place. Clearly it was not
the Areiopagos. If it was the Delphinion, then
Eratosthenes must have pleaded some justification
of the homicide; but he admits its guilt, and lays
the blame on his colleagues (§ 24). If it was an

---

[1] Blass notices especially the
heaping together of homoioteleuta
in §§ 41 and 35. Markland observes on Or. XIV § 47, μεγάλη δ'
εὐτυχία τὸ τοιούτων πολιτῶν ἀπαλλαγῆναι πόλει, 'hi non sunt numeri
Lysiani: ille potius scripsisset
μεγάλη δ' εὐτυχία τῇ πόλει τοιούτων
πολιτῶν ἀπαλλαγῆναι (ap. Reiske
O. A. v. 553). The absence of ἦθος
and χάρις is the more general accusation—a vague one.

ordinary heliastic court under the presidency of
the Eleven, then there must have been an arrest
(ἀπαγωγή) by the Eleven ; but this does not seem
to have taken place[1].

The other supposition offers less difficulty. A
special clause in the Amnesty of 403 B.C. excluded
the Thirty Tyrants, the Ten who had succeeded
them, and the Eleven who had served them. But
any one even of these might enjoy the Amnesty if
he chose to stand a public inquiry, and was acquitted[2].
When the oligarchy was finally overthrown, Pheidon
and Eratosthenes were the only members[3] of it who
stayed at Athens. As they dared to do this, they
must have availed themselves of the permission to
give account of their office. And Lysias could have
had no better opportunity for preferring his accusation than that which would be given by the public
inquiry into the conduct of Eratosthenes. Two
things in the speech itself tend to show that it
was spoken on this occasion. First, its general

[1] The arguments against the
hypothesis of an ordinary γραφὴ
φόνου are well given by Blass (*Att.
Ber.* pp. 540—1.) Scheibe (*ib.*) thinks
that the trial was 'fortasse apud
heliastas ad Delphinium;' Rauchenstein apparently (*Introd.* p. 16)
before an ordinary heliastic court.
Francken also (*Comment. Lys.* p.
79) seems to reject the idea of an
accusation at the εὔθυναι.

[2] Xenophon (*Hellen.* II. iv. 38)
mentions the exclusion from the
Amnesty of the Thirty, the Eleven,
and 'the Ten who had ruled in the
Peiraeus.' Andokides (*De Myst.* §

90) gives the words of the Amnesty:
καὶ οὐ μνησικακήσω τῶν πολιτῶν
οὐδενί, πλὴν τῶν τριάκοντα καὶ τῶν
ἕνδεκα [καὶ τῶν δέκα]· οὐδὲ τούτων
ὃς ἂν ἐθέλῃ εὐθύνας διδόναι τῆς ἀρχῆς
ἧς ἦρξεν. Francken cannot be
right in referring τούτων here to
τῶν ἕνδεκα *only* (*Comment. Lys.* p.
79). The words τῶν δέκα are added
by Sauppe and Baiter with Schneider and others.

[3] Pheidon had been one of the
Thirty and also one of the Ten.
Eratosthenes had been one of the
Thirty, but *not* one of the Ten.
This is clear from §§ 54, 55.

scope. It has a wider range, and deals more generally with the history of the Anarchy, than would
be natural if it was concerned exclusively with
an ordinary indictment for murder. Only the first
third of the speech relates to Polemarchos; thenceforth to the end his name is not mentioned, even
in the peroration; the political offences of Eratosthenes are exclusively dwelt upon. It may be
noticed, too, that at the commencement Lysias
speaks in the plural of 'the defendants' and their
hostility to Athens, as if Eratosthenes was only in
the same predicament with several other persons.
Secondly, an expression in § 37 should be noticed.
The speaker there says that he has done enough in
having shown that the guilt of the accused reaches
the point at which death is deserved. He would
not have said this if death had been the necessary
penalty in case of conviction. But he might well
say it if his charge was preferred, among many others,
when Eratosthenes was giving his account, and when
the question was what degree of punishment, if any,
he was to suffer[1].

---

[1] The view that Lysias accused
Eratosthenes at his εὐθῦναι is taken
by Blass (*Att. Ber.* p. 540) and by
Grote (vol. VIII. p. 402). I have
purposely abstained from bringing
into the question the fact that
Lysias was only an isoteles. On
the one hand, as Rauchenstein
says, a resident alien was probably
allowed to prosecute personally,
instead of being represented by
his προστάτης, when the duty of
avenging blood came upon him as
the nearest relative. On the other
hand, it can hardly be doubtful that
a resident-alien would, as Blass
thinks, have been allowed to prefer an accusation at the euthunae of
any official whose acts had touched
him: it certainly is not doubtful
that such a man as Lysias would
have been allowed, under the democracy which he had just helped
to restore, to impeach one of the
Thirty Tyrants.

The date must be 403 B.C., the year of Eukleides. After their flight from Athens the Thirty maintained themselves for a short time at Eleusis. Soon after the restoration of the democracy, an expedition was made against Eleusis; the generals of the Thirty, who came out to ask for a parley, were seized and put to death; and the Tyrants, with their chief adherents, fled from Attica[1]. But it is clear from § 80 of the speech that this expedition had not yet taken place.

Again, in §§ 92 f. Lysias addresses successively two distinct parties—the 'men of the city' who remained in Athens under the Thirty, and the 'men of the Peiraeus.' The line of demarcation could have been drawn so sharply only while the war of parties was quite recent; not two or three years later, when exiles and oligarchs had long been fused once more into one civic body. It was, no doubt, remembered for years who had been on one side and who on the other. But in a speech made (say) in 400 B.C., we should not find the 'men of the city' and the 'men of Peiraeus' addressed separately as if they still formed two distinct camps.

The speech falls into two divisions. The first and shorter (§§ 1—36) deals with the special charge against Eratosthenes; the second, with his political character and with the crimes of the Tyrants generally.

I. §§ 1—36.

The difficulty here is not how to begin, but where to stop. Ordinarily the accuser is expected to show that he has some motive for hostility to the accused. Here it would be more

---

[1] Xen. *Hellen.* II. iv. 43.

natural to ask the accused what motive he and his fellows
have had for their hostility to Athens (§§ 1—3).

Lysias then enters on his narrative of the facts. His
father had been invited by Perikles to settle at Athens as a
resident-alien, and had lived there peaceably for thirty years.
His family had never been involved in any troubles until the
time of the Thirty Tyrants. Theognis and Peison, members
of that body, suggested the policy of plundering the resident-
aliens. These two men first paid a visit to the shield-manufactory of Lysias and his brother, and took an inventory of
the slaves. They next came to the dwelling-house of Lysias,
and got all his ready money, about three talents. He managed
to slip away from them, and took refuge with a friend in the
Peiraeus; then, hearing that his brother Polemarchos had been
met in the street by Eratosthenes and taken to prison, he
escaped by night to Megara. Polemarchos received the usual
mandate of the Thirty—to drink the hemlock; and had a
beggar's burial. Though he and Lysias had yielded such
rich plunder, the very earrings were taken from the ears of
his wife (§ 19). Now the murderer of Polemarchos was
Eratosthenes (§§ 4—23). Here he is briefly cross-examined:—

'Did you arrest Polemarchos or not?' 'Terrified by the
orders of the authorities—I proceeded to do so.' 'And were
you in the council chamber when we were being talked
about?' 'I was.' 'Did you support, or oppose, those who
advised our execution?' 'Opposed them.' 'Opposed our
being put to death?' 'Yes.' 'Considering such treatment
of us to be unjust—or just?' 'Unjust.'

Lysias comments indignantly on these answers. If Eratosthenes had really protested against the sentence, he would
not have been selected to make the arrest. He was one of
the Thirty themselves and had nothing to fear. All the
circumstances disprove his pretence of good-will; instead of
contenting himself with a visit to the house of Polemarchos,
he seized him in the street; he gave him no friendly hint
beforehand. If it is true that he opposed the sentence, he
must at least prove that he did not make the arrest, or did
not make it in a harsh manner. The judges are then re-

minded of the importance which their decision will have as
an example for both citizens and foreigners.   The fate of the
generals who conquered at Arginusae is contrasted with the
deserts of those who profited by the defeat at Aegospotami.
If those suffered death, what is due to these?   (§§ 24—36.)

II.   §§ 37—100.

To say more is superfluous: the guilt of Eratosthenes
has already been shown to be capital.   But lest he should
appeal to his past life, this must be exposed.   In the first
oligarchy [411 B.C.] he had to fly from the Hellespont
after an unsuccessful attempt to corrupt the democratic crews
of Athenian vessels there.   After the defeat of Athens [405
B.C.] he and Kritias were first among the Five Ephori and
afterwards among the Thirty Tyrants.   Perhaps he will say
that he obeyed the Thirty through fear.   No, in the cause of
Theramenes he dared to oppose them.   But this opposition
was not patriotic; all the quarrels among the Thirty were
selfish.   The so-called moderate party to which Theramenes
belonged was represented by the later Board of Ten.   And
the Ten, instead of promoting peace, waged war with the
exiles more bitterly than the Thirty (§§ 37—61).

Theramenes is the man whom Eratosthenes takes credit
for having defended.   It can be fancied how eagerly he would
have claimed friendship with Themistokles, who built the
walls of Athens, if he is proud of friendship with Theramenes
—who pulled them down.   Theramenes, when a member of
the first oligarchy, betrayed his own closest friends, Antiphon
and Archeptolemos; after Aegospotami, he undertook to
make peace without loss of honour, and yet it was he who
proposed at Sparta that Athens should lose her walls and her
fleet; it was he who advocated the proposal of Drakontides
for the establishment of the Thirty; and it is this man—
twice the enslaver of Athens—whom Eratosthenes glories
in having defended! (§§ 62—78.)

This is no season for mercy.   The man who condemned,
untried, the fathers, sons, brothers of those who now judge
him, does not deserve even a trial.   His advocates can urge

no merits either of his or of their own. His witnesses are mistaken if they think that they can shield from peril of death the men who made it dangerous to attend a burial. They will say that Eratosthenes was the least criminal of the Thirty. Is he to escape because there are twenty-nine greater villains in Greece? (§§ 79—91.)

Lysias now addresses himself, first, to those who remained in Athens during the Anarchy, then to the exiles who returned from the Peiraeus—speaking as if he had before him two definite bodies of men. He reminds each party of their peculiar reasons for hating the Thirty. The 'men of the city' should hate that despotism; for it shared with them nothing but its shame, and forced upon them an unholy strife. The 'men of Peiraeus' should hate it: it proscribed them, persecuted them, severed them from country and kinsfolk. Had it triumphed, no sanctuary would have protected them, nothing could have saved their children from outrage at home or slavery abroad. But it is needless to speak of what might have been: what has been is too great for words. It can only be *felt*—felt, with boundless resentment for the shrines which these men desecrated, for the city which they humbled, —for the dead, who are listening now to mark if the judges will avenge them.

'I will cease to accuse. You have heard, seen, suffered:— you have them:—judge.' (§§ 92—100.)

The result is unknown. But as the accused had *Result of the Trial.* evidently strong support, and as Lysias complains of the difficulty which he had experienced in finding witnesses to some of the principal facts, it is probable that the penalty of death, at least, was not inflicted[1].

The Speech Against Eratosthenes must take the *Character of the Speech.* first place among the extant orations of Lysias. In

---

[1] Grote vol. VIII. p. 402: Rauchenstein *Introd.* p. 16: Blass *Att. Ber.* p. 542. As to the number of men who supported Eratosthenes, see §§ 51, 56, 65, 87, 88, 91. As to the difficulty about witnesses, §§ 46, 47. See Or. x (Against Theomnêstos) § 31, and the remarks on it below.

the two parts into which it naturally falls the speech presents, in perhaps unique combination, two distinct styles of eloquence,—first, the plain earnestness of a private demand for redress—then the lofty vehemence of a political impeachment. The compass of the power shown may best be measured by the two passages which mark its limits —on the one hand, the account of the arrest of Polemarchos, which has almost the flow of Herodotean narrative;—on the other hand, the passionate appeal to the two classes of men who had suffered from the Thirty—worked up with all the resources of a finished rhetoric. As regards the first, what may be called the private, division of the speech, it is very noticeable how little attempt Lysias makes to excite compassion; he contents himself with a bare recital of facts. He relies less on the atrocity of the wrong itself than on its significance as part of that system of organised crime which he sees personified in Eratosthenes. He therefore throws his whole weight upon the second, the public, division of his subject; and here he gives us, first, two political biographies, the lives of Eratosthenes and Theramenes—then, a retrospect of the government to which they belonged. In one sense this speech of Lysias may be compared with that of Demosthenes On the Crown. The question at issue involves a whole chapter of Athenian history, in which both the parties to the case were actors. But there is a difference. Demosthenes, the statesman, reviews the train of events with which he deals from the level of one who has helped to determine

their course. Lysias stands on the lower ground
of a private person ; he sees the events of the
Anarchy as they were seen by the masses who
suffered, but were powerless to control ; he does
not discuss two rival lines of policy, but recalls,
as a common man, experiences familiar to thousands.
It is just because he speaks from among the crowd
that he is so successful in denouncing Eratosthenes,
and leaves the impression that in his attack upon
the worst of close oligarchies he was the spokesman
of an entire people[1].

2. *Against Agoratos.* [Or. XIII.]—Agoratos, VI. 2. *Against Agoratos.*
son of a slave, had gained the Athenian citizenship
by pretending to have had a hand in the assassination
of Phrynichos in 411 ; a merit to which, according
to his accuser, he had no claim. (§ 76.) For six
years afterwards he had lived at Athens, exercising
the trade of informer, and laying 'all conceivable
indictments' (τὰς ἐξ ἀνθρώπων γραφάς § 73) before
the law-courts. He is now charged with having
slandered away the lives of several distinguished
citizens just before the establishment of the Thirty.

It was in the spring of 404 that Theramenes came
back from Sparta with the hard conditions of peace.

---

[1] Perhaps sceptical criticism has
produced no greater marvel than
an essay *De oratione in Erat-
osthenem Trigintavirum Lysiae
falso tributa,* by A. Hecker (progr.
Gymn. Leid. a. 1847—8). After
proving to his own satisfaction
the spuriousness of this speech,
the author ends by regretting
that he has spent some time
in emending the speech Against
Agoratos; 'quam suppositam esse
a Graeculo ludimagistro idoneis
argumentis evincam. *Antiphonteae
omnes et omnes pariter Andocideae orationes spuriae sunt. Quae
brevi singula persecuturus sum.*'
Literature has lost a curiosity by
the non-fulfilment of this promise.

Athens had been suffering for months the extreme of
famine and misery; the mass of citizens were thank-
ful for relief on any terms. But there were still a few
men, influential by their position and service, who
stood out against the bargain which the oligarchical
party were about to strike with Sparta. The oligarchs, impatient to get rid of their opponents, had
recourse to the aid of Agoratos. It was arranged
that he should himself be charged with plotting to
defeat the peace, and should then denounce a certain
number of other persons as his accomplices. One
Theokritos accused him before the Senate. A party
of senators went to the Peiraeus to arrest him. Agoratos, feigning alarm, took sanctuary at the altar in
the temple of Artemis at Munychia. Certain citizens
who suspected him to be the victim, or the agent, of
a plot, gave bail for him, and offered to take him out of
Attica to await quieter times. He declined this proposal, and appeared before the Senate to give information. He denounced, first, the men who had
bailed him; then several of the Generals and taxi-
archs (§ 13), among whom were the General Strombi-
chides, Dionysiodôros (kinsman of the accuser in this
case), and probably Eukrates[1] the brother of Nikias;
also a number of other citizens. These, with Agoratos himself, were imprisoned; and it was decreed
that they should be tried both by the Senate and by
a special court of Two Thousand. Immediately afterwards the peace with Sparta was ratified[2].

[1] Eukrates is not named in this
speech; but see § 5 of Or. xviii.,
which refers to the confiscation of
his property.

[2] That, according to Lysias, the
informations of Agoratos were
made *before* the acceptance of the
peace and the surrender of the

The government of the Thirty having been established, the prisoners were tried; but not by the
Two Thousand; only by a new oligarchical Senate.
They were all condemned to death, except Agoratos,
who was banished. In 404 he joined the democratic
exiles at Phylê, and afterwards returned to Athens

city, appears distinctly from § 17,
εἵλοντο πρὶν τὴν ἐκκλησίαν τὴν
περὶ τῆς εἰρήνης γενέσθαι τού-
τους (the popular leaders) εἰς δια-
βολὰς καὶ κινδύνους καταστῆσαι.
It follows also from § 16.

Grote (VIII. p. 320) believes that
Lysias has misdated the informations of Agoratos, placing them
before the surrender, whereas they
were, in fact, given *after* it. He
remarks: (1) That it is difficult to
suppose an interval sufficient for
these accusations between the return of Theramenes and the ratification of the peace, for which the
people were most impatient. (2)
That the bailers of Agoratos could
not have proposed to convey him
away by sea from Munychia, when
the harbour was blocked up. (3)
That the expression 'till quieter
times' (ἕως κατασταίη τὰ πράγματα,
ib.) would have been inappropri-
ate at a moment just before the
surrender.

Now, (1) all that Lysias relates
about the informations need not
have occupied more than one day;
there is room for them, then, between the return of Theramenes
and the ratification of the peace (on
the day after his return, Xen.
Hellen. II. ii. 22). Lysias describes
the capitulation and entrance of
Lysandros into Athens as following
immediately on the act of Agora-

tos, § 34. (2). We do not know how
strict the blockade established in
November 405 may have been in
March 404 : the 'two boats' may
have lain ready at some point in
Munychia outside the harbour. (3)
The third objection I do not understand. Surely the time just *before*
the surrender—when Athens was
full of misery and faction—might
be called a troubled time.

No doubt Lysias had a motive
for placing the informations of Agoratos before the capitulation, and
thus representing him as responsible for it. On the other hand, it
may be observed that the oligarchs
would not have had the same
motive for suborning Agoratos
when the peace, which gave them
the ascendancy, had been ratified.

An ingenious attempt has been
made (by Christian Renner, *Comment. Lysiac. cc. duo*, Gottingen
1869) to show that it is consistent
with the narrative of Lysias to
suppose that the peace had been
accepted, and that the popular
leaders, when denounced by Agoratos, were only agitating for a
revision of it. But the words in
§ 17 bar this view. Renner can
get over them only by supposing
them corrupt. He proposes with
Frohberg to strike out the words
τὴν περὶ τῆς εἰρήνης after ἐκκλησίαν.
This is to cut the knot.

with them; but appears to have been ill received (§ 77). He is now accused of murder by Dionysios, cousin and brother-in-law to Dionysiodôros.

Mode of procedure. The procedure was not by an indictment before the Areiopagos or the Delphinion, but by an information (endeixis) laid before the archon, followed by a summary arrest (apagogê)—precisely as in the case of the Mitylenean charged with the murder of Herodes, for whom Antiphon wrote a defence; the case was therefore heard by an ordinary court under the presidency of the Eleven. There had, however, been a slight informality. Strictly speaking, endeixis and apagogê were applicable only in cases where the accused had been taken in the act; though, as appears from this and from the Herodes case, the limitation was not always observed. Here the accuser had left out the words ἐπ᾽ αὐτοφώρῳ in drawing up the indictment; but had been compelled to add them by the Eleven, although in this instance they had no real meaning (§§ 84, 86).

Date. The trial took place 'long after' the events to which it referred (§ 83); and the condemnation of Menestratos, who himself suffered on the same account 'long after' his offence (§ 56), is mentioned as if it was not very recent. At least five or six years, then, must have elapsed since 404 B.C. The speech cannot be placed earlier than 400; probably it may be placed as late as 398[1].

Analysis. The speaker begins by explaining that both on private and on public grounds he is entitled to be the accuser of

---

[1] Rauchenstein *Introd.* p. 55: Blass *Att. Ber.* p. 557.

Agoratos. On private grounds, since Dionysiodôros was his cousin and brother-in-law; on public, because the crime of Agoratos affects the whole State (§§ 1—4).

The narrative of the facts (§§ 5—48) falls into four parts. (i) From the defeat at Aegospotami in 405 to the moment when Agoratos made his accusations, in the spring of 404: §§ 5—34. (ii) The trial and condemnation of the accused: §§ 35—38. (iii) Their last injunctions to their relatives: §§ 39—42. (iv) The sequel of their deaths—the reign of terror, which they had foreseen and endeavoured to avert: §§ 43—48.

The pleas which Agoratos may set up in his defence are next considered. He may deny the fact of having informed; but the decrees of the Senate and of the ekklesia will confute him. He may pretend that he informed in the interest of the State: but the events disprove that. He may say that he was forced to inform; but the circumstances of his arrest show that he did so willingly. He may throw the blame on Menestratos, who also informed. Nay, Menestratos was afterwards a victim of Agoratos, whose turn it is now to suffer himself. Compare the conduct of Agoratos with that of Aristophanes, who died rather than turn accuser (§§ 49—61).

The eminent men whom Agoratos destroyed may be contrasted with himself and with his family. His three brothers have all suffered death for base crimes; he himself obtained the citizenship by pretending to have assassinated Phrynichos. It is a dilemma; let him suffer for the murder or for the fraud (§§ 62—76).

He will perhaps claim sympathy as having joined the exiles at Phylê and returned with them. The fact was that, when he appeared at Phylê, they would have put him to death, had not the general Anytos interfered; and when, at the entry into Athens, he presumed to bear arms in the procession, Aesimos, its leader, came and snatched away his shield (§§ 77—82).

Or he will raise technical objections. He will say that the time which has elapsed ought to exempt him from penalties; but there is no statute of limitations (προθεσμία, § 83)

here. Or he will say that the words ἐπ' αὐτοφώρῳ were
omitted in the indictment; which is much the same thing as
arguing that he is guilty, indeed, but was not caught in guilt.
Or he will plead the Amnesty. This is in itself a confession.
Moreover, the Amnesty was a covenant between the oligarchs
in the city (§§ 83—90) and the democrats of the Peiraeus:
it has no force as between two democrats.

The judges, the whole people, are bound by the solemn
injunctions of the dead. To acquit Agoratos would be to
confirm the sentence by which they perished. A democratic
court must not be in unison with the courts of the Tyrants.
By condemning Agoratos, the judges will mark the difference
between them; will avenge their friends; and will have done
right in the sight of all men (§§ 91—97).

*Character
of the
Speech as
compared
with Or.
XII.*
In historical interest the speech Against Agoratos
stands next, perhaps, to the speech Against Eratosthenes; but it is conceived in a totally different
spirit. No transition from a private to a public character, like that which is so marked in the other case,
occurs here. From beginning to end the accuser of
Agoratos confines himself to his special task, that of
demanding vengeance for the death of his kinsman.
Much of the general history of the time is necessarily
introduced, and the speaker of course avails himself
of the great advantage which he possesses in being
able to represent the slander of Agoratos as treason
to the State. But there is no such large view of a
whole period as is given in the speech Against Eratosthenes. The historical references are scattered,
not concentrated, and, instead of forming pictures,
are only picturesque; individual interests are in
the foreground throughout. Lysias accusing Eratosthenes hardly attempts to excite a personal sym-

pathy; he relies rather on the hatefulness of that
system of crime to which this particular crime belonged; Dionysios accusing Agoratos describes the
wives, mothers, sisters of the condemned visiting
them in prison, and receiving their last messages of
vengeance—a passage which strikingly resembles in
conception and tone the prison-scene in the speech of
Andokides On the Mysteries. The arrangement of
the topics here, as usually with Lysias when he
takes pains, is clear and good; though perhaps the
speaker tries to make too many distinct points towards the end, and thereby rather impairs the breadth
and strength of his argument. This is particularly
the case in §§ 70—90; where the sophism about the
Amnesty—that it was not meant to hold good between two men of the same party—is a curious
exception to the usual tact of Lysias in argument.

3.   *On the Death of Eratosthenes.*   [Or. i.]— VI. 3. *On
*the Death
Euphilêtos, an Athenian citizen of the humbler sort, *of Eratos-
thenes.
had slain one Eratosthenes of Oea (Οἴηθεν, § 16), whom
he had taken in adultery with his wife. He is now
prosecuted for murder by the relatives of Eratosthenes; and pleads in his defence the law which
allowed the husband, in such cases, to kill the adul-
terer[1] (§§ 30, 31). As the law was clearly against
them, the accusers were driven to allege that Euphilêtos had himself decoyed Eratosthenes into his
house (§ 30); and that the real motive of the homicide
was fear, enmity, or cupidity. This line of argument may have had some plausibility if Athenian

---

[1] Dem. *in Aristocr.* § 53 ἐάν τις   δάμαρτι, κ.τ.λ....τούτων ἕνεκα μὴ
ἀποκτείνῃ ἐν ἄθλοις ἑκών...ἢ ἐπὶ   φεύγειν κτείναντα.

husbands were in the habit of compromising such cases [1]. But the assertion of the accusers would be hard to prove; and Euphilêtos speaks throughout like a man confident of a verdict.

The cause would be tried, probably by heliastic judges [2], at the Delphinion, the court for cases in which an admitted homicide was defended as justifiable. There is nothing to indicate the date.

Analysis. The accused asks the judges to imagine themselves in his place: all Greece, he says, would recognise the justice of his act. He had no motive for it but the dishonour done to his wife, his children and himself (§§ 1—4). Then comes the narrative (§§ 5—28), followed by the citation of witnesses and laws (§§ 29—36). He meets the suggestions of the defendants; as (i) that Eratosthenes was decoyed into the house, §§ 37—42; (ii) that the homicide was prompted by a former enmity, or by cupidity, §§ 43—46. In any of these cases, he would not have slain him before witnesses. The decision of the judges will have a good effect if it accords with the laws; if it does not, then these laws should be annulled, since citizens are only entrapped (ἐνεδρεύονται) by them. His life and property are at risk because he trusted to the laws of the city (§§ 47—50).

Social interest of the Speech. The first part of this speech (§§ 5—28) is curious as a vivid picture—vivid with almost Aristophanic life—of a small Athenian household [3]; especially as

---

[1] In one instance, at all events, we find that the injured husband λαμβάνει μοιχόν...καὶ εἰς φόβον καταστήσας πράττεται τριάκοντα μνᾶς—not an excessive sum: Dem. *in Neaer.* § 65. As Blass notices (*Att. Ber.* p. 577) this case of Eratosthenes happens to be the only recorded example of that extreme and summary vengeance which the law allowed.

[2] After the year of Eukleides, heliastic judges sat at the Palladion : see Isokr. *adv. Callim.* § 54, Dem. *in Neaer.* § 90. Probably at the Delphinion also they had taken the place of the Ephetae.

[3] The passage §§ 6—18 may be noted as a locus classicus on the architecture of Athenian houses.

illustrating the position of a married woman of the lower class. The husband says that, at first, his wife gave him entire satisfaction as a housekeeper; on his part, he 'watched her as far as possible, and gave all reasonable attention to the subject;' at length, however, at her mother's funeral, she for once left the house; and hence the intrigue. Lysias has been clever in making the defence homely and at the same time dignified; Euphilêtos, the plain citizen, feels strong in the law of the city.

4. *Defence Against Simon.* [Or. III.]—The ac- VI. 4.
Defence
Against
Simon. cused, an elderly Athenian of good family and fortune (§§ 4, 47), is accused by one Simon of having wounded him in a quarrel about one Theodotos, a young Plataean. The indictment was for Wounding with Intent (τραύματος ἐκ προνοίας), a charge which, in this case, seems to have been made merely in the sense of 'wounding deliberately[1].' But, as the accused justly says, the 'intent' to which the law referred was not merely intent to wound, but intent to kill (§§ 40—43). It was for this reason that the Areiopagos had jurisdiction in such cases, as well as in those of actual murder[2]. The present trial took place before that

---

[1] The τραύματος γραφή seems to have been notorious as an instrument of false accusation. Cf. Dem. *adv. Boeot.* II. § 32 ἐπιτεμὼν τὴν κεφαλὴν αὐτοῦ τραύματος εἰς Ἄρειον πάγον με προσεκαλέσατο, ὡς φυγαδεύσων ἐκ τῆς πόλεως. Aeschines charges Demosthenes with having brought a false γραφή of the same kind against one Demomeles (*De F. L.* § 93, *in Ctes.* § 51); indeed, he says, this was one of his ha-

bitual villanies—τὴν μιαρὰν ταύτην κεφαλὴν καὶ ὑπεύθυνον ... μυριάκις κατατέτμηκε καὶ τούτων μισθοὺς εἴληφε τραύματος ἐκ προνοίας γραφὰς γραφόμενος (*in Ctes.* § 212). Compare Lucian *Timon* § 46 ΓΝΑΘΩΝΙΔΗΣ. τί τοῦτο; παίεις, ὦ Τίμων· μαρτύρομαι. ὦ Ἡράκλεις, ἰοὺ ἰού. προσκαλοῦμαί σε τραύματος ἐς Ἄρειον πάγον.

[2] For the law see Dem. *in Aristocr.* § 22. In [Lys.] *in Andoc.*

Date.

court (§§ 1, 3) ; the penalty was banishment (§ 47), and further (as appears from Or. IV. § 18) confiscation of property. The battles of Corinth and of Koroneia had already been fought (§ 45) ; the speech is therefore later than 394 B.C.

Analysis.

After observing that Simon ought to be defendant rather than prosecutor, and requesting the indulgence of the court for the weakness which had involved him in so unpleasant a dispute (§§ 1—4), the accused gives his own account of the quarrel between himself and the prosecutor (§§ 5—20). He then refutes the account given by Simon (§§ 21—39). The formula, 'wounding with intent,' does not, he says, apply to this case (§§ 41—43). He wishes that he was at liberty to give illustrations of Simon's character [the Areiopagos not allowing the introduction of irrelevant matter]. As it is, he will mention only one fact—that Simon was dismissed from the Athenian army at Corinth (§§ 44, 45). Simon, he concludes, is one of those informers 'who force their way into our houses, who persecute us, who snatch us by force out of the street.' He appeals to the services of his ancestors, and to his own ; and says that compassion is due to him, not only in the event of being condemned, but for the very fact of having been brought to trial (§§ 46—48).

VI. 5. *On Wounding with Intent.*

5. *On Wounding with Intent.* [Or. IV.]—The first part of this speech has been lost[1], and with it the original title. It is a defence before the Areio-

---

§ 15 it is loosely said that 'according to the laws of the Areiopagos' the penalty was banishment ἄν...τις ἀνδρὸς σῶμα τρώσῃ κεφαλὴν ἢ πρόσωπον ἢ χεῖρας ἢ πόδας—the mention of the πρόνοια being omitted.

[1] The loss must have taken place before the Palatine MS. was written. Sauppe (*O. A.* p. 73), regarding the speech as complete in its present shape, thinks that it

was the last or at least the second ('epilogus vel deuterologia') made for the defence. In that case, as Blass says (*Att. Ber.* p. 590), the preceding speech or speeches can have contained little more than the narrative ; since our speech deals with the proof. Francken (*Comment. Lys.* p. 37) and Scheibe (Blass *l. c.*) agree in thinking the speech imperfect.

pagos on a charge of wounding with murderous intent in a quarrel for the possession of a slave girl. The defendant asserted that the slave was the joint property of himself and the accuser; the latter claimed sole ownership (§ 10). The penalty threatening the accused was banishment and confiscation of property (§ 18).

The speech, as now extant, begins at the point where the defendant is answering the assertion that a personal enmity of long standing accounts for the murderous character of the assault. It is not true, the defendant says, that they were at this time enemies; they had been reconciled. He had been called upon to perform a costly leiturgia, and had challenged his present accuser either to undertake it himself or to exchange properties (ἀντίδοσις); and this had been cited by the accuser in proof of the alleged hostility. But it has been shown that this exchange was never actually made; friends mediated, and the defendant took the leiturgia. The accuser had, indeed, already received some property of his, with a view to the exchange; but had returned it when the reconciliation took place. Another proof is given that they were on good terms. The accuser had been nominated by the defendant as judge of the prizes at the Dionysia. Unfortunately, when lots were drawn, he was not among the judges elected. If he had been, his goodwill to the defendant would have been publicly shown; for he was prepared to give the prize to the defendant's tribe, and left a written memorandum of that resolve[1] (§§ 1—4).

Analysis.

---

[1] § 3 ἐβουλόμην δ' ἂν μὴ ἀπολαχεῖν αὐτὸν κριτὴν Διονυσίοις, ἵν' ὑμῖν φανερὸς ἐγένετο ἐμοὶ διηλλαγμένος, κρίνας τὴν ἐμὴν φυλὴν νικᾶν· νῦν δὲ ἔγραψε μὲν ταῦτα εἰς τὸ γραμματεῖον, ἀπέλαχε δέ:—' I could have wished that he had not missed the lot to be judge at the Dionysia, as then he would have proved to you that he was reconciled to me, by adjudging the victory to my tribe. As it was, he made a note of it in his tablets, but failed to draw the lot.'

The reference is apparently to a private compact between the defendant and the accuser. The judges of the prizes at the Dionysia were nominated by the Senate; the names of all the nominees were

Assuming, however, that this personal enmity did exist, yet the very circumstances of the assault exclude the idea of premeditation. The accuser had made the utmost of a black eye ($\dot{v}\pi\dot{\omega}\pi\iota\alpha$ § 9), and had pretended illness. At the same time he has refused to allow the slave, who was the cause and the eyewitness of the quarrel, to be put to the question (§§ 5—11). After dwelling further on the refusal of this challenge ($\pi\rho\dot{o}\kappa\lambda\eta\sigma\iota\varsigma$) as presumptive evidence in his own favour (§§ 12—17), the defendant ends by contrasting the gravity of his danger with the worthlessness of its cause, and begs the court not to award so disproportionate a penalty to him, and so excessive a triumph to his unjust accuser (§§ 18—20).

Special points illustrated by the Speech. This fragment has at least some antiquarian interest. It is curious to find from § 2 that the fact of having offered a man the antidosis could be quoted in court as presumptive evidence of ill-will towards him. The difficult passage in § 3 regarding the appointment of judges at the Dionysia has already been noticed. Section 4 illustrates a point in the peculiar procedure of the Areiopagos—that no witness could be examined who did not swear either to or against the guilt of the accused in regard to the particular facts before the court.

Taylor's doubt of its genuineness. Taylor's suspicion that in this piece a sophistic writer has imitated the Defence against Simon seems gratuitous[1]. If the fragment which has been pre-

put into an urn, and lots were then drawn (Isokr. *Trapez.* § 33). The defendant—being at the time a senator—had so nominated the accuser, under a compact that he should award the prize to the chorus furnished by the defendant's tribe. The accuser had registered this compact; but, in the end, his name was not drawn.

This is Francken's explanation (*Comment. Lys.* p. 38); and no better has been offered. The shock which the candour of the defendant must have given to the Areiopagos is perhaps not a decisive objection.

[1] 'Multis modis mihi videtur haec declamatiuncula in umbra Scholae $\mu\epsilon\lambda\epsilon\tau\hat{\alpha}\sigma\theta\alpha\iota$, ad imaginem

served is neither clear in arrangement nor strong in argument, it has at least the vigorous simplicity by which Lysias knew how to make the appeal of a commonplace man effective without making it rhetorical.

VII. CAUSES RELATING TO IMPIETY (γραφαὶ ἀσεβείας, ἱεροσυλίας κ.τ.λ.).

1. *Against Andokides.* [Or. VI.]—This is cer- VII. 1.
tainly not the work of Lysias; but in any survey of $\overset{Against}{Andokides.}$
his works its claim to be ranked with them must
at least be examined. It is probable that it was
really spoken against Andokides at his trial in 399
B.C. The occasion and the circumstances of that
trial have already been discussed[1]. Of his three
accusers—Kephisios, Epichares and Melêtos—one,
Kephisios, is mentioned by the speaker (§ 42): it is
possible that the speaker himself may have been one
of the other two[2]. Two lost pages of the Palatine
MS. contained probably the latter part of the speech
Against Kallias, and the first part of this speech
Against Andokides. But it is not likely that the
part thus lost was so large as to include, besides the
proem, a connected statement of the whole case. It
remains to suppose that such a statement had been
made by a previous speaker and is only supplemented

superioris orationis elaborata, cui deinde ob argumenti affinitatem in scriptis codd., ut fieri solet, perpetuo adhaesit.' Taylor ap. Reiske *Or. Att.* v. p. 164. Blass (p. 594) answers some objections raised by Falk to the arrangement of the speech; by Scheibe, to the weakness of the πίστεις and to some points of expression.

[1] pp. 114 ff.

[2] All that can be gathered from the speech about the speaker is that he was the grandson of one Diokles, whose father Zakorus had held the office of ἱεροφάντης, or initiating priest at Eleusis: § 54.

here. This is what might have been expected; Kephisios, the chief accuser, would properly have made the leading speech.

Analysis. The fragment begins in the middle of a story told to show how surely the goddesses of Eleusis resent an insult. A certain man cheated them of an offering; and there came upon him this doom, that he starved amid plenty; for though good food was set before him, the goddesses made it seem loathsome to him. Let the judges beware, then, of showing mercy to Andokides, whose punishment is claimed by these same deities (§§ 1—3). If he should be acquitted, and, as Archon Basileus, should some day conduct the festival of the Mysteries, what a scandal for comers from all parts of Greece! For he is known to them, not only by his deeds at Athens, but by his conduct during his exile in Sicily, in Italy, in the Peloponnesus, at the Hellespont, in Ionia, at Cyprus §§ 4—8).

He will say that the decree banishing him from the agora and the temples has been cancelled. Let the advice of Perikles be remembered, that impious men should be liable not only to written laws, but to the unwritten laws of the Eumolpidae. Andokides has aggravated his offence against the gods by presuming to make himself their champion. Before he had been ten days at Athens, he accused Archippos of having defaced a Hermes, and withdrew the charge only on receiving money (§§ 9—12). He will say that it is hard if the informer is to suffer when the denounced have been pardoned. The court is not responsible for that pardon; besides, these men denied their guilt; he confesses it. A man is banished for injuring his fellow; shall he not be banished for injuring the gods? Diagoras of Melos mocked the religion of a strange land; Andokides outraged the religion of his own. It is a further proof of atheism that, not dreading his own crimes, he committed himself to the dangers of the sea. [A notable petitio principii.] But the gods were reserving him for a late reckoning. Let the judges consider what his life has been since his first great crime. Imprisoned, and escaping only by betraying kinsmen and friends; dis-

franchised and banished; rejected by oligarchy and by democracy at home, ill-treated by tyrants abroad; and now, in
this same year, twice brought to trial! Men ought not to
lose faith in the gods because they see Andokides surmount
so many dangers: the life of pain thus spared to him is no
life (§§ 13—32).

But he is not content to have escaped punishment; he
dares to meddle in public affairs, even in the concerns of
religion (§§ 33, 34). And now he will be ready with various
pleas. That his informations relieved Athens from distress:
—but who had first caused it? That the Amnesty shields
him: but it was only political. That Kephisios is as bad as
he is: perhaps so, but that is irrelevant. That no one will
inform in future, if he suffers: nay, he has had his reward—
he saved his life. He is now in danger because he has forced
himself upon Athens—more shameless than Batrachos, the
informer of the Thirty, who at least hid his infamy abroad
(§§ 35—45).

Why should Andokides be acquitted? Not for his services in war, for he has never made a campaign. Not for
services rendered by his boasted wealth; for at the citizens'
sorest need he did not so much as buy them corn (§§ 46—49).
[Here, after the ἀνταποδούς, follows a lacuna: see above, p. 201.]

The profanation of the Mysteries is an old story now, and
men's horror of it is faded: but let them for a moment imagine Andokides mocking the awful rites of the Initiated, and
then remember the priests standing with their faces to the
west, and waving the crimson banners as they cursed him!
The city must be purged and the gods appeased by his expulsion. Once, when it was proposed that a Megarian guilty
of impiety should be put to death without trial, Diokles said
that he ought to be tried indeed, but that every judge must
come into court resolved to condemn. And now, let not the
judges be moved by entreaty. Compassion is not for murderers but for their victims (§§ 50—55).

The doubt with which Harpokration twice[1] names

---

[1] s. vv. κατάπληξ, φαρμακός. It
may be an accident that in a third
citation, s. v. ῥόπτρον, the words
εἰ γνήσιος are not added.

this speech is the only clue to the opinion of the
ancients. Modern critics are all but unanimous in
rejecting it.

The speech not by Ly- sias.

The diction shows many words and phrases which
Lysias could hardly have used[1]; but it is not by the
diction nor by the composition[2] that his authorship
is disproved. The question is decided by broader
characteristics. In arrangement Lysias was not fault-
less; but he would not have tolerated the chaotic
disorder which is found here. Again, in several of
those passages which dwell on the crimes of Andokides and on the vengeance of the gods there
is a certain hollow pathos, a certain falseness and
affected elevation, which are utterly remote from
the style of Lysias. Further the whole speech has
what may be called (in the Greek sense) a *sycophantic*
tone; it is rancorous, palpably unfair and prodigal
of unproved assertion. Lastly it is singularly deficient in the foremost general quality of Lysias—in
tact; it is preeminently a blundering speech. The
accuser makes at least four mistakes. First, he
recites at length the sufferings which Andokides has
been enduring without respite for the last sixteen
years; intending thereby to prove the displeasure
of the gods, but forgetting that he was more likely

---

[1] *e. g.* §§ 4, 44 ἀθῶος: §§ 18, 48
κομπάζειν: § 30 ἀλώμενος: § 50
καταπλῆγες: § 49 ποῖα ἁμαρτήματα
ἀνακαλεσάμενος, ποῖα τροφεῖα ἀπο-
διδούς. Blass further notes as non-
Lysian such redundancies as § 53
τὴν πόλιν καθαίρειν καὶ ἀποδιοπομ-
πεῖσθαι καὶ φαρμακὸν ἀποπέμπειν
καὶ ἀλιτηρίου ἀπαλλάττεσθαι, &c.

(*Att. Ber.* p. 574).

[2] The *composition*, indeed, is not
very different from that of Lysias.
It is free from the diffuse periods
of the later rhetoric—such as those,
for instance, of the speech Against
Alkibiades attributed to Andokides—undoubtedly a late sophistic
work.

to move the compassion of men. Secondly, he observes that, strange to say, Andokides has always come safely through his perils; but that it would be wrong to suppose the gods capable of protecting him;—an awkward allusion to the natural inference, and almost a prophecy of acquittal. Thirdly, in noticing the charges brought by Andokides against Kephisios, he allows that there is something in them, and objects to them only as irrelevant; thus needlessly throwing over his own colleague, the leader of the prosecution. Fourthly, he ends by begging the court to remember a saying of his own grandfather—that, in certain cases, it was the duty of the judges to be prejudiced against the accused. Any one of these faults would have been striking: taken together, they·make the authorship of Lysias inconceivable.

It is a further question whether this Accusation *Was the author a contemporary of Lysias or a later sophist?* was written by a contemporary of Lysias and was actually delivered in the Mysteries-trial, or is merely a rhetorical exercise of later date. Those who take the latter view, lay stress upon the discrepancies between this speech and the speech of Andokides On the Mysteries. Two of these discrepancies are important. (1) Andokides complains of having been specially charged with denouncing his own father (*De Myst.* § 19): here, he is only accused generally of denouncing his kinsfolk (§ 23). Again (2) he speaks of having been charged with placing a suppliant's bough in the temple at Eleusis (*De Myst.* § 110); here nothing of the kind is mentioned. But in regard to such differences, it should be remem-

bered that this speech, itself mutilated, was not the
only one for the prosecution; and that, where the
subjects of accusation were so large and covered so
many years, it would have been strange if every
point had been touched by every accuser. On the
other hand a rhetorician who had prepared himself
by studying the Speech On the Mysteries would
have aimed at a more exact correspondence with it.
He would probably have taken the charges against
Andokides in the order set by his model, and have
given paragraph for paragraph, or at least topic for
topic. He must have been a subtle artist indeed,
if with a general agreement he combined so many
intentional differences of detail. It may be noticed
that in § 46 Andokides is said to be 'upwards of
forty years old.' This statement has been used
as an argument for the late origin of the speech
by those who identify the orator Andokides with
the general named by Thucydides (I. 51) as holding
a command in 435 B.C. But if, as is most probable, the general was the grandfather of the orator,
and the age of the latter in 399 B.C. was really
about forty, then the statement in § 46 is one
reason the more for ascribing the speech to a contemporary of Andokides[1]. As regards the faults
of expression, of method or of general tone, these
help to disprove the authorship of Lysias; but they
are not of a kind which help to prove that the

---

[1] See above, p. 71. The inference is strengthened by the fact
that the mistake which is *not* made
by this speaker seems to have been
a common mistake in later times.
The author of the Plutarchic Life
of Andokides, for instance, puts
his birth in 468 B.C.

author was a late sophist. Bad taste is of no age;
and the fact of being contemporary with Lysias
need not have given a good style to Epichares or
Melêtos.

2. *For Kallias.* [Or. v.]—The shortness of VII. 2. *For Kallias.*
this speech does not necessarily prove it to be a
fragment. It opens with an express statement that
the case for the defence had already been fully
argued by others; and it ends with a completed idea.
Since, however, two pages of the Palatine MS. have
been lost just at this place, comprising the first part
of the speech Against Andokides, that For Kallias
has probably suffered also[1]. As it now stands, it
gives no direct clue to the special nature of the
case. The traditional title, 'Defence on a Charge of
Sacrilege,' must therefore have been taken from the
part now lost. The accused is a resident alien (§ 2),
an elderly man (§ 3), against whom his own slaves, in
hope of being rewarded with liberty, have informed.

In the view of sacrilege taken by Attic law, its *Sacrilege —how viewed by Attic law.*
aspect as a robbery seems to have been more pro-
minent than its aspect as an impiety. Thus it is
mentioned in the same category with ordinary theft,
housebreaking, kidnapping and like offences[2]. In

---

[1] Harpokration s. v. τίμημα has:
—τίμημα ἀντὶ τοῦ ἐνέχυρον καὶ
οἷον ἀποτίμημα (*i. e.* 'instead of
'*security*,' or almost in the sense
of '*mortgage*,') Λυσίας ἐν τῷ ὑπὲρ
Καλλίου· οὗτοι δὲ φάσκοντες
πλείονος μισθώσασθαι καὶ τίμημα καταστήσασθαι. Sauppe
thinks that these words are a
fragment from our speech; οὗτοι

being the slaves of Kallias, who
accused their master of having
agreed to rent some sacred land
('fundum sacrum') at a higher rate
than he himself admitted (*O. A.*
II. p. 192).

[2] Xen. *Mem.* I. ii. 62 ἐάν τις φανερὸς γένηται κλέπτων ἢ λωποδυτῶν ἢ
βαλαντιοτομῶν ἢ τοιχωρυχῶν ἢ ἀνδρα-
ποδιζόμενος ἢ ἱεροσυλῶν, τούτοις

this instance it appears from the address, ἄνδρες δικασταί (§ 1), that the trial was not before the Areiopagos. The cause must have been heard by an ordinary heliastic court, under the presidency either of the Thesmothetae or of the Eleven[1].

Analysis. The speaker says that, were it not a case of life or death, he would have forborne to come forward, considering the defence to be already complete; as it is, he desires to give a public proof of friendship for Kallias (§§ 1, 2). He then refers very briefly, first, to the high character of the accused; secondly, to the worthless nature of the informations. It is the hope of winning freedom which has prompted the calumny of the slaves. If they are believed, servants who desire liberty will henceforth think, not how they are to oblige their masters, but what lie they can tell against them (§§ 3—5).

Conjecture suggested by § 4. The phrase used by the speaker in reference to Kallias—'those who bring themselves into danger by lending their services to the Treasury' (τῷ δημοσίῳ βοηθοῦντες § 4)—is noticeable. It suggests that the 'sacrilege' of which the title speaks may have been connected with the sacred treasury on the Acropolis. Kallias may have had some employment under the Stewards of the sacred fund (ταμίαι τῆς θεοῦ, τῶν ἱερῶν χρημάτων) which gave him access to the inner

---

θάνατός ἐστιν ἡ ζημία. *Id. Apol. Socr.* § 25 ἐφ' οἷς γέ μην ἔργοις κεῖται θάνατος ἡ ζημία, ἱεροσυλίᾳ, τοιχωρυχίᾳ, ἀνδραποδίσει, πόλεως προδοσίᾳ.

[1] Meier and Schömann suggest that ἱεροσυλίας γραφαί may have been tried (1) by the Areiopagos, when, besides the question of fact, there was a further question as to

whether the fact, if established, would amount to sacrilege: (2) by heliasts with the Thesmothetae for presidents, when the question was of the fact only, the alleged act being clearly sacrilegious: (3) by heliasts with the Eleven for presidents, when the committer of sacrilege had been taken in the act (*Att. Proc.* pp. 306 ff.).

chamber (ὀπισθόδομος) of the Parthenon; and may have been accused of profiting by that opportunity to commit a theft.

3. *On the Sacred Olive.* [Or. VII.]—The man (VII. 2) for whom this defence was written—a rich Athenian citizen (§§ 21, 31)—had originally been charged with destroying a *moria*, or sacred olive, on a farm which belonged to him. As to do this was a fraud upon the public Treasury, the form of the original accusation had been an apographê (ἀπεγράφην, § 2). But the charge was not supported by the persons who had rented from the State the produce of the moriae on this farm (οἱ ἐωνημένοι τοὺς καρποὺς τῶν μορίων, § 2). The accusers had therefore changed their ground. They now charge the defendant merely with uprooting the *fenced-in stump* (σηκός) of a moria; and they lay against him an indictment for impiety. The chief accuser is one Nikomachos[1].

Throughout Attica, besides the olives which were private property (ἴδιαι ἐλαῖαι, § 10), there were others which, whether growing on public or on private lands, were considered as the property of the State. These were called *moriae* (μορίαι)—the legend being that they had been propagated (μεμορημέναι) from the original olive which Athene herself had caused to spring up on the Acropolis[2]. This theory was convenient for their conservation as State property; since, by giving them a sacred character, it placed them directly

---

[1] Not the Nikomachos of Or. XXX, who had held public office in 411 B.C.; whereas this Nikomachos was a youth in 399 B.C. (§ 29).

[2] The μορίαι were under the special protection of Ζεὺς Μόριος (Soph. *O. C.* 705).

under the care of the Areiopagos, which caused them
to be visited once a month by Inspectors (ἐπιμεληταί,
§ 29) and once a year by special Commissioners (γνώ-
μονες, § 25). To uproot a *moria* was an offence
punishable by banishment and confiscation of goods
(§ 41)[1].

Technical terms.

The technical terms used in this speech need
definition : see especially §§ 20, 24. Ἐλαία was the
generic term. Common olive-trees were called, either
ἐλαῖαι simply, or ἴδιαι ἐλαῖαι ; sacred, either μορίαι
ἐλαῖαι, or μορίαι simply. Σηκός properly meant the
enclosure or fence intended to guard the stump
(στέλεχος) of a moria which had been cut down or
burnt down (πυρκαιά, § 24)—as often happened in
the raids of the enemy during the Peloponnesian War[2]
(§ 6). Then σηκός came to denote the fence with the
stump itself; and this is the sense which it bears
in this speech : see § 11, σηκὸν ἐκκεκόφθαι[3]. In §§ 2,
5 ἐλαία *as opposed to* σηκός means a full-grown
moria.

The case is tried by the Areiopagos under the
presidency of the Archon Basileus. The offence was
alleged to have been committed in the archonship

Date.

of Suniades (§ 11), Ol. 95. 4, 397 B.C. To judge from

---

[1] In such cases the ἀγών was
ἀτίμητος, and there was no fixed
period (προθεσμία) after which the
liability of the offender ceased :
Meier and Schömann. *Att. Proc.*
p. 307.

[2] On the vitality of the olive, see
Her. VIII. 55, Verg. *G.* II. 30, 181.

[3] It is true, of course, that as
Rauchenstein says (Introd. to this
speech, p. 171) σηκός was never a
mere equivalent for the 'stump'
or 'stock ;' on the other hand, an
Athenian could say σηκὸν ἐκκόπ-
τειν, thinking rather of the στέλεχος than of the fence itself.
This is probably what Harpokration
means when he says loosely σηκὸν
δέ, ὡς ἔοικεν, καὶ μορίαν ὀνομάζουσι
τὴν αὐτήν.

§ 42 (τοσούτῳ χρόνῳ ὕστερον) the trial took place not earlier than 395 ; probably later.

A quiet life, the defendant had thought, was its own *Analysis.* protection ; but he has been taught that hired informers have a power which the unborn might dread (§§ 1—3). He will have done enough if he can show that there has been neither moria nor stump of moria on the farm since it came into his possession. This he proves by the evidence of tenants who had rented it from him (§§ 4—11).

After commenting on the unlikelihood of his having done a deed which could hardly have escaped detection (§§ 12—18), he observes that the accuser has failed to bring any witnesses (§§ 19—23). The defendant has several other farms, on which olive-trees abound ; but, notwithstanding the strict watch kept by the Areiopagos, he has never been accused of any such offence as this. And here the risk would have been peculiarly great. It is strange if Nikomachos has discovered what escaped the regular Inspectors (§§ 24—29).

He then speaks of his own public services; of the accuser's refusal to give up his slaves for torture, and of the absence of witnesses for the prosecution. He describes the malice of his enemies who had bribed Nikomachos to bring this charge ; and refers to the cruel sentence which hangs over him (§§ 30—41). He then concludes with a short review of the whole case. It depends upon an unproved assertion, which the accuser has refused to bring to the test (§§ 42, 43).

One attraction, which elsewhere seldom fails Lysias, is wanting in this speech ;—there is no narrative, for there is no story to tell, except the former history of the farm. In this, one rather curious point may be noticed. The farm had belonged, it seems, to Peisandros ; had been confiscated ; and had then been given as a public gift to Apollodôros of Megara. Now Apollodôros, as is known from the speech Against Agoratos (§ 71), was

one of the two men who planned the assassination
of Phrynichos; and so it appears that he had been
rewarded for destroying one leader of the Four
Hundred by receiving the property of another. As
Ethos of the speaker. regards the character of the defendant, Lysias has
described with a few touches the quiet citizen who
shrinks from publicity (§ 1), but with whom, at
the same time, it is a point of honour to discharge
his public duties in the best way (§ 34); a man
who, in Greek phrase, is at once ἀπράγμων and φιλό-
τιμος. Photios says that some critics doubted the
authenticity of this speech: and that the rhetorician
Paulos of Mysia, in particular, absolutely denied
its genuineness, for the unconvincing reason that
he could not understand a word of it[1].

---

[1] Phot. *Cod.* 262 ἀμφιβάλλεται
παρ᾽ ἐνίοις ὁ περὶ τοῦ σηκοῦ λόγος.
Παῦλος δέ γε ὁ ἐκ Μυσίας τὸν περὶ
τοῦ σηκοῦ λόγον, οὐδὲν τῶν εἰρη-
μένων συνιείς, τῆς γνησιότητος
τῶν Λυσιακῶν ἐκβάλλει λόγων.

CHAPTER XI.

LYSIAS.

WORKS.

Forensic Speeches in Private Causes.—Miscellaneous Writings.—Fragments.

O F the speeches of Lysias in private causes only four are extant; but each of these four represents a class.

I.   Action for Defamation (δίκη κακηγορίας).

Against Theomnêstos. [Or. x]—The occasion of this action was as follows. (1) Theomnêstos, a young Athenian, had been indicted by one Lysitheos for throwing away his shield in battle; but had been acquitted. The present speaker had been among the witnesses of Lysitheos; and in the course of the trial had been called a parricide by Theomnêstos. (2) A certain Dionysios, also a witness of Lysitheos, was next prosecuted by Theomnêstos for perjury; and was sentenced to disfranchisement (§ 22).   (3) The present speaker then brought his action against Theomnêstos—which was thus the third of a series.

The Athenian law against Defamation (κακηγορίας) punished with a fine of 500 drachmas (about £20) the utterance of certain reproaches classed as ἀπόρρητα (§ 2). To call a citizen a murderer, a

I. Against Theomnêstos.

Law against Defamation.

striker of father or mother, or to charge him with having thrown away his shield in battle, were among these[1]. The present case had already been submitted to arbitrators (§ 6); it now came before an ordinary court, under the presidency of the Thesmothetae[2].

Date.   From § 4 the date is certain. The speaker had been thirteen years old in the time of the Tyrants (404—3 B.C.), and was now thirty-three: the speech belongs therefore to 384—3.

Analysis.   Witnesses can scarcely be needed, since many of the judges themselves heard the libel when it was uttered in court. The prosecutor holds it mean and pettifogging (ἀνελεύθερον—φιλόδικον) to go to law about abusive words; but the taunt of *parricide* has driven him to it (§§ 1—3). He then proves by witnesses that he was only thirteen years old at the time of his father's death; and that he was directly a sufferer by it, since he became the ward of his father's elder brother, Pantaleon[3], who has defrauded him (§§ 4, 5).

Theomnêstos owns that he used the taunt; and the taunt has been proved false. But Theomnêstos argues that it is not, in the view of the law, a libel. He said only 'slew:' not 'murdered.' Is it lawful, then, the speaker asks, to reproach à man with 'flinging' away his shield? The law speaks only of 'throwing.' He gives further instances; and then observes that, in the procedure of the Areiopagos, 'slaying'

[1] See the speech §§ 6—9: ἀνδροφόνος—πατραλοίας—μητραλοίας—ῥίψαι τὴν ἀσπίδα. From Dem. *in Eubul.* § 30 it appears that to reproach a citizen with trading in the marketplace (τὴν ἐκ τῆς ἀγορᾶς ἐργασίαν) came under this law.

[2] Meier and Schömann, *Att. Proc.* p. 67.

[3] The language in § 5 leaves it ambiguous whether Pantaleon was uncle or brother of the speaker;

Sauppe assumes the former, which is more likely. The speech of Lysias κατὰ Πανταλέοντος (*Frag.* v.) may, he thinks, have had this man for its object. He conjectures that the father of the speaker—who is said in § 27 to have died for the democracy—may have been that Leon of Salamis who was put to death by the Thirty (*Or. Att.* II. p. 202).

is the term always used (§§ 6—14). Not content with this exposure of the quibble, he adds some illustrations from the old laws of Solon. These are full of obsolete words ; but their meaning is the same now as ever (§§ 15—20).

If Theomnêstos got satisfaction for having been charged with cowardice, much more should the plaintiff get satisfaction for having been charged with parricide. Theomnêstos has had one favour done him already :—Dionysios, a brave man, has been his victim. For the plaintiff, what could be so shameful a reproach as to be accused of murdering his father —a man who, after serving the democracy all his life, died for it at the hands of the oligarchs ? His bravery has to this day its memorials in the temples of Athens ; even as the cowardice of Theomnêstos and of *his* father have their memorials—in the temples of the enemy (§§ 21—29). The plea that the libel was uttered in anger is no defence at law (§ 30). Let the court bear in mind that he, who is now accused of murdering his own father, had in his youth impeached the Tyrants before the Areiopagos. Remembering this, the laws and their oaths, let the judges stand by his father and him (§§ 31, 32).

If not one of the most artistic or the most powerful, this is at least one of the most spirited of the speeches of Lysias[1]; and the doubt of its genuineness which seems to have existed in antiquity[2] must be explained—as in the case of the speech For the Invalid—by the slightness of the matter on which the case turned. The verbal quibble of Theomnêstos is, indeed, treated at somewhat excessive length ; but the absurdity of the defence was perhaps felt to be

The Speech suspected in antiquity —but probably genuine.

---

[1] 'Oratio prior in Theomnestum ad optimas Lysiae referenda,' says Francken : which is true so far, certainly, that 'indignationis et iusti plena doloris est oratio' (*Comment. Lys.* p. 72).

[2] Harpokration adds εἰ γνήσιος to his citation of the speech s. vv. ἀπίλλειν, ἀπόρρητα, πεφασμένης, ποδοκάκκη : but *not* s. vv. ἐπιορκήσαντα, οἰκέως.

among the best supports of the complaint. The conclusion of the speech bears the sure stamp of genuineness. It was a characteristic of Lysias that he loved
to end, not with a rhetorical appeal, but with a definite point, put in the fewest and plainest words.
Just such an ending we have here. There are besides in the speech several passages quite worthy of
Lysias;—for instance, the opening remarks (§§ 1—3);
—the reference to the fate of Dionysios (§§ 24, 25);—
and the speaker's tribute to his own father (§§ 26—28).

Reference in § 31 to the Tyrants.'   The reference in § 31 is of some interest. The
speaker says that, immediately on reaching the age of
eighteen—that is, in 399 or 398 B.C.—he had prosecuted 'the Thirty' before the Areiopagos. Now
when the Thirty Tyrants left Athens in 403 B.C.,
Pheidon and Eratosthenes alone of their number
are known to have stayed at Athens. If the allusion here is to them, then we see that Eratosthenes
escaped at least the penalty of death when impeached by Lysias in 403.

The 'Second' Speech an Epitome.   The so-called Second Speech Against Theomnêstos
[Or. XI.] is merely an epitome of the First, made by
some grammarian later than Harpokration[1]. The
epitome preserves for the most part the very
words of its original, with which it corresponds as
follows :—

Epitome	§§	1— 2	= Speech	§§	1— 5
....	§§	3— 6	=	§§	6—20
....	§§	7—10	=	§§	21—29
....	§§	11—12	=	§§	30—32

[1] Who in no one of his six references to the speech Against Theomnêstos (see above) distinguishes
it by α'.

II. ACTION BY A WARD AGAINST A GUARDIAN
(δίκη ἐπιτροπῆς).

Against Diogeiton. [Or. XXXII.]—After describing II. *Against Diogeiton.*
in detail the characteristics of Lysias, Dionysios illustrates his criticism by giving extracts from a Forensic,
an Epideictic and a Deliberative Speech. The Olympiakos and the Defence of the Constitution (Or.
XXXIV.) supply his examples of the two latter classes.
The speech Against Diogeiton is chosen by him to *Special*
prestige of
represent the distinctive excellences of Lysias in the *this Speech.*
forensic style[1]. Photios, too, says expressly that it
was among the most admired of all its author's
works[2]. It belongs to a class of private speeches
to which Dionysios gives a special title—the ἐπι-
τροπικοί, or those made in actions brought by wards
against their guardians[3].

Diodotos, an Athenian citizen, went to the coast *Occasion*
and Date.
of Asia as a hoplite under the command of Thrasyllos in 410 B.C.[4],—the year of the battle at Kyzikos.
In 408 he was killed at Ephesos, when the troops
under Thrasyllos were defeated by the allies of Sparta[5].
Before leaving Athens he had entrusted his two sons

---

[1] Dionys. *de Lys* cc. 20—27.

[2] Phot. *Cod.* 262 θαυμάζονται
μέντοι γε αὐτοῦ ἄλλοι τε πολλοὶ
λόγοι καὶ δὴ καὶ ὁ πρὸς Διογείτονα
ἐπιτροπῆς. After praising it in
detail, he concludes—καὶ ἁπλῶς
ὅλος ὁ λόγος ἄξιος θαυμάσαι κατά τε
τὰ σχήματα καὶ τὰ νοήματα καὶ τὰ
ὀνόματα καὶ τὴν ἐναρμόνιον τούτων
συνθήκην, καὶ τὴν εὕρεσίν τε καὶ
τάξιν τῶν ἐνθυμημάτων τε καὶ ἐπι-
χειρημάτων.

[3] *De Lys.* c. 20 ἔστι δὲ ὁ λόγος
ἐκ τῶν ἐπιτροπικῶν.

[4] Γλαυκίππου ἄρχοντος, Dionys.
Lys. c. 21, in his ὑπόθεσις to the
speech.

[5] Xenophon distinctly refers the
battle at Ephesos, in which the
troops of Thrasyllos were engaged,
to the archonship of Euktêmon in
Ol. 93. 1, *i.e.* 408 B.C.: see *Hellen.*
I. ii. 1 and 7. Blass (*Att. Ber.* p.
620) puts the battle in 410; Grote
in 409 (vol. VIII. p. 174). But the
statement of Xenophon, at least, is
clear. I once thought that in §
7 of the speech we might read

and his daughter to the care of Diogeiton, who was at once their uncle and their grandfather, since Diodotos had married his own niece, the daughter of Diogeiton. Eight years (§ 9) after his father's death—that is, in 400 B.C.—the eldest son attained his majority. Thereupon he was informed by Diogeiton that the property left by Diodotos was exhausted, and that he and his brother must shift for themselves.

This action was brought—probably in 400 B.C.— by the eldest son. It is contended that Diodotos had left altogether 15 talents and 26 minae. Diogeiton had at first represented the sum left as only 20 minae 30 staters, *i. e.* 26 minae altogether. But he had since confessed to 7 talents and 40 minae additional, *i. e.* 8 talents 6 minae in all. His accounts, however, made him out to have spent 8 talents 10 minae on his wards in eight years; so that, instead of having a balance to hand over to them, he was 4 minae out of pocket.

The speech is directed to showing, first, that the property left by Diodotos was about double of that to which Diogeiton owned; secondly, that his alleged outlay was incredible.

The speaker is husband of the daughter of Diodotos and brother-in-law of the plaintiff. An action of this kind was τιμητή,—that is, the plaintiff named the sum which he claimed; as Demosthenes, for instance, claimed ten talents from his guardians.

Ἐρέσῳ instead of Ἐφέσῳ: since Eresos in Lesbos was in fact attacked by Thrasyllos in 411 B.C. (Thuc. VIII. 100). But this, on the other hand, does not agree with the ἐπὶ Γλαυκίππου ἄρχοντος of Dionysios.

It does not appear what precise sum was claimed from Diogeiton. The case would come before an ordinary court; and, as a ward was suing his guardian, the president of the court would be the first Archon.

The speaker begins by explaining the necessity which *Analysis.* forces him to appear against a relative. His brothers-in-law, cruelly wronged, have besought his aid. Their grandfather Diogeiton had rejected all attempts at mediation; they were therefore driven to seek a legal remedy for his flagrant abuse of his trust (§§ 1—3).

The narrative of facts falls into two parts:—(i) The circumstances under which Diogeiton was appointed guardian, and his assumption of the office on the death of Diodotos: §§ 4—8. (ii) The disclosure made by him to his eldest ward on the latter coming of age, and the interview which followed between the young man's mother and her father Diogeiton: §§ 9—18.

These facts having been proved by witnesses, the speaker turns to the case set up by the defence. The defendant (i) has denied receiving part of the property; and (ii) professes to account for the rest:—§ 20. This account is scrutinised in detail, and shown to be absurd. On the most liberal reckoning, a balance of six talents should have been forthcoming (§§ 19—29).

Here the extract given by Dionysios ends. The statement of the defendant as to the amount which he had originally received must have been the next topic; followed, probably, by the peroration.

This speech—or fragment—is admirable for two *The twofold merit of the Speech.* things; the compact marshalling of a mass of intricate details, so that the broad result is made triumphantly clear; and the artistic treatment of character. Nothing could be better fitted to disarm prejudice, or even to create one favourable to the speaker, than the simple opening words. They show no bitterness against Diogeiton,—on the contrary, annoyance at having to appear against him—a necessity for which no one but himself is to blame. But the rhetorical skill is highest in the dramatic passage where the plaintiff's mother is brought in upbraiding her father Diogeiton with his purpose of disinheriting her sons, and the effect of the pleading on those who heard it is described (§§ 12—18).

III. Trial of a Claim to Property (διαδικασία).

III. On the Property of Eraton.

On the Property of Eraton. [Or. XVII.[1]]—This is the only extant speech of Lysias in a diadikasia,—*i.e.* in a case of a disputed claim (διαδίκασμα, § 10) to property either between two private persons or between a private person and the State. Here the dispute lies between a private claimant and the State.

The speaker's grandfather had lent two talents to Eraton, who died without having repaid them. Eraton's three sons, Erasiphon, Eraton, and Erasistratos, failed to pay the interest. The speaker's father therefore brought an action against Erasistratos, the only one of the three brothers who was at Athens; and obtained an order for the payment of the entire debt, principal and interest.

---

[1] The title in the MSS. is περὶ δημοσίων ἀδικημάτων. Reiske (*Or. Att.* v. 588) thinks that this title is common to our speech and to the next (περὶ δημεύσεως τῶν τοῦ Νικίου ἀδελφοῦ): and that it may have stood originally thus—ΛΥΣΙΟΥ ΠΕΡΙ ΤΩΝ ΠΡΟΣ ΤΟ ΔΗΜΟΣΙΟΝ ΑΔΙΚΗΜΑΤΩΝ ΛΟΓΟΙ. Dobree concurs in this view (*Adv.* I. p. 233). Sauppe follows Schott (*O. A.* I. p. 110) in changing ἀδικημάτων to χρημάτων and so prints it in his edition; but this is unsatisfactory. Hoelscher (ap. Blass, *Att. Ber.* p. 628) suggests πρὸς τὸ δημόσιον περὶ τῶν Ἐράτωνος χρημάτων (better περὶ τῶν Ἐ. χρ. πρὸς τὸ δ.); and this would be a better title

His father having died about this time, the speaker, in right of the verdict, took possession of certain lands of Erasistratos at Sphettos, and claimed at law certain other lands at Kikynna, which the representatives of Erasiphon, the eldest brother, refused to give up to him.

Meanwhile—for what reason is not stated—all the property which had belonged to the elder Eraton[1] was confiscated by the State. The speaker was obliged to give up the lands at Sphettos, which he had already for two years been letting to tenants (§ 5,) and to withdraw his claim to the others.

He now brings an action against the Treasury for the partial satisfaction of his claim upon the property of Eraton. The whole of this property was (he says) insufficient to satisfy his claim. Yet he is ready to give up two-thirds of it to the State; and rates the remaining third, which he demands for himself, at 15 minae (§ 7);—*i.e.* one-eighth of the sum originally lent by his father to Eraton.

The case is heard by an ordinary court, of which the fiscal board of syndici (§ 10) were presidents. Since the action against Erasistratos fell in the archonship of Xenaenetos (§ 3), *i.e.* in 400 B.C., and *Date.* three years had elapsed since (§ 5), the date is 397 B.C., of which the winter months had already passed (*ib.*).

The plaintiff begins by expressing a fear that the judges *Analysis.* give him credit for powers of speech which he does not possess—an exordium which suggests that he was at least

---

[1] In § 6 'Ερασιφῶντος must be altered to 'Εράτωνος (meaning the   elder Eraton), as appears from §§ 4 f.

in some way distinguished (§ 1.) He then gives a narrative, in three parts, of the facts just stated, witnesses being called at the close of each part: (i) § 2: (ii) § 3: (iii) §§ 4—9. He ends by simply asking for a verdict (§ 10).

No ground for supposing this to be an epitome.

In this short speech there is no argument; the proofs are all 'inartificial,' ἄτεχνοι πίστεις : *i.e.* derived directly from witnesses and documents. But there is certainly no reason for suspecting that we have here merely an epitome of a longer oration, like the so-called 'Second' speech against Theomnêstos[1]. Short as it is, the speech is in every respect complete and clear. There is nothing of that crowding which is generally apparent in a summary; the whole is on a small scale, but the symmetry of the parts is perfect. Besides, each section of the narrative is followed by a short recapitulation (§§ 3, 4, 10). An epitomist would have left out epitomes.

IV. Answer to a Special Plea (πρὸς παραγραφήν).

IV. Against Pankleon.

Against Pankleon. [Or. XXIII.]—The speaker had formerly indicted Pankleon, a fuller living at Athens (§ 2), for some offence not specified; and believing him to be a resident-alien, had summoned him before the Polemarch, who heard cases in which foreigners were concerned. Pankleon thereupon put in a 'plea to the jurisdiction,' on the ground that he was a Plataean by birth, and, as such, entitled at Athens to the rights of an Athenian citizen : and

---

[1] Francken (*Comment. Lys.* p. 123) says 'probabile mihi videtur, esse hanc orationem commentarium, aut potius *excerptam* esse ex genuina Lysiaca;' and at p. 238 he describes it as 'epitome.'

that, therefore, the action ought not to have been brought before the Polemarch. This plea (παραγραφή) gave rise to a previous trial to decide whether the action, in its original form, could be brought into court (§ 5). In such a case the first speech was usually made by the maintainer of the special plea[1]: here it is evidently made by the opponent[2]. The date is uncertain.

With a promise that he will be brief, the speaker comes *Analysis.* to the facts. Pankleon, on being summoned before the Polemarch, stated himself to be a Plataean by birth, son of Hipparmodôros, and enrolled in the Attic deme of Dekeleia. On inquiry[3], the speaker learned that Pankleon was in fact a runaway slave of a Plataean named Nikomêdes. A few days afterwards, Nikomêdes actually claimed Pankleon as his slave; but the latter was rescued by a gang of bullies (§§ 5—12). He had once before been brought before the Polemarch by a certain Aristodikos, and had blustered, but had eventually given in. Before doing so, he had withdrawn for a time to Thebes—a signal proof that he was no Plataean (§§ 13—15). If the judges bear in mind these plain facts the speaker is confident of a verdict (§ 16).

As in the last speech, so here all is narrative;

---

[1] See *e.g.* the speeches of Demosthenes For Phormio and Against Pantaenetos, and that of Isokrates Against Kallimachos.

[2] Meier and Schömann, *Att. Proc.* p. 648. The speaker makes a full statement of the facts. He would have assumed a *general* knowledge of the case on the part of the judges, and would have addressed himself rather to particular points, if Pankleon had spoken before him.

[3] The particulars of the inquiry are curious. The speaker goes to look for the Dekeleia men at a barber's shop in the Hermae street (leading from the Old to the New Market-place), a regular resort for the men of that deme—τὸ κουρεῖον τὸ παρὰ τοὺς Ἑρμᾶς ἵνα οἱ Δεκελεῖς προσφοιτῶσιν (§ 3). He seeks the Plataeans, again, at the cheese market in the Old Agora—hearing that on the first of every month ἐκεῖσε συλλέγονται οἱ Πλαταεῖς (§ 6).

there is no argument but the logic of facts. These are not stated with the same conciseness and clearness as in the former case; but there is no better ground here than there for suspecting, with Francken, the work of an epitomist[1].

Miscellaneous Writings.

1. *To his Companions: a Complaint of Slanders.* [Or. VIII.]—A friend addresses friends who have wronged him—states his grievances—and formally renounces their acquaintance.

Analysis. The opportunity is favourable for approaching this painful but unavoidable subject. He has before him both those whom he wishes to accuse and those whom he wishes to witness the accusation (§§ 1—2). His so-called friends have spoken of him as having thrust his society upon them (§§ 3—8). They have also persuaded him to buy an unsound horse, and have since taken part with the seller (§§ 9—13). Lastly, they have charged him with inciting others to slander them (§§ 14—17). For all these reasons he renounces their friendship. He will be safe now—for they attack only their friends (§§ 18—20).

It is scarcely worth while to inquire how this curiously absurd composition first came among the works of Lysias. As it is too uniformly dreary to be mistaken for a joke, not even a grammarian's conception of his sportive style can explain the imputation. The person who could thus take leave of his friends is certainly hard to imagine; but it is

---

[1] *Comment. Lys.* p. 238 '*excerpta ex Lysiaca.*' At p. 164 he says only 'equidem spondere ausim, hanc Lysiacam esse; sed aut non satis ab auctore aut satis superque ab aliis refictam.' Dobree notices, and appears to endorse, a doubt of its genuineness; but without assigning grounds (*Adv.* I. 245).

perhaps equally difficult—notwithstanding the amplitude of fatuity conventionally supposed in 'the late sophist'—to fancy any one taking such a subject for an exercise [1].

2. *The Erotikos in Plato's Phaedros* (pp. 230 E —234 c).—Plato makes Phaedros read to Sokrates a speech of Lysias in which the claims of the non-lover are urged as against those of the lover. Even to ask whether this speech is or is not an actual work of Lysias might seem at first sight to argue a want of sympathy with the broad literary characteristics of the dialogues. This speech of Lysias, it might be assumed, is as much Plato's own creation as the funeral speech by Aspasia which Sokrates repeats in the *Menexenos,*—or as the discourses put into the mouths of the sophists in the *Protagoras,*—or as those delivered by Aspasia, Agathon, Aristophanes and others in the *Symposium.* The gravity of the imitation is, of course, perfect ; but only a matter-of-fact reader could be misled by it.

This is probably the light in which the question would appear at first to most readers of Plato. But a nearer examination of the *Phaedros* brings out two points which seem to distinguish this case in an important way from cases apparently analogous.

The Erotikos in the Phaedros.

[1] Benseler—a very close observer of the style of Lysias—points out that in this Eighth Oration there are hardly any examples of *hiatus,* and that such as do occur can easily be removed—*e. g.* in § 7 by reading εὐνοοῦντες for εὖνοι ὄντες. Here, then—in this marked avoidance of hiatus—we have at least one definite mark of a post-Lysian style (Bens. *de hiatu,* pp. 182 f.). In § 17, again, one may recognise very distinctly the ring of the scholastic rhetoric—ᾤμην γὰρ ἀπόθετος ὑμῖν εἶναι φίλος, κ.τ.λ. Some phrases in §§ 2, 14 again—ἐναντίον τῆς ἐλπίδος—ὁ δὲ τοσοῦτον ὑπερεῖδε τὸ δι' ἐμέ—are not like the Attic of Lysias.

The first point is the elaborate dramatic preparation made for such a recital of the speech as shall
be *verbally exact.* Phaedros is asked to repeat it
from memory—makes excuses—is pressed; and presently it turns out that he has the book with him.
Now if the speech was merely Plato's imitation of
Lysias, surely this preface would be somewhat heavy
—inartistic, indeed, as forcing attention too strongly
upon the illusion. It is perfectly fitting, on the
other hand, as the dramatist's apology for bringing
into his own work of art so large a piece of another's work[1]. There is surely a special emphasis
here :—

Phaedr. What do you mean, Sokrates? How can you
imagine that I, who am quite unpractised, can remember or
do justice to an elaborate work, which the greatest rhetorician of the day spent a long time in composing. Indeed,
I cannot; I would give a great deal if I could.

Sokr. I believe that I know Phaedros about as well as
I know myself, and I am very sure that he heard the words
of Lysias, not once only, but again and again he made him
say them, and Lysias was very willing to gratify him; at
last, when nothing else would satisfy him, he got hold of the
book, and saw what he wanted—this was his morning's occupation—and then when he was tired with sitting, he went
out to take a walk, not until, as I believe, he had simply
learned by heart the entire discourse, which may not have
been very long....Therefore, Phaedros, as he will soon speak
in any case, beg him to speak at once.

Phaedr. As you don't seem very likely to let me off
until I speak in some way, the best thing that I can do is to
speak as I best may.

---

[1] *Phaedr.* p. 228. It may be
noticed that at p. 243 c the speech
of Lysias is designated, with the
same emphasis which I recognise
in the opening scene, as ὁ ἐκ τοῦ
βιβλίου ῥηθείς.

Sokr. That is a very true observation of yours.

Phaedr. I will do my best, for believe me, Socrates, I did not learn the very words; O no, but I have a general notion of what he said, and will repeat concisely, and in order, the several arguments by which the case of the non-lover was proved to be superior to that of the lover; let me begin at the beginning.

Sokr. Yes, my friend; but you must first of all show what you have got in your left hand under your cloak, for that roll, as I suspect, is the actual discourse. Now, much as I love you, I would not have you suppose that I am going to have your memory exercised upon me, if you have Lysias himself here[1].

The second point to be observed is the closeness of the criticism made by Sokrates on the speech—corresponding to the elaborateness of the contrivance for an accurate report of it. General criticism of expression or of moral drift would have been perfectly in place even if the speech had been fictitious. But detailed criticism—recognition, on the one hand, of 'clearness,' 'roundness,' 'polish' in every phrase—on the other hand, ridicule of the chaos of topics, of the repetitions, and especially of the beginning which is no beginning—would this have much meaning or force if the satirist were merely analysing his own handiwork?

Sokr. Well, but are you and I expected to praise the sentiments of the author, or only the clearness, and round-ness, and accuracy, and tournure of the language?...I thought, though I speak under correction, that he repeated himself two or three times, either from want of words or from want of pains[2]....

2. *Character of the criticism.*

---

[1] pp. 234 E—235 A. (From the Translation by Professor Jowett.)

[2] p. 235 E.

Again, further on :—

Sokr. Read, that I may have his exact words.

Phaedr. (*reading*). 'You know my views of our common interest; and I do not think that I ought to fail in the object of my suit because I am not your lover, for lovers repent of the kindnesses which they have shown, when their love is over.'

Sokr. Here he appears to have done just the reverse of what he ought; for he has begun at the end, and is swimming on his back through the flood of words to the place of starting....Then as to the other topics—are they not a mass of confusion ? Is there any principle in them ? Why should the next topic or any other topic follow in that order ? I cannot help fancying in my ignorance that he wrote freely off just what came into his head[1]....

Then comes the comparison of the speech to the epitaph on Midas, and Phaedros can bear it no longer :—

You are making fun of that oration of ours.

Sokr. Well, I will say no more about your friend, lest I should give offence to you[2]....

It is surely clear that the speech of Lysias is both so introduced and so handled by Plato as to stand on a wholly different ground from such dramatic fictions as those in the Protagoras, where the sophists are persons of the drama, imitated in their general method and style of discourse ; or from the fiction of Aspasia's authorship in the Menexenos—a fiction, indeed, which Plato has taken so little trouble to keep up that he makes her allude to the Peace of Antalkidas[3]. It would not be much to the purpose to analyse the composition of the Erotikos, or to

---

[1] p 263 E. [2] p. 264 D. [3] *Menex.* p. 245 C.

show that it bears the special marks of the style of
Lysias[1]. This could prove nothing. Plato could have
imitated Lysias, if he had chosen, without much
danger of being found out by us. It is the evidence
of the dialogue, not the evidence of the speech itself,
which is important.

Lysias is the earliest known writer of Erotic discourses[2]; and he is in a twofold sense the object of
Plato's attack in the Phaedros. The primary subject
of that dialogue is the antithesis between the false
and the true Rhetoric. The true Rhetoric springs
from Dialectic, and Dialectic from love of the ideas.
Hence the secondary subject of the dialogue is the
antithesis between false and true Love. Lysias is
by his profession a representative for Plato of the
false Rhetoric; by his Erotikos in particular he is the
representative of the false Eros. Plato could have
imitated well enough for his purpose the general
rhetorical characteristics of Lysias; but he embodied
the Erotikos in his dialogue, because, further, he
wished Lysias to speak for himself upon a special
subject[3].

[1] Blass (*Att. Ber.* p. 422) points
out that, plain as the style of the
Erotikos is on the whole, there is
rather more rhetorical ornament
of the type made popular by Gorgias than Lysias usually employed:
see *e. g.* p. 233 E ἐκεῖνοι γὰρ καὶ
ἀγαπήσουσι καὶ ἀκολουθήσουσι
καὶ ἐπὶ τὰς θύρας ἥξουσι | καὶ μά-
λιστα ἡσθήσονται καὶ οὐκ ἐλα-
χίστην χάριν εἴσονται καὶ πολλὰ
ἀγαθὰ αὑτοῖς εὔξονται. In such
a piece as this—written very likely,
as Grote suggests (*Plato* I. 254),

simply for the amusement of
friends — it was natural enough
that Lysias should have drawn
upon the ληκύθια of the Sicilian
school rather more than he would
have allowed himself to do in a
graver performance.

[2] Dr Thompson, *Phaedr.* p. 151
note 3.

[3] In the foregoing discussion I
have purposely abstained from at-
tempting to examine several arguments, turning on more or less fine
points of style, which have been

FRAGMENTS.

Three hundred and thirty-five fragments of every kind, from speeches, letters or unknown works, are arranged and examined by Sauppe, *Oratores Attici*, vol. II. pp. 170—216. Of this number, 252 represent 127 speeches of known title. Six of the 127 are represented by fragments more considerable than the rest. These six demand a few words of notice.

brought forward on each side. The fact that we have to do with such a literary artist as Plato seems to minimize the value of any argument which might be founded on the internal evidence of the speech. As to external evidence, we know only (1) that Dionysios and the pseudo-Plutarch mention ἐρωτικοί among the works of Lysias; (2) that this particular ἐρωτικός was thought really his by Diogenes Laertius (III. 25), by Hermeias p. 63 (quoted in Spengel's συναγωγὴ τεχνῶν, p. 126); and (as Dr Thompson points out, *Phaedr.* p. 184, Appendix III.) by Cornelius Fronto—who took it as one of his models in his extant ἐρωτικός to Marcus Aurelius. I would add that the reference of Hermogenes (περὶ ἰδ. I. 12, Sp. *Rh. Gr.* II. 331) makes it plain that he thought the ἐρωτικός authentic. The evidence

of the dialogue in which the speech is set must decide the question. This is, to my mind, conclusive for the authenticity.

Modern critics have been much divided. Among those who believe the Erotikos genuine are Sauppe (*Or. Att.* II. p. 209), Spengel (συν. τεχνῶν, p. 126), Blass (*Att. Ber.* p. 416—423—where L. Schmidt is quoted as agreeing)—and Dr Thompson in his edition of the *Phaedros:* see esp. Appendix I. Among those who regard the discourse as fictitious are Stallbaum (*Lysiaca ad illustrandas Phaedri Platonis origines*, Leipz. 1851); C. F. Hermann (*Gesammelte Abhandlungen*, pp. 1 ff.); K. O. Müller (*Hist. Gr. Lit.* c. 35, vol. II. p. 140 ed. Donaldson); and Professor Jowett, in his Introduction to the dialogue (Translation, vol. I. p. 553).

In a Public Cause.

1. Against Kinesias [LXXIII., LXXIV. Frag. *Speeches.*
   143 in Sauppe].

In Private Causes.

2. Against Tisis [CXIX. 231, 232].
3. For Pherenikos [CXX. 233, 234].
4. Against the Sons of Hippokrates [LXII.
   124].
5. Against Archebiades [XIX. 44, 45].
6. Against Aeschines [I. 1—4].

1. *Against Kinesias.*—Harpokration mentions 1. *Against Kinesias.*
two speeches of Lysias against Kinesias. One of
these was probably identical with that speech of
Lysias 'For Phanios' from which Athenaeos (XIII.
p. 551 D) gives an extract. Phanios had been accused by Kinesias of proposing an unconstitutional
measure (παρανόμων). The short extract in question
is a personal attack upon Kinesias, whose impiety, and unfitness, therefore, to be the champion of
the laws, are set forth. He is described as having
belonged to a club the members of which styled
themselves κακοδαιμονισταί—'the Mephistophelians'
—in ridicule of societies who chose carefully euphemistic names[1]. As the latter held their meetings on
the first of the month, the seventh, or some such
auspicious day, so this society made a point of meeting on one of the black days of the calendar (ἀπο-
φράδες ἡμέραι). Kinesias is satirised by Aristophanes,

---

[1] Such as the νουμηνιασταί men-   νιαστῶν κακοδαιμονιστὰς σφίσιν
tioned in *Frag.* 143—ἀντὶ νουμη-   αὐτοῖς τοὔνομα θέμενοι.

partly for his dithyrambs, partly for his atheism[1];
and enjoyed the distinction of having a whole comedy
written about him by Strattis[2].

The next four fragments have all been preserved
by Dionysios; who quotes the first of them in comparing Lysias with Demosthenes—the other three,
in contrasting Lysias with Isaeos.

*2. Against
Tisis.* 2. *Against Tisis.*—Tisis, a young Athenian, had
quarrelled with one Archippos at the palaestra; had
treacherously invited him to supper afterwards; and
then tied him to a pillar and flogged him. Archippos
brought an action for assault and battery (αἰκίας
δίκη); and the present speech was written for him by
Lysias. The extract given by Dionysios[3] contains the
narrative of the facts, which he compares with the
similar narrative in the speech of Demosthenes against
Konon (§§ 3—9). The critic remarks that to other
excellences Demosthenes joined those which distinguished the narrative style of Lysias—clearness
and naturalness.

*3. For
Pherenikos.* 3. *For Pherenikos.*—This fragment is concerned
with historical names. Plutarch[4] mentions Pelopidas,
Androkleidas, Pherenikos as the principal of the Thebans who fled to Athens when the Kadmea was seized
by Phoebidas in 382 B.C. It appears that Androkleidas had died soon after their arrival, and that
Pherenikos had taken possession of his property. He
was sued for it by a rival claimant, probably also
a Theban; and the present speech was made in his

---

[1] Ar. *Ran.* 366: *Eccl.* 3ː0: *Lys.* 227 f.
838, 852.
[2] Meineke, *Com. Graec.* I. pp.
[3] *De Demosth.* c. 11.
[4] *Pelop.* c. 5.

defence by an Athenian citizen, who had been hospit-
ably received at Thebes by Kephisodotus, father
of Pherenikos, in the exile of 404 B.C. Dionysios
expressly says that the speech was made for Pherenikos as for a ξένος—which is against the improbable
statement of Aristeides[1] that the Athenian franchise
had been given to the Theban exiles on this occasion.
As the exiles were restored to Thebes in 379, this
speech must belong to the year 381 or 380, and is
therefore the latest known work of Lysias. Quoting
a passage of the same kind from a lost oration of
Isaeos[2]—in which the advocate explains the motives
of gratitude which have prompted him to come forward—Dionysios compares it with this extract. In
Isaeos, we hear the rhetorician ; here it is the private
friend who recounts in the simplest but most telling
words the great services which Pherenikos and his
father had rendered to the Athenian refugees.

4. *Against the Sons of Hippokrates.*—A guardian
is here defending himself against a charge of malversation in his trust which had been brought against
him by his wards. Dionysios[3] places an extract from
the opening of this speech beside a defence written
by Isaeos for a guardian ; and remarks upon the difference between the styles in which they respectively
resent the imputation. The client of Isaeos uses
elaborate phrases ; the client of Lysias speaks like a
plain man, expressing a natural sense of hardship

4. Against the Sons of Hippokrates.

---

[1] *Panath.* p. 300 c.
[2] ὑπὲρ Εὐμάθους, εἰς ἐλευθερίαν
ἀφαίρεσις. Dionys. *de Isae.* c. 6.

On this and the two next Fragments, see vol II pp. 2.7 f., 365 f.
[3] *De Isaeo* c. 6.

at the recompense which his wards are giving him.

5. *Against Archebiades.*—A young Athenian citizen who has lately succeeded to a fortune by his father's death is sued by Archebiades for a debt alleged to have been contracted by his father. The point of the contrast which Dionysios[1] illustrates by an extract from this speech is the same as in the two last cases. Isaeos, too, had once occasion to write for a young client inexperienced in lawsuits. Yet even here he could not prevent his artificialism from showing itself. Lysias, on the contrary, has given to the life the character of a man who was never in a law-court before, who does not deserve to be there now, and who hopes never to be there again.

6. *Against Aeschines.*—The Aeschines in question here is that disciple whom Sokrates once advised 'to borrow from himself by shortening his commons'[2]. Athenaeos[3] quotes a curious passage from this speech by way of exemplifying the truth that philosophers are not always philosophers. 'Who would have supposed,' he says, 'that Aeschines the Sokratic had been such a character as Lysias makes him in one of his speeches on contracts?' (ἐν τοῖς τῶν συμβολαίων λόγοις.) The 'contract' to which the speech cited by Athenaeos referred was a debt, due from Aeschines to the speaker. It is not clear, as Blass remarks, how Aeschines came to be plaintiff instead of defendant

---

[1] *De Isaeo* c. 10.

[2] Diog. Laert. II. 62, φασὶ δ' αὐτῷ λέγειν Σωκράτην, ἐπειδήπερ ἐπιέζετο ὑπὸ πενίας, παρ' ἑαυτοῦ δανείζεσθαι τῶν σιτίων ὑφαιροῦντα.

[3] XIII. p. 611 D.

in the action; that he was so, however, is plain from
the opening words. Aeschines had applied for a
loan to help him to set up in business as a distiller
of perfumes (τέχνην μυρεψικὴν κατασκευάζεσθαι). The
speaker had lent him the money, 'reflecting that
this Aeschines had been a disciple of Sokrates, and
was in the habit of discoursing impressively concerning Justice and Virtue.' Then come some scandalous
stories about Aeschines. The genuineness of the
speech has been elaborately attacked by Welcker[1],
who takes it to be the work of a later rhetorician,
inspired by hatred of philosophers generally. He
thinks it too coarsely defamatory for Lysias. This
kind of argument is scarcely satisfactory when not
supported by particular evidence; and in this case
there is none. Sauppe and Blass seem right, then,
in holding the fragment to be genuine. The broad
comedy of the latter part is remarkable[2].

Letters are mentioned among the writings of *Letters.*
Lysias by Dionysios, by the pseudo-Plutarch and

---

[1] The substance of his view, as
explained in an essay, *Unächtheit
der Rede des Lysias gegen den
Sokratiker Aeschines,* is given by
Sauppe, *O. A.* II. p. 170.

[2] Besides this fragment — to
which Athenaeos (XIII. p. 611 D)
gives the title, πρὸς Αἰσχίνην τὸν
Σωκρατικὸν χρεώς—two others are
cited by the lexicographers; viz.
(1) κατ' Αἰσχίνου .περὶ τῆς δημεύσεως τῶν 'Αριστοφάνους χρημάτων:
Harpokr. s. v. Χύτροι: and (2) πρὸς
Αἰσχίνην βλάβης : Bekker *anecd.*
p. 132, 23. Sauppe thinks that
neither of the two latter was

against the Sokratic. Aeschines
was one of the commonest names.
Diogenes Laertius (II. 64) mentions
eight bearers of the name who
were all more or less distinguished. The speech περὶ συκο-
φαντίας which Diogenes notices
in the same chapter as having been written by Lysias
against the Sokratic Aeschines is
very likely that from which our
fragment comes : see its opening
words—νομίζω δ' οὐκ ἂν ῥᾳδίως αὐτὸν ἑτέραν ταύτης (δίκην) συκοφαν-
τωδεστέραν ἐξευρεῖν.

by Suidas[1]. The last-named speaks of seven; one, 'a
business letter' (πραγματικήν), is generally identified
with the letter to Polykrates cited by Harpokration.
In the other six may probably be included the letter
(or address) in the *Phaedros*; the Erôtikos quoted
by Harpokration; and the letters to Asybaros and
Metaneira. A few short sentences are all that remain. But two of these are interesting; each belongs, apparently, to a letter written after some cool-
ness or misunderstanding with a friend; and each
of them shows in the writer a characteristically eager
warmth towards friends.

[1] Dionys. *De Lys.* c. 3, cf. c. 1:
[Plut.] *Vit. Lys.*: Suidas *s. v.* Λυσίας.

[2] The two fragments are nos.
260, 261 in Sauppe, *O. A.* II. p. 210.
In the second there is a striking
phrase:—'I thought I was knitted
to you by such friendship'—ὥστε
μηδ' ἂν τὴν Ἐμπεδοκλέους ἔχ-
θραν ἰσχῦσαι διαστῆσαι, *i. e.*, 'that
not the Principle of Enmity itself
could have parted us.'

END OF VOL. I.